THE COMPLETE IDIOT'S GUIDE® TO

Understanding Judaism

Second Edition

by Rabbi Benjamin Blech

ALPHA

A member of Penguin Group (USA) Inc.

ALPHA BOOKS

Published by the Penguin Group

Penguin Group (USA) Inc., 375 Hudson Street, New York, New York 10014, U.S.A.

Penguin Group (Canada), 10 Alcorn Avenue, Toronto, Ontario, Canada M4V 3B2 (a division of Pearson Penguin Canada Inc.)

Penguin Books Ltd, 80 Strand, London WC2R 0RL, England

Penguin Ireland, 25 St Stephen's Green, Dublin 2, Ireland (a division of Penguin Books Ltd)

Penguin Group (Australia), 250 Camberwell Road, Camberwell, Victoria 3124, Australia (a division of Pearson Australia Group Pty Ltd)

Penguin Books India Pvt Ltd, 11 Community Centre, Panchsheel Park, New Delhi—110 017, India

Penguin Group (NZ), cnr Airborne and Rosedale Roads, Albany, Auckland 1310, New Zealand (a division of Pearson New Zealand Ltd)

Penguin Books (South Africa) (Pty) Ltd, 24 Sturdee Avenue, Rosebank, Johannesburg 2196, South Africa

Penguin Books Ltd, Registered Offices: 80 Strand, London WC2R 0RL, England

Copyright © 2003 by Benjamin Blech

International Standard Book Number: 1-59257-131-X
Library of Congress Catalog Card Number: 2003106940

09 08 07   8 7 6

Interpretation of the printing code: The rightmost number of the first series of numbers is the year of the book's printing; the rightmost number of the second series of numbers is the number of the book's printing. For example, a printing code of 03-1 shows that the first printing occurred in 2003.

Printed in the United States of America

Note: This publication contains the opinions and ideas of its author. It is intended to provide helpful and informative material on the subject matter covered. It is sold with the understanding that the author and publisher are not engaged in rendering professional services in the book. If the reader requires personal assistance or advice, a competent professional should be consulted.

The author and publisher specifically disclaim any responsibility for any liability, loss, or risk, personal or otherwise, which is incurred as a consequence, directly or indirectly, of the use and application of any of the contents of this book.

Most Alpha books are available at special quantity discounts for bulk purchases for sales promotions, premiums, fund-raising, or educational use. Special books, or book excerpts, can also be created to fit specific needs.

For details, write: Special Markets, Alpha Books, 375 Hudson Street, New York, NY 10014.

Publisher: *Marie Butler-Knight*
Product Manager: *Phil Kitchel*
Senior Managing Editor: *Jennifer Chisholm*
Senior Acquisitions Editor: *Randy Ladenheim-Gil*
Senior Production Editor: *Christy Wagner*
Copy Editor: *Michael Dietsch*
Illustrator: *Jody Schaeffer*
Cover/Book Designer: *Trina Wurst*
Indexer: *Tonya Heard*
Layout/Proofreading: *Angela Calvert, Megan Douglass, Donna Martin*

Contents at a Glance

Contents

Foreword

The Jewish story is a wondrous and complex journey. Jewishness is a peoplehood, a civilization, a legal system, a philosophy, a tribe—even gastronomy. There are multiple explanations for every tale, multiple interpretations for every commandment. At times, it appears to be a game of telephone gone berserk. But when the cacophony dims and a clear message is sent, its import is magnificent, stirring enough to inform civilization.

In a deceptively easygoing and humorous way, a master teacher named Blech manages to convey the grand picture and the nuance of Judaism—in paperback, no less. Rabbi Blech taught me that Judaism is a religion of deed, not creed. In this volume, he explains the creed of deed. He shows how the Jewish lifecycle and lifestyle, informed by Torah, creates a sacred self-consciousness that adds value to life.

At a time of profound existential loneliness and emptiness, he provides an invitation into a complex philosophic ecosystem that answers the "meaning" question through "knowing Jewish" and "doing Jewish." In one volume, the reader is provided with a tour through Jewish life that is not only descriptive, but also explanatory. Each chapter is almost an excuse to introduce the reader to the panoply of Jewish thinkers who have informed Jewish life, and to present those ideas in memorable ways. An ongoing sidebar is called "Let There be Light," in which basic terms and concepts are explained. In a larger sense, the whole volume is enlightening—it's for the uninformed as well as for those knowledgeable of Judaism. The shaping of the pieces into a holistic tapestry of Jewish meaning is a great accomplishment for such an unassuming book.

Benjamin Blech is a teacher extraordinaire. Learning from him, I am reminded of the cartoon light bulb that illumines when something comes clear. Rabbi Blech is a storyteller and a concept-sharer. As a master teacher, he has the ability to appeal to readers of enormously different backgrounds, and make it appear that he has written each one a personal letter. With his profound scope and knowledge, he fashions the various colors of Jewish thought into a Technicolor rainbow. Through a unique blend of stories, midrash, legal principles, and history, we are invited into the Jewish world.

Rabbi Blech simplifies without being simplistic. He expresses complex ideas in ways which make the ideas seem obvious. He both makes the profound seem simple, and teases the profound out of the simple. Here is a work almost masked as a "How to" book, that not only explains "How to," but also "*Why* to." It succeeds at both, and makes it fun.

Richard M. Joel

Richard M. Joel served as president and international director of Hillel: The Foundation for Jewish Campus Life from 1988 until 2003, at which time he assumed the prestigious position of president of Yeshiva University. He had previously been associate dean and professor of law at the Benjamin Cordozo School of Law, Yeshiva University; director of University Alumni Affairs, Yeshiva University; and assistant district attorney and deputy chief of the Appeals Bureau in the Bronx, New York. The *Forward* newspaper has written of Richard M. Joel: "When people speak of resuscitating organizations that seem to have lost their relevance or passed their prime, they often invoke the metaphor of doing what Richard Joel did for Hillel."

Introduction

Suppose someone told you he knew the secrets of life. How to be happy. Why life is worth living. What it means to be human. Who created us. What happens after death. Would you be interested in finding out the answers to these, as well as to a host of other equally fascinating questions?

Well, Holy Moses—and Jews believe that's exactly what Moses was—that's just the offer that Judaism makes to its followers. Judaism isn't just a religion that teaches us how to relate to God. It's a way of life that is meant to make us wiser, happier, and better people. It touches on almost every imaginable topic: how to raise children; how to develop to the fullest of our potential; how to love others and how to be worthy of being loved; how to find contentment and peace of mind; and yes—believe it or not—how to have great sex, with advice that's even better than what Dr. Ruth can give you.

What makes Judaism so smart? No one should ever forget that the Jewish Bible and Judaism are synonymous. The teachings, the laws, the values, and the principles of Judaism all have their source in the book of books almost universally recognized as the greatest masterpiece of wisdom and insight. The Bible has stood the test of time. It is revered today as it was in ancient times. And, remarkably enough, not only has the Bible survived, but so have the people who took its message as divine prescription for living.

Mark Twain wondered:

> All things are mortal but the Jew; all other forces pass, but he remains. The Egyptians, the Babylonians and the Persians rose, filled the planet with sound and splendor, then faded to dreamstuff and passed away; the Greeks and the Romans followed and made a vast noise, and they are gone; other peoples have sprung up and held their torch high for a time but it burned out, and they sit in twilight now, or have vanished. The Jew saw them all, survived them all, and is now what he always was, exhibiting no decadence, no infirmities of age, no weakening of his parts, no slowing of his energies, no dulling of his alert and aggressive mind. What is the secret of his immortality?

The Jew would answer simply, "Judaism is the secret of our survival. It is not we who have kept our faith, but our faith that has kept us."

This book will help you understand what makes Judaism so different from other religions, how Judaism enabled a small people to outlast the mightiest empires, and why Judaism has had such a profound impact on human history and contemporary civilization. You'll see why the rabbis of the Talmud (a book you'll read about in Chapter 8) said of the Jewish religion, "Delve into it and delve even more into it—for everything is in it." Psychology and philosophy, sociology and theology, medicine and mysticism, behavior modification and self-fulfillment—all these and more are dealt with in ways that believing Jews consider divinely revealed wisdom.

Hopefully, when you finish this *Complete Idiot's Guide*, you'll grasp why Jews feel themselves privileged to live for their faith and, when necessary, are honored to die for it.

Just one word of caution: Before you start on what I promise will be a fascinating journey of enlightenment and discovery, remember that Judaism is simply too large a subject to be covered fully in one volume. Consider this a first step. To truly do the subject justice, you'll need at least a lifetime—and for the mystics who believe in reincarnation, you'll have to keep coming back again and again until you get it all.

My goal here is to introduce you to a little bit of a tremendous number of areas with which Judaism deals. The key to this book is that it's user friendly. With a light touch, I'll take you through the most serious questions of life. My prayer is that as you proceed, you'll want to know more and more. In Judaism, we never speak of a "wise person"; the kind of individual we revere is known as a *Talmid Chacham*—a student of wisdom. To know that there is always more to know is what makes someone truly wise. So, let me accompany you as we start to travel from darkness to the ever greater and brighter light of understanding.

What You'll Find Inside

This book is divided into eight sections that summarize the major areas you should become familiar with.

Part 1, "The World According to God," introduces you to the most important ideas of Judaism. What does monotheism really mean? Is God always good? How can we be sure He really exists—and why do we say He instead of She? You'll spend some time reading about man and woman, how they differ, and what we mean when we say we are created "in God's image." You'll find an analysis of the role of human beings in a social setting; how religion deals not only with our relationship to God, but our interactions with fellow human beings.

You will read about the meaning of law in Judaism and why it's so important to have rules instead of relying on our instincts. I'll explain why God gives us commandments—and what difference it can possibly make to Him whether we obey them. Finally, you'll explore the purpose of life and how it should be lived. And also how Judaism contrasts with Christianity and how a sin for one religion is considered a sacred act for another.

In short, Part 1 will offer you a cram course on God, men and women, society, law, and life. Whew, that's a tall order—but a prerequisite for moving on to the details of Judaism as a way of life.

Part 2, "Read All About It," is a guided tour through the texts that serve as the source of the Jewish religion. You'll learn about the Bible—its main books, its major teachings, its most important personalities, and its lasting contributions. You'll get to know how rabbis and scholars added their insights and contributed to the Oral Law, as exemplified by the Talmud. You'll find out how intellectual creativity was encouraged throughout the ages and see examples of modern-day problems resolved by reference to ancient principles. The link between law and lore, the rational and the mystical, will make you aware of the broad scope of Judaism's scholarly interests.

Part 3, "The Time of Your Life," will explain how the Jewish calendar works and then introduce you to the important holidays and festivals. You'll become familiar not only with the reasons why so many days are special, but also discover the rationale for the various customs, ceremonies, and traditions associated with all the holidays—from Passover, the first festival given to the Jews when they became a people and celebrated their freedom—right up to the newest holiday, *Yom Yerushalayim*, observed since 1967 as the day of liberation of Jerusalem.

Part 4, "From the Cradle to the Grave," takes you through the lifecycle of a Jew, from the *mazel tov* at birth to the tearful observance of *shiva*, the mourning period of seven days for a departed loved one. Here you will find information about circumcision, details about preparing a wedding and its rituals, as well as the views of Judaism on death and dying.

Part 5, "All in the Family: The Home," walks you through a Jewish household and demonstrates the vital role Judaism plays in every room. You'll learn about the little box on the doorway called the *mezuzah*; you'll find out all you need to know about a kosher kitchen; you'll be introduced to the special menus for all the holidays that turn your dining room into a gourmet heaven (including a great recipe for chicken soup—the Jewish penicillin); a sex manual for the bedroom that comes with a Godly guarantee for better performance and pleasure; and finally, a summary of the most important principles of child-rearing rooted in Jewish tradition.

Part 6, "The Synagogue," will ensure that you will never again feel like a stranger in the contemporary version of the Jerusalem Temple of old. You'll learn not only about synagogue architecture and religious functionaries like the rabbi and cantor, but also about why we should pray, how prayer can work, and a little about the most beautiful prayers in the *siddur*, the Jewish prayerbook. Synagogue fashion will be clarified, so you'll never need wonder again about prayer shawls, fringes, and funny little boxes worn on the arm and the head by some Jews during prayer.

Part 7, "The Crucial Questions," is where you'll get the answers to the contemporary queries everyone wants to know but may be afraid—or ashamed—to ask. What is really the difference between Orthodox, Conservative, Reform, Reconstructionist, and Hassidic Judaism? Are secular Jews really Jewish? And who *is* a Jew? What's most important in the Jewish religion? Does a Jew have to live in Israel? What does being holy mean? How do you sanctify God's name? And if you had to choose between *mitzvot* (different commandments), which one, if any, has priority?

This part, like any good lecture, closes with questions "from the floor"—20 questions, to be precise (typical ones usually asked at the hundreds of lectures I've given on Judaism), from the permissibility of organ transplants to whether a nice Jewish boy or girl could become an astronaut.

Part 8, "Welcome to the Twenty-First Century," will bring you up to date as you'll discover how changing times have brought important changes to Jews as they grapple with contemporary challenges to Judaism as well as to Jewish survival. You'll see how the major movements of Judaism have attempted to cope with the new realities of our times. You'll learn all about the new problems that have taken center stage. Finally, you'll have a chance to look into a crystal ball and contemplate what lies in store for a religion that has managed to defy all predictions about its imminent demise throughout the centuries.

Some Bonuses

To make reading this book an even more enjoyable experience, you'll find little sidebars scattered throughout—boxes of interesting and helpful information. These include the following:

Pulpit Story
Admit it. There's nothing like an anecdote, a joke, or a story to bring an idea to life. You don't need a pulpit to tell them, or even a lectern; any speaker will tell you such tales are the frosting on the cake. I know you'll love these—please be sure to share them with your friends.

 From the Mountaintop

The Jews learned so much from the mountaintop of Sinai. When God shared His truths with the Jews there, it was called Revelation. Important ideas that didn't make it into the text but that should be "revealed" to you will be "gifts" to you in these boxes.

Ask the Rabbi _____

Yes, that caricature is really me (but I hope I'm just a little better looking). My editor convinced me that this would be the most effective way to issue tips and warnings. So with the help of the drawing, picture me standing over your shoulder—probably pointing my finger—as I add a note of caution or offer some fatherly and rabbinic advice.

Schmoozing _____

Schmoozing is a Yiddish word for talking with somebody, but it means a little more than just having a conversation. It conveys warmth, friendship, and a real need on the part of both participants—speaker and listener—to dialogue. These boxes will contain quotes that illuminate ideas in the text. They will let you meet people whose ideas you should know and whose thoughts deserve to be heard.

Let There Be Light _____

Definitions of words you may never have heard that have great significance in Judaism.

And a Final Note of Thanks

I've had the good fortune of writing three books in the *Complete Idiot's Guide* series: *The Complete Idiot's Guide to Jewish History and Culture, The Complete Idiot's Guide to Learning Yiddish,* and the first version of this book, *The Complete Idiot's Guide to Understanding Judaism.* There is no way to put into words the rewards of these efforts. Clearly, all three books filled an all-important need on the part of tens of thousands of readers. It would have been hard to imagine or hope for the kind of positive response they drew forth from so many readers.

Most gratifying of all has been the impact that *The Complete Idiot's Guide to Understanding Judaism* has had until now. In these few years since its first publication, it has consistently been at the top of best-selling lists of books on Judaism; it's become one of the most recommended books by rabbis and educators when asked for suggested reading; it's used as text in hundreds of courses in adult education and Hebrew high school programs (as far away as Japan, where it's the required book for the course); and it's probably the most widely used book today for teaching prospective converts the basics of Judaism.

What a thrill, then, to be asked to revise this book for a newer version that would bring it up to date. It isn't very often that an author gets a chance to actually act on all those moments when he thinks, "Oh, if only I could have had the opportunity to include this … if only I could have written some things with the perspective that these past few years have given me … if only I could have shared with my readers the most recent developments that are so important for understanding Judaism *today*."

What you're holding in your hands right now is not just the book that has gained a devoted following round the world but *an improved and even more information-filled, entertaining, and easy-to-read version.* Of course I can't be objective, but I firmly believe that even people who have already bought the first book will gain a great deal by getting this newer version as well (and it won't only help you—it will help me as well).

In my preface to the first version, I made clear how much respect I had for the people with whom I had the pleasure to work for Alpha Books: The editorial director, Gary Krebs; my editor, Carol Hupping; my production editor, Suzanne Snyder; my copy editor, Clifford Shubs; together with my colleague and technical editor, Rabbi Allen Schwartz, all of whom blessed me with their talents and their total dedication to this project. In conjunction with this new version, I want to express gratitude to the Penguin Group, the new publishers of this series, and single out for very special thanks the two people who are most responsible for this effort: Randy Ladenheim-Gil, who worked with me every step of the way and encouraged me throughout the entire project, and Marie Butler-Knight, whose commitment to this book made it all possible. Copy editor Michael Dietsch and senior production editor Christy Wagner were great help on the revised edition as well.

Special thanks are also due to my super-efficient typist, Eileen Greeley, who is truly indispensable.

I dedicate this book to the 10 generations of rabbis who are my direct ancestors and, in particular, to my father, Rabbi Ben Zion Blech, of blessed memory. It is my father who taught me by example that a life lived by Divine Law is truly divine. I pray that this book gives his soul the satisfaction of knowing that his values and wisdom have been faithfully transmitted to others.

Special Thanks to the Technical Reviewer

The Complete Idiot's Guide to Understanding Judaism, Second Edition, was reviewed by an expert who not only double-checked the accuracy of what you'll find in this book, but also added valuable insight. Our special thanks go to Rabbi Allen Schwartz.

Rabbi Schwartz is senior rabbi at Congregation Ohab Zedek in Manhattan. Ordained at Yeshiva University, he now holds the Raymond J. Greenwald Chair of Jewish Studies there and teaches Bible. Rabbi Schwartz writes Bible curriculum for Jewish Day Schools and lectures extensively for the Board of Jewish Education of New York. He serves on the executive board of the Rabbinical Council of America, is chairman of the Midtown Board of Kashrut, and vice president of the Council of Orthodox Jewish Organization of Manhattan's West Side.

Trademarks

All terms mentioned in this book that are known to be or are suspected of being trademarks or service marks have been appropriately capitalized. Alpha Books and Penguin Group (USA) Inc. cannot attest to the accuracy of this information. Use of a term in this book should not be regarded as affecting the validity of any trademark or service mark.

Part 1

The World According to God

Judaism isn't just a religion. It's a special way of living and looking at life.

For some people, the meaning of life is a mystery and because of this its definition is tragedy. Without any purpose, human existence is no better than a disease, the whole world is a hospital, and death is the final physician who brings our suffering to a close. Judaism, however, replaces pessimism with hope and existential despair with belief in divine providence.

To the perplexed, Judaism offers answers to five of humankind's most frequently posed questions: What is God? What's so special about human beings? How are we supposed to relate to other people? Why do we need laws? What's the meaning and purpose of life?

Part 1 will help you understand why Jews have found inspiration, comfort, and guidance from the unique ways in which the oldest religion in the world deals with these subjects.

Oh, My God

In This Chapter

- ◆ The first Jew and the discovery of God
- ◆ Creation according to religion and science
- ◆ What Judaism believes about God and what it rejects
- ◆ The meaning of ethical monotheism
- ◆ Whether God can be proved

Judaism begins with a man and a revolutionary idea. The man was Abraham, a Mesopotamian nomad who lived almost 4,000 years ago. The idea was a concept so daring, so original, and so groundbreaking that it would be almost universally recognized as a turning point in the history of the world.

Abraham discovered nothing less than God Himself—or, although it may shock you to hear this, God *Herself* (a concept that you will learn more about later in this chapter).

Of course, you don't have to be Jewish to believe in God, but the God of the Jews, as Abraham defined Him and as Judaism would worship Him, is unique in many ways. That's why when Jews pray, they always begin by addressing the "God of Abraham." And what Judaism says *about* God is probably even more important than the simple belief that there *is* a God.

In the Beginning

The story, strangely enough, isn't even in the Bible. The *Midrash*, an ancient collection of rabbinic legends and stories, tells us how Abraham came to his profound spiritual revelation. Walking some way from the populated area of his city of Ur, he came across a magnificent palace. For the briefest of moments, he thought to himself, "No one is here. The palace must have come into being by itself." Then he laughed at his own stupidity. A palace just doesn't come into being. A magnificent structure requires an architect and a builder. And with a flash of intuition, he made what in retrospect was the obvious connection: The world, too, in its complexity, magnificence, and splendor surely required a creator as well.

Let There Be Light

Midrash is the "searching" of Scripture to discover its deeper meaning. The word has come to refer to the collection of rabbinic interpretations of the Bible as well as stories relating to it.

The Bible considers Abraham's conclusion so important, it makes it the theme of its opening verse:

> In the beginning, God created the heavens and the earth. (Genesis 1:1)

The world hasn't always existed. It had a beginning. It came into being. For that to happen, there had to be a Creator. That is the first thing we mean when we use the word *God*—an all-powerful being who preceded the universe and is responsible for bringing it into existence at a specific moment in time.

Until the middle of the twentieth century, scientific theory firmly clung to the view that the world was eternal. The idea of *creatio ex nihilo*—creation out of nothing—which is at the core of Judaism's belief in a divine Creator, was considered impossible. Science and religion seemed to be locked in a duel with no hope for a clear victor. After all, how could we ever be certain of what happened such a long time ago?

In 1946, George Gamow stunned the scientific community with a radically new theory. Instead of the accepted assumption of the constancy of the universe—that what we observe today has always existed and will always exist in essentially its present form—Gamow expressed his conviction that the universe began *at a fixed moment in time, 15 billion years ago, out of nothing.*

Schmoozing

From a historical point of view, probably the most revolutionary aspect of the modern theory of cosmology is the claim that matter and energy were literally created. This claim stands in marked contrast to centuries of scientific tradition in which it was believed that something cannot come from nothing.

—Professors Alan Guth of Massachusetts Institute of Technology and Paul Steinhardt of the University of Pennsylvania

Gamow didn't try to explain the source of the original enormous burst of energy or light, popularly known as the "Big Bang," but he did show convincingly that when something—or *Someone*—said, "Let there be light," the tremendous energy that came into being formed the basis of all matter that now exists in the entire universe.

By the 1960s, it had become technically feasible to detect the electromagnetic radiation predicted by the Big Bang theory and to validate its conclusions. In 1978, Arno Penzias and Robert Wilson, Gamow's collaborators, were awarded the Nobel Prize in Physics for their fundamental discovery. Unfortunately, George Gamow couldn't share in this honor because he died in 1968, and the rules of the Nobel Prize do not permit posthumous awards.

That's also probably why Abraham wasn't even considered as co-recipient, even though he was the first one to teach that at a specific moment in time the world was created out of nothing—an idea that Nobel Laureate Professor Steven Weinberg of Harvard University calls "one of the most important scientific discoveries of the 20th century."

Somebody Had to Do It

Science so far only agrees with part of the first sentence of the Bible. Yes, as Professor P. A. M. Dirac, Nobel Laureate from Cambridge University, writes, "It seems certain that there was a definite time of creation." But physicists will not presume anything beyond that fact.

Stephen Hawking, of Cambridge University, who probably stands at the very head of his profession, says quite simply, "The actual point of creation lies outside the scope of presently

Schmoozing

The foundation of foundations and the pillar of wisdom is to know that there is a prime Being and that it is He who has brought everything into being and that all creatures in heaven and earth owe their existence to His true existence.

—Moses Maimonides (1135–1204), philosopher and theologian

known laws of physics." And where physics dares not tread, faith demands to be heard: "In the beginning, God created the heavens and the earth." Creation without a Creator didn't make sense to Abraham. If you call that a belief you can't prove, Judaism says that the opposite view, that there is no Creator and "everything just happened by itself," is also a belief you can't prove—but one that is far more improbable and illogical.

There's an apocryphal story about Maimonides (1135–1204), the great Jewish philosopher, physician, and rabbi, that powerfully makes this point. Maimonides tried to convince an atheist that there had to be a God who created the world. When hours of debate proved unsuccessful, the nonbeliever excused himself for a few moments to "take care of some personal business." When he returned, Maimonides took out a parchment on which was written a beautiful poem with perfect rhyme and meter, expressing brilliant ideas. "What a strange thing happened while you were out of the room!" Maimonides said to his guest. "The ink happened to spill over on my desk and, as it blotted, it created these words by accident." The man laughed and asked Maimonides why he wanted him to believe such a foolish impossibility.

"Why do you reject what I'm telling you?" Maimonides asked. "Because," the man answered, "these words so carefully thought out with such great sense and meaning, obviously had to be composed by someone with great intelligence. They didn't appear here by accident. Somebody had to do it."

"Let your own ears hear what your mouth has said," Maimonides answered. "If you can't believe that a simple poem could have come into being by a quirk of fate, how much more so the entire universe, whose wisdom encompasses so much more than these few words and whose profundity surpasses all human understanding."

From the Mountaintop

In the 1980s, when Sir Fred Hoyle, the renowned British scientist, was asked whether it was possible that given enough time we could see the spontaneous emergence of a single-cell organism from random couplings of chemicals, he said, "It's about as likely as the assemblage of a 747 by a tornado whirling through a junkyard."

That's why science isn't really in conflict with religion. The more that science makes us aware of the complexity of the universe, the more apparent it becomes that the intricate orchestration of atoms and molecules, of DNA and of chromosomes, of life, nature, and human beings could never be the result of an undirected "big bang" or an unguided, accidental evolutionary development. That's what Louis Pasteur must have meant when he said, "A little science estranges men from God; much science leads them back to Him."

Judaism calls God *Ribono Shel Olam*—the Creator of the World. The phrase not only describes *what* Jews believe about God, but also *why* they believe in Him. To be an atheist is simply to refuse to acknowledge reality. It is a far greater leap of faith to believe that a poem "wrote itself" by accident than to accept an intelligent First Cause responsible for a brilliantly designed and structured universe.

Just One

It isn't enough to believe that God created the world. Judaism insists that for this to have meaning, you also have to accept that He did it alone. To believe in many gods is almost as meaningless as believing in none. "Hear O Israel," reads the most important line of the *Sh'ma*, the Jewish prayer repeated by every observant Jew twice a day, morning and night, "the Lord is our God, the Lord is One." Monotheism—the rejection of many gods in favor of a belief in the existence of only one—was the logical consequence of Abraham's recognition of God as the First Cause and Creator of the World.

False Gods

The Midrash again gives us a more profound insight into this truth by way of a story. Abraham's father, Terach, as tradition has it, owned a thriving business selling idols. He was extremely successful (who knows, maybe like McDonald's, he had a huge billboard proclaiming "over 1 million gods sold"—with the numbers changing from month to month) and he hoped some day to pass the corporation over to his son. To teach him the business, Terach allowed Abraham to run the store all by himself one day.

Picture his shock when upon his return the next day he found all the idols in the shop smashed to pieces. "Who broke the idols?" he screamed in anger. Abraham, who had used the opportunity of his father's absence to express his contempt for these false gods, had taken the precaution of leaving one large idol standing in whose carved hands he placed an axe. "While you were gone," Abraham told his father, "a terrible thing happened. The large idol got angry at all the others and destroyed them."

Furiously, Terach rejected the explanation. "How dare you tell me something so stupid. That's just an idol. He couldn't possibly do anything." What a great opening for Abraham to reply, "But if idols can't do anything, why should we worship them?"

The Midrash was meant to be much more than a story. It speaks as a metaphor. It marks Abraham as the man who had the courage to break with the paganism not only of his age but also of his own ancestors. His courage came from his conviction that idols are powerless. Not only because they are statues or carvings, made of metal and wood, but because in their multiplicity they clearly aren't the one creator of the universe.

Many gods, Abraham reasoned, would naturally fight each other. Everyone would try to protect his own turf. Larger ones would pick on the smaller ones. Paganism could only produce conflict. Pagan gods, by definition, could not be all-powerful because there were other gods alongside or in opposition to them. The world is a harmonious whole. Its parts are not at war with each other; it functions as one. So "Hear O Israel, the Lord is our God, the Lord is One."

Not Two

Polytheism is a belief in many Gods. *Dualism* is the belief that there are only two. Pretty close to monotheism, you might say. After all, it's only off by one. Yet Judaism considers dualism as the heresy that presents it with its most formidable challenge.

What made dualism pick just two as the number of gods? Well, dualism was the attempt of Zoroastrianism, an ancient Persian religion founded by Zoroaster about

Let There Be Light

Polytheism is a belief in many Gods. **Dualism** is the belief that there are only two.

3,500 years ago, to deal with the most fundamental religious problem: How can one God be responsible for both the incredible good as well as the horrible evil that seem to coexist on this earth? Just as every day has both light and darkness, sunshine and blackness, so do our lives seem to be filled with both blessings and curses.

Dualism tries to solve the problem of a seemingly schizophrenic God by concluding that there are really two CEOs who run the universe. One is a God of Light who loves to do good. The other, like a wicked twin, is the God of Darkness who gets his kicks playing dirty tricks on people and gleefully watching the results of his mischief as he causes human tragedy.

What dualism could never successfully explain, however, is how these two opposing and contradictory forces ever got along well enough to create the world in the first place; how they managed to agree to some guidelines to determine their respective areas of control; and how they could be just exactly equal in power so that neither one eliminates the other. A good guy and bad guy squabbling endlessly throughout all of history with neither one clearly winning and both supposedly having absolute power seems too incredible to imagine.

The Jewish God is one, even though that forces Judaism to find other ways to solve the problem of good and evil. One God who is good may at times allow bad things to happen for reasons we cannot understand. As a famous Jewish philosopher once said, "If I could understand God, I would be God." Evil may simply be a blessing in a not-yet-recognized form. But *monotheism* shouldn't be rejected just because there are times when we think we could have written a better script for God to follow.

Let There Be Light

Monotheism is a belief in one supreme Being as Creator and Ruler of the universe.

Not Three

Polytheism and dualism are pretty much passé in the Western world today. *Trinitarianism*, however, the belief that there are three to the essence of God, is a belief accepted by all contemporary Christians. Judaism strongly disagrees. It stands firm in maintaining that God is One—without partners, self-sufficient, and indivisible. As important as it is to find common ground among different faiths, it is both foolish as well as disrespectful to disregard their major differences.

Religions may rightfully disagree with each other. Much as we talk about a common Judeo-Christian heritage, we have to be realistic enough to acknowledge that One is not Three and Three is not One. So strongly do Jews and Christians differ on this point that during the Middle Ages there were many Jews who chose martyrdom rather than to renounce their monotheistic faith for a belief in the Father, the Son, and the Holy Ghost.

Let There Be Light

Trinitarianism refers to the Christian understanding of God as a unity of three persons—Father, Son, and Holy Spirit—distinguished in their relations to one another and yet equally God.

Jews understand that the idea of the Trinity is not the same as *tritheism*—a belief in three gods. That, of course, would be a heresy for Christians as well—whose understanding of the Trinity is that the three, though separate, are in actuality one. Yet Judaism has serious difficulties with a number of Trinitarian major premises:

♦ God is not human. Man is not God. The Christian doctrine of the Incarnation, that God assumed human form, goes against the fundamental Jewish belief that God is incorporeal—that He has no body and cannot be affected by any of the weaknesses of the flesh. To say that God then died on the cross seems incomprehensible. God cannot die—just as He does not "live" in human form.

♦ To worship Jesus as God is to violate the commandment that "You shall have no other gods before Me." The greatest leader of the Jewish people, Moses, was buried by God in an unmarked grave. As the Bible says, "And no man knew his burial spot to this very day." No matter how great a man Moses was, God did not want him to be revered in a way that would have people confuse him with divinity. "And the *man* Moses ..." (Numbers 12:3)—his name is prefaced by the adjective describing his mortal limitations. God was careful to delineate the difference between Himself and human beings. Jews can't accept that a man or a woman could possibly be God.

♦ Most disturbing of all to the Jewish idea of monotheism in the Trinity is that Judaism recognizes no intermediary between God and man. The first of the Ten Commandments, "I am the Lord *your* God," is written with a Hebrew word that implies a singular "your." God speaks to every person directly and says, "I am accessible to you without any middle man." For the Jew, this means he has an open line to God Himself. Praying to the Son to get to the Father goes against one of the major beliefs of Judaism, as later codified by Maimonides: "To Him and to Him alone shall you pray directly." A Jew believes that no one else is supposed to talk for him, live for him—and certainly not die for him.

It is true, as the great Jewish historian, Joseph Klausner (1874–1958), made clear, that "Jesus remains even for the Jews a great teacher of morality and an artist in parable." Jews can accept Jesus as someone who attained heavenly heights—but not as a being who came down from heaven. He may well have been a man who walked with God on earth—but according to the Jewish faith, he was not a god who walked on earth like a man. He is for Jews to be respected as a man who lived divinely, but not revered as a God who lived humanly.

The King and I

You can believe everything you've learned until now that Judaism teaches about God—that God is an all-powerful Being who created the universe, One, not many, not two, and not three—and still be totally irreligious if you are a deist. Deists have no trouble believing in God. They just can't believe that an all-powerful God could be interested in us.

Deism compares the relationship of God to the world to that of a watchmaker and a watch that he made. A craftsman may produce a magnificent timepiece, but that doesn't mean he'll have an ongoing relationship with it. The deist asks, "Could the Creator of the whole universe really be interested in little old me?" He rejects a belief in a personal God who continues to be concerned and involved with His creations and feels quite comfortable in ignoring a Creator he is sure doesn't care about him.

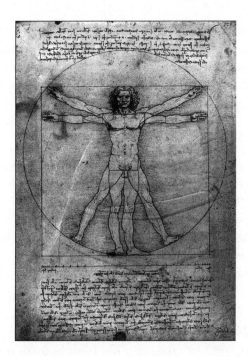

Vitruvian man—*anatomical study by Leonardo da Vinci.*

(Art Resource, NY/Alinari)

It's interesting that the very first of the Ten Commandments, in which God identifies Himself, obviously addresses not only the atheist but the deist as well: "I am the Lord your God who took you out of the land of Egypt, the house of bondage." Not only does God use the pronoun, "I," to express His existence as well as His personhood (to teach you that God is not just an abstract force or concept), but He makes it clear that He is a God of history who maintains an ongoing relationship with human beings.

As a matter of fact, God not only refers to His role as Redeemer of the entire Jewish people from "the land of Egypt," but He also stresses His intervention in every "house of bondage." God tells us He is concerned with what happens in every home. He may be the King of the Universe, but "The King and I" is the best description of our relationship.

Jews refer to God as the God of Abraham not just because Abraham discovered Him. What we mean in a deeper sense is that the very God who created the world isn't too busy or

Ask the Rabbi

"Jews For Jesus" are willing to recognize Jesus as Messiah, in accord with Christian doctrine. Judaism believes that Messiah has yet to come, because the Messianic age and its blessing of universal peace and acceptance of God have still to be fulfilled. Guess we'll continue to respectfully disagree until God Himself gives us His final word on the matter.

too distant from His creation to be involved with the details of the life of Abraham. And not just Abraham. "I am the Lord *your* God." That means every one of us. God knows, God cares, God plays a role in everything that happens to us. How can one person possibly do so much? Did you forget?—He's not a person. That's what makes Him God!

God Is Good

If God were a human being, there's one thing we wouldn't have expected of Him. In the course of history we've seen that the maxim of Lord Acton is invariably correct: "Power corrupts; absolute power corrupts absolutely." When rulers like Saddam Hussein can do whatever they please, we don't expect them to be paragons of virtue. That's why it's so remarkable to realize that Abraham gave us the gift not only of a belief in one God, but the concept of *ethical monotheism* as well.

Let There Be Light

Ethical monotheism is the belief that there is only one God who chooses to limit Himself to acting only in a just and ethical manner.

From the Mountaintop

In the musical *Fiddler on the Roof*, Tevye not only talked to God throughout the day, but sometimes even argued with Him. Too daring? Not at all. He took his cue from Abraham who also argued with God. God, for a Jew, can be held to his commitment to justice.

The very word *God* in English is a contraction of a longer word *good*. God who *could* be anything *chose* to be good. So strongly does Judaism hold this to be true that the Bible records one of the most remarkable debates between a human being and the Almighty. When God informs Abraham that He is about to destroy the cities of Sodom and Gomorrah for their wickedness, Abraham has the absolute gall to say to Him, "Will the judge of the whole world not act justly?" What about the innocent people in these cities, Abraham wants to know. To paraphrase him just a bit, it's almost as if Abraham complains to God, "God forbid you should do such a thing." It might not seem so unusual to us, steeped as we are in a centuries-old tradition of belief in a righteous God. Just imagine, though, how daring it must have been for Abraham to make this assumption at a time when it was common for kings to dictatorially do as they pleased, without regard to any ethical or moral considerations. Abraham accepted God as the Creator of the whole universe, yet he was unwilling to believe that this God might act in an unjust manner!

What's even more striking is that God agreed with Abraham. You didn't understand, God explains. If there would indeed be a minimum number of good people in these wicked cities, God admits He wouldn't be able to destroy them. What Abraham suspected, the Bible later reveals as the essence of God's nature and character: "The Rock [God], His work is perfect; for all His ways are justice; a God of faithfulness and without inequity, just and right is He." (Deuteronomy 32:4)

When Moses asks God to share with Him a little bit more about His personality, God lets Him know His attributes: "The Lord, the Lord, a compassionate and gracious God, slow to anger, rich in steadfast kindness, extending kindness to the thousandth generation, forgiving iniquity, transgression and sin; acquitting the penitent." (Exodus 34:6–7)

If that's what it means to be God, say the rabbis, these attributes must be holy. If God is good, then humankind has to imitate Him. And that's why adding the adjective "ethical" to the belief in monotheism is probably the most relevant of all the Jewish beliefs about God.

Schmoozing

Belief in a cruel God makes a cruel man.

—Thomas Payne (1737–1809), American patriot

Two Names: Tough Love

So if God is One, how come He has two names? I don't mean just in English—Lord and God—but even in Hebrew, in the Bible itself. There are times when God is referred to as *Adonay*—the word usually translated as "Lord." Other times, He is called *Elohim*—the word translators render as God.

Stranger still, the very quote from the Bible that Judaism requires to be recited twice a day as an affirmation of monotheism mentions both names in the very same sentence! We'll get the phrase a number of times in this book, so let's write the transliteration of the Hebrew now: *Sh'ma Yisroel Adonay Elohenu Adonay Echod—Hear O Israel the Lord our God, the Lord is One.* So if He really is one, why confuse us with two different designations?

From the Mountaintop

Observant Jews don't pronounce the name of God as it is written in Hebrew. It's just too holy. Instead of *Adonay*, they will say *Hashem*—the name; instead of *Elohim*, they will intentionally mispronounce it as *Elokim*. Be careful not to take God's name in vain.

Different Names for Different Strokes

The answer of Jewish philosophers adds a final piece to the puzzle of our understanding of God. One person can have a number of names to describe different relationships. I can be daddy to my children, honey to my wife (depending on the day), rabbi to my students, and Benny to my friends. Because God has two main ways in which He relates to the world, He is either *Adonay* or *Elohim*—Lord or God. When we perceive Him as kind, merciful, and compassionate, we say, "Thank the good Lord." Win the lottery and, of course, it was the Lord who appeared to you. In Hebrew, you would praise *Adonay*. But let something bad happen—miss a plane, stub your toe, catch a cold—and you exclaim, "Oh, my God!" The name *Elohim*, God, is used to describe moments when God relates to us in ways we consider strict, harsh, judgmental, and perhaps even cruel.

Why would a God of love, the Lord, choose at times to be tough, almost harsh, strict, and seemingly unloving? For the same reason that parents from time immemorial have been seen by their children not only as loving but "too strict, too rigid, too stuck on stupid rules." The one line that is probably heard in households around the world from parents to children is: "Someday when you get older and have children yourself you will understand." And the line is, of course, repeated from generation to generation.

 Ask the Rabbi

Of course when we say male or female, we refer to sexual identity of body that's totally inappropriate for God. God has no physical form. Yes, God has characteristics that we ascribe to man or woman. Then why call God a "He"? You're right, "She" is really just as appropriate. When English catches up to Hebrew grammar which uses God in feminine form, we'll hopefully be able to interchange gender when we write about Him/Her.

I guess even God hopes that when He has to be God—the strict disciplinary parent—His children will some day understand that it's only because He loves us so much that He has to act firmly and toughly. "Tough love" isn't just the name of an international movement that has proven successful in dealing with rebellious teenagers. It's a description of the duality of approach God/the Lord has chosen as the most productive way to deal with His children.

Father and Mother

What's even more fascinating is that in Hebrew the name for the Lord, *Adonay*, has a feminine ending. A merciful God is more like a mother. The Hebrew for God, *Elohim*, has a masculine ending. It suggests that God is also a father. The Jewish concept of Lord/God is a combination of male and female attributes. The Almighty is a

He *and* a She, harmonizing the best of both sexes so that human beings can be blessed not only with a Father, but also with a Mother, in heaven. (This is what I meant when I said God *Herself*, in the beginning of this chapter.)

How Do We Know It's True?

People say "seeing is believing." That's not true. Seeing is knowing. Believing is choosing to accept one opinion as more credible, more *believable*, than another.

Religion is based on belief. Faith is not the same as facts. That's why we have *atheists* and *agnostics*.

Theologians ask, if God wants the world to believe in Him, why doesn't He make Himself clearly known, why doesn't He appear in full glory so that no one could dispute His existence? The answer is simple. If God were to do that, no one would *believe* in Him. People would simply be forced to accept His reality.

That's why proof of God's existence not only isn't possible, it isn't desirable. If by proof we mean incontrovertible demonstration as a scientific proof would demand, God will remain forever undiscovered. But if by proof we mean proving the most logical of two alternatives, neither of which can be ascertained as fact, then God can be "proven" as the more logical of two possibilities. A world with God has meaning, has purpose, has a way to explain its existence. To believe that the mathematical precision of the universe is the result of chance or coincidence requires a blind faith far more demanding than a religious disciple can muster.

Schmoozing _____

Nature is too thin a screen; the glory of the omnipresent God bursts through everywhere.
—Ralph Waldo Emerson

Atheists, goes an old Yiddish saying, can't find God for the same reason that a thief can't find a policeman. Plato put it more powerfully: "Atheism is a disease of the soul before it becomes an error of the understanding." And a Jewish atheist, of course, is someone like the apocryphal Jew who is proud of his rebelliousness and proclaims to everyone within earshot, "Thank God, I'm an atheist." Guess it's not easy to totally disbelieve!

Let There Be Light _____

An **atheist** believes there is no God. An **agnostic** says that the question of God's existence is unknowable—and therefore he doesn't take a stand on the issue one way or the other. Both share this trait: Neither of them has any invisible means of support.

The Least You Need to Know

♦ Judaism begins with Abraham, who recognized one God as the Creator of the World.

♦ The Big Bang theory of creation accepted by most scientists today agrees with the Judaic teaching that the world suddenly came into being "out of nothing," but does not offer any judgment about how it happened.

♦ Judaism insists that God, the Creator, is only one—a belief in monotheism that rejects the many gods of paganism, the two gods of dualism, and the three persons of the Trinity.

♦ Judaism believes that God, the Creator, is also God the Carer—a God who maintains an ongoing personal relationship with every one of His creations.

♦ Judaism believes that God is by definition good; ethical monotheism views the All-Powerful Creator as a being who voluntarily chooses to be guided solely by the principles of truth, kindness, and justice.

♦ The two Hebrew names for God that translate into the English names "Lord" and "God" refer to two harmoniously blended traits: the more feminine attribute of kindness and the more masculine aspect of strict justice.

♦ One hundred percent proof of God is neither possible nor desirable, for that would eliminate belief; Judaism accepts the certainty of God's existence as the most logical of all possible alternatives.

Man and Woman

In This Chapter

- ◆ Why God started the world with only one person
- ◆ The relationship of body and soul
- ◆ What "man is created in God's image" means
- ◆ Why God created man and woman
- ◆ The concept of free will
- ◆ The role of human beings on earth

Atheists claim man created God in his image. Judaism, together with almost all other religions, teaches that God created man in *His* image. What we think about the essence of God and the real meaning of man depends ultimately on which side we take in this crucial controversy.

As you read in Chapter 1, Judaism begins with the premise that there is a God. People may argue His existence but we can't question our own. We know that we're here on this Earth, but we're still trying to figure out why. What's our purpose in life? Who are we really? Are we just one of the countless creatures on earth, different only in appearance, or are we qualitatively a breed apart: Godly beings—the true goal of creation? Are we truly better than all the beasts of the field or just egomaniacs who let our minds rationalize that we are the greatest beings in the universe?

Judaism is not just a religion that values questions. It also has answers for these most fundamental problems of human existence.

One God—One Man

Why we need God is obvious. Why God needs man and woman is a mystery. It's hard to believe that God was just bored or simply needed some laughs, so he put into motion the human comedy. Perhaps, suggest Jewish philosophers, a God who is by definition good had to *actualize* His goodness by creating and by giving of Himself to others.

What we do know is that God wanted people. Surely it would have been just as easy for Him to start with a million or more. Instead, the creation of humankind begins with one. And that, Judaism teaches, is the very first way in which God chose to tell us a number of very important truths about ourselves:

♦ "Whoever saves one life, it is as if he saved the entire world." That was the message from the *Talmud* with which Steven Spielberg chose to close his masterpiece film about the Holocaust, *Schindler's List.* The most powerful proof of the infinite value of human life is the fact that the whole world originally started with one life. If anyone would have killed Adam, there would have been no future generations. Every human being today is a potential Adam. Kill a person and you cut off a future world. Save one person and you are responsible for saving an entire world.

Let There Be Light

The **Talmud** is the "teaching" of Jewish law and lore by rabbinic sages in the academies of Israel and Babylonia, which existed from the beginning of the Common Era (C.E.) to approximately the end of the sixth century. (C.E. is the way Jews refer to years after Jesus—instead of A.D., which means Anno Domini, or the year of our Lord.)

♦ The Talmud also teaches: "Only one person was originally created for the sake of peace among human beings, so that no man should be able to say to his fellow man, 'My father is greater than your father.'" Hatred between people is often based on claims to greater ancestry. Many cultures have caste systems, depending on heredity. People of noble birth are privileged; those born to the poor are often pariahs. Class distinctions make no sense when you realize we all come from common parentage.

♦ The popular parlor game *Six Degrees of Kevin Bacon* describes how the prolific actor is linked to every other Hollywood star. (Bet you didn't think you'd see bacon mentioned in a book on Judaism!) One father for all humankind, however, makes everyone on earth brothers and sisters in the truest sense of the word. Jewish prophets could later preach peace on earth and goodwill toward all based on the simple premise that we are all basically "one big happy family."

◆ Adam, as the first human being, was not just one man—he was every man. Christian and Jew, black and white, American and Asian—every later way in which people would come to differentiate themselves from others appears insignificant in light of the recognition that the one from whom all of us are descended was created by God "in His image."

◆ One last Talmudic insight: "And one man was created first to proclaim the greatness of God. If a human being stamps several coins with the same die, they all resemble one another. But the King of kings, the Holy One, praise be He, stamps all human beings with the die of the first man and yet *not one of them is identical with another*. Therefore, every individual is obligated to say, 'For my sake was the world created!'" Adam was meant to be a symbol of every person in the future. Adam was unique, and so are you. If you wouldn't have something special and distinctive to contribute to the world, you wouldn't have been created. Realize how important you are. Know your own worth. That is the final message Judaism sees in the story of man's creation.

What Is a Human Being?

As the Bible tells it, man and woman were created last in God's scheme of creation. Mark Twain said he wasn't surprised to read this: "Man was made at the end of the week's work, when God was obviously tired." The Talmud put a much more positive spin on the story. Human beings came last because they are the purpose of all of creation. Just as a king would make all the necessary preparations before inviting an honored guest to his palace, so, too, God made sure everything was ready for people as soon as they appeared on earth.

But God didn't want all this to go to our heads. Excessive pride is a religious sin. So God called the first man Adam, from the Hebrew word *Adamah*, which means "earth." It was God's way of telling Adam—and through him

From the Mountaintop

From where did God take the earth with which He created Adam? From all the four corners of the Earth—so that Adam's descendants should feel at home no matter where they choose to make their residence.

all of us, his descendants—always to remember where we came from: "Then the Lord God formed man of the dust of the ground …." (Genesis 2:7)

Creation of Adam *detail by Michelangelo.*

(Art Resource, NY/Alinari)

What makes man so special, though, is the last part of that sentence: "And He breathed into his nostrils the breath of life, and man became a living soul." Dust and divine breath, body and soul define the duality of a human being and explain the biblical view of God's final creation: "What is man, that You are mindful of him? And the son of man, that You think of him?—Yet You have made him a little lower than the angels, and have crowned him with glory and honor?" (Psalm 8:5–6)

Everything about the human condition, Judaism believes, is based on the two sources of our being. Half dust, half deity, we spend the rest of our lives trying to decide which one will be master. For Sigmund Freud in the twentieth century, it would come down to the battle between the id and the superego. For the rabbis, it would be the struggle between the *yid*, the subconscious desire of the soul to be true to its essence, and the bodily cravings for pleasure and material fulfillment.

> **Schmoozing**
>
> The soul must not boast that it is more holy than the body, for only in that it has climbed down into the body and works through its limbs can the soul attain to its perfection. The body on the other hand may not brag of supporting the soul, for when the soul leaves, the flesh falls into decay.
>
> —Martin Buber (1878–1965), German theologian

Ideally, body and soul should learn that cooperation is far more beneficial than conflict. God created both of them because alone neither can accomplish what God has in mind for man. A body without a soul is an animal. A soul without a body can't live on earth. That's why Jewish law demands treating both with great care, with reverence and respect.

Take Care of Your Body

A story from the Talmud: The first-century scholar, great sage Hillel finished giving a lecture and rushed off to what was obviously an important appointment. "Master," his disciples asked, "may we ask where you are going?" "To fulfill a religious obligation," Hillel answered. Hoping to learn from their teacher, and perhaps to imitate him as well, they pressed on: "What is this religious obligation?"

Hillel replied: "I am going to the bath house in order to take a bath." The students were astonished. "A bath? Our master is running to take a bath? And he calls that a religious obligation?"

Hillel responded: "Most assuredly, yes! If somebody appointed to scrape and clean the statues of the king that stand in the theaters and circuses is paid for the work and even associates with the nobility, how much more should I, who represents God on this earth and whose body was created by Him not make certain that it is kept in pristine and pure condition."

It may just be a body, but it's the receptacle of the soul. God's spirit lives in it. You don't allow the noblest and most sublime thing on Earth to live in an unkempt slum. Cleanliness isn't just next to Godliness, it's a precondition for spirituality. Before God met with the Jews at Mount Sinai and gave them the Ten Commandments, He made sure to tell them to prepare for this holy moment by sanctifying themselves—bathing and washing their garments.

Healthy in Body

More important even than keeping the body clean is keeping it healthy. It's no coincidence that every Jewish mother's dream is that her son become a doctor. Healing the body is a religious act, a *mitzvah*.

The man Jews admire as the closest to Moses in the Bible, the twelfth-century Spanish rabbi,

Let There Be Light

A **mitzvah** is a "commandment" of the Torah, traditionally incumbent upon all Jews.

philosopher, and scholar, Moses Maimonides (1135–1204), was a great physician by profession. He authored a book summarizing all of Jewish law, the *Mishneh Torah*. In it, he wrote: "Since it is impossible to have any understanding and knowledge of the Creator when one is sick, it is one's duty to avoid whatever is injurious to the body and to cultivate habits that promote health and vigor." He then went on to list medical do's and don'ts that read like the *Health Letter* from the Mayo Clinic—and that have become part of the Jewish Code of Law!

Pulpit Story

The first Jew ever to be elected president of the United States (it's just a story) invited his mother to come to the inauguration and made sure she had a front row seat. Proudly, he watched her gesturing to him as she animatedly spoke to people all around her. He asked one of his aides to find out what she was saying. The aide came back to report that she was telling everyone, "See that man up there? He's the brother of my other son, the doctor!"

Schmoozing

There is no wealth like health.
—Apocrypha: Ben Sira 30:16

Let There Be Light

Kosher is the Hebrew term meaning "fit," usually referring to food that is permitted according to Jewish religious law. In a broader sense, it may refer to anything that is legitimate or legally permissible.

Do Not Desecrate

The Bible forbids tattooing as a dangerous and unwarranted desecration of the body. It commands: "You are the children of the Lord your God—You shall not cut yourselves nor make any baldness between your eyes for the dead." (Deuteronomy 14:1) Pagans would deliberately disfigure their bodies as a sign of mourning. The Bible, speaking just like a Jewish mother, reminded us that we are "children of the Lord." It's almost as if God was saying, "It hurts Me if you hurt yourselves."

That's why, if the Surgeon General warns that cigarettes are dangerous to your health, Jews have to know that Joe Camel isn't just giving bad advice. He's teaching children to do something that *religiously* isn't *kosher*.

Watch Out for Your Soul

Judaism added something to Newton's discovery of gravity. Men and women are unique because they are governed by a *double* law of gravitation—one pulls them down to earth, the other pulls them up to heaven. Gravity is another way of saying that everything has a natural pull to go back to its original source. That's why things that come from the earth go back to the earth. Without interference, material things will fall to the ground.

The same thing should happen to man and woman, but they walk around with a soul that has a gravitational pull upward, to its heavenly source. That will keep man and woman elevated until the moment of death when the soul returns to where it came from, leaving the corpse, without its support, to drop to the ground.

The soul not only elevates the body physically; it also elevates it spiritually, giving it direction and purpose. The soul is what defines man, just as a book tells the world about its author. The soul, in Jewish thought, remembers where it once was and tries to make man and woman what they are capable of becoming.

The soul, just like the body, needs to be nurtured. The physical body needs food. The soul requires spiritual nourishment. Good deeds, acts of kindness, and imitating God's ways all make it flourish. Starving the soul of its supplements makes it wither. "A sound soul in a sound body" is the most important maxim of the Jewish religion.

In His Image

One more thing we know about man: "… And He created man in His image, in the image of God He created him." (Genesis 1:27) If that means we look like Him, it's not very clear whether we're talking about Brad Pitt or Bela Lugosi. What's even more difficult to figure out is how all of the billions of people in the world who look so different from one another could all still be said to be "in the image" of the One who created them.

Does God Look Like Us?

Clearly, when we talk about human likeness to God we can't possibly mean physical similarity. One of the fundamental beliefs in Judaism is that God has no body or any attributes of physical form. A body is limiting; it restricts us in space. If we're six feet tall or even a million, it would mean at some point our body reached its outermost limit. That can't be true for God, who is everywhere.

That's why Jewish philosophers explain that every time the Bible speaks of "the hand of God" or uses a similar comparison to human features, it's meant as a metaphor. God's hand is His power. "God descended" doesn't mean He took an elevator; it means He chose to make Himself more visible on Earth. The Bible uses anthropomorphisms—it couches in human terms those concepts about God that would otherwise be incomprehensible to us.

Sorry to break this to you, but even if someone tells you that you look divine, it can't be literally true. Appearance is something we simply can't share with a God who has no face or figure. Yet the Bible did state very clearly that we are "in His image." What can that possibly mean? It means that we can be like someone else because we *are* like them, not necessarily because we look like them. People can share characteristics without sharing physical features. And that's what God meant when He let us in on the secret that we are like Him.

Are We Just Like God?

So what exactly is this trait with which human beings were endowed that makes us different from all the rest of creation? What did God put into us that makes us like Him?

Strangely enough, God didn't tell us. But then again, if we are in His image we probably should be smart enough to figure it out. In Jewish tradition, there are two major interpretations of how we are in God's image that have gained acceptance. And just because they're different from one another doesn't mean that one interpretation is right and the other is wrong. In all probability, the truth is a combination of both.

- ◆ **We have God's intellect.** Maimonides, widely recognized as the preeminent Jewish philosopher and scholar, believed that man shares with God His divine intellect. As a philosopher, Maimonides felt that what separates man from the beast is the gift of reason. Animals may "think" on a certain level called instinct but they cannot conceptualize. They cannot dream dreams, they cannot change the world, and like God, they cannot be themselves creators. It's been said that a human being is the only animal that laughs and weeps—because he is the only animal that is struck with the difference between what things are and what they ought to be. This knowledge, this level of awareness, this ability to understand the world and even come to discover God Himself—this is the meaning of the divinity within ourselves that defines us as being in God's image.

- ◆ **We have souls.** Nachmanides, Rabbi Moses ben Nachman, the great Spanish rabbinic scholar, physician, and theologian (1194–1270), thought that reason alone isn't enough to explain what makes human beings unique. There's only one thing within mortals that is not mortal. Our bodies, composed of perishable matter, are finite. But our souls, breathed into us by God, contain His very essence and like Him live on forever beyond our deaths. That's what God meant when He told us we are in His image. Every person on earth carries within himself or herself a little bit of God. Imagine how important every single human being is and realize that when we say God is in our midst, we mean it literally—by virtue of *all the people around us, including ourselves.*

Hasidim Versus Mitnagdim

Jewish history records two major movements of the late Middle Ages that differed in their emphasis on mind or on soul, on the priority of wisdom or of spirituality in serving the Almighty. The *Hasidic* movement chose the heart. Spirit meant more than study. The *Mitnagdim* were adamant in insisting that only by sharpening one's intellect and spending every waking moment of the day using one's mind could we fulfill our mission on earth. What each of these movements did was to take hold of one of the interpretations of man in God's image and grant it exclusive legitimacy.

There's a famous legend about the leaders of these two respective movements—the *Ba'al Shem Tov* who founded the Hasidic movement and the *Gaon* of Vilna who stood at the head of the Mitnagdim. As they quarreled bitterly over whose interpretation of Judaism was correct, a meeting of reconciliation was arranged. For reasons unknown, the two never got together, and their disciples continued their disagreement.

With the intuitive wisdom of common Jews, an oft-repeated saying arose: Had the two leaders succeeded in meeting and bridging their differences in compromise, the Messiah would have come! Which is another way of saying that after centuries of disputing the meaning of man's uniqueness "in the image of God," we should at long last realize that we are godly because we are blessed with both a mind and a soul.

 Let There Be Light _____

Hasidism, the religious movement originating in Eastern Europe in the late eighteenth century and founded by Israel Ba'al Shem Tov, stresses spirit over study and the heart over the intellect. *Hasidim* are members of the movement. **Mitnagdim,** "opponents" of Hasidism formed after Rabbi Elijah, the Gaon of Vilna, placed the Hasidim under a ban because of their displacement of Torah study as the ultimate priority in Judaism.

One God—Two Sexes

The author of this couplet, often quoted, remains anonymous—probably because he was afraid for his life—but it offers one humorous reaction to the final act of God's creation of humankind:

> Whilst Adam slept, Eve from his side arose:
> Strange his first sleep should be his last repose.

Judaism teaches that one of the noblest goals is to imitate God. The first two professions we see practiced by the Almighty Himself are activities that remain to this day profoundly Jewish occupations: medicine and matchmaking.

No sooner did God create man than He wanted to play doctor and perform surgery—a clear proof, say some (with tongue in cheek), that God is Jewish. The next thing God realized was that "it is not good that man should be alone." (Genesis 2:18) Adam may have been in the Garden of Eden but without another human being there, even Paradise is Hell. So God created once more, and as some people would have it, proved that even He got better with practice.

From the Mountaintop

The first woman, Eve, was in Hebrew called *Chavah*, Hebrew for "mother of all living things." Man's name, Adam, "from Earth," referred to his past. But the name Eve speaks of woman's role for the future. Only in their union, explained the rabbis, can past and future be brought together to create a present of meaning.

Schmoozing

There is no pleasure for man unless woman shares it.

—Aristophanes (ca. 450–385 B.C.E.), Athenian dramatist

It's foolish to think that the only purpose for the creation of woman is for the reproduction of the species. Asexual reproduction could just as well have been chosen by God as the means to populate the earth. Nothing prevented God from cloning not just sheep but even Adam so that he could say "Hello Dolly" to his descendants. But God chose Eve, proving what the Talmud would later turn into a Jewish proverb: "Without woman, man is only half a man, incomplete."

Eve was meant to be man's best friend. She would take away from Adam the curse of loneliness. More than that, it would be her biblically designated destiny to be "Ezer K'negdo." (Genesis 2:20) English translations render the phrase "a helpmate for him." But rabbinic commentators make it a point to emphasize that that is not its real meaning. In Hebrew, *K'negdo* means not *for* him, but rather *opposite* him.

The Bible long ago answered Rex Harrison's bewildered question in the musical *My Fair Lady:* "Why can't a woman be more like a man?" A woman wasn't meant to be just like a man. There already was one of those on earth. A woman was meant to be different. She is to be man's *opposite*, balancing out man's deficiencies with her dissimilar nature. Man and woman are meant to be complementary—and to realize that they ought to be *complimentary* as well. Their differences are *intentionally* mandated by God. We ought to be smart enough, with the French, to say *"Vive la différence."*

Vive La Différence

There's a delightful Scottish nuptial song that almost sounds like it's taken from the pages of the Jewish Midrash:

> The woman was not taken
> From Adam's head, you know
> So she must not command him
> 'Tis evidently so;
> The woman was not taken
> From Adam's feet, you see
> So he must not abuse her—
> The meaning seems to be.
> The woman she was taken
> From under Adam's arm
> Which shows he must protect her
> From injury and harm.

The rabbis gave the same reasons for why Eve wasn't created from Adam's head or feet. The punch line though, is, I think, more powerful and more profound: God took a portion from Adam's rib so that man would always remember his mate must stand at his side as an equal, neither higher nor lower.

Bone Is Stronger Than Dust

The Midrash takes note of another difference between man and woman: Man was created from the dust of the earth, woman from a bone of Adam. Bone is stronger than earth; an earthenware jar when it falls shatters into many pieces; a vessel of bone remains firm and whole. Woman, concludes the Midrash, is blessed with greater emotional inner strength. A remarkable observation for an ancient text considering that Ashley Montagu, the respected American anthropologist and social biologist, wrote the following in the twentieth century: "Though women *are* more emotional than men, men are emotionally weaker than women; that is, men break more easily under emotional strain than women do. Women bend more easily, and are more resilient."

It may not be politically correct today to speak of innate differences between the sexes. At the very least, though, it should be of interest to note what Jewish texts believe, based on an analysis of biblical sources. When the Bible describes God taking the rib from man and "building" it into a woman, it uses a Hebrew word, *Va'yiven*, which is related to the word for profound understanding. Based on that, the Talmud concludes, "The Holy One, blessed be He, endowed women with more insight and intuitive intelligence than men."

And when the Talmud wonders why, at the time of Revelation, God told Moses to first "speak to the daughters of Israel" before addressing the men, and to ask *them* whether they wished to receive the Torah, the response is: "Because the way of men is to follow the opinion of women." (Guess the world hasn't changed that much after all in thousands of years!)

Woman is seen to have one more attribute in much greater measure than man. The Hebrew word for kindness, *Rachamim*, has as its root the word *rechem*, which means "womb." The English language, by contrast, took the root for womb, *hyster* (as in hysterectomy) and used it as the basis for the words hysteria and hysterical. As we've seen, the very name of God that expresses this characteristic of mercifulness and compassion appears in Hebrew with a feminine ending. God Herself chooses sometimes to be more like a woman.

Separate, but Not Always Equal

All of this, of course, doesn't mean that throughout Jewish history women were treated equally or acknowledged for their superior traits. Jews were affected by their environments as well as by the currents of foreign cultures in which they lived. Yet Judaism rather than Jews always taught the nobility of women (as we will see in Chapter 10). It even made it a requirement for every Jewish husband to sing a song of praise to his wife on Sabbath eve extolling her virtues and calling her a "woman of valor."

You Have a Choice

Man and woman, both made by God and both "in His image," were given a mind and a soul, as well as one more great gift, which would define their kinship with their Creator: Put into Paradise, they were told they could *choose*—because God imbued them with free will.

Let There Be Light

Mishneh Torah is the name of the Code of Jewish Law written by Maimonides to summarize the legal ruling of Judaism.

Adam and Eve were given a commandment: They were not permitted to eat of a particular tree in the garden and were informed that the way they would act would bring them either curse or blessing. In this, Maimonides, together with all other Jewish philosophers and theologians, concludes that God does not preordain what we do. Human beings are free to act as they will—and either reap the rewards or suffer the consequences of their choices. Maimonides, in his *Mishneh Torah*, Laws of Repentance (5:4), says:

> If God decreed that a person should be either righteous or wicked, or if there was some force inherent in his nature which irresistibly drew him to a particular course ... how could God have commanded us through the prophets, 'Do this and do not do that, improve your ways, and do not follow your wicked impulses,' when, from the beginning of his existence a person's destiny had already been decreed? ... What room would there be for the whole of the Torah? By what right or justice could God punish the wicked or reward the righteous? "Shall not the judge of all the earth act justly." (Genesis 18:25)

Gotta Have Free Will

Isaac Bashevis Singer, the Nobel Prize–winning Yiddish author, was asked, "Do you believe in free will?" He wryly replied, "Of course! Do I have a choice?" Judaism is even more definitive in its answer.

Is everything determined by heredity? The Talmud describes how at the moment of conception, an angel takes the drop of semen and brings it before God. He asks, "Master of the Universe, what will be the fate of this drop? Will it develop into a strong person or a weak one? A wise person or a fool? A wealthy person or a poor one?" But whether the person will be wicked or righteous, this the angel does not ask.

Of course, the Talmud is saying, some things are clearly predetermined by our genes. I've come to grips with the fact that never in my lifetime will I hit 70 home runs in a season or dunk the ball the way Michael Jordan does. But whom I choose to be, my character, and, bottom line, my worth as a human being, remain up to me. And the same is true of you.

The "Officer Krupke" excuse found in the musical *West Side Story* is roundly rejected by Judaism:

> Dear kindly Sergeant Krupke
> You gotta understand
> It's just our bringing up-ke
> That gets us out of hand.
> Our mothers all are junkies
> Our fathers all are drunks
> Golly Moses! Naturally we're punks.

If your parents are criminals and your neighbors are crooks, nothing prevents you from following what your soul really wants you to do. It's not written in the stars nor predestined by circumstances. Judaism teaches that you and you alone are the author of your autobiography.

"You're a Good Man, Charlie Brown"

Making the right choices isn't all that hard. Judaism rejects the Christian view that, "In Adam's fall/We sinned all." Jews don't begin life with the mark of Cain or the guilt of original sin.

Schmoozing

In spite of everything, I still believe that people are really good at heart.

—Anne Frank, from her diary entry of July 15, 1944

Every morning, religious Jews start their daily prayer service with the following words: "My God, the soul you placed within me is pure. You created it, you fashioned it, you breathed it into me." It is the very opposite of the belief that people are born to be wicked, that humankind is evil by nature. We begin life with a pure soul and a clean slate. God tells us, as He told Adam, "I set before you two possibilities … the blessing and the curse. Choose life."

A Partner with God

The Talmud tells of a rabbi who was also an excellent healer. One day someone criticized him: "If God wanted that man to be well, he certainly wouldn't allow him to be sick. How dare you interfere with God's will and cure someone the Almighty has chosen to be ill!" (The critic's line of reasoning would find an echo many years later in the philosophy of Christian Science.)

The rabbi was quick to reply: "If God doesn't want me to succeed, He will surely make my efforts fail. In the meantime, it is God who is responsible not only for the man's sickness but also for the medicines which I am using, as well as for the intelligence and the skill God has given me to practice my profession. God did not create a perfect world. He left it imperfect so that man may play a role in it and serve as partner to God in the act of creation. I am fulfilling my function as God's partner in the way He intended."

A World Left Unfinished

God closed the biblical account of creation by declaring that He finished "what He created to do." (Genesis 2:3) The "to do," explain the commentators, implies an ongoing obligation for man. Because our role is to imitate God, the most powerful way we can do that is to be creative.

When the Wright Brothers invented the airplane, critics condemned their efforts as being ungodly. "If God would have wanted man to fly," they said, "God would have given man wings." Not true. God didn't give man wings because He wanted him to discover through his own ingenuity how to soar to the heavens. Had God *not* wanted man ever to overcome his earthbound limitations, He would have simply created the laws of physics in such a way as to make flying impossible.

> **Schmoozing**
>
> The universalistic dream of a transformation and healing of the world, the belief that peace and justice are not meant for heaven but are this worldly necessities that must be fought for, is the particularistic cultural religious tradition of the Jews.
>
> —Michael Lerner, from *Tikun* magazine

All of scientific progress—all of humankind's inventions and discoveries—are justified and even mandated by Judaism's insistence that humans are supposed to strive to imitate God. A world purposely left imperfect by a God who chose to "rest" on the seventh day and leave His work incomplete waits with anticipation for the one created in God's image to complete the task.

"Tikun Olam"

Two Hebrew words summarize this obligation: *Tikun olam* means to fix the world. It is Judaism's two-word summary of human beings' obligations on Earth.

A Hasidic rabbi was asked: "You have taught us that everything God created has a divine purpose. I can understand that for most things, but there is one matter which troubles me greatly. Why is there such a thing as atheism in this world? What purpose could a lack of belief in the Almighty possibly have?"

The rabbi replied: "Yes, strange as it seems, even atheism has a very important purpose in life. It is for all the times when people are tempted to say they need do nothing because God will take care of it, God will do it for them. God allows a spirit of agnosticism to exist so that man will understand there is a need for him to play a role as well."

The Least You Need to Know

◆ God created one man at first so that all humankind could share in a common ancestry and recognize the unique worth of every single individual.

- A human being is fashioned by God from a mixture of earthly and heavenly sources, so man and woman must revere and take special care of both body and soul.

- Man in "the image of God" refers to his uniqueness of mind and of soul.

- Man and woman are different and both, with their complementary natures, are required for a full expression of humanity.

- Humankind is granted free will and for that reason people are responsible for their actions.

- Human beings come into this world with a pure soul, unburdened by original sin or guilt.

- God left the world unfinished and imperfect so that we might have an opportunity to complete the divine act of creation.

Chapter 3

Friends

In This Chapter

◆ The two purposes of religion

◆ Choosing between person and God

◆ The difference between charity and the Jewish concept of *tzedaka*

◆ How to help people without giving them money

◆ Collective responsibility and the mission of the Jew

Spinoza, the great Jewish philosopher of the seventeenth century, observed that, "Man is a social animal." The world may have started with Adam but there's a good reason why one of the top TV shows today is *Friends*. We just can't live our lives without other people. The worst punishment prisons have for inmates not bothered by anything else is total isolation. So Judaism, which, as we've seen, gave us unique insights into God and humankind, shares with us some very important ideas about society and our relationship to others.

A great rabbi, Hillel, who lived at about the time of Jesus at the beginning of the Common Era, summed up the teachings of the *Torah* with this profound observation: "If I am not for myself, who will be for me? And if I am *only* for myself, what am I?" To be for oneself isn't egotistical; it's simply fulfilling the obligation of self-preservation. But to be *only* for oneself and not be concerned with anyone else in the world is to turn yourself into a what?—a parasite who only takes and never gives and has lost the right even to call him- or herself human.

Take Two Tablets

The Ten Commandments are the shortest summary of the ideals of the Bible. Way before David Letterman came up with his Top Ten lists, God presented the Jews with two tablets bearing ten laws that told the Jews what He expected of them.

These laws, the people were told, are God's prescriptions for a sick society. They were meant for the spiritual health and well-being of the world. Just like doctors today, God was advising us to take two tablets—and call Him in the morning if we still weren't any better.

Let There Be Light

Torah, literally, "instruction," narrowly refers to the five Books of Moses, which are also the first five books of the Bible (see Chapter 6). In its broader usage, it includes not only the entire Jewish Bible, but the oral law and the transmitted teachings accompanying the Bible as well (the Talmud, etc.).

What should give us pause, though, is why God chose to put this list of ten major principles on two separate tablets. Why didn't God simply put them all on one? To say they wouldn't all fit is surely the wrong answer. So Jewish scholars respond with an answer that not only explains something extremely profound about the *Decalogue*, but also offers a breakthrough in Judaism's understanding of the very word *religion*.

Two Kinds of Commandments

Let's review the laws that appear on each one of the tablets before I explain why they were divided into two.

Let There Be Light

The **Decalogue,** literally "the 10 words," is the name given to the Ten Commandments that appear on the two tablets handed by God to Moses on Mount Sinai.

Here are the five commandments that comprise tablet number one:

1. I am the Lord your God who took you out of the land of Egypt, the house of bondage.

2. You shall have no other gods before me. You shall not make unto yourself a graven image, nor any manner of likeness of anything that is in heaven above or that is in the earth below

or that is in the water under the earth; you shall not bow down unto them nor serve them.

3. You shall not take the name of the Lord your God in vain.

4. Remember the Sabbath day to keep it holy.

5. Honor your father and your mother so that your days may be long upon the land which the Lord your God gives you.

This is where God stopped and said "Let's continue on a different tablet of stone." The next five read as follows:

6. You shall not murder.

7. You shall not commit adultery.

8. You shall not steal.

9. You shall not bear false witness against your neighbor.

10. You shall not covet your neighbor's house; you shall not covet your neighbor's wife, nor his manservant, nor his maidservant, nor his ox, nor his ass, nor anything that is your neighbor's.

From the Mountaintop

Christians have a different way of numbering the Ten Commandments. For Catholics and Protestants both, "I am the Lord" is an introductory statement and not a commandment. Protestants make up for the missing one by splitting the second commandment into two separate parts. Catholics divide the commandment concerning coveting (#10 listed earlier) into two, one referring to the neighbor's house and the other referring to the neighbor's wife.

Look at these laws carefully, say the rabbis, and you will see that they have totally different concerns. Those on the first tablet all deal with obligations that a human being has to his or her Creator. Those on the second tablet all deal with relationships of people to people.

Okay, if you're really smart you'll object, just as someone did in a Talmudic academy long ago, and ask, "What about commandment number five? Why does that one belong on the tablet

 ### Schmoozing

If I want to come closer to God, it is only by my coming closer to my fellow human being. If I am your friend, I am God's friend. If not, I am the enemy of both God and His creatures.

—Elie Wiesel (b. 1928), Nobel Prize–winning author

From the Mountaintop

Cotton Mather, the famous Puritan preacher in colonial America, was concerned with the problem of people who fervently worshipped God but ignored the ethical commandments toward fellow man. "Woe to those," he said, "who pray with all their hearts to God on Sunday and then prey upon their fellow man throughout the rest of the week."

outlining obligations to God since parents are also human beings?" The answer is simple: The first tablet explains not only what we owe our Creator above but also our creators below here on Earth. Parents gave us life and are entitled to a kind of respect comparable to the Almighty.

What God did, in short, was to visually demonstrate that *religion isn't restricted to our dealings with Him.* Religion, as defined by the revelation at Mount Sinai, legislates our relationships with others as much as it is concerned with our relationship to God. To be religious means to be ethical as much as it does to be pious. A religious thief is as much an oxymoron as an atheist believer.

Why Noah Wasn't the First Jew

As if it weren't daring enough to declare that how we deal with other people is as important as how we treat God, Jewish tradition went one step farther. People occasionally are an even higher priority. That explains why Abraham was the first Jew, though the Bible itself records that someone "walked with God" 10 generations before Him.

Noah, it would seem, had all the right qualifications. His resumé reads like a super-Jew who certainly deserves to be considered the founder of Judaism. Who could be better than a man described as "righteous, perfect he was in his generations"? (Genesis 6:9)

Yet the rabbis realized that something about him wasn't fully kosher. He was perfect "in *his* generation"—implying, Jewish commentators infer, that if he would have lived in the generation of Abraham he wouldn't have amounted to all that much. And why is that? Because Noah lived in a generation of corrupt people and obviously wasn't involved enough with others to influence them or to save them. His philosophy of life was to live "in his own little ark," self-satisfied to be pious for himself and not really concerned with the rest of mankind.

The final Jewish verdict on the man whose neighbors were all destroyed by a flood for their sins is that he may have been wonderfully observant of the laws that appear on the first tablet but woefully lax in appreciating the demands of those on the second.

The definitive story of Abraham goes like this: Abraham is hosting God, who came to visit him during his recuperation from his circumcision, when he suddenly sees three strangers in the distance. Abraham presumes they are Arabs—total strangers—weary from their travels and desperately needing food and lodging. So he leaves God to take care of these people. At first glance that seems like a horrible perversion of priorities. Men over God? But Abraham understood that because God is so great, He's never in need. People who need people *should* be taken care of before serving the omnipotent Creator.

A "Pious Fool"

The Talmud has a great example to illustrate this idea. It asks: Would you like to know who is a pious fool? It is a man who stands by the seashore, wrapped in his *tallit* and devoutly engrossed in prayer. Suddenly, he hears screams from a person drowning and pleading for help. Knowing he could rescue the man if he jumps in, he continues to stand in his place—for how could he forsake the God he's conversing with merely to aid a human being in distress? In response to this kind of behavior, the rabbis call him a "pious fool," which I guess is a more polite way of saying, "What an idiot!"

Let There Be Light

A **tallit** is the prayer shawl with fringes on its four corners, as ordained by the Bible (Numbers 15:37–41), used by Jews during prayer.

Judaism on One Foot

This idea may even be the deeper meaning of a famous story in which Hillel (here he is again) is the hero. A non-Jew, the Talmud tells us, went first to Shammai, a famous rabbinic figure of the time, and asked if he could be taught the entire Torah "on one foot." Shammai turned him away. He didn't believe in teaching a crash course in Judaism.

Then the non-Jew went to Hillel, who was known for his patience and kindness. Of course, it was a formidable task to boil Judaism down to one major teaching. But Hillel wouldn't turn the man away, so he tackled the question: "On one foot, the most important idea of Judaism is not to do to your fellow man what you would not want him to do to you." The master teaching of our religion, he explained, is what stems from the verse in Leviticus (19:18), "You shall love your neighbor as yourself." Hillel then advised the man to go and study more. It turned out that he became so impressed by everything else he learned that he eventually converted.

A simple reading of the story implies that the questioner was just a man in a hurry. His request for the information on one foot meant he didn't have time to stand around. There is, however, a far more profound interpretation: Judaism rests on two foundations, represented by the fact that the Decalogue was written on two tablets. The non-Jew was deeply intrigued by the idea that this religion he had heard about was committed to both. He understood that Judaism requires service to God and to man. But what he wanted to know was on which of these two feet did Judaism put more emphasis. If someone has to make a choice between them, what would Judaism decide?

Shammai thought this question impertinent. There are two tablets and they are both equally valid. Shammai didn't want to have to choose between them. Hillel understood more clearly why the man was so persistent. What he really wanted to know was whether Judaism was God-centered or man-centered. When it came to the nitty-gritty, would the religious priority be the first or the second tablet?

Judaism does in fact have two major verses demanding man's allegiance. One is in Deuteronomy (6:5): "And you shall love the Lord your God with all your heart, and with all your soul, and with all your might." The other is the one in Leviticus that asks people to love their neighbors. Remarkably enough, Hillel did not tell the non-Jew the sentence about the need to love God. Hillel didn't quote both sentences because the man had insisted he wanted to know the essence of Judaism on one foot. What he really wanted to know was which of the two ideals is more important. So Hillel said, if I'm forced to make a choice, let me tell you God is more interested in people being good to each other than in worshipping Him. God can always manage, but His greatest concern is for people, so He is ready to set aside His own honor for the greater good of the world.

Two Temples Destroyed

History proves that Hillel was right. Twice in the long story of the Jewish people their holiest site was destroyed. The First Temple was torched by the Babylonians in 586 B.C.E.; the second, by the Romans in the year 70 C.E. The Jews understood that both of these terrible tragedies were caused by their sinfulness. Prophets made clear that these were punishments for a nation that didn't deserve God in its midst because they rejected His teachings.

Yet each one of these tragedies had a different cause; the specific sin that angered God wasn't the same for these two major catastrophes of Jewish history. The First Temple was destroyed because Jews worshipped idols. They had forsaken the God of their ancestors. Simply put, they broke the first tablet. The second time around, Jews were "religious" and deeply pious in their allegiance to God, but profoundly insensitive to ethical behavior among themselves. The Second Temple was destroyed, the rabbis realized, because of needless hatred between Jew and fellow Jew. The values of the second tablet were the ones disregarded.

Each of these desecrations was punished. Each one was a rejection God could not allow to pass unpunished. Yet Jews couldn't fail to notice a major difference between the severity of God's retribution. The effects of the first sin, that of idolatry, lasted for 70 years. The Second Temple was rebuilt just one generation later. The aftermath of the Second Temple's loss, however, is still felt to this day. Obviously, God can forgive insults to Him far more readily than He is willing to overlook people's cruelty to each other.

It's More Than Charity

That probably explains why the Talmud concludes that "charity is equal in importance to all the other commandments combined." And even as it states this remarkable law, it uses a word in Hebrew that makes it clear that Judaism doesn't even accept the notion of "charity."

An 1860 alms box from Hungary.

(Art Resource, NY/The Jewish Museum, NY)

Charity, from the Latin word *charitas*, meaning "high regard," or "love," conveys the idea of doing something more than you have to. It's a noble gesture, a deed that comes from the heart, an act that's praiseworthy precisely because it's completely voluntary. That's not at all what its Jewish counterpart, the word *tzedaka*, implies. Tzedaka is literally justice or righteousness. It's not just a good thing to do, but a necessary, required act—an obligation, a mitzvah.

The Scotsman, goes the story, when asked by his minister to "give till it hurts," responded, "The very thought of giving makes me sick." And so he refused to open his purse. The Jew simply has no choice. Like it or not, Judaism requires ten percent of one's earnings to be set aside for the poor. Generally known as *tithing*, this amount is the minimum, a commandment whose source is in the Bible.

From the Mountaintop

The performance of every *mitzvah*, every religious commandment, is prefaced with a blessing. "Why," the rabbis ask, "is there no blessing preceding the giving of charity?" "Because," they answer, "that would delay helping a human being in need with words directed to God. God can wait; a poor person can't."

The difference between giving charity and tzedaka is profound: With a perspective of charity, the one who gives is to be exceedingly praised; the one who doesn't has merely omitted performing a nice gesture. With the concept of tzedaka, the giver has done his duty; the one who failed to respond is guilty of a grievous sin that makes him spiritually unworthy of his wealth.

That's probably why there are so many stories of impoverished Jews accepting funds as if they were coming to them. For instance, did you hear the one about the poor collector who came around regularly for alms every year but this time suddenly appeared with another, far-younger man at his side? When asked who this additional supplicant was, he answered simply, "This is my new son-in-law. I promised to support him for the next two years."

Schmoozing

It often happens that when one is eager to perform a mitzvah, the evil impulse says to him: "Why do you want to reduce your wealth?" The truth is that just as the light on the lamp is not diminished even if a million candles are lighted from it, so will one who gives never suffer a diminution of his possessions.

—Midrash, commenting on the verse, "The life breath of man is the lamp of the Lord." (Proverbs 20:27)

Or the one about the wife of a rabbi who said to her husband, "Your prayer was lengthy today. Have you succeeded in bringing it about that the rich should be more generous in their gifts to the poor?" Her husband replied, "Half of my prayer I have accomplished. The poor are willing to accept them."

Beggars treated their donors almost as if they were doing them a favor by accepting their money and allowing them to do a good deed. And who knows, if charity is tzedaka, maybe they really were!

From the Mountaintop

The Rabbi of Punid, a Polish town, sold all his belongings in a year of famine to aid the poor. His wife hid the Sabbath candlesticks and waited until better times came before she took them out of their place of concealment. When the rabbi saw them, he fainted. On being revived, he asked with a sigh, "How many of the poor could have been fed with the money these candlesticks would have brought?"

It's Not Just Money

Leo Tolstoy, the great nineteenth-century Russian novelist and social reformer, was asked by a beggar for some coins. Tearfully, Tolstoy replied, "My brother, it pains me deeply to tell you that I have nothing to give you." Without hesitation, the poor man said, "But you have already given me more than any other person. You have called me your brother."

Judaism understands this great truth and expanded the mitzvah of tzedaka into an even more noble category called *g'milat chesed*—acts of loving kindness. G'milat chesed, the rabbis taught, is greater than charity in three ways:

1. Charity, tzedaka, is accomplished with money; loving kindness is practiced with one's person—spending time with the sick, cheering up the depressed, making people feel they are important.

2. Charity, tzedaka, is given only to the poor; g'milat chesed can be given both to the poor and to the rich—consoling those who are in mourning, comforting those who are suffering, being a friend to those who are lonely or spiritually starved even as they are financially blessed.

3. Charity, tzedaka, is given only to the living; g'milat chesed is shown both to the living and to the dead—arranging for a proper burial, attending a funeral, or visiting the graveside of a friend or a member of the family.

One of the greatest practitioners of g'milat chesed was Rabbi Akiva, a leading Talmudic scholar of the first century. When his student, Judah bar

Schmoozing

If people would realize that Judaism is not a matter of obeying or pleasing God, it is a matter of changing the world by investing ordinary moments with holiness and making our lives matter in the process, then living Jewishly would no longer be an obligation. It would be an irresistible answer to one of life's most pressing questions.

—Harold Kushner (1935–), rabbi, author

Ila'i, witnessed his martyrdom, he was certain that the power of his master's acts of kindness would ensure him eternal reward in the heavens. The words he wrote at that moment best sum up Judaism's view of the greatness of g'milat chesed:

Rock is strong
But iron shatters it.
Fire melts iron
Water extinguishes fire.
Clouds carry away water,
And wind drives away clouds.
Man can withstand the wind,
But fear conquers man.
Wine dispels fear,
But sleep overcomes wine.
And death rules over sleep.
But more powerful than all ten
Are sweet acts of charity and loving kindness.

We're All in One Boat

People must help each other. "All Jews are responsible for one another" isn't just a powerful United Jewish Appeal slogan. It's a law from the Talmud. And it means exactly what it says—not only that Jews are obligated to help each other but are also *responsible* one for another. Other people's failings are partly my fault if I could have done something to correct them and didn't.

The Midrash tells the story of a group of people sitting in a ship. One of them took a drill and began to bore a hole under his seat. When his shipmates protested, he said to them, "What has this got to do with you? I'm boring the hole under my own seat!" The point, of course, is obvious. In life, all of us are in the same boat. What one person does affects everybody else. Someone can say it's just under his seat that he's drilling a hole—as he chooses a life of crime, of drugs, of ignorance, or of cruelty—but his choice can sink all of society if we don't intercede. "No man is an island unto himself" is the way the English poet John Donne put it. "All men are brothers" is the Jewish way of alerting us to the fact that Cain was wrong, and we are indeed, all of us, our brothers' keepers.

 Schmoozing

The world is based on three things: on Torah, worship, and loving kindness.

—Simeon the Just, Mishna, *Ethics of the Fathers* 1:2

The Jew and the World

There's a Yiddish joke that has a Jew complaining to God: "O Lord, you have chosen us from among all the nations. So tell me, what do you have against us?"

Yes, Jews do believe they are different from the rest of the world. It isn't based on any feelings of racial superiority, as some people have claimed. That obviously isn't true because Judaism admits converts. As a matter of fact, one of the most famous converts of all had a book of the Bible named after her, the Book of Ruth. And this formerly Moabite woman then became the ancestress of King David. One of the greatest Jews of all didn't even come from Jewish parents! Judaism is a religion, not a race. Jews are a people by virtue of their faith, not their forebears. Their uniqueness rests not in their being chosen but in the fact that they had the wisdom to choose correctly.

The Midrash pictures God turning to all the peoples of the world and asking them if they want to accept His Torah. Each one asks, "What is written in it?" and when informed of some of the strict laws, refuses it. For some, it was adultery; for others, theft or murder. Culturally, morally, and ethically, the nations at the time of Revelation (thirteenth century B.C.E.) just weren't ready. Only the Jews willingly accepted the law. That's what makes them the *choosing*, not the *chosen*, people.

A Kingdom of Priests

God told Moses to tell the Jewish people when they were about to accept the Torah, "And you will be to Me a kingdom of priests and a holy nation." (Exodus 19:6) The biblical commentators ask: But the Jews weren't *all* priests? Only a limited number served in that capacity among the people. Why does God give them all that title? The answer: What the priests were to the rest of the Jewish people, the Jewish people as a whole were to become to the entire world. That's what the prophet Isaiah meant when, many years later in the eighth century B.C.E., he told the Jews that their mission was to be a "light unto the nations." (Isaiah 9:6) Jews aren't meant to ignore the rest of the world. They have an obligation to inspire it. Jews shouldn't feel superior to the rest of humanity. They should only feel an obligation to serve as a moral example so that others follow in their ways. To be a Jew, as Jews understand it, is not so much a gift as a responsibility. It's an obligation to teach others and to share their wisdom—not just with other Jews, but with all of humankind.

> **Schmoozing**
>
> The Jewish Messianic faith is the seed of progress which has been planted by Judaism throughout the whole world.
>
> —Joseph Klausner, Russian Israeli historian (1874–1958)

The Messianic Vision

This commitment to perfecting the world is what serves as the source for the Jewish vision of the end of days. A Jewish optimist isn't somebody who just says the glass is half full instead of half empty. A real Jewish optimist says, "Wait just a little bit longer and you'll see, the glass will be completely full."

For some, history is a sad saga recounting the decline and fall of a series of empires. For the Jew, history is a story with a script written by God that has a preordained happy ending. The Messianic vision assures us that a time will come when "nation will not lift up sword against nation neither shall they learn the art of war anymore." People will live together in peace and tranquility, learning to live by the commandments written on *both* of the tablets. Jews can't just wait for that time to come. They know it's their responsibility to make it happen.

The Least You Need to Know

- Jewish law, as summarized on the two tablets bearing the Ten Commandments, concerns itself with our obligations both to God as well as to our fellow man and woman.

- Judaism places greater priority on helping people than worshipping God because God is never in need but people are.

- The destruction of the Second Temple was far more serious and long-lasting than the destruction of the First because the sin that caused it was hatred between people rather than idolatry.

- Helping people monetarily is tzedaka, a just and required act, rather than charity, a voluntary act of kindness.

- Even higher than tzedaka is the concept of g'milat chesed, acts of kindness that go beyond material gifts.

- Jews are not so much the *chosen* people as they are the *choosing* people, whose uniqueness rests on their willingness to be the first to accept God's laws upon themselves.

- The Messianic vision places upon Jews a responsibility and a mission to perfect the world and to serve as a light unto the nations.

Chapter 4

Law and Order

In This Chapter

- ◆ The Christian God of love and the Jewish God of law
- ◆ The final judgment
- ◆ The source of ethical behavior and morality
- ◆ The laws that do and the laws that don't make sense
- ◆ The purpose of the Commandments

Christianity has long claimed that the difference between it and Judaism is that Christianity is a religion of love and Judaism is a religion of law. The comparison was meant to put Judaism in a less favorable light. Jews, however, accept this analysis not as a criticism but rather as a compliment.

For Jews, a religion that stresses God's love even for those who continue to sin too readily takes for granted that man and woman can't be better. It emphasizes humankind's great faith in God but diminishes God's faith in humankind. A God of law forces people to recognize that their blessings impose obligations, that privileges carry responsibilities, and that obeying rules is the rent we pay for the gift of being allowed to live here on earth.

Because there is a God (Chapter 1), because we were created in His image (Chapter 2), and because we relate to others (Chapter 3), we have a responsibility to be true to God, to ourselves, and to fellow humans. It is a God of law who teaches us how to live up to these responsibilities because, after all, responsibility is nothing more than our response to God's ability.

The Final Exam

President John F. Kennedy won a Pulitzer Prize for his book, *Profiles in Courage.* As he reflected on the lives of great people who can serve as heroes, he wrote: "Of those to whom much is given, much is required. And when at some future date the high court of history sits in judgment on each one of us—recording whether in our brief span of service we fulfilled our responsibilities ... our success or failure will be measured by the answers to four questions: Were we truly men of courage ... were we truly men of judgment ... were we truly men of integrity ... were we truly men of dedication?"

I doubt whether the thirty-fifth president of the United States was aware of an eerily similar passage in the Talmud. Thousands of years before Kennedy wrote that we will be judged by our answers to four questions, the rabbis recorded the following:

> In the hour when an individual is brought before the heavenly court for judgment, the person is asked:
>
> Did you conduct your business affairs honestly?
>
> Did you set aside regular time for Torah study?
>
> Did you ensure continuity of the world by having children?
>
> Did you look forward to the world's redemption?

The bad news is that all of us have to be prepared to take a final exam once we finish our lives on Earth. The good news is that it's a test for which we are given the questions in advance. God doesn't want to surprise us. And the important points this Talmudic passage makes have to be studied not only so that we can get a good grade for the Academy on High, but also so we understand how our lives will ultimately be judged at the entrance to eternity. Here, at a minimum, are the ideas we should stress from this remarkable passage:

- ◆ A God of law holds us responsible for the kind of life we lead. Because we were given the gift of life, we are held accountable to a Higher Authority. We must be true to the basic demands of morality and fulfill our purpose on Earth or be deemed failures by the only standard that matters. The famous slogan on T-shirts is wrong. It's not, "Those who die with the most toys win." It's "Those who can answer the questions on the final exam correctly win."

◆ The first question—were you honest?—isn't at all what we would expect. It doesn't deal with God, or for that matter anything else on the first tablet (remember the previous chapter?). Before God checks to see whether you were a saint, He wants to know if you were a *mensch*—an honorable human being. I guess decency counts even more than devotion.

◆ The second question—whether you set aside regular time for Torah study—has as its focus not the way you treat others but the way *you regard yourself*. Not to develop and grow intellectually and spiritually is to make your years meaningless, your days fulfilling no purpose. Sammy Davis Jr. said, "I've got to be me." God says it more strongly: You've got to be you; you've got to become all that you are capable of becoming. And if you don't, when you look back after death you're going to have to admit that you made a mess of your life.

◆ The third question—relating to family—asks whether you understood that you had to think of more than yourself. As Isaac Peretz, the Yiddish novelist (1852–1915), so beautifully put it, "Children constitute man's eternity." We are, all of us, a link in a chain that, according to Judaism, leads from Adam to Messiah. Those without biological children can adopt. But those too egotistical or too miserly to willingly desire family or be concerned with the future are failures.

◆ Notice the progression: Dealing ethically with others; being true to yourself; preparing for family and future. It is the fourth question that broadens one's perspective and makes us realize that everyone, in his or her own small way, has an obligation while we are here on earth to do something to bring the entire world closer to redemption. The temple, say the rabbis, was built brick by brick. So, too, the entire world will become a holy habitation when every single individual does his share. We can all be heroes of history if we live up to the obligations imposed upon us by our destinies. The *Mitzvah of Tikun Olam*, the commandment to improve and to perfect the world, is the final obligation by which the totality of our lives is measured.

> **Schmoozing**
>
> The Jew who fails to understand the importance of law misses the very essence of his people's contribution to humanity.
> —Solomon Goldman (1893–1953), *Reflex*, American rabbi

For Judaism, God is a God of love who forgives imperfect people even when they don't get it 100 percent right. At the same time, He is a God of law who has enough confidence in man's ability to demand that he get at least a passing grade.

Deed over Creed

Christianity, it's often been said, is a religion of creed. As the New Testament puts it, "Believe in the Lord Jesus Christ and you will be saved." Judaism differs because it places deed over creed. Here again, because God is a God of law, He is more concerned with what you *do* than with what you *think*.

As Moses Mendelssohn (1729–1786), the German philosopher and biblical scholar, pointed out: "There is not in the Mosaic Law a single command, 'Thou shalt believe' or 'not believe.' Faith is not commanded. Only actions are."

The Feast of the Rejoicing of the Law, *1850, by Solomon Alexander Hart.*

(Art Resource, NY/The Jewish Museum, NY)

The Torah is a manual of behavior, not a catechism of beliefs. Revelation in Judaism means that God told Moses to teach the Jewish people 613 laws (see Chapter 8). The same God who had just taken the Jews out of the slavery of Egypt and shared with them the value of freedom now demanded that they be bound by the discipline of divine commandments.

Contradiction? Not at all. God wanted the Jews to learn what Will Durant, the great historian, claimed is the greatest lesson of history: Man became free when he recognized that he was subject to law.

You Can Do It!

Laws only make sense if they don't make impossible demands on people. If man is by inclination a sinner, there's hardly any point in commanding him not to sin. But as we saw, Judaism believes in free will. "The devil made me do it" is a cute Flip Wilson line, but not a theologically acceptable excuse. The devil isn't Mike Tyson; he has no power over those who really *want* to defeat him. The first killer in history, Cain, wanted to use this argument. God told him in no uncertain terms: "Sin crouches at the door, and unto you is its desire—but *you may rule over it*." (Genesis 4:7)

Here again is another major difference between Judaism and Christianity. Christianity believes that the laws in the Old Testament were given to prove that they cannot be kept. Man needed to see that he couldn't gain salvation on his own. Or as the New Testament puts it: "If uprightness could be secured through the law, then Christ died for nothing." (Galatians 2:21)

Jesus, claims Christianity, had to die in order to gain forgiveness for man's sins because mankind was incapable of deserving God's favor by compliance with the law. Judaism disagrees. Law, with all of its stringent demands, was given to man because God was demonstrating his belief that "You can do it!" More than man believing in God, the very concept of Torah demonstrates the idea of God believing in man.

Do We Need God to Be Good?

The fact that we *can* be good doesn't, unfortunately, mean that we *will* be good. Judaism believes that God gives us laws as commandments because without them we'd all figure out ways to do whatever we pleased and somehow be able to rationalize them.

The philosophy of secular humanism believes that you don't need God to be good. People can on their own know the difference between right and wrong. Religion isn't necessary because civilized and cultured people will come to correct ethical conclusions. Even without the Bible or the belief in a Supreme Being, people know that murder is wrong and morality is the obvious, intelligent choice.

Schmoozing

On your way through life you'll meet men who cling to reason, but reason gropes like a blind man with a white cane, stumbling over every pebble, and when it comes against a wall it stops short and tries to tear it down brick by brick. ... We, on the other hand, believe in the power of faith and ecstasy and no wall can stand against us.
—Elie Wiesel

Dostoevsky, in his classic novel *The Brothers Karamazov*, best summarized the opposite of secular humanism, which is the Jewish view: "Where there is no God, all is permitted." If there is no God, objective good and evil simply do not exist. What remains are subjective opinions concerning desired and undesired behavior. If there is no God, what we call right and wrong are just euphemisms for personal taste. You don't like stealing, so you call it wrong. I like stealing, so I call it right.

But those are no more than labels for personal taste. To use an extreme example, without God, you can't say the Nazis were wrong. Because if there were no God, then there were no divine commandments or objective laws of the universe for them to violate. All you can say is that you don't like what they did. The Nazis thought they were right and you don't. They considered racial purity a higher goal than the rights of those they considered an inferior people.

We Need Help!

Society as a whole can't be counted on to come to the right conclusion about what is ethical or moral. Nazis, Communists, and proponents of "ethnic cleansing" to this day prove that people can find ways to collectively justify even genocide. The Germans were highly cultured, but that didn't stop them from carrying out the Holocaust. Rabbi Joseph Soloveitchik, one of the leading Orthodox theologians of our generation, pointed out that the greatest lesson of the twentieth century is that we can no longer confuse civilization with civility, knowledge with wisdom, and culture with morality.

In Nazi Germany, civilized and intelligent surgeons performed sadistic experiments on human beings. Ardent opera lovers and devotees of Bach and Beethoven forced Jewish musicians to play for them and then tortured them to death. As Romain Gary, in his book *The Dance of Genghis Cohn*, put it: "The ancient Simbas, a cruel, cannibalistic society, consumed their victims. The modern-day Germans, heirs to thousands of years of culture and civilization, turned their victims into soap. This, this desire for cleanliness, that is civilization."

From the Mountaintop

Dennis Prager, the contemporary author and radio talk show host, asked high school seniors around the country the following question: "Would you save your dog or a stranger first if both were drowning?" In every instance, he says, one third voted for the dog, one third for the stranger, and one third didn't know. Without a belief in God and the concept of man created in God's image, Prager concludes human life is obviously no more sacred than that of a dog.

Lighting Our Way

In the aftermath of the Holocaust, when we learned that culture and crematoria are not mutually exclusive, Jews see the clearest indication of the death of secular humanism. When man eats of the Tree of Knowledge of Good and Evil and decides on his own the parameters of right and wrong, he is expelled from Paradise. Divine Law is God's way of preventing man from using his reason to rationalize the most obscene behavior. Religion and revelation, Judaism believes, are necessary to light our way out of darkness.

As Will Herberg (1901–1977), U.S. theologian and social critic, wrote in his book *Judaism and Modern Man:*

> The attempt made in recent decades by secularist thinkers to disengage the moral principles of western civilization from their scripturally based religious context, in the assurance that they could live a life of their own as a "humanistic" ethics, has resulted in … our "cut-flower culture." Cut flowers retain their original beauty and fragrance, but only so long as they retain the vitality that they have drawn from their now-severed roots; after that is exhausted, they wither and die. So with freedom, brotherhood, justice, and personal dignity— the values that form the moral foundation of our civilization. Without the life-giving power of the faith out of which they have sprung, they possess neither meaning nor vitality.

Laws That Don't Make Sense

The new preacher who came to town, the story goes, gave his first sermon on the sin of stealing. It was a rousing success and the congregants praised his talk. The next Sunday the clergyman expanded on his theme just a little bit and spoke on the topic, "Thou shalt not steal chickens." His farm community immediately rode him out of town. "Now," they said, "you've gone from preaching to meddling."

We can smile at how people may agree with laws on an abstract level but reject them as soon as they become relevant. That's a good reason why, as I explained, laws need divine sanction to make them applicable in every situation, even when people want to rationalize that *in this case*—when it means them—the law wasn't meant to be in effect. The Ten Commandments aren't the ten *suggestions*. They are meant to be binding, whether we agree or not, and in *every* situation.

But God's book of law for the Jews, the Torah, also has laws that don't make sense. It's not that we don't agree with the reason given for them. They are laws that God doesn't explain at all and without any reason they seem—well, just unreasonable. Why *not* eat pig? Why shouldn't *Kohanim*, Jewish priests, come in contact with the dead? Why should Judaism, a religion that prides itself on logic, demand that its adherents abandon logic for some of its observances?

Let There Be Light

The **Kohanim** (singular, *Kohen* or *Cohen*) are descendants of Aaron whose family was designated as priests. With the absence of the Temple, the Kohanim no longer have "priestly functions" but still retain special honorary status and are subject to a number of special restrictions, such as being forbidden to come in contact with the dead or to marry a divorcee.

Let There Be Light

A **chok** (plural, *chukim*) is a law for which no reason is offered. Jewish philosophers disagreed as to whether it was permissible for us to offer a possible explanation when the Bible didn't do so. Majority opinion sides with the view of Maimonides, that we may suggest interpretations, provided we make clear that they are merely our ideas—and God may have had many other reasons we still don't understand for giving us the law.

Jewish scholars give several answers to explain the category of laws known as *chukim* (singular, *chok*), laws without reason:

- Chukim are not laws that are unreasonable; they are laws for which we do not as yet know the reasons. Revelation, the giving of Torah, is God's gift of a shortcut to ultimate wisdom. We don't know everything yet. We'd have to be God to do that. God does know what we don't, even in the twenty-first century. If God told Jews not to eat pig for all time, it isn't just because He knew about trichinosis and warned Jews millennia before its link with pork was discovered, to stay away from this disease-bearer. It's because God knows things we still haven't figured out about pork that He gave us a commandment not to eat it—a commandment that isn't irrational but super-rational, not *against* reason but *beyond* reason as we know it today.

- Chukim are God's way of allowing us to express confidence in His superior wisdom. If we only obey what we understand, we are worshipping *our* knowledge. Someone who says, "I'll do it if I agree with you," implies that when he doesn't like what you're saying, he'll do it his way. Chukim are a test of faith. God purposely doesn't tell you why in order to see whether you really believe He is smarter than you.

- Chukim may also be a great way to train people in self-discipline. "Just say no" isn't only a slogan for an antidrug program. Human beings are more than animals because we can master our desires, we can control our impulses, we can put off immediate gratification for higher goals. The Marines promise to toughen their enlistees and turn them into "real men" by rigorous discipline. The Torah asks for sacrifices and teaches you to say no so that you can become not only a man or a woman, but a more spiritual "mensch."

Schmoozing

The most precious of all possessions is power over ourselves: Power to withstand trial, to bear suffering, to front danger; power over pleasure and pain; power to follow our convictions.

—John Locke (1632–1704), English philosopher

Does God Really Care?

Why is it so important to God that people follow His laws? What difference can it possibly make to the Creator of the entire world whether a person keeps the Sabbath, eats kosher food, or fasts on the Day of Atonement, *Yom Kippur?* If God is all-perfect and all-powerful, can anything we do really affect Him?

The answer is obvious. What we do doesn't affect Him, it affects us. And because God loves us so, He wants us to do the right thing. In that way, all Jewish Law is not God-centered but human-centered. God tells us the choice before us is not between obedience or disobedience but between blessing or curse. The only reason God cares what we do is because He cares about us.

The Mitzvah and the Golden Mean

The Greek philosopher Aristotle came to the conclusion that the ideal way of life is "the golden mean." Happiness can come only from moderation. Fasting and excessive feasting are both equally bad. The ability to enjoy life comes from taking the middle road.

Maimonides used this concept as the rationale for all of Jewish law. He applied it to the 613 rules that, according to the Torah, regulate human life and showed that the purpose of *mitzvot* (plural of mitzvah, or "commandment") was to create the proper balance between potentially dangerous extremes. Asceticism and hedonism both have no place in Judaism. As

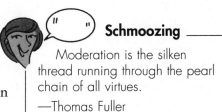

Schmoozing

Moderation is the silken thread running through the pearl chain of all virtues.

—Thomas Fuller

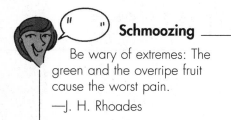

Schmoozing

Be wary of extremes: The green and the overripe fruit cause the worst pain.

—J. H. Rhoades

Maimonides puts it, "Good deeds are good deeds precisely because they are equally balanced between the *too much* and the *too little*."

Don't drink wine at all and you're being disrespectful to God. After all, when He created everything He said, "Behold it is good," and your rejection is almost a personal affront. Drink too much and both your head and body will tell you that you made a mistake.

What does Jewish law demand? You *must* drink wine every Friday night to usher in the Sabbath, acknowledging God's great "spiritual" gift to the world. But you can't drink too much because you have to be sober enough to recite the blessings at the end of the meal. The laws for moderation in the consumption of wine are a paradigm for all the other laws as well. The ideal is moderation, and Jews believe in it so much that—we'll drink to that!

From the Mountaintop

When Noah planted the first vineyard in history, Satan happened along and suggested they go into partnership. Satan then slaughtered first a lamb, then a lion, followed by a pig and a monkey. The blood of each soaked under the vine, and Satan then shared with Noah his secret: "Whenever in the future man will drink of the vine, he will first feel innocent as a lamb; then strong as a lion; more than that and he will resemble a pig; and if he drinks to the point of intoxication he will behave like a monkey."

The Least You Need to Know

- Human beings face a final examination after death, according to Judaism, which demands accountability in four major areas.

- Judaism differs from Christianity in its emphasis on a God of law over a God of love and its priority of deed over creed.

- Judaism differs with secular humanism in its belief that God is necessary as an ultimate source for ethical and moral behavior.

- Jews accept laws that don't make sense, not as *irrational*, but *super-rational* rules, demanding faith rather than reason as the basis of their acceptance.

- God commands us, not for His sake but for our benefit, with a set of commandments, the major goal of which is moderation and the golden mean.

Chapter 5

It's a Wonderful World

In This Chapter

- ◆ How Judaism views life
- ◆ Joy and Judaism
- ◆ More ways Judaism differs from Christianity
- ◆ The importance of life
- ◆ Suicide and death

The musical *Fiddler on the Roof* made the Jewish toast famous: "To life, to life, *L'Chayim*." Jews don't just pray for life, they treasure it and revere it.

Christianity stresses the words of Jesus, "My kingdom is not of this world." The here and now is not important; the hereafter is what we should be after. Again, Judaism disagrees. Remarkably enough, a people that has perhaps suffered more than any other in the course of history believes that life is the greatest gift and that God must be thanked every day for it.

Let There Be Light

Chayim, the Hebrew word for "life," is in the plural. The singular is *chai.* The reason, explain the rabbis, is that life alone is impossible; it is only when shared with others that life is truly lived.

Mark Twain couldn't understand why we rejoice at a birth and grieve at a funeral. His answer was, "Because we aren't the person involved." If life, as Woody Allen would have it, is "divided into the horrible and the miserable," we should only be glad when our journey is finally over. Judaism teaches that to be dissatisfied with life is to be critical of the God who created it. "We thank thee O Lord who has kept us alive, permitted us to survive and allowed us to reach this day" is an all-important blessing the Jew is obligated to recite at all the major moments of life.

"And Behold, It Was Good"

The Bible tells us that after every day of creation God reviewed what He did and proclaimed, "It is good." When He was finished, "God saw everything that He had made, and behold it was very good." (Genesis 1:31) The first evaluation we have of the world comes from no less a critic than God Himself, and He gave it five stars— or whatever rating is the divine standard for ultimate excellence.

That's why this statement in the Talmud, the Jewish book of law (see Chapter 2), is remarkable: In the future world every person will have to give an accounting for all the good things created on earth that he or she denied him- or herself from enjoying.

Never stop to admire a sunset? How could you be oblivious to the wondrous painting God makes to appear in the heavens every day for your benefit? Never travel to see the Grand Canyon, the Great Barrier Reef, the Alps, or any of the famous scenic wonders of the world? God made them for you, and it's almost disrespectful to ignore them. Don't have time to smell the flowers? When they put them on your grave it will be too late to enjoy their fragrance or their beauty. God decorated His house so magnificently. Judaism believes He takes it personally if you don't share His excitement and joy in everything He has put on Earth.

Enjoy Yourself

Religion somehow has gotten a bad rap. People think that its purpose is to restrict pleasure, to limit fun, to make life a dull and dour experience. Nothing could be farther from the truth, at least as far as Judaism is concerned. Over and over again, the Bible repeats the refrain, "And you shall rejoice before the Lord your God." For the Jews, asceticism not only isn't praiseworthy, it's a sin.

The Torah has a fascinating section of law dealing with a person who wants to be holier-than-thou. A *nazir* is the name given to a man who wants to consecrate himself to the Lord by abstaining from wine and strong drink. He knows, as the Book of Psalms tells us, that "wine gladdens the heart of man" (Psalm 104:15), but he'd rather be sad.

The Bible tells him to keep his vow for whatever number of days he pledged because people should keep their word even when they promise to do something the Bible doesn't really approve of. At the conclusion of the period of *nazir*-ship, however, the law is that this man must bring a sin offering. (Numbers 6:14) God is angry, the Talmud explains, because, "Were the restrictions found in the Torah not sufficient for you?" Unnecessary abstention is a sin.

> **Schmoozing**
>
> No one should, by vows and oaths, forbid to himself the use of things otherwise permitted.
>
> —Maimonides, *Laws of Character Development and Ethical Conduct*

A Hasidic story says it best. A young man came before his teacher and prided himself on his extremely pious behavior: "I always dress in white; I drink only water; I place tacks in my shoes for self-mortification; I roll naked in the snow; and I order the synagogue caretaker to give me forty strikes daily on my bare back."

Just then a white horse entered the courtyard, drank water, and began rolling in the snow. "Observe," said the rabbi, "this creature is white; it drinks only water; it has nails in its shoes; it rolls in the snow; and receives more than forty strikes a day. Yet it is nothing but a horse." Human beings, the message is, serve God with joy, not with mortification. God doesn't love masochists and He isn't a sadist.

Christian Ideals, Jewish Sins

The old proverb has it that "one man's meat is another man's poison." A more modern version is, "Different strokes for different folks." So because Judaism believes so strongly that what God created is meant to be enjoyed, it considers three concepts that Christianity idealizes to be nothing less than sins.

The Sin of Celibacy

Jesus taught His disciples: "The people of this world marry and are married, but those who are thought worthy to attain the other world at the resurrection of the dead neither marry nor are married." (Luke 20:34–35) True, marriage is permitted for Christians. Yet Paul instructed the Corinthians: "To all who are unmarried and to widows I would say this: It is an excellent thing if they can remain single as I am, but if they cannot control themselves, let them marry. For it is better to marry than to be on fire with passion." (1 Corinthians 7:9) In Christianity, marriage is at best a compromise with the sexual drive. True holiness is expressed by those who can live under the constraints of a vow of celibacy.

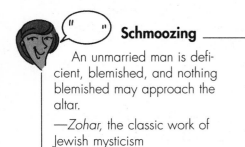

Schmoozing

An unmarried man is deficient, blemished, and nothing blemished may approach the altar.

—*Zohar*, the classic work of Jewish mysticism

In Judaism, sex cannot be sinful. It is the source of all life, and life itself is holy. Everything created by God must be used for some divine purpose. The sexual drive is included in what God saw that He had created, and behold "it was very good." Marriage is not just permissible, it is a mitzvah, a divine commandment. "Therefore shall a man leave his father and his mother, and shall cleave unto his wife, and they shall be one flesh." (Genesis 2:24)

It's not true, as the old joke goes, that a bachelor is somebody who hasn't made the same mistake once. For Jews, he's someone to be pitied because he doesn't realize that Paradise is only Paradise when viewed through four eyes, not two. Anyone who is unmarried, according to the verdict of the Talmud, "lives without joy, without blessing, and without goodness."

The Sin of Poverty

Tevye, in *Fiddler on the Roof*, fantasizes, "If I were a rich man ..." In Judaism, that's a permissible dream. Money is nothing to be ashamed of not just because, as the Yiddish writer Sholem Aleichem humorously observed, "If you have money, you're wise and handsome—and you can also sing." Money allows a person to fulfill many mitzvot. Just like anything else, it can of course be misused. But money isn't the root of all evil. It's the source of countless blessings when spent the right way.

Schmoozing

The act of sexual union is holy and pure. The Lord created all things in accordance with His wisdom and whatever He created cannot possibly be shameful or ugly. When a man is in union with his wife in a spirit of holiness and purity, the Divine Presence is with them.

—Nachmanides, Rabbi Moses ben Nachman (1194–1270), Spanish Talmudist, theologian, and philosopher

Christianity idealizes the vow of poverty. The New Testament says: "It is easier for a camel to go through the eye of a needle than for a rich man to enter the Kingdom of Heaven." (Matthew 19:23) In Judaism, poverty is not glorified as a good and wealth is not considered a sin. "And God blessed Abraham with all things." Abraham *was* a rich man. That's why he was able to invite strangers and feed them, clothe them, and then bring them closer to God. A Jew should strive for possessions. Once he gets them he should be guided by Jewish law to give charity and to transform his blessings into a blessing for humankind.

The Sin of Solitude

On the mountain of Sinai, perhaps the very spot on which the Torah was revealed by God to man, there sits a Christian monastery. Its occupants have taken a vow to remove themselves from the world and never to leave this holy site. Even after death, their bones remain in one of the rooms so as not to break their commitment. The monks affirm their dedication to holiness by their total separation from the profane world.

Judaism believes, as the great sage Hillel expressed it in *Ethics of the Fathers* (2:5), "Do not separate yourself from the community" (see Chapter 8). Holiness is not achieved in isolation. God doesn't want us to remove ourselves from earth to get closer to heaven; He prefers that we take the teachings of heaven and bring them down to Earth. We're not supposed to renounce the world, but repair it. Moses, say the rabbis, was asked to come up to Mount Sinai to receive the Torah and then to bring it down to the people. To stay on top of the mountain is to complete only half the journey. "Tell it to the world" is the Jewish slogan for a truly spiritual human being.

> **Schmoozing**
>
> An avowal of poverty is no disgrace to any man; to make no effort to escape it is indeed disgraceful.
>
> —Thucydides, Greek historian, circa 400 B.C.E.

Life Above All

In Chapter 4, I mentioned an interesting law. The *Kohanim*, the priests, are not permitted to come into contact with the dead. We call that a chok—a law with no apparent reason. There is no explanation given, but in light of Judaism's emphasis on life, I can share with you an intriguing possibility.

In so many other religions, the major focus is not on life but on death, not on this world but the world to come. Pagan priests concentrated their efforts on contacting the spirits or helping people cope with the mystery of death. Imagine what it meant when Jewish law said that its rabbis, the priests of old, were not permitted to have any contact with the dead. What then was supposed to be their function? It was, of course, to deal with life. In Judaism, God says to humankind, "My kingdom is of *this* world." Live your life well on this Earth, and what follows doesn't have to concern you now.

Pulpit Story

Tragically, three friends die in a car crash, and they find themselves at the gates of heaven. Before entering, they're each asked a question. "When you are in your casket and friends and family are mourning upon you, what would you like to hear them say about you?" asks the angel. The doctor says, "I would like to hear them say that I was a great doctor of my time and a great family man." The teacher says, "I would like to hear that I was a wonderful husband and a teacher who inspired children." The rabbi replied, "I would like to hear them say, "Look! He's moving!"

Please Break the Law

How important is life? Important enough to permit the breaking of all other religious laws to preserve it. (There are only three exceptions, as you'll discover in Chapter 8.) Jews are supposed to fast on Yom Kippur; it's a biblical law. Yet if a person isn't feeling well and not eating would be a threat to his or her health, then not only is eating permitted on that holiest of days, it's a mitzvah.

In 1848, a cholera epidemic broke out in the city of Vilna, Poland. The local rabbi, Israel Salanter, was one of the leading luminaries of his time. Doctors advised him that not only those already sick but everyone else should eat so they would have their strength and be less susceptible to the raging disease. Rabbi Salanter didn't think it sufficient to issue a public proclamation that all Jews that year should eat on Yom Kippur. He was afraid that some "pious" people might take it upon themselves to disregard this seeming leniency.

Instead, he strode to the pulpit of the synagogue on the holiest day of the year, took wine and cake, recited the proper blessings, and then drank and ate in front of the entire congregation. He told them that what he was doing was not being lenient with the laws of Yom Kippur but rather strict with the laws of preserving one's health. And so that's the famous story of how an entire congregation feasted instead of fasted on the Day of Atonement and, as tradition has it, made God glad by their decision.

The Talmud records it as a basic principle of law: The saving of life takes precedence over everything else. The laws were given, they explained, "to live by them" (Leviticus 18:5)—and not that you die because of them.

The Sin of Suicide

Poets pen words about suicide, but suicide is a grave sin. Why? Eleventh-century Jewish moralist and philosopher, Joseph ibn Pakuda put it best: "The nearer the relation to the murdered person, the more heinous the crime … and man is closest to himself. A suicide is a sentinel who deserted his post."

To the person who claims the right to choose his own death by declaring, "It's my life, isn't it?" the Jewish response is, "Not!" Life comes from God and can only be ended by Him. So strongly does Judaism feel about this that it teaches, "A suicide loses a share in the world to come."

From the Mountaintop

Jewish law severely condemns suicide in order to prevent it from happening. After the fact, however, Jewish Law is compassionate and does not condemn one who has taken his or her own life. Judaism accepts that, in all probability, suicide was the result of an act of temporary insanity.

After the Final Curtain

As precious as life is, the world to come is even better. The rabbis teach in *Ethics of the Fathers* (4:17): "More beautiful is one hour in the world to come than all the goodness of a lifetime here on earth." Why then should people weep when they take leave of this earth? Why cry if you're moving to a better location?

One of the sages of the Talmud, Rabbi Yehudah, explained it to his students on his deathbed, "I am weeping because of the Torah and the meritorious deeds that I will no longer be able to perform." Death deprives us of the ability to continue to serve God and to accomplish acts of kindness. Life presents us with opportunities for personal growth; death brings to a close our ability to achieve our fullest potential.

A Hasidic story with a supposed "inside look" at what happens upstairs after death, makes the point clearly:

A very rich but miserly man passed away and was standing in line waiting to hear his final judgment. As he watched the procedure with those in line before him, he became far less fearful. He noticed that reported acts of charity had tremendous influence on the divine decree; gifts given during one's lifetime could outweigh many sins. And so, when it was his turn to stand before the heavenly Judge, he said: "It's true I may not have done all I should while I was on earth, but permit me to take out my checkbook and write out very large sums for any worthy institutions you recommend." To which the Judge replied, "Here we do not accept checks. We only accept receipts."

So maybe it is a Jew, after all, who's responsible for the graffiti that reads, "Do it now!"

The Least You Need to Know

- Because God looked and saw that "the world is good," man has an obligation to revere life and to enjoy it.

- Judaism considers celibacy, poverty, and solitude as sins, removing people from the world and its full enjoyment.

- Judaism is a religion of life, not of death, and the preservation of life takes precedence over other Jewish laws.

- Suicide is a severe sin, considered an act of murder.

- Although life after death offers great joy, it lacks the opportunity for humankind to grow and to perform any more good deeds.

Part  2

Read All About It

What do we mean when we say "Judaism believes"?

Judaism speaks to us through its books, which, according to traditional belief, convey the message of God. The Bible is the beginning. The five Books of Moses are followed by the works of the Prophets and the writings of divinely inspired geniuses. The power of their words is best illustrated by their influence to this very day.

Jews have studied and analyzed, argued and debated, and explored and expounded on every thought, every word, every letter of Scripture throughout the centuries.

Part 2 will help you to understand why the Bible is considered by many the greatest book ever written. It will also explain how Jews have made its teachings the focus of their lives, their culture, their traditions, and their way of looking at the world.

The World's Best-Seller

In This Chapter

- ◆ The structure of the Jewish Bible
- ◆ Why the Bible is the world's biggest seller of all time
- ◆ The biblical heroes and heroines
- ◆ The most important biblical stories
- ◆ Major themes of the Bible and all-important laws

Patrick Henry should be remembered for more than, "Give me liberty or give me death." He said something else that is surely the source of his commitment to freedom and the ideal that serves as the foundation of American democracy. "There is a book," he declared about the Bible, "worth all the other books that were ever printed."

President John Quincy Adams, as so many others, echoed the same idea: "I speak as a man of the world to men of the world, and I say to you: Search the scriptures! The Bible is the book of all others, to be read at all ages and in all conditions of human life; not to be read once or twice or thrice through, and then laid aside, but to be read in small portions of one or two chapters every day, and never to be intermitted, unless by some overruling necessity."

The Bible is universally acknowledged as the best-selling work of all times. It is the classic of classics, translated into every language and found in most

r some, it is the literal word of God, dictated by the Al-
s, its holiness derives from the fact that it was written with

t because they were its original recipient. "Speak to the chil-
nt refrain. Jews study it daily; they read it publicly in the
sis, completing its five books every single year. The Torah is
ews. The Torah is the book that teaches Jews what it means
ay "Hear what Judaism believes," we really mean "Hear what

A Pentateuch, Not a Pentium

When Jews use the word *Torah*, or Bible, it can have three meanings. Its most restricted sense, and probably the way it's most often used, is as a synonym for the five books of Moses. That encompasses the text that Orthodox Jews believe stands in a place all by itself as the direct communication of God to man and woman, every letter divine.

In this chapter, when I speak of the Bible, I am referring to the five books of Moses.

The Torah that's found in the ark of every synagogue (more about that in Chapter 22) is a copy, painstakingly handwritten on parchment, of these five holy books, which together are called the *Pentateuch*. The word *Pentateuch*, of course, comes from the root word, *penta*, which means "five." In computer-speak, everyone knows that the Pentium chip is a master at retrieving information. No matter how powerful a Pentium is, however, Jews would rather have the Pentateuch as their source of wisdom.

From the Mountaintop

Please don't call the Jewish Bible the *Old Testament* because that's the name Christians gave it, and for Jews it comes with an uncomplimentary connotation. Many Christians believe that the special covenant between God and the Jewish people was taken away from them and given from Old Israel to the new Israel of the Church. The Bible of the Jews, Christians claim, was also superseded by a new and improved version, the *New Testament*, which made much of the former Testament "old" and outdated. What makes the Bible so precious for Jews is that it remains always new, fresh, and relevant in every generation. It's not the "old" Testament for Jews—it's the "only" Testament.

The Torah can also refer to the later books of the prophets appended to the five books of Moses; together, these form what is usually referred to by Jews as the Bible.

In this larger version, what we call the Bible has 24 books, which you'll read about in the next chapter.

Now don't get confused, but Torah has one last meaning based on its literal definition. Torah is a teaching, a doctrine, or a law. Any discussion of the Bible, any analysis that helps us to understand the Bible better, is a teaching and also deserves to be called Torah. So I have great news for you: What you're reading right now is also Torah because it helps you to understand Judaism and God's words—and that's why you're fulfilling a great mitzvah at this very moment!

Take a Good Shot

Because Torah is such an important word, it's worth taking a small tangent to explore its deeper root meaning. Students of the Hebrew language are intrigued by the fact that Torah comes from the root *yarah*, meaning "to shoot" (such as at a target). When somebody shoots at a target, he's trying to direct an arrow. So the root meaning of the word *Torah* is "correct direction." The Torah wants to point you in the right way. The best English language parallel is probably when we praise somebody as being a "straight shooter."

Remarkably, the Hebrew root of the word for sin, *chet*, means "to miss." To sin means to miss the mark, and to do the right thing is to hit the bull's eye.

"Give Me Five"

In poetic metaphor, the Pentateuch, with its five books, was God extending His hand to man in greeting. "Give me five" is the slang expression today for stretching out a hand of friendship. The five books represent five "fingers of God"—ways in which we can get to "hold on" to a little piece of His essence.

In English, the names of the five books are Genesis, Exodus, Leviticus, Numbers, and Deuteronomy. The titles are descriptive, summarizing the major theme of each of these works:

- ◆ **Genesis,** from the word for "beginning": The book takes us from Creation and the beginning of world history through the founding fathers of the Jewish people and the beginning of the story of the children of Israel.

- ◆ **Exodus,** the going-out: The second book deals primarily with the exodus of the Jews from Egypt, where they had been enslaved.

- ◆ **Leviticus,** after the Tribe of Levi, those appointed to serve in the Temple: The third book gives the detailed instructions of Temple service and sacrifices.

- **Numbers,** the fourth book, gives us a census of the Jews in the desert and follows their wanderings as they approached the Promised Land.

- **Deuteronomy,** literally "the second law": The final book of the Pentateuch is the lengthy last speech of Moses to his people, his farewell address, recapitulating what had happened to the Jews until now, as well as the covenant they made with God that would ensure their survival.

Jews refer to these books in Hebrew by the first important word written in them. Here is the list of the five books of Moses as a Jew would write them in Hebrew:

- *B'reishit,* "in the beginning": From the first verse, "In the beginning, God created the heavens and the earth."

- *Sh'mot,* "names": From the first verse, "And these are the names of the children of Israel who came to Egypt with Jacob; every man came with his household."

- *Va'yikro,* "and He called": From the first verse, "And He called to Moses and the Lord spoke to him …."

- *Bamidbar,* "in the desert": From the first verse, "And the Lord spoke to Moses in the desert of Sinai in the tent of meeting on the first day of the second month, in the second year after they were out of the land of Egypt …."

- *D'vorim,* "words": From the first verse, "These are the words that Moses spoke unto all of Israel beyond the Jordan."

Why use first words instead of the major theme? Perhaps, as some have suggested, because the very idea of a *major* theme for a book in which every word ought to be equally precious is improper. It is as if to say we love every word in this book, so we'll remember it by its initial word of greeting.

One more thing. A Jew who's looking for a copy of the five books of Moses is almost certainly not going to say, "Please pass me a Pentateuch." The word that's used is *Chumash,* from the Hebrew *Chamishah,* which means "five." So if you're sitting in a synagogue and someone asks you to pass him a Chumash, "give him five" and hand him the book that goes from *B'reishit* through *D'vorim.*

Seek and You Shall Find

So what can these five-books-in-one possibly contain that make them worthy of raves from some of the greatest minds in every generation? Lord Tennyson said, "Bible reading is an education in itself." But an education in what? What is its subject?

The answer of the Talmud says it all: "Turn it and turn it, for *everything* is in it." Seek and you will find no matter what your field of interest. History and philosophy; psychology and sociology; science and physics; law and ethics—it's a veritable shopping mall of ideas with every item in stock. That's why the Jewish people are known as "the people of the book." To study the Torah is the quintessential mitzvah because only through it can a person learn how to live as a Jew.

The Fox and the Fish

A story in the Talmud says it best: Once the wicked government (the Romans) issued a decree forbidding the Jews to study and practice their faith. Pappus Bar Judah saw Rabbi Akiva publicly bringing gatherings together and teaching Torah. Pappus said to him, "Akiva, aren't you afraid of the government?" Akiva answered, "I will explain it to you with a parable."

"A fox was once walking alongside of a river, and he saw fish swimming from one place to another. He said to them, 'From what are you fleeing?' They replied, 'From the fishermen's nets.' The fox said, 'Would you like to come up onto the dry land so that you and I can live together as my ancestors lived with your ancestors?' The fish replied, 'And they call you the cleverest of beasts? You are a fool! If we are frightened being in water, the element in which we live, how much more so in the element in which we would die?'"

"You see," said Rabbi Akiva, "it is the same with us. If we are in trouble when we sit and study the Torah, imagine how much worse off we would be if we were to neglect it. The Torah is compared to water and only by swimming in its sea do we have the slightest chance of surviving."

Schmoozing

The existence of the Bible, as a book for the people, is the greatest benefit which the human race has ever experienced. Every attempt to belittle it is a crime against society.

—Immanuel Kant (1724–1804), German philosopher

Some of My Best Friends Are Jewish

Summarize *War and Peace?* Show five minutes of *Casablanca* or *Gone with the Wind?* It's too dangerous to mess with a classic by trying to abridge it. You'll have to read it in full to get its real flavor. What I can do is introduce you to some of the Bible's heroes, a few of its key stories, and a little bit of its major ideas.

The Biblical Heroes

This list isn't meant to be comprehensive. (All I need is to get to the other world and have some biblical personality accost me in anger because he wasn't included in *The Complete Idiot's Guide to Understanding Judaism!*) So without any claim to complete coverage, let me tell you a little about a few of these people.

Abraham

You already met Abraham; he's the founder of the Jewish people and was originally called Abram. In English, it may seem funny to realize that when Abram became a believer, God added "ham" to his name. In Hebrew, though, the name change had an all-important meaning: Abram, Hebrew *Avrom*, means "father of Arom." It restricts his leadership to a small group. *Avrahom*, Abraham, is a contraction of the phrase *av hamon goy'im*—"father of many nations."

Accepting monotheism, Abraham was now charged with spreading the word. As a believer, Abraham was given a mission. Abraham's new name was meant to teach him not to simply "keep the faith." The real religious message is, "If you've got it, flaunt it"—spiritual truths are meant to be shared with the entire world.

Schmoozing

I am profitably engaged in reading the Bible. Take all of this book that you can by reason and the balance by faith, and you will live and die a better man. It is the best book which God has given to man.

—Abraham Lincoln

From the Mountaintop

In Judaism, every number has a special meaning. The significance of numbers 1 through 5 follow a logical sequence: *One* is God, the Source. *Two* are the tablets; they contain ideas illustrated in the lives of the *three* patriarchs, Abraham, Isaac, and Jacob, as well as the *four* matriarchs, Sarah, Rebecca, Rachel, and Leah. The lives of the three and the four are the basis of the *five*—the five books of Moses.

Sarah

Abraham's wife, Sarah, also had another name before her "conversion to Judaism." She used to be *Sarai*, "my princess." (Not the politically incorrect JAP, Jewish American Princess, but the legitimate princess of Abraham, accorded a title worthy of a Jewish wife.) With Abraham's mission, Sarai was to become a co-partner in the work of spreading God's word. No longer would she be "my princess," Sarai, but Sarah—princess without qualification to the rest of humankind.

Isaac and Rebecca

Their son Isaac—in Hebrew, *Yitzhak*—carried forward the spiritual teachings of his parents. His name, from the Hebrew root for laughter, was given because it seemed like a joke when an angel told Abraham, at age 100, and Sarah, 90, that they would be blessed with a child. Yitzhak's birth proved that when God promises, nothing is impossible. He would be proof of the religious truth that he who laughs, lasts.

Rebecca—Hebrew *Rivkah*—from the Hebrew for "to bind," tied her future to Isaac/Yitzhak, the man who loved God so much he was willing to be bound on the altar as a sacrifice.

> **From the Mountaintop**
>
> In Abraham's times, infanticide—slaying children as a form of worship to pagan gods—was common. Abraham was told to offer his son, but then was commanded to stop. The God of Abraham made clear that for him human sacrifice was abhorrent.

Sixteenth-century prayer book depicting the sacrifice of Isaac.

(Art Resource, NY/The Jewish Museum)

Jacob

In Hebrew, Jacob is *Ya'akov*, from the Hebrew for "heel." He was, with his twin brother Esau, child of Isaac and Rebecca. Passive, introverted, and nonconfrontational in his early years, his name fit him perfectly; he was somebody people readily stepped on. Only later in life did he come to the realization that wimps can't win. God doesn't fight all your battles for you if you're not willing to try to fight for yourself.

> **Ask the Rabbi**
>
> "Turn the other cheek" is not a Jewish ideal, as the name **Israel,** "fighter for God," implies. The Talmud says that if you turn the other cheek after someone hits you, you share responsibility for the second blow.

In the traumatic moment when Jacob finally realized this truth and fought with his attacker, his name was changed to *Yisrael*, in English Israel, which means "fighter for God." The observation that "nice Jewish boys don't fight" may have been a culturally created fact of Jewish history when they were an impotent minority outnumbered by powerful anti-Semites. But that is not the religious perspective that is supposed to guide the "children of Israel," descendants of a man who finally learned that failing to fight evil is what permits evil to triumph.

Rachel

From the Mountaintop

Jacob didn't love Leah as much as he loved Rachel. That's why the rabbis teach that Leah was blessed with more children than her sister. God loves those who are downtrodden and tries to make it up to them in other ways.

She was the love of Jacob's life. Her name (same in Hebrew) is from the Hebrew for "beloved ewe." When his prospective father-in-law, Laban, made him work seven years for Rachel's hand, he didn't hesitate to fulfill his end of the bargain. Unfortunately, Laban switched brides on him, and Jacob found himself married to Leah, Rachel's sister. This was while he was still *Ya'akov*, the one used to being stepped upon, so he didn't put up much of a fuss. He worked another seven years for his true love. And because bigamy wasn't yet banned, he ended up doubly blessed.

The Twelve Tribes

The next 12 biblical heroes came in rapid succession: Reuben, Simeon, Levi, Judah, Issachar, Zebulan, Dan, Naftali, Gad, Asher, Joseph, and Benjamin. These are the children of Israel (formerly Jacob) who would each have such large families they would become the twelve tribes. Every one was as different as … well … the 12 months of the year. As a matter of fact, the different tribes *are* linked with the months, according to the mystical teachings of the *Kabbalah*.

Let There Be Light

Kabbalah, literally "received," is the esoteric tradition passed on among Jewish mystics that deals with the secrets of the universe.

When the Jewish people later settled in Canaan, the Promised Land of Israel, the country was divided into 12 sections so that every tribe had its own area. The result was something like the United States of America, a confederation of states maintaining some of their own identity while sharing common ideals and remaining one nation.

Moses

Three generations after the children of Israel were born, Amrom, the grandson of Levi, married Yocheved, and they had a child named Moses. Unfortunately, they didn't even have the opportunity to give their son that name. In a time of persecution with echoes of the modern-day Holocaust, the parents had to hide their newborn child in a little ark, or boat, to prevent his being killed by the decree of the pharaoh, and hope for Godly intervention. Because nothing is impossible when God wills it, Pharaoh's daughter, ironically enough, found the ark floating in the water. (Maybe she shrieked, "Holy Moses," when she discovered a baby inside.)

It was the daughter of Pharaoh, like the modern-day saint Raoul Wallenberg, who rescued the Jewish child, named him Moses because she said, "from the water I drew him," and raised him in the very place where he would later play such a prominent role for his people. Who could have known that this would be the man who would not only "play the palace" with such success, but also become the greatest leader in all of Jewish history!

Aaron

Let's not forget that Moses had a brother, Aaron. It must be pretty tough, as Aaron discovered, to have a kid brother who outshines you. But Aaron was a great man in his own right and was also given a position of prominence by God. He became the High Priest in the temple in charge of the religious services. (Perhaps God, in his wisdom, by dividing political and religious leadership, was giving us a hint of the benefits of separation of church and state.)

From the Mountaintop

Aaron, as high priest, wore a breastplate over his heart. This, say the rabbis, was to acknowledge the purity of his heart and his greatness in not being envious of his brother's superior role.

Stories with a Message

The Bible is filled with stories—but it's not meant to be a storybook. Whatever appears in this book is only there, all the commentators agree, because it has a message, an important idea to teach us. For entertainment, we can read novels. But for inspiration, we should reflect on the novel ways in which the Bible teaches us by example how to live our lives. Generation after generation has learned crucial truths from stories like these:

- Cain, the first murderer in history, is cursed by God. Crimes can't be committed without being seen by someone—if not here on Earth, then by God above.

- The flood was God's way of teaching people that corruption has consequences, that punishment can be not only personal, but collective as well. Nations and entire countries are held accountable for their sins.

- Abraham, Isaac, and Jacob were just individuals, but one person dedicated to a cause, one lonely voice in the wilderness, can change the entire world.

- Sibling rivalry can destroy families, and the story of Joseph and his brothers illustrates the horrible effects of brothers hating one another. Never lose sight of the fact that it was because of the Joseph story that the children of Israel ended up in Egypt—where they had to face the first attempted genocide of their people.

- The reconciliation of Joseph and his brothers shows that change is possible, that people can turn from their wicked ways, that repentance can repair wrongs and hatred can be replaced by love.

- The slaves in Egypt rebelled and were able to regain their freedom. The American colonists used this story as their inspiration. With the slogan, "Rebellion against tyrants is obedience to God," they identified themselves as the children of Israel of their day and proclaimed their "Declaration of Independence" as an expression of the ideals they discovered in the Bible.

- The 10 plagues and the splitting of the Red Sea remind us that sometimes we are witness to "wonder of wonders, miracle of miracles." It may not happen all the time—miracles are reserved for very special occasions—but they are *possible*. And they don't always have to come in a form that suspends the laws of nature. Sometimes miracles are hidden in the language of what some choose to call coincidence. Those who are more spiritually sensitive, however, realize that coincidences can be nothing more than God's way of choosing to remain anonymous.

- The Torah was given in the desert because without law the world is a desert—arid, unproductive, and desolate. But law transforms a wasteland into fertile ground. God is not just an idea; He is a moral code. Religion is not merely a faith; it's a prescription for proper human behavior.

- When the Jews insisted on sending spies to scout out the land of Canaan and they then accepted their pessimistic report that they weren't strong enough to conquer the land, they were doomed to spend the next 40 years in the desert. God waited until that entire generation of pessimists passed away. There was no point in their going to the Promised Land, because even though God promised they would succeed, *you can't accomplish your goal if you don't believe in yourself.*

- Even the greatest of leaders has critics. Yes, Moses himself wasn't immune. True leadership—by definition—means that you lead, not follow the masses, and that's why it's impossible for you not to make enemies. "If you can't stand the heat," Harry Truman was smart enough to realize, "get out of the kitchen." True greatness is judged not by contemporaries but by posterity.

- Before the Israelites entered Canaan and conquered the land, two and one-half tribes, Reuben, Gad, and part of Menasseh, an offshoot of Joseph, decided they were happy east of the Jordan and willing to stay there. They wanted to avoid the hardship of battle and let the rest of the tribes go on without them. The answer of Moses remains to this day a stirring reminder of communal responsibility: "Shall your brothers go out to war and shall you sit here?" "All for one, one for all" isn't a motto invented by the Three Musketeers. It has its source in the Bible. It's not Dumas, but divine.

Ideas Worth Remembering

More than individual stories, there are some major themes that serve as refrains, almost like magnificent musical chords that keep being repeated and set the mood for God's symphony. From hundreds of these, let me just mention a few that I think are particularly significant:

- There is a covenant between God and man. "Let's make a deal," is the way God put it. He'll keep His part of the bargain if we keep ours. Over and over again, God reminds us that if we listen to Him, He will take care of us. And what does God want of us? There may be 613 laws in total, but Isaiah summarizes them all in just two principles: Do justice; carry out acts of righteousness. (Isaiah 56:1) And as the Talmud concludes: "When the prophet Habakkuk came, he summed up the 613 commandments in but one principle, "The righteous shall live according to his faith." To live by one's faith isn't asking all that much. For that, God promises His constant care, divine guidance, and blessing.

- Measure for measure is the divine principle for punishment and reward. The Egyptians drowned Jewish babies in the Nile. They were punished by drowning in the Red Sea. Jacob fooled his father in order to receive the blessing. Jacob was later fooled by his father-in-law Laban and given the wrong bride, as well as by

> **From the Mountaintop**
>
> Measure for measure is the theme of later biblical stories as well. In one of these, Samson sinned with his eyes, lusting after Philistine women. Captured by the Philistines, they tortured him and took out his eyes.

his own children, who told him that a wild beast had devoured his beloved son Joseph. Miriam, the sister of Moses, waited to see what would happen to the ark her brother was in so that she might be of help to whomever found it. When she was struck with leprosy many years later, she was rewarded for her good deed as the entire Jewish people waited for her instead of continuing on their journey. The consequences of our actions eventually catch up with us—for good and for bad.

♦ Worth and not birth is what determines our fate. In ancient times, the firstborn son automatically assumed rights and privileges by virtue of heredity. Yet in the Bible there is a long list of older brothers who give way to younger siblings who are more deserving. Cain was older than Abel; Ishmael was older than Isaac; Esau was older than Jacob; Reuben was older than Judah and Joseph. The eldest was passed over because the democratic ideal of the Bible does away with automatic entitlement. Like the commercial says, "We do it the old-fashioned way; we earn it."

♦ "Remember you were slaves yourselves in the land of Egypt." The memory of our past demands empathy with the downtrodden. Jews must understand the importance of freedom because only those who were not free really grasp the true horror of slavery.

From the Mountaintop

The wicked Esau was Jacob's twin brother. They had to be genetically alike, yet they were morally different. Is this the Bible's way of teaching us that we can't blame who we are simply on heredity?

Ask the Rabbi

Who are you supposed to love? If you have to "love your neighbor as yourself," then the first person you *really* have to love is yourself. Then you will be able to love others as well. The Bible suggests that those who are, deep down, incapable of loving others actually hate themselves.

♦ Peace is the greatest blessing of all. The word *shalom* has become the "Jewish password," used for both hello and good-bye. It is one of the most repeated words in the Bible and an ideal that concludes the priestly benediction: "May the Lord bless you and keep you; may the Lord make His face to shine upon you and be gracious unto you; may the Lord lift up his countenance upon you and grant you peace." Peace between nations, peace within families, and peace of mind for oneself are the goals of a godly life.

"It's the Law"

Together with the messages couched in stories and the concepts repeated as themes are statements of law that succinctly remind us what it means to be human, to be decent, to be children of God:

♦ "You shall not take vengeance nor bear any grudge … You shall love your neighbor as yourself."

♦ "You shall not steal nor shall you deal falsely, nor lie one to another."

♦ "You shall not oppress your neighbor nor rob him; the wages of a hired servant shall not abide with you all night until the morning."

♦ "You shall not curse the deaf, nor put a stumbling block before the blind, but you shall fear your God."

♦ "You shall do no unrighteousness in judgments; you shall not respect the person of the poor nor favor the person of the mighty, but in righteousness shall you judge your neighbor."

♦ "You shall not go up and down as a talebearer among your people; neither shall you stand idly by the blood of your neighbor."

♦ "You shall not hate your brother in your heart; you shall surely rebuke your neighbor and not bear sin because of him."

♦ "When you reap the harvest of your land, you shall not wholly reap the corner of your field, neither shall you gather the gleaning of your harvest; and you shall not glean your vineyard, neither shall you gather the fallen fruit of your vineyard; you shall leave them for the poor and for the stranger."

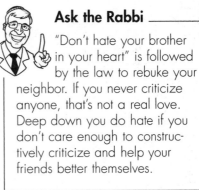

Ask the Rabbi

"Don't put a stumbling block before the blind" means far more than its literal interpretation. Don't hand a drink to someone who can't handle liquor; don't make drugs available to an addict; don't tell a secret to somebody who can't keep one. All these people are "blind" to the consequences of their actions, and you can't be a party to making them stumble.

Ask the Rabbi

"Don't hate your brother in your heart" is followed by the law to rebuke your neighbor. If you never criticize anyone, that's not a real love. Deep down you do hate if you don't care enough to constructively criticize and help your friends better themselves.

This is but a small part of the constitution of Judaism. Just imagine what the world would look like if these divine commandments became the accepted basis of international law.

The Beginning and the End

Because I can't do justice to the whole Bible in just a short overview, I'll try to summarize it the way the Talmud does. The Bible teaches us something about God, who is our role model, in the opening and closing chapters, which serve as a key to all of our obligations. In the beginning of B'reishit, Genesis, God clothes the naked Adam and Eve in the Garden of Eden. His last act, at the end of D'vorim, Deuteronomy, is to bury the dead, as God fulfills this final tribute to Moses. The message? Man is to clothe the naked and bury the dead—as well as everything else that expresses compassion and love that is found in the pages between these two recorded acts of God's goodness.

The Least You Need to Know

♦ The Pentateuch, the Chumash, or the five books of Moses, is the holiest book of the Jewish religion and the source of all its major teachings.

♦ The Jewish Bible consists of the Torah, the name usually used for the first five books, Genesis through Deuteronomy, with the addition of the later prophetic works from Joshua through Chronicles.

♦ Biblical heroes and stories serve as illustrations of important ethical principles, as well as messages relevant to this day.

♦ The laws found in the Bible are the sources of democratic principles and universally recognized concepts of kindness and compassion.

♦ The stories of God's deeds at the beginning and end of the Bible circumscribe the major message of biblical and Judaic concern.

Chapter 7

There's More to the Bible

In This Chapter

- ◆ The 24 books of the Jewish Bible
- ◆ The messages of the prophets
- ◆ The Psalms and prayer
- ◆ The Song of Songs, the Book of Job, and the wisdom of the Proverbs

The word *Bible* in English is misleading. From the Greek word for "book" and written in the singular, it makes it seem like we're talking about a single work by one author. That isn't true. The Bible is a collection of books produced over many centuries by different hands and in different places. Only its very first portion, the part you read about in the previous chapter, known as the Pentateuch, the Chumash, or the five books of Moses, is traditionally considered to have a single author and dates from the time of Moses in approximately the thirteenth century B.C.E.

But Scripture didn't stop with the death of Moses.

For centuries afterward there were other great men known as prophets. God spoke to them, and they left us a record of His revelations to them. Some may choose to doubt the words of these men who claimed they were the privileged recipients of divine communication. Yet many millions have been so moved by the power, the brilliance, the spiritual insights of these spokesmen for God that they are convinced that the Creator really did want to continue a conversation with His creations until such a time as we finally got His message.

Sir Isaac Newton was smart enough to discover the Law of Gravity. Let's give him credit for being right again when he came to the conclusion that, "There are more sure marks of authenticity in the Bible than in any profane history."

Bring Down the Curtain

So how many books are there in the Bible? And at what point was it decided to "bring down the curtain" on a book that would stand apart from all others? With so many different authors writing over so many hundreds of years, how did anyone know when to say, "This is the end"?

From the Mountaintop

Why did prophecy cease? Children need to be told, but maturity demands the ability to learn from the past and to stand on your own two feet. The rabbis believe that the close of the prophetic period is a compliment to man and woman's stature and growth.

The word that describes the official closing of the Bible is *canonization*. It was a decision made by the leading rabbis and scholars who met at a synod in the city of Jabneh in approximately 100 C.E. Strangely enough, although Jews are used to arguing about almost everything, the stature of the rabbis involved in this decision was so great that their decision has been accepted to this day without dispute.

The Canon, or Sacred Books, was officially closed with the 24 prophetic books written to that time because, with the destruction of the Second Temple, the spirit of prophecy was no longer granted to humankind.

The Three Levels

The Hebrew name for the *entire* Bible is *T'nakh* (with the last two letters pronounced as if you were clearing your throat). The word is an acronym for the three different categories of books that comprise the Hebrew Bible: The *T* is for the word *Torah*, used in its restricted sense as the five books of Moses; the *N* is for the Hebrew word *Neviim*, the prophets; the *K* is for *Ketuvim*, writings. The threefold division is meant to distinguish between degrees of holiness.

The five books of Moses represent direct communication from God. This is the work read from beginning to end in synagogues throughout the course of the year. The second category, Neviim, or the books of the prophets, contains communications from God but is written in the words of the authors themselves. The Ketuvim, the writings, are also sacred but come from a less intense form of communication known as the Holy Spirit.

Religious Jews acknowledge this three-tiered division by observing an interesting law: Since it's improper to place something less holy on something holier than it, Jews will never put a copy of one of the biblical books listed in the Ketuvim on top of a book from the prophets, nor either one of these two on top of any of the five books of Moses.

Just so that you know which books belong in which division (you might have to stack them up some day) and so that you have a simple guide to which books made "the final cut," here's the official list:

Torah

1. Genesis

2. Exodus

3. Leviticus

4. Numbers

5. Deuteronomy

Neviim

6. Joshua

7. Judges

8. Samuel 1 and 2

9. Kings 1 and 2

10. Isaiah

11. Jeremiah

12. Ezekiel

13. The Book of the Twelve: Hosea, Joel, Amos, Obadiah, Jonah, Micah, Nahum, Habakkuk, Zephaniah, Haggai, Zechariah, and Malachi

> **Schmoozing**
>
> I draw meaning to my life not from Marxism or any other secular philosophy, but from the prophets of Israel. The ethic of Judaism is integral to my Christian faith. The exhortation of the prophets, "Justice, justice, shall you pursue," rings constantly in my ears.
>
> —Martin Luther King Jr.

> **From the Mountaintop**
>
> The entire Bible ends with King Cyrus, a non-Jew, acknowledging God as the Creator of the heavens and the earth. When universal recognition of God is achieved, Jews will consider their Bible complete.

From the Mountaintop

Just like the Jewish Bible, *The Odyssey* and *The Iliad* of Homer have 24 books. For Jews, the number 24 has special significance: It's a multiple of 12, the number of the Tribes of Israel. By their books, the children of Israel become twice what they were!

Schmoozing

The whole history of humanity has produced nothing which can be compared in the remotest degree to the prophecy of Israel. Through prophecy, Israel became the prophet of mankind.

—Karl Heinrich Cornill (1854–1920), German Protestant theologian

Ketuvim

14. Psalms

15. Proverbs

16. Job

17. Song of Songs

18. Ruth

19. Lamentations

20. Ecclesiastes

21. Esther

22. Daniel

23. Ezra and Nehemiah (treated as a single book)

24. Chronicles 1 and 2

Don't be confused by the fact that the English translation of the Jewish Bible usually lists these same books as a total of 39. It's just a matter of how the list is broken down, but the 39 is just another way of numbering the same 24 that make up the Jewish Bible.

We're Not a "Nonprophet" Organization

When Chaim Weizmann, the first president of the State of Israel, wanted to explain who Jews are, he said:

> "We are perhaps the sons of dealers in old clothes, but we are the grandsons of prophets." The world may take pride in ancestors who were kings. Jews prefer to find glory in their descent from those who taught mankind a passion for justice, a belief in the universal brotherhood of man, and a Messianic vision of peace on earth when "the Lord will be King over the entire earth, and in that day He will be One and His name will be One."

It is the Bible, and in particular the section of Neviim, that serves as a constant reminder that the only profit in life is to live according to the ideals of the prophets. Of the many spokesmen for God who left an everlasting impact, five stand out for us because of the contemporary relevance of their messages.

Nathan

The prophet Nathan was witness to a horrible crime committed by the king. David lusted after Bathsheba (was it just a coincidence that he spotted her while she was taking a bath?) and believed that kings (just like presidents?) didn't have to be bothered with conventional morality. Bathsheba was married, so when she became pregnant by David, he ordered her husband Uriah into the front lines of battle where he was sure to get killed. It was a grievous sin that combined both adultery and murder. Yet it was the king who committed these crimes, and it was long before anybody had ever heard the word *impeachment.*

In any other society of the time, it would have been unthinkable to face the king and condemn him. The prophet Nathan, however, knew that he had no choice but to confront the sinner. His story is a true profile of courage. Nathan tells the king he must ask him for his advice on a simple matter:

> "There were two men in the same city, one rich and one poor. The rich man had large flocks and herds, while the poor man had only one little lamb he had bought. He tended it, and it grew up together with him and his children. It shared his morsel of bread, drank from his cup, and nestled in his bosom. One day, a traveler came to the rich man, but the rich man hesitated to take anything from his own flocks and herds to prepare a meal for the guest. So he forcibly took the poor man's lamb away and prepared it for the man who had come to him. How shall we deal with this matter?" King David flew into a rage. "As the Lord lives," he shouted, "the man who did this deserves to die." To which Nathan responded: "You are the man!"

The prophet confronted the king. The voice of religion spoke out against the voice of power. The representative of the spirit was not frightened by the wielder of the sword. Nathan didn't just tell us that might doesn't make right. He showed us that we dare not fear to speak out against evil no matter how powerful the perpetrator. And what makes the message that much stronger, the Bible tells us, is that Nathan succeeded. The king acknowledged he was wrong, begged forgiveness, repented, and was forgiven by God.

Isaiah

The United Nations isn't particularly known for its friendship to Israel. Yet when its founders needed a quote to express its ultimate goal and its vision, they couldn't find anything better than the words of the Jewish prophet Isaiah: "Nations shall not lift up sword against nation, neither shall they learn the art of war anymore." (Isaiah 2:4)

With the practiced wisdom of diplomats, however, they posted the quote on the wall but didn't identify its source so as not to offend anybody who might be angered by the use of a verse from the Jewish Bible.

From the Mountaintop

Isaiah predicted, "And the wolf and the lamb shall lie down together." Woody Allen added, "But the lamb won't get any sleep."

What the United Nations wouldn't acknowledge we can certainly take pride in. Isaiah not only dared to dream the impossible dream of an end to war and of a time when people "shall beat their swords into plow shares and their spears into pruning hooks," but to proclaim that the impossible is very possible and every person has a role to play in making it speedily come to pass.

Isaiah stressed the power of individuals to affect the future of the world. Society is changed by the small revolutions of little acts of kindness. How do we create a new world? By changing ourselves: "Cease to do evil, learn to do good. Devote yourselves to justice. Aid the wronged. Uphold the rights of the orphan. Defend the cause of the widow." Let enough people decide to be better and all of humankind would be transformed—because the world is nothing more than the sum of its parts.

Isaiah took special pains to preach to the Jewish people and to tell them that their spiritual status demanded even more of them. Their covenant with God gave them greater obligations. Jews, Isaiah said, have a mission to be an *or laGoyim*, "a light unto the nations." The messianic ideal needs a messenger. The Jews believe that God's script calls for them to play that role.

Jeremiah

Jeremiah came to teach us that sometimes *jeremiads* are justified. The English word, named after the prophet who spent most of his life offering tragic predictions, refers to complaints and lamentations. Nobody likes to hear bad news, and you can bet that Jeremiah wasn't too happy about having to be the bearer of sad tidings. But being an ostrich isn't a better alternative. Jeremiah is the prophet who reminds us that to stick your head in the sand and deny reality is to invite destruction.

From the Mountaintop

Jeremiah didn't only criticize and weep. He also predicted that "Again there shall be heard in this place [Jerusalem] the sound of mirth and gladness, the voice of bridegroom and bride." Jeremiah's words are still sung at every Jewish wedding.

Had the people listened to Jeremiah's warnings, they could have prevented their downfall. Jeremiah tried to get people to see that moral decay is the real reason for military defeat. Spiritual strength is more meaningful than mighty armies. The tragedy of the destruction of the First Temple in 586 B.C.E. was in no small measure due to the fact that the Jews didn't listen to Jeremiah. Many of the tragedies of history to this day probably share in this same failing.

Elijah

Elijah brought us a message about where God is *not* to be found and where He *is* waiting to be discovered. Elijah searched for God in the grandeur of a whirlwind, in the majesty of thunder and lightning, in the awesome manifestations of nature. Metaphorically, he thought God was most accessible where there were "lights, camera, and action." He eventually came to the conclusion that God was present in the still, small voice that is within all of us. Three-ring circuses are for the Ringling Brothers. God much prefers a spiritual setting without trumpets and fanfare, not playing to the crowds, but rather responding to the inner stirrings of your soul.

Ezekiel

Ezekiel had a vision that may have allowed him to peer into the twentieth century. It's possible, say some modern commentators, that he saw both the Holocaust and the birth of Israel. To him was given a vision of a valley with lifeless, dry, and dead bones. It was clear to him that these bones could never again come back to life. But God told Ezekiel, "Say to the breath, thus says the Lord God, 'Come, oh breath from the four winds, and breathe into these slain, that they may live again.'" Amazingly enough, the corpses then stood on their feet. The dead lived once again.

Then God explained to Ezekiel what the vision meant: "Oh, mortal, these bones are the whole house of Israel. They say our bones are dried up, our hope is gone; we are doomed." Thus says the Lord God: "I am going to open your graves and lift you out of the graves, oh my people, and bring you to the land of Israel … I will put my breath into you and you shall live again … I will set you upon your own soil."

Ezekiel was speaking to the Jews of Babylonia. They felt they had no hope: They were bones who would no longer live. They believed Jewish history was at an end. For them, Ezekiel

Ask the Rabbi

Elijah is the one prophet who, according to tradition, didn't die. He is sent back to earth many times to perform heavenly missions. Tradition has him visiting at every circumcision and at every Passover seder. Wait for him also to be the bearer of the good news that Messiah is on His way.

expressed the prophecy of *Hatikvah*—the Hope. Ezekiel's vision proved to be correct for the Jews of his day. Babylonian Jewry returned to their land and reclaimed their heritage.

European Jewry in the mid-1940s believed that with six million slaughtered they, too, were faced with a valley of dry and dead bones that could no longer come back to life. Yet the words of Ezekiel were there to encourage them. The State of Israel was born three years after the end of the Holocaust. Jews returned to the Promised Land where they adopted as their national anthem the song known as *Hatikvah*. Hatikvah, Hebrew for "the hope," is the national anthem of the State of Israel, based on a poem by Naftali Herz Inber.

Prophet Ezekiel *(detail) by Michelangelo.*

(Art Resource, NY/Alinari)

"Psalm" of These Days

In most of the Bible, God speaks to us. In the Book of Psalms, we speak to God and to our own hearts. In 150 chapters, most of them written by King David, we find expression for all the sorrows, troubles, fears, doubts, hopes, pains, perplexities, and stormy stresses to which the souls of men are tossed. Faith is challenged and proves victorious. The human spirit reels from the threats and defeats of life and surmounts them with brilliant spiritual insights.

Small wonder that in every country, the language of the Psalms has become part of the daily life of nations, passing into their proverbs, mingling with their conversation, forming the major text of their prayers, and used at every critical stage of their existence. As Theodore Robinson, the English historian, has noted, "The Psalms are the songs of the human soul, timeless and universal; it is the sacred poets of Israel who, more than any others, have well and truly interpreted the spirit of man."

From the Mountaintop

"We spend our years as a tale that is told."
   "They that sow in tears shall reap in joy."
      "They that go down to the sea in ships. ..."
Where do all these lines come from? The Book of Psalms, of course. Read it to find many familiar expressions.

Jews designate the Book of Psalms as *Sefer Tehillim* (often simply contracted to *Tehillim*, the Book of Praises). In all probability, selections from Psalms were the feature of the religious service in the Temple of old, sung by a choir of Levites, accompanied by string and wind instruments. With the destruction of the Temple, the synagogue service became a substitute for sacrifices, and Psalms to this day form a major portion of the liturgy.

More significantly, Jews have adopted Tehillim as their best script for conversing with God in every time of personal need. Whenever someone is ill, family and friends will recite Tehillim for his or her speedy recovery. Organized groups stand ready to offer their services on a 24-hour-a-day basis as prayer vigils when necessary. Thanks to modern technology, there's even an opportunity to use the Internet and e-mail to have Tehillim delivered to the Western Wall, site of the ancient Temple, and from there presumably to ascend directly to God. The Western Wall is the only portion of the ancient Temple to survive after its destruction by the Romans in 70 C.E. It is one of the holiest sites in the world for Jews and prayers offered alongside of it are considered especially worthy of being answered by God.

From the Mountaintop

The 23rd Psalm may well be the most famous of all. "The Lord is my shepherd, I shall not want; He makes me to lie down in green pastures; He leads me beside the still waters; He restores my soul." These words are read at every Jewish funeral, as well as by people of all faiths who seek comfort in tragedy.

While so much of the book is a cry from the heart, it's interesting to note that the very first word in the Book of Psalms is *happy*. The goal of Jewish spirituality is to find joy in life. To be at one with God is the best way to ensure inner peace and contentment. As the opening verses declare:

> Happy is the man that has not walked in the council of the wicked,
> Nor stood in the way of sinners,
> Nor sat in the seat of the scornful.
> But his delight is in the law of the Lord;
> And in His law does he meditate day and night.
> And he shall be like a tree planted by streams of water,
> That brings forth its fruit in its season,
> And whose leaf does not wither;
> And in whatsoever he does he shall prosper. (Psalm 1:1–3)

It is fitting that this biblical book, which has been called the grandest symphony of praise to God ever composed on Earth, should close with the verse: "Let everything that has breath praise the Lord, Hallelujah."

To read it, to experience the book's power, to imbibe its ideas and to become intoxicated with its spiritual intensity is to ensure that the day of universal acknowledgment of praise to God is coming ever closer.

Too Sexy for the Bible?

One book of the Bible almost didn't make it into the final version. The canonizers of Scriptures were a little nervous about the Song of Songs. After all, reading it superficially, it seems better to be inserted as a centerfold.

Schmoozing

The Song of Songs and Ecclesiastes seem like a love song and a pamphlet of Voltaire found astray among the folios of a theological library. This is what gives them their value.

—Ernest Renan (1823–1892), French historian and theologian

The story it tells is of a passionate love relationship between a beautiful peasant maiden and a shepherd. Like every real love story, this biblical Romeo and Juliet have to deal with disapproving family and neighbors. There's even another man, the king himself, who falls violently in love with the heroine and tries to dislodge her love for her humble shepherd. But true love wins out, if not always in reality, at least in this biblical story.

The Most Sacred of All

So what in the world does this have to do with religion, with God, and with the Jewish people? That's what some rabbis thought, and they believed the Song of Songs had no part in a holy book. Thankfully for us, the opposing view prevailed. Not only was the book incorporated into the Bible, but, as Rabbi Akiva put it, "If the other books of the Bible are holy, the Song of Songs is 'holy of holies.'" As if this weren't praise enough, this greatest of Jewish sages added that "the whole world attained its supreme value only on the day when the Song of Songs was given to Israel."

The reason? It was clear to the rabbis that this work, traditionally assumed to be authored by King Solomon, is a magnificent metaphor for the relationship between God and the Jewish people. The book acknowledges that the strongest emotion in the human heart is that of love. Its power can totally transform us. That is why it must find expression both in the sacred as well as the profane.

Think of what the greatest love means between people who spend every moment thinking only of each other when they are apart. Transfer that emotion to the feelings we ought to have for God to whom, symbolically, we became wed at the moment of Revelation, when God revealed His Torah to the Jewish people of Mount Sinai. Israel is the bride and God is the groom. If Jews worship other gods they are no less than adulterous. Faithfulness is the key to blessed family life as well as to spiritual salvation.

Sex Is Beautiful

The sensual parts of the book didn't pose any problems. Sex, as we will see later in Chapter 20, isn't something to be dismissed or denigrated. Sex is beautiful, and anything created by God, by definition, can't be dirty. So the Song of Songs speaks of breasts and of scarlet lips, of comely mouths and of a loved one's neck that is "like the Tower of David." What an image—mixing a sexy spot with a spiritual site! But that's probably why the Song of Songs is not only in the Bible but read by religious Jews every Friday night as they prepare themselves for the spiritual ecstasy of the Sabbath, as well as the sensual delights of physical union with their spouses as commanded by Jewish law.

Why Do Good People Suffer?

So tell me, if you believe in a loving and all-powerful God, why do bad things happen to good people? It's the question of questions and the ultimate test of every religious person's faith. Those looking for easy answers will always be disappointed. When

Harold Kushner, an American rabbi who faced the death of his teenaged son, wrote a best-selling work dealing with this problem, he called it *When Bad Things Happen to Good People*. Most people remember the title as *Why Bad Things …*, but Kushner made it a point to emphasize that all he was capable of dealing with was *when* bad things, not *why*. For the why, there simply are no simple solutions.

The Trial of Job

The Bible obviously can't ignore the most fundamental human difficulty with God. So it presents us with the Book of Job, which describes a holy and saintly man who goes from great success to loss and tragedy for no apparent reason.

Ask the Rabbi

Confronting death, Jews have for centuries used the words of Job to express acceptance in the face of unalterable tragedy: "The Lord hath given and the Lord hath taken away, blessed be the name of the Lord."

In what is perhaps the most powerful message of the book, it's made clear that what Job's "friends" believed happened is wrong. Job's acquaintances, with their limited understanding of theology, consider Job's affliction a certain proof of sin. If you're suffering, in their view, then surely you deserve it. Really good people don't have bad things happen to them, they claimed. But they were wrong. Job *was* righteous. Good people *do* suffer. As the friends openly deride Job and call him a hypocrite, we, the readers, are appalled at their insensitivity and their sanctimonious preachings.

From the Mountaintop

On the way to catch a plane for an important business meeting, a man's car was suddenly halted by a flat tire. He cursed his fortune and wept because he missed his plane. Hours later he heard that his plane had crashed, killing everyone onboard. What he previously thought was a catastrophe turned out to have been a blessing in disguise. The story is true. Variations of it happen to us all the time, but we aren't usually smart enough to realize it.

For that alone, the Book of Job deserves its popularity. Sometimes it's just as important to know what isn't the correct answer as what is. It can even be a source of comfort to know that bad things do happen to good people—although we don't understand why. What we do have to realize is that suffering and misfortune are not necessarily negative appraisals from God about the worth of a human being!

We Can't Know It All

The only conclusion the Book of Job offers us as to the right answer for the moral dilemma of injustice on this earth is the need to acknowledge human ignorance:

> Where were you when I laid the foundations of the Earth? Declare, if you have the understanding. Who determined the measures thereof, if you know? Or who stretched the line upon it? … Have you commanded the morning since your days began, and caused the day springs to know its place; that it might take hold of the ends of the Earth, and the wicked be shaken out of it? (Job 38:4–5, 12)

As Jewish philosophers would later summarize the idea, "If I could understand God, I would be God." Man is incapable of judging God's wisdom in managing the world simply because man lacks God's wisdom.

With Job, we can only root our confidence in the perception that:

> The fear of the Lord, that is wisdom;
> And to depart from evil is understanding. (Job 28:28)

You Heard It Here First

When Solomon was young, he wrote the Song of Songs. It is only natural, say the rabbis, for youth to write songs of love. As he advanced in years, Solomon gained wisdom and learned to couch his thoughts in maxims and aphorisms. These became the Proverbs that would help to instruct humankind throughout all generations.

Temple of Solomon reconstruction.

(Art Resource, NY/The Jewish Museum, NY)

Cervantes, the Spanish novelist, called Proverbs "short sentences drawn from long experiences." Who better than Solomon, a king, a warrior, the man who built the Second Temple and who was responsible for the age of the greatest international power and influence of the Jewish people, to give us the benefit of his reflections and wisdom.

The Book of Proverbs may be a book of the Bible but it is not a "Jewish" book. It's been pointed out that the word *Israel* doesn't appear even once. The word *Adam*, referring to man in the universal sense, is mentioned 33 times. The instructions and insights are applicable to all people, everywhere. No part of life, no aspect of human relationship, is overlooked. The tradesman in his store, the farmer in the field, the king on his throne, husband and wife, parents and children, all receive attention and advice. That's why so many of Solomon's sayings have entered everyday speech and become part of the universal language of humankind.

Have a "Nosh" of Wise Sayings

To get some idea of the flavor of Proverbs, try these for a sampler:

- "Go to the ant, thou sluggard; consider her ways, and be wise: which having no guide, overseer or ruler, provides for meat in the summer and gathers for food in the harvest." (Proverbs 6:6–8)

- "Wisdom has builded her house, she has yewn out her seven pillars." (Proverbs 9:1)

- "Reprove not a scorner, lest he hate you; rebuke a wise man, and he will love you." (Proverbs 9:8)

- "Stolen waters are sweet, and bread eaten in secret is pleasant." (Proverbs 9:17)

- "Hope deferred makes the heart sick." (Proverbs 13:12)

- "The way of a fool is right in his own eyes." (Proverbs 12:15)

- "Righteousness exalts a nation." (Proverbs 14:34)

- "A soft answer turns away wrath." (Proverbs 15:1)

- "A merry heart makes a cheerful countenance; but by sorrow of the heart the spirit is broken." (Proverbs 15:13)

- "Pride goes before destruction, and a haughty spirit before a fall." (Proverbs 16:18)

- "He that is slow to anger is better than the mighty; and he that rules his spirit than he that takes a city." (Proverbs 16:32)

- "Where there is no vision, the people perish." (Proverbs 29:18)

These are just a few of the reasons why Jewish tradition maintains that Solomon was the wisest of all men.

The Least You Need to Know

- The complete Jewish Bible, finished in the first century C.E., consists of the five books of Moses (Torah), the Prophets (Neviim), and the Writings (Ketuvim). Altogether it's called the *T'nakh*.

- God's words and the messages of the prophets still have strong relevance to this day—especially the words of Nathan, Isaiah, Jeremiah, Elijah, and Ezekiel.

- The Psalms of David remain the liturgy of the Jew and much of the world.

- The Song of Songs, with its sensuality and erotic suggestions, is included in the Bible as a powerful metaphor for the relationship between God and the Jewish people.

- The Book of Job is the biblical response to the problem of why good people suffer.

- The wisdom of Solomon is manifest in his many Proverbs, which serve as a biblical guide to daily issues of life.

Chapter 8

The Laws and the Legends

In This Chapter

♦ How the Oral Law became written text

♦ The themes of the Mishna

♦ Studying a page of the Talmud

♦ A sampler from the legends of the Midrash

With the close of the Bible, Judaism entered a new era. Jews no longer depended on men known as prophets to hear the voice of God for them. Instead, they looked to the Torah texts, which were interpreted for them by rabbis and scholars. In the Bible, God spoke *to* man. In the Mishna, the Talmud, and the major Jewish works that followed, God would speak *through* man, allowing His will to filter through the intellectual faculty of those who studied His words.

What resulted were texts that weren't simply one-sided. The religious writings after the Bible were dialogues, conversations that recorded not only God's requests but also man's responses. The ancient rabbis loved to argue among themselves—after all, they were Jews—and they came to specialize in what would to this day be called "Talmudic hair-splitting."

They would debate seemingly minor issues as if their lives depended on it—because they felt that when it came to religious matters, nothing was petty and their lives did depend on coming to correct conclusions.

It's as if these rabbinic scholars could just imagine God sitting in the heavens, watching them creatively interpret the Torah and smiling at His children's ingenuity as they carried His words to ever higher levels! Small wonder that Jews came to regard their scholars very often as even greater than prophets. Prophets repeated what they heard; scholars showed the beauty of combining man's wisdom with God's.

From the Mountaintop

Jewish mystics note a remarkable "coincidence" about the word *Mishna*. The Hebrew letters, when rearranged, make the word *Neshama*, or "soul." The written text corresponds to the body, but the Oral Law, the Mishna, is the very soul of Judaism.

The Mission of the Mishna

The first major text containing the views of rabbinic scholars is the *Mishna* (from the root *shanah*, to repeat, and hence, to learn) edited by Rabbi Judah the Prince in approximately the year 200 C.E. It was certainly no coincidence that the Mishna was divided into six Orders, or major divisions. Since the Torah, the Pentateuch, had five books, the work meant to explain it and to apply its laws to everyday life was its "follow-up number," six.

Six Parts of the Mishna

In broad strokes, these are the names and the themes of the six Orders of the Mishna:

- *Zera'im* (seeds), dealing with agricultural laws, laws for food and blessings.

- *Mo'ed* (appointed times), dealing with the Sabbath and the Festivals.

- *Nashim* (women), dealing with marriage, divorce, sexual relations, and issues between men and women.

- *Nezikim* (damages), dealing with civil law, such as buying and selling, civil suits involving claims and damages, as well as criminal law.

- *Kodashim* (sacred things), dealing with the sacrificial system.

- *Tohorot* (purities), summarizing the laws of ritual purification for service in the Temple.

It's the Doing That Counts

What the list doesn't make clear is the broad scope of all of these subjects. It is from the Mishna that we can grasp the uniqueness of Judaism as far more than a faith, much more than what we normally mean by the word religion.

As the famous saying goes, Judaism is not a noun, it's a verb. Its laws take Jews from the moment they open their eyes in the morning and are required to recite a special blessing to the way in which they are told to lie down in their bed at night. Jewish law, as recorded in the Mishna, turns every waking minute into a spiritual experience: managing one's business affairs, dealing with one's parents, mate, and children, and arranging the days and years of one's life. The Mishna, in short, is a manual for living.

What gave the Mishna its authority to speak in God's name? What allowed its rulings to become not only the law of the land in civil and criminal matters, but even the ultimate judge of all human actions, in the privacy of one's bedroom, as well as the personal moments of solitude? To understand the power of the Mishna, you have to know the meaning of the Oral Law.

What's Oral Law?

Until now, when we spoke of Torah, we meant the written text. But a text is always deficient. Words lend themselves to different interpretations. In English, we even have the expression, "reduced to writing." Writing restricts meaning to the limited vision of the reader. Lewis Carroll understood it well in *Alice's Adventures in Wonderland:*

> "When *I* use a word," Humpty Dumpty said in rather a scornful tone, "it means just what I choose it to mean—neither more nor less."

> "The question is," said Alice, "whether you *can* make words mean so many different things."

> "The question is," said Humpty Dumpty, "which is to be master—that's all."

Words in a text couldn't suffice for God. That was much too dangerous. So God accompanied the text with an Oral Torah (*Torah She-B'al Peh*) that traditional Judaism believes "Moses received on Sinai, and transmitted to Joshua, and Joshua to the Elders, and the Elders to the Prophets, and the Prophets to the Men of the Great Assembly ...." (*Ethics of the Fathers,* 1:1)

The Oral Torah explained exactly what God wanted the words to mean. What is the work that is forbidden to be done on the Sabbath? (You'll learn more about that in Chapter 10.) How are we supposed to slaughter animals in a kosher way if all the

Bible tells us is to do it "as I have commanded you," with no further information in the text? (More on that in Chapter 18.) What do we put inside the mezuzah that's supposed to be placed on the doorpost (see Chapter 17)? What isn't in the text is taught. The Oral Law was, as the name indicates, transmitted orally from teacher to student throughout the generations.

Don't Write It Down!

Here's a law that's going to shock you: The Oral Law *had* to remain oral. It was forbidden to write it down. As a transmitted tradition, it required a living relationship. You couldn't simply hand a student a book and tell him to memorize its contents. Since it had to be given over by word of mouth, every Jewish child learned Judaism from a human being, not a book.

What an educational concept! A book doesn't know how to hug you when you get the right answer. A book can't tell you it cares whether you open or close its pages. A book can only tell you the rules, but it can't serve as a role model. And a book doesn't know whether you misunderstood what it was trying to tell you.

So how did the Mishna ever get written? Remarkably enough, the first major book summarizing Jewish law only came into being because the rabbis were daring enough to break a law! Sometimes we have to be smart enough to know that even good rules have to be overridden because of a greater priority. Rabbi Judah the Prince understood that with the destruction of the Temple and the imminent dispersal of the Jews around the world, the teachings of Torah would be lost if they weren't recorded.

Schmoozing

Were it not for the men who produced the Mishna and the Talmud, the Torah of our God would have long since been lost and forgotten. It was they who confirmed the commandments and elucidated them thoroughly.

—Abraham ibn ["son of"] Ezra (1092–1167), Hebrew poet and scholar, Spain

Since scholars couldn't be everywhere, at least their words could accompany Jews in their enforced travels. The Mishna may have "reduced" the Oral Law to writing, but it made possible the continuation of Jewish scholarship, the Talmud, and—as most people would agree—the survival of the Jewish people.

Ethics of the Fathers

The Mishna deals mainly with laws. As the saying goes, "God is in the details." Yet there is one portion of the Mishna that turns from specifics to broader visions, from what happens when one ox injures another to how people should live their lives and how they should grasp the essence of a spiritual and ethical outlook. These are the insights and the succinct maxims of the section known as *Ethics of the Fathers*. It's been said that studying these Mishnas make you more than a Jew; they turn you into a *mensch*.

How many of these have you heard or wish you had?

Let There Be Light

A **mensch** is a Yiddish word that's almost untranslatable. Simply, it means a human being. What it implies is a decent, caring, kind, understanding person—you know what I mean, a mensch.

◆ Say little and do much.

◆ Don't judge your fellow man until you are in his place.

◆ Don't say "I will study when I have time," lest you never find the time.

◆ It is not your responsibility to finish the work, but you are not free to desist from it either.

◆ The world rests on three things: on Torah study, on prayer, and on the doing of kind deeds.

◆ Who is wise? He who learns from every person.

◆ Who is strong? He who subdues his personal inclinations.

◆ Who is rich? He who is happy with his lot.

◆ Who is honored? He who honors others.

◆ The more possessions, the more worry.

◆ The day is short, the task is abundant.

◆ A protective fence for wisdom is silence.

◆ Let the honor of your student be as dear to you as your own; the honor of your colleague as the reverence for your teacher; and the reverence for your teacher as the reverence of heaven.

Pulpit Story

Rabbi Yosi ben Kisma recounted that once, while walking on the road, he was met by a man who made him the following offer: "Rabbi, would you be willing to live with us in our place? Leave your city of scholars, and I will give you thousands upon thousands of golden dinars, precious stones, and pearls." Rabbi Yosi replied, "Even if you were to give me all the silver and gold, precious stones, and pearls in the world, I would dwell nowhere but in a place of Torah."

" " Schmoozing _____

Before studying ethics, I blamed the whole world and justified myself; after I started the study, I blamed myself and also the world; but finally now, I blame only myself.

—Rabbi Israel Salanter (1810–1883)

- When your enemy falls, be not glad, and when he stumbles, let your heart be not joyous.

- Do not look at the vessel, but what is in it.

And if you're having trouble concentrating on so many ideas, as good as they are, then we should close with this one: The reward is in proportion to the exertion—or, like they say at the health club, "no pain, no gain."

The Wisdom of the Talmud

For 300 years, scholars gathered in informal schools known as _yeshivot_ (singular _yeshiva_, from the Hebrew for "sitting") discussing the laws of the Mishna. Very often they digressed and talked about whatever captured their fancy. Sometimes they told stories and shared personal observations. Other times they reflected on philosophical and theological issues. It was almost a running stream of consciousness for which the Mishna was just a point of departure. (Amazingly enough, even before Linda Tripp was born, people "taped" all these discussions mentally.)

" " Schmoozing _____

The Bible has been compared to water, the Mishna to wine, and the Gemara to liqueur. All three are necessary, and a rich man enjoys them all.

—Talmud: Soferim, 15:7

And Then There Was the Gemara

Eventually, under the editorship of Rabbis Ravina and Rav Ashi, they compiled the _Gemara_ (from the root for "to complete") that completed the much shorter summary of law that Rabbi Judah the Prince popularized three centuries before. The Gemara appended to the Mishna together became the _Talmud_ (from the root _lamad_, "to learn"), 63 volumes that would become the core of the Jewish curriculum, next to the Bible, for all serious students of Judaism to this day.

Talk About Dedication

Imagine this: a book written in Aramaic without any punctuation, moving from subject to subject in language so sparse it sometimes takes hours to decode a line or two, dealing with subjects that sometimes seem as irrelevant to contemporary life as men from Mars. Yet for centuries Jews have pored over its pages, often dedicating their lives to mastering every nuance of this complicated text. In the *shtetl*, the Jewish communities of Poland and Russia immortalized by *Fiddler on the Roof*, little children spent most of their days mastering legal texts that in other cultures would be considered difficult for aspiring lawyers.

Such a Catch!

When a young man was ready to "pop the question" and ask for someone's hand in marriage, it was customary for him to be given a test on his knowledge of the Talmud to see whether he deserved the bride. The more desirable the girl—prestigious family, wealth, beauty—the more learned the suitor had to be. You can imagine what an incentive that was for Torah study!

And if the young man was lucky enough to pass his exam (the ultimate irony: if he was truly a scholar, he *lost* his bachelor's degree!), they would announce a wedding date and the groom would be given the traditional gift presented by the father of the bride to his new son-in-law— the gift of, what else?—a complete set of the Talmud.

 **Schmoozing**

When two merchants exchange goods, each one surrenders part of his stock; but when two students exchange instruction, each one retains his own learning and acquires also the other's. Is there a bigger bargain than this?

—Rabbi Simeon ben Lakish, Talmudic scholar

A Page a Day

To this day, around the world, tens of thousands of people, not just rabbis, but doctors, stockbrokers, accountants, salesmen—you name it—are part of a program called *Daf Yomi*, literally "a page a day." It takes over seven years of intensive and disciplined study, at the very minimum an hour a day, to finish the entire Talmud at the rate of a page a day. Daf Yomi participants all study the very same page no matter where they are around the globe.

When they finally finish, as they last did in 1997, Madison Square Garden in New York, the Hollywood Bowl in Los Angeles, and major arenas all over the world were packed to capacity with people who didn't come to see an NBA playoff game, but who celebrated the continuing commitment of the Jewish people to one of their most treasured texts.

Let There Be Light

Yeshiva, the name for a school of Jewish study, runs the gamut from academies for children of kindergarten age to scholars who devote their lives to study until the day they die.

From the Mountaintop

The tractate of the Babylonian Talmud named *Sanhedrin,* after the Supreme Court of Judaism, deals with matters of criminal justice, capital punishment, and civil law.

What's So Interesting?

So what is in the Talmud that could make it so interesting and so beloved in spite of the fact that it's so user-*un*friendly? The best I can do is give you an example of a sample text. You won't have to struggle through the Aramaic; I'll translate it for you and add some commentary—explanations, questions and answers, clarifications—just the way Talmudic scholars would do it. Imagine yourself sitting in a *yeshiva,* picture a friendly rabbi (that's me), and don't make yourself too comfortable because you're going to need to give this your full attention …

Question Everything

You've read the text and now, if you're a good student, the first thing you should do is ask a good question. What in the world were they doing in an attic? And why was it important for this Talmudic passage to tell me such a seemingly irrelevant piece of information in its introduction?

Let's think about that for a moment. There's always an explanation. The beauty of Talmudic passages is that they challenge you to think and to come up with a logical answer. Since we're not really sitting together, I can't wait for your response, so I'll have to tell you. If the rabbis were in an attic and not in the house of study, they obviously were in hiding. It must have been a time of persecution. For them, the subject of martyrdom wasn't just a theoretical question but an issue they had to deal with on a practical day-to-day level.

What the Talmud is beautifully pointing out in an almost casual manner is that a decision of law that teaches us when we must be prepared to give up our lives can't possibly come from scholars safely seated in a luxury villa deciding the fate of others far less fortunate than they. For the lottery, "You've got to be in it to win it"; for the law of martyrdom, you've got to be personally affected if you teach others that Jewish law demands you give up your life to preserve a sacred ideal.

From the Mountaintop

In many yeshivot there is no degree to which its students aspire, nor a fixed number of years for the curriculum. Torah study is viewed as a legitimate lifetime pursuit with its goal the accumulation of a portion of knowledge of the infinite wisdom of God.

The Talmud teaches in the tractate *Sanhedrin 74A:* Rabbi Yochanan taught that they voted and concluded in the attic of the House of Nitzeh in the City of Lod as follows: Regarding all sins in the Torah, if someone says to another, "Transgress so that you will not be killed," he may transgress and not be killed, except in three instances. In the case of idolatry or immorality or murder, one must be prepared to die rather than to transgress. These three and these three alone demand martyrdom rather than violation.

But Why Is That the Law?

"Aha, now I understand the opening line, and I think I can proceed a little bit further," you say. "For any other sin, the law is that I may transgress and not be killed. Why is that?" I wonder. Someone in the study group remembers and quotes the appropriate text. (Remember that you learned this in Chapter 5.) The saving of life takes precedence over everything else because the Bible says "And you shall live by them"—and not die because of them.

Yet three sins (idolatry, immorality, or murder) are exceptions to the rule. Better to die in holiness than have these transgressions stain our souls. Even the Talmud can't just unequivocally record a law of such importance without indicating the source for this decision.

In an analysis of different biblical verses, the Talmud proves that idolatry and sexual immorality are exceptions to the rule of "your life above all." They can't, however, seem to find proof that if someone commands you to murder another person, you're supposed to die rather than do it. In frustration, the question is asked: "How did the rabbis who rendered that decision in the attic know this law?"

The response is stunning in its simplicity. This is a law that doesn't require a biblical verse as

Schmoozing

I hope the time will come when the laws and literature of the ancient Hebrews will be studied in all of our schools as now are studied the laws and literature of the ancient Greeks and Romans, and that it will be universally recognized that no man ignorant of the laws and literature of the ancient Hebrews is a well-educated man.

—Lyman Abbott

basis because *it is logical*. After all, in a succinct phrase that would become a Jewish proverb, "Who says your blood is redder than his?"

Thousands of years ago, the Talmud considered this ruling obvious. Yet it took the Nuremburg Trials, the Nazi war crime trials, of the twentieth century to finally codify this idea for modern man. Germans sought to be excused for their killing sprees because they "were only acting under orders." Had they not murdered Jews, they pleaded, they themselves would have been killed. That, for them, seemed to be sufficient justification.

But the Nuremburg Trials concluded that what was obvious to the rabbis of ancient Talmudic times is in fact correct: You have no right ever to murder an innocent person, even to save your own skin, because "who says your blood is redder than his (or hers)?"

How broad is this ruling? What if you're smarter than the one you're told to murder—or younger, better looking, a different gender, or any one of a thousand other reasons people might give to value one person's life over another? None of them matter. The law is the most powerful expression of the democratic concept of Judaism that "all men and all women are created equal."

Two Men in the Desert

Talmudic scholars don't just study one passage at a time. They remember citations from other volumes of the Talmud, and if they see an apparent contradiction, they have to find a way to resolve it. Because you've come so far in studying a sample selection, let me take you just one step further and show what a discussion in a yeshiva might sound like after some very bright students completed the previous text.

The Talmud seems to have told us that it's better to be killed than to kill, better to be victim than villain. We disagree with Paul Simon's lyrics in *El Condor Pasa* that, "I'd rather be a hammer than a nail, yes, I would, I really would, if I only could." Yet our noble sentiment, that it's morally superior to be the nail than the hammer, seems contradicted by another important ruling:

> If two men are traveling on a journey far from civilization, and one has a pitcher of water sufficient only to save him until they can reach civilization, but if both drink they will die, what is the law? The son of Patura taught: It is better that both shall drink and die, rather than that one should behold his companion's death.

> That was the view until Rabbi Akiva came and taught: The Bible says that "thy brother may live with thee"—your life takes precedence over his life. "With you" implies you are to save yourself first, and that your friend only has a right to your help after you have assured your own survival.

The ruling seems to make clear that self-preservation is the greatest priority. If that's true, why then shouldn't the law be that if your life is threatened you may kill somebody else in order to save yourself? Isn't there a logical contradiction between these two rabbinic rulings?

Here's where you get a chance to add your own creative insight. And that's what makes study of the Talmud so absorbing and exciting.

Did you figure it out yet?

There is a significant difference between the two cases. In the desert story, you drink your own water and passively witness your friend's death. It's tragic, but you didn't do it. You drank your own water because to do otherwise would be committing suicide. In the other story, however, you were given the choice of becoming murderer or victim. Between those two, the decision is clear: It's better to be an innocent nail than a murderous hammer.

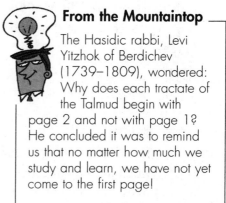

From the Mountaintop

The Hasidic rabbi, Levi Yitzhok of Berdichev (1739–1809), wondered: Why does each tractate of the Talmud begin with page 2 and not with page 1? He concluded it was to remind us that no matter how much we study and learn, we have not yet come to the first page!

The Concentration Camp Question

Unfortunately, these Talmudic discussions became all too relevant during the Holocaust. Many are the stories of Jews turning to their rabbis and asking what Judaism required of them as they were presented with horrible choices by their captors. Amuse Nazi officers by participating in some terrible atrocity or be executed for refusing? Work on the Sabbath or die? Shoot a fellow prisoner as commanded or have the death sentence carried out on yourself?

Rabbis remembered the relevant texts, and they wept as they gave the answer of martyrdom when required. They stood in awe—even as we who read about these events do now—of those who wanted only to know what was required of them by law.

The Insights of the Midrash

The Talmud is primarily law; the Midrash is mainly legends. Written at about the same time as the Talmud and recording the statements of most of the same rabbinic figures, the Midrash is more interested in theology than commandments, the meaning of biblical texts as opposed to their practical applications. The Talmud forces you to focus your mind; the Midrash inspires, entertains, and speaks to your soul.

Start your study of the Bible with the Midrash, and you learn things like these:

◆ Why is the opening letter of the Torah a *bet*, which is the second letter of the alphabet—rather than the *aleph*, which is the first letter? It is to teach you that this is not the first world created by God and also to inform you that God created two worlds, life here on Earth and the one that awaits us after death.

From the Mountaintop

The English word alphabet has in it the names of the first two letters of the Hebrew "alpha-bet." Hebrew begins with the *aleph*, which is assigned the number one because of its position. The second letter, *bet*, stands for two. In this way, every letter of the Hebrew alphabet also conveys a numerical message—an idea used by Jewish mystics to convey biblical codes and deeper layers of meaning to simple texts.

◆ How could the Bible tell us God created light on the first day if the sun wasn't created until the fourth? Explains the Midrash, this was a celestial light far more intense than sunlight, a light reserved for the righteous in the Messianic Age and a light that allows us to "see," to intuit and to truly understand the world around us.

◆ On the sixth day of Creation, the Bible says, "And God said, 'Let us make man in our image …'" The Midrash asks: Why did God say "let *us*"? Surely there is only one God; what is meant by this plural? The Midrash answers, although God created man by Himself, He nevertheless took council with the ministering angels. But does God need advice? Of course not, but He meant to teach us an important lesson: One should always consult others before embarking on major new initiatives. So important is this idea that God is not deterred by the possibility that some might read this verse and find in it a sacrilegious implication of the plurality of God.

◆ Adam and Eve were placed in the Garden of Eden "to work it and to guard it." The Midrash asks: If this was Paradise, why were they commanded to work? From here we may deduce, the Midrash teaches, that human beings can only find happiness when their life has purpose, when they must fulfill obligations. A life of total ease is no life; work is as much a necessity to us as are eating and drinking. Without it, we are parasites; with it, we gain a measure of self-respect.

◆ What motivated Cain to kill his brother Abel? The Bible simply says: "And Cain said to Abel his brother." It leaves the rest blank, so the Midrash offers three fascinating possibilities: They fought over a woman. They fought over division of property. Or they fought over which one of them would be given the honor of having the Temple of God built on his land.

In analyzing the first murder of history, the rabbis were obviously trying to determine the most powerful drive for man's actions. Is it the sexual drive as Freud in the twentieth century would claim? Is it the lust for more money and possessions, as Karl Marx would conclude in *Das Kapital?* Or is it overzealousness in the pursuit of religious ideals as Crusaders and religious fanatics throughout the ages have so often demonstrated? The Midrash opens our minds to these possibilities and introduces us to modes of thought that would become the intellectual coin of philosophers many centuries later.

Schmoozing

We don't consider manual work as a curse or a bitter necessity, not even as a means of making a living. We consider it as a high human function, as the basis of human life, the most dignified thing in the life of a human being, and which ought to be free, creative. Men ought to be proud of it.

—David Ben-Gurion (1886–1973), first prime minister of Israel

Ingenious comments accompany every biblical verse. They amaze us with their profundity. They delight us with their wit and their wisdom. Sometimes they are fanciful, meant to be allegories or parables. Other times they record traditions passed down from generation to generation, elaborating on events only briefly touched upon in the text. The message of Judaism can't be captured by the study of Talmud alone. Only by combining Midrash with Talmud have Jews been able to grasp the magnificent panorama of Jewish law and legend, Jewish culture and faith.

From the Mountaintop

If Cain and Abel were the only two people other than their parents, where did they find mates for sex and reproduction? The Midrash has the answer: They were born with twin sisters and one of them even had a triplet! Who was the extra woman for? Aha, that's what the fight was all about.

The Least You Need to Know

◆ The Mishna, edited by Rabbi Judah the Prince, is the Jewish Oral Law, written down only by the fear that exile might cause its teachings to be forgotten.

◆ The six major sections of the Mishna cover every aspect of life.

◆ The *Ethics of the Fathers*, a small portion of the larger Mishna, is an especially beautiful collection of rabbinic maxims and guides to what Judaism considers a good life.

◆ The Talmud adds to the Mishna 300 years of discussion by the sages, known as Gemara, that illuminates Jewish law and relates its principles to situations contemporary to their times.

◆ The Midrash, a collection of legends, is both educational and entertaining and complements Talmudic legalism with rabbinic theology.

The Later Voices of Judaism

In This Chapter

- Biblical commentaries throughout the generations
- The secrets of mysticism and the Kabbalah
- The emphasis on law and doing the right thing
- Modern-day dilemmas answered by responsa

"My, you look so young!" That's a line you surely wouldn't expect anyone to say to a religion that's more than 3,000 years old. To be relevant for every age, including our own, has to be the greatest challenge Judaism faces in every generation. Religion, if it's to be meaningful, can't be out-dated. It has to learn the secret of the fountain of youth for its ancient texts so that people can always relate to its "new" insights and fresh ideas. And remarkably enough, Judaism discovered what Ponce de Leon couldn't—a way to remain youthful and relevant into the twentieth century.

What miraculous elixir made possible this amazing result? The many voices that spoke to their times in the language of the day but with the biblical concepts of the past. The beauty of Judaism and, in all probability, the secret of its longevity, is the ability of its disciples to continually find creative new ways to make its message appealing and its teachings vital.

Great rabbis are most often known by the acronym of their names. *Rashi* is short for Rabbi Shlomo ben Isaac. *Rambam* is a contraction of Rabbi Moses ben Maimon. *Ben* is Hebrew for "son of," and in each instance the acronym includes the person's name, as well as that of his father.

Judaism survived and survives because of the many different approaches its spokespeople have found to popularize its profound concepts.

Explaining the Texts

"The greatest" is almost always an accolade that lends itself to argument. You'll never get everyone to agree on who is most deserving of an Oscar. Yet Jews—who love to argue about almost everything—will almost universally agree on the man who deserves the title "the greatest teacher." There simply has never been anyone like Rashi—Rabbi Shlomo ben Isaac.

Rashi's Wisdom

Rashi was born in Troyes, France, in 1040, and a remarkable legend surrounds his birth. A year before Rashi was born, his father was carrying a precious gem when he was accosted by Christians who demanded the stone for idolatrous purposes. Rather than give it up to be misused, he threw the gem into the sea. With that, a heavenly voice was heard to proclaim that as reward for his pious act, a son would be born to him who would enlighten the world with his wisdom.

The real point isn't whether the story is true, it's that it was repeated for centuries because of the awe in which Rashi was held. What seems almost impossible to believe is the magnitude of his work, combining a lengthy, almost linear, commentary on the entire Bible, together with a similarly erudite and comprehensive work on the entire Babylonian Talmud. More to the point, these commentaries made the Bible alive and the Talmud comprehensible. They were the doors for both laymen and scholars to peruse the basic books of Judaism. Without him, these works were simply too difficult, too formidable, and too intimidating to understand.

His Commentary Everywhere

I do not know of any printed text of the Talmud or of the Torah that is not accompanied by Rashi's commentary. No Jewish curriculum fails to incorporate Rashi into its program of study. Jewish law demands that every week a portion of the five books of Moses be reviewed twice, together with commentary, so that it can be completed in the course of a year. The commentary chosen for this requirement is invariably that of Rashi. No wonder that his commentary was the first Hebrew work ever printed (in 1475).

What makes a great teacher? Read Rashi's commentary and learn. Rashi is succinct and to the point. He seems to realize exactly what problem the reader would be troubled by and how best to resolve it. He always knows when to add the light touch of a story and when to add a dash of profundity. His books deserve to be studied, not simply for content, but for perfection of style, educational methodology, and the art of communication.

Believe it or not, Rashi, like most rabbis throughout history, earned his living from another profession. As a good Frenchman, he owned vineyards and produced some of those famous French wines. Just like the product of his business venture, we can say of his scholarly works that they keep improving with age and are more revered as time goes by.

From the Mountaintop

How could Rashi possibly have written so much? He was blessed with three daughters who served as his scribes. His daughters knew the entire Bible, as well as the Talmud—not only the text but the commentary of Rashi as well!

From Rashi to Einstein

Rashi paved the way for literally thousands of others to offer their interpretations and explanations of ancient texts. Seeing a verse in a new light was called a *chidush*, and it became the goal of every commentator to offer something different. In this way, the Bible kept revealing new faces that Jewish scholars maintained were always there waiting anxiously for future generations to uncover.

In this spirit, new commentaries regularly appear with fresh interpretations of the Bible. They amaze us with their ability to introduce modern concepts in order to make sense of texts that troubled less-scientifically sophisticated readers for centuries. Take, for example, this analysis of a verse in Genesis by Professor Nathan Aviezer, Chairman of the Department of Physics at Bar-Ilan University in Israel, from his *In the Beginning: Biblical Creation and Science:*

> We read in Genesis (1:3) that God created light. Presently known sources of light include the sun and the stars and the light produced when one strikes a match or turns on a light switch. But on the first day, there was no sun, no stars, no man. The nature of this light is a complete mystery. We read that God subsequently

Let There Be Light

A **chidush** is a "new" interpretation. Tradition has it that every Jew is born to add at least one new insight to the way in which the Torah is understood. Only in this way is one's life truly justified. (Have you figured out your chidush yet?)

"separated" the light from the darkness (1:4). Darkness is not a *substance* that can be separated from light. The word "darkness" simply denotes the *absence* of light. If there is darkness, then there is no light; if there is light, then there is no darkness. Thus, there is no logical content to the notion of the separation of light from darkness.

Professor Aviezer explains the concept of the primeval fireball that marks the beginning of the universe according to the Big Bang Theory.

> The fireball was an intense concentration of pure energy. According to Einstein's formula $E=mc^2$, not only can matter be converted into energy, but energy can also be converted into matter. It is the initial energy present in the primeval fireball that was the source of all the matter that now exists in the entire universe.

> However, when matter was initially formed, it didn't exist in the form of atoms. The enormous temperature of the primeval fireball would have instantly disintegrated any atom. Therefore, matter existed in a different form called a "plasma." The important distinction between these two forms of matter is that an atom is electrically neutral, whereas a plasma consists of particles having either positive or negative electric charges. The properties of charged particles are such that a charged plasma "traps" light and prevents its free passage. For this reason, a plasma always appears dark to an outside observer.

> The universe initially appeared dark because of the plasma. The sudden transformation of the plasma into atoms shortly after Creation caused the electromagnetic radiation ("light") of the primeval fireball to "separate" from the previously dark universe and shine freely throughout space. This separation is called decoupling in scientific terminology.

> The biblical passage, "And God separated the light from the darkness," may be understood as referring to the decoupling of the light from the dark fireball-plasma mixture. It is this decoupled radiation ("light") that was eventually detected 15 billion years later by Penzias and Wilson, earning them a Nobel Prize.

So there was the verse in Genesis waiting for Nobel Prize winners to decode its meaning and allow us to grasp the deepest truth of a verse that had been read in a far more superficial way for so many centuries! That's how modern commentaries and the ancient texts on which they're based continue to amaze us.

Exploring the Secrets

There's yet another way in which more profound meanings have been found in the Bible. It was the mystics who, from the Middle Ages until today, have explored secrets that seem too incredible for some to believe and too remarkable for others to be simply ignored.

The evil twin of mysticism has always been superstition. Charlatans have found it easy to prey on the gullible in the guise of being clairvoyant and having access to secret information. But con men shouldn't be allowed to discredit an ancient tradition just because they distort it. Mysticism has had many saintly spokesmen, and its insights add another significant dimension to the perspective of Judaism.

Signs of the Zodiac—*a fifth-century mosaic from Beth-alpha, Israel.*

(Art Resource, NY/The Jewish Museum)

Mysticism and the Kabbalah

The Talmud has a famous story about four great sages who entered "the orchard," a metaphor to describe a mystical experience, in which they sent their souls "to the heavens" to gaze on the celestial spheres. As a result of this intense experience, the Talmud tells us, one of the sages died, one became insane, one became a heretic, and only Rabbi Akiva walked away whole.

It was the Talmud's way of warning us that overinvolvement with mysticism is dangerous. Its esoteric knowledge isn't for everybody. For that very reason, the teachings of Jewish mysticism are known as *Kabbalah*, literally "received." These ideas were only to be received by direct word of mouth from master to disciple so that the one who transmits its information could be certain of the worthiness and the emotional maturity of the one receiving it.

Kabbalistic plaque.

(Art Resource, NY/The Jewish Museum, NY)

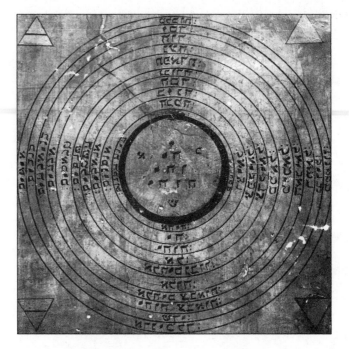

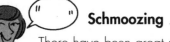 **Schmoozing**

There have been great mystics, attractive figures, who cannot easily be disposed of as self-deluded fools.

—Jawaharlal Nehru (1889–1964), Indian prime minister

In time, it was even suggested that there is a minimum age requirement for receiving this secret knowledge: No one under the age of 40 was permitted entry into the club of kabbalistic students.

Just a little before the year 1300, in Spain, a book made its appearance that for the first time revealed some of the mysteries of this tradition. Its authorship is unclear. Some claim it was penned by the second-century Palestinian teacher, Rabbi Simeon bar Yochai, a kabbalist who lived in a cave as a hermit for

13 years, and who hid his work from public view until it was miraculously discovered many centuries later. Others believe that the man responsible for "revealing" the book, the Spanish Kabbalist Moses de Leon, was in fact the author.

Written in Aramaic and, intentionally, in a style that is very difficult to comprehend, the *Zohar* ("illumination") has been called the Bible of kabbalists. It is the disciples of the Zohar and of Kabbalah who deal with those subjects of spirituality, of communion with God, of angels and the afterlife, of prophecies and predictions that are left unexplored in the Jewish texts meant for the general populace.

"My Little Monster"

Legend has it that Kabbalah also empowers its practitioners. Rabbi Judah Loew of Prague (1525–1609) knew how to arrange the secret names of God in such a manner that he was able to create a *golem*, a "man" brought to life out of clay, to serve his bidding and protect the Jewish people. True or not, it became the inspiration for Mary Shelley to write a book called *Frankenstein*. So even though you didn't realize it, when you saw the movie, you were watching an idea created by the masters of the Kabbalah!

Let There Be Light

Golem means "unformed clay." The golem came alive when Rabbi Loew wrote the word for "truth," *emet*, on his forehead. When it was time for the golem to be returned to dust, the rabbi erased the first letter, leaving only the word *met*, or "death."

The Bible Codes

More recently, another insight of Jewish mysticism that had previously been accessible only to a select few became known worldwide with the publication of a book on Bible codes. Studying the Torah by way of a special system that takes note of sequences of letters, mystics see predictions revealed, including events like the assassination of Prime Minister Yitzhak Rabin.

Don't believe it? No one says that you have to. Judaism doesn't mandate belief, only action. Mysticism isn't a must; it's only for those who choose to believe in its teachings. Before you reject out of hand Kabbalah's insistence that, since the Bible has everything in it, it even predicts contemporary events, see what you make of this example:

Biblical sentences correspond to years, and important moments of history are alluded to in the verses that correspond to the Hebrew year in which they take place. The State of Israel in modern times was established in the Hebrew year 5708. The 5,708th verse in the Bible is Deuteronomy 30:5. It reads: "And the Lord your God will bring you into the land which your fathers possessed and you shall possess it; and He will do you good and multiply you above your fathers."

Coincidence? You're a good Jew whether you believe it or not. And you're a candidate for the study of Kabbalah if you're excited by the concept.

Challenging Faith

When Nobel Prize winner Isador Isaac Rabi returned from school as a little boy, he remembers his mother asking him, "Did you ask any good questions today?" Jews don't just like answers; they encourage questions as well. Judaism believes that true faith is not imposed, but the result of inquiry. Self-enforced blinders don't let you see. So the great giants of Jewish history authored works of philosophy that dared to challenge fundamental religious premises and came to religious conviction after intellectual struggle. The result was a Judaism of choice, not of chance.

Men like Maimonides showed that to have faith was not to suspend reason but rather to allow reason to come to its most logical conclusions.

Who was Maimonides? A popular saying puts it best: "From Moses to Moses, there was no one like Moses." Moses ben Maimon, the *Rambam* (or Maimonides, son of Maimon), accomplished so much in his lifetime (1135–1204) that it seems almost impossible to believe that he wasn't a university like Harvard.

 **From the Mountaintop**

In 1985, to commemorate the 850th anniversary of his birth, a UNESCO Conference was held in Paris, and a Maimonidean scholar, Shlomo Pines, confidently asserted that, "Maimonides is the most influential Jewish thinker of the Middle Ages, and quite possibly of all times." A Soviet scholar, Vitali Naunkin, said at the same gathering, "Maimonides is perhaps the only philosopher in the Middle Ages, perhaps even now, who symbolizes a confluence of four cultures: Greco-Roman, Arab, Jewish, and Western."

Maimonides lived by the creed of the Talmud not to make a living out of religious calling, so he served professionally as the full-time physician to the Sultan of Egypt. No one understands how he found time, after providing medical care to all the prominent people in the palace, to write the voluminous works that still serve as the core of the curriculum for every budding Jewish scholar.

Maimonides had at his fingertips all the vast body of Jewish law and lore that preceded him. But he was not content with his mastery of the Talmud and Bible. He knew intimately the philosophic writings of Plato and Aristotle, as well as the great thinkers of other cultures. Combining his Judaic and secular wealth of knowledge, he created the masterpiece of Jewish philosophy, the *Guide to the Perplexed*.

Not only did he fulfill his goal of leading the religiously perplexed out of their confusion, he also demonstrated for all time that Judaism doesn't fear philosophic questioning, that faith is not a first option of the timid but a final conclusion of the intellectually bold and daring.

The Thirteen Principles

It is to Maimonides that we owe the most concise summary of the basic belief of Judaism. This list was eventually turned into one of the best-known prayers in the synagogue, the *Yigdal*. Its power derives not only from its brilliant encapsulation of Judaism's most important ideas, but from the fact that its author was bold enough to question, and that these 13 Principles of Belief represent the answers accepted by perhaps the most brilliant mind of the ages. No book on Judaism is complete without their inclusion:

1. I believe with complete faith that the Creator, Blessed is His Name, creates and guides all creatures, and that He alone made, makes, and will make everything.

2. I believe with complete faith that the Creator, Blessed is His Name, is unique, and there is no uniqueness like His in any way, and that He alone is our God, Who was, Who is, and Who always will be.

3. I believe with complete faith that the Creator, Blessed is His Name, is not physical and is not affected by physical phenomena, and that there is no comparison whatsoever to Him.

4. I believe with complete faith that the Creator, Blessed is His Name, is the very first and the very last.

5. I believe with complete faith that the Creator, Blessed is His Name—to Him alone is it proper to pray, and it is not proper to pray to any other.

6. I believe with complete faith that all the words of the prophets are true.

7. I believe with complete faith that all the words of the prophecy of Moses our teacher, peace upon him, was true, and that he was the father of the prophets—both those who preceded him and those who followed him.

Statue of Maimonides in Cordoba, Spain.

(Art Resource, NY)

8. I believe with complete faith that the entire Torah now in our hands is the same one that was given to Moses, our teacher, peace be upon him.

9. I believe with complete faith that this Torah will not be exchanged nor will there be another Torah from the Creator, Blessed is His Name.

10. I believe with complete faith that the Creator, Blessed is His Name, knows all the deeds of human beings and their thoughts, as it is said, "He fashions their hearts all together, He comprehends all their deeds."

11. I believe with complete faith that the Creator, Blessed is His Name, rewards with good those who observe His commandments, and punishes those who violate His commandments.

12. I believe with complete faith in the coming of the Messiah, and even though he may delay, nevertheless I anticipate every day that he will come.

13. I believe with complete faith that there will be a resuscitation of the dead whenever the wish emanates from the Creator, Blessed is His Name and exalted is His mention, forever and for all eternity.

From the Mountaintop

What gave many Jews faith during the darkest days of the Holocaust was a song that they sang even as they were led to their deaths. The words were those of the twelfth of Maimonides' Thirteen Principles of Faith: "I believe in perfect faith in the coming of Messiah." Knowing that the coming of the Messiah would be preceded by a time of unprecedented horror, they prayed that their pain would be the prelude to the long-awaited time of the redemption.

Applying the Laws

Ideas are wonderful, but they mean nothing if they aren't turned into action. Philosophy only becomes Judaism when it is joined to the fulfillment of mitzvot, a commandment of the Torah. That's why most of Jewish scholarship, creativity, and commitment was focused on works of law—books whose purpose was not to tell you what to think but to help you know what to *do*.

Jewish theologians came to an interesting conclusion about the relationship between thought and deed. "The heart," they said, "is drawn after the actions." It's not so much that thinking leads to doing as that doing leads to thinking. As clinical psychologist Dr. Paul Pearsall put it, coming to the same conclusion as the rabbis of old: "Going through the motions alters the emotions. If you behave lovingly, you will feel love. You change your behavior first." That's why Judaism stresses the deed. The creed will follow.

Schmoozing

Even as there are laws of poetry, so there is poetry in law.
—Abraham Isaac Kook (1865–1935), Chief Rabbi of Palestine

"The Strong Hand"

Maimonides, the great philosopher, understood this clearly. Before he wrote his *Guide to the Perplexed*, he completed his master work on Jewish Law. He called it the *Yad Ha'chazakah*, "the strong hand," to emphasize that only through obedience to law and performance of mitzvot is our obligation to God fulfilled. It is our "hand" that makes us good Jews far more than our convictions.

From the Mountaintop

Another name for the *Yad Ha'chazakah*, written by Maimonides, is *Mishneh Torah*, literally "a second Torah." Maimonides hoped that after reading the original Torah text, people would be able to refer to this "second" concise summary of its laws for practical guidance.

The *Yad Ha'chazakah* was the first code to systematically arrange all the laws scattered throughout the Talmud into a readily available and clear summary of *halacha*, proper practice. Before the publication of this work, you had to be a scholar or ask a scholar how to observe the law. Maimonides made it possible for every Jew to find the answers him- and herself. That's why his first work, before his philosophic *magnum opus*, was also a guide to the perplexed—not for confusion of faith, but rather for behavior and practice.

Let There Be Light

Halacha, literally "the going," is the Hebrew word for law, the legal way "to go."

"The Prepared Table"

Maimonides began the process of codifying Jewish law. In the sixteenth century, Rabbi Joseph Karo (1488–1575) wrote the book that would become the standard legal work of Judaism to this day. Karo was able to incorporate not only the rulings of Maimonides, but also of all the other great rabbis who preceded him.

His encyclopedic scope coupled with his erudite scholarship produced a masterpiece that deserves its title, *The Shulkhan Arukh*, "The Prepared Table." What the author wanted to achieve was to present Judaism in a format as accessible as a prepared table and as delectable and appealing as well. Its universal acceptance by world Jewry to this day proves how successful he was.

To give you an idea of how much it covers, I can't do better than quote its opening line: "A person should rise in the morning like a lion in order to strive to fulfill the service of his Creator …" Before the invention of alarm clocks, it was the law that made Jews hear an inner voice telling them they had to quickly jump out of bed to begin fulfilling all their obligations to God. What to do next, how to pray, what restrictions governed their jobs and their professions, what happened if they were involved in disputes with others about money matters, how to observe festivals … the list is as large as the possibilities of life.

From the Mountaintop

Rabbi Joseph Karo wrote *The Shulkhan Arukh*, "The Prepared Table," as a code of law from the perspective of a Sephardic Jew, one whose ancestors lived in Spain and Portugal. Jews from Ashkenazic tradition, of Franco-German descent, wanted their own traditions and different customs to be included in this work. Rabbi Moses Isserlis (1525–1572), therefore, wrote an addendum to the prepared table that, with a delicious sense of humor, he called *Mapa*, "The Tablecloth."

Non-Jews find it hard to understand Judaism's obsession with law. The law books in the secular world are meant to be studied only by lawyers. Jews are different. Laws teach us the Godly disciplines of life. They accompany men and women every waking hour—and even teach us how to sleep. Laws, say the sages, are what make us greater than animals. So even little children who don't dream of becoming lawyers or rabbis are regularly brought to "the prepared table" and encouraged to take from it some spiritual nourishment. That way their lives will gain the beauty of discipline and the joy of serving God as He intended.

Personal Questions

The law books are for everyone. They offer general rules and guidance for most occasions. But central to the word *life* are the two letters "if." Life is filled with so many imponderables, no book could possibly cover them all. And life also changes for every generation, with new discoveries, new scientific advances, new medical procedures, all of which offer ethical questions and religious problems that were never thought of before.

It is to address issues like these that a vast body of literature was produced throughout all the centuries known as the *responsa*. Responsa (singular, *responsum*) are the answers of the leading luminaries of every age to specific questions posed by Jews who wanted to know "the law"—what it was that God wanted them to do in their particular situation.

> **Schmoozing**
>
> The Law as a whole is not the means to an end, but the end in itself; the Law is active religiousness, and in active religion lies what is specifically Jewish.
>
> —Louis Ginzberg (1873–1953), American Talmudic scholar and professor

"Dear R-abby"

Dear Abby letters aren't a modern-day discovery. The mounds of mail regularly sent to this modern-day "philosopher" reflect a strongly felt need on the part of people to ask for wise counsel. Abby is smart, but she relies solely on her own judgment. Rabbis were at least as wise, but they responded not only with their own opinions but also from the vast corpus of knowledge scattered throughout the Torah and Talmud.

The kinds of questions people addressed to rabbis reflect the social conditions of the times, new situations seemingly not covered by ancient law, and stories that appear to have no parallel in rulings of the past. The twentieth century, perhaps more than any other, prompted queries that required careful consideration, analysis, and rabbinic rulings. To give you some idea of their scope, let me share with you some fairly modern responsa.

> ### From the Mountaintop
>
> When the sick man explained his ailment to his visitor, the visitor said: "Oh, that's really interesting. My father died of the same disease." The sick man became very depressed, but the visitor said, "Don't worry, I'll pray to God to heal you." To which the sick man answered: "And when you pray, add a prayer that I may be spared visits from any more stupid people." It's not enough to visit the sick. You have to do it right for it to be a true mitzvah.

Can I Do It by Phone?

Question: My best friend lives out of town. She is quite ill, and I can't possibly leave my family to fly to her home and fulfill the mitzvah of *bikkur holim*—visiting the sick. Is it possible for me to fulfill this commandment by calling her on the telephone?

Responsum: There is no doubt that calling a sick person on the telephone is considered a visit. Maimonides classifies the mitzvah of visiting the sick under the heading of "loving your neighbor." This being the case, any favor you do for your friend, even if you do it by telephone, is a manifestation of "loving your neighbor." Nevertheless, it would be preferable to go to see the patient since seeing her will stir your feelings more than speaking on the telephone. It will cause you to pray more fervently for her recovery, and you will see more clearly what her needs are and be able to take care of them.

—Rabbi Yonatan Steif (1877–1958)

Can I Buy Insurance?

Question: I want to buy insurance, but I am concerned that this might be a sin. Does it exhibit a lack of trust in God's ability to make a person wealthy so that he will have a large estate to leave to his heirs?

Responsum: Man must strive to earn his livelihood. He may not say, "If I don't do anything, God will provide somehow." How does he know that he has earned this great merit? Besides, it is forbidden to rely on miracles. Although man should be mindful that whatever he earns from his labor derives from God, it is

God's decree that He provides a livelihood only when it is earned through labor, as it says, "By the sweat of your brow you will eat bread." And so an insurance policy is like any business that one does to provide for his family. It is permitted to buy a policy because it is a form for providing for your family.

Since God enlightened the recent generations to design the concept of insurance so that people should have money for their old age and heirs, it is beneficial and appropriate to obtain it for all God-fearing and observant Jews who place their trust in God. The same holds true for fire, theft, and automobile insurance; there is no question of lack of faith.

—Rabbi Moshe Feinstein (1895–1986)

Must He Atone for His Sin?

Question: During the Holocaust, the Nazis evacuated a concentration camp in fear of the approaching American Army. They hounded the inmates, forcing them to march at top speed to prevent them from being liberated. It was a death march in which those who were too weak to continue were shot on the spot. Many times, during one of the brief rest stops, a prisoner fell asleep and didn't immediately respond to the marching orders. Instantly, the Nazis put a bullet through his head. This prompted the prisoners to devise a buddy system, taking turns sleeping so that one could wake up the other.

One man was in this march together with his younger brother. During a rest stop, he told his brother to take a nap and that he would watch over him and wake him. However, he, too, fell asleep. When the Germans screamed for them to start moving, he scrambled to line up with the others and instantly the column began to move. When he remembered his brother, it was too late to go back, as he surely would have been shot. He never saw his brother again, and he is certain that the Germans killed him. For the last 13 years he has been reproaching himself for his brother's death, and he is depressed with feelings of guilt. He wants to know whether or not he must atone for this.

Responsum: His guilty feelings stem from two sources: that he failed to wake up his brother when he himself was aroused from sleep, and that he did not go back to wake him up after he had joined the column. The fact that he told him to take a nap is of no consequence. The brother was so exhausted that he would have gone to sleep anyway. Proof of this is the fact that he himself fell asleep.

Throughout *halachik* literature—writings about Jewish law—the rabbis discussed the question of whether forgetting is due to negligence or is an unintentional, unavoidable circumstance. In this case, where the man blames himself for not waking his brother, it is abundantly clear that it was not due to negligence. We are dealing here with prisoners who were tired, weak, and totally exhausted from the long march, and who were overcome by sleep. Of course their sleep was an unavoidable circumstance.

Regarding his concern for not having gone back to wake him up after having joined the column, this is analogous to the Talmudic discussion of the two men in the desert, with only one of them possessing a jug of water. The conclusion there is, "Your life takes precedence over your brother's life." The brother clearly did not have to jeopardize his life to save his brother.

I want to conclude by stating that in the present case the brother should have no pangs of conscience since this leads to grief and despair, which is an even greater sin, for it distresses him and prevents him from serving God. We must serve God with gladness.

—Rabbi Mordechai Yaakov Breisch (1895–1976)

Pulpit Story

Why can't a Jew be an astronaut? The first religious Jew offered the job had to refuse when he heard how many times the capsule orbits the earth: "I won't have any time to do any work for you," he explained. "All I'll have to do is morning prayer, afternoon prayer, evening prayer. Morning prayer, afternoon …"

Modern-Day Problems

Science moves forward at a dizzying pace. What was science fiction only years ago is often reality today. Organs are transplanted, sheep are cloned, babies are created in test tubes, and we are contemplating establishing colonies in space. Can ancient legal systems deal with these contemporary ethical problems? Responsa literature produces voluminous works dealing with every one of these questions—and thousands more.

The Talmud may not have directly discussed travel in space. Contemporary Jewish scholars, however, are proving that implicit in the legal system that has guided Jews for ages is the divine wisdom that will allow us to discover a moral compass for the future.

The Least You Need to Know

♦ Biblical commentators of every generation perceive new truths in ancient writings as they explain verses from their own perspective and fulfill the mission of merging human intellect with divinely transmitted text.

♦ Students of the Kabbalah, inspired by the Zohar, add a mystical dimension to our understanding of God and the world.

♦ Jewish laws turn ethical concepts into practical daily application and are the focus of countless works attempting to teach Jews how to "do the right thing."

♦ Responsa make Jewish law relevant to modern life as they apply ancient principles to contemporary situations.

Part 3

The Time of Your Life

Judaism sees the calendar filled with drama, with memories, with vivid recollections of important moments that can inspire us, enlighten us, and probably even change our lives.

Part 3 takes you on a tour of the days of the year. You will explore "the best of times and the worst of times." You will see why holidays are so important to Jews and why every one of the holidays has its mood and its message. You will discover the real meaning of the High Holy Days, the Pilgrimage Festivals, Hanukkah, and Purim, as well as the newest Jewish holidays—Israel Independence Day and Yom Yerushalayim (the commemoration of the liberation of Jerusalem).

Prepare yourself not only for the time of your life, but also for the realization that eventually dawns on every one of us: That time *is* your life.

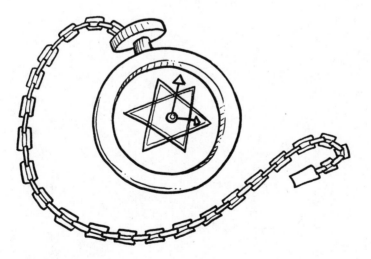

Chapter 10

The Jewish Calendar

In This Chapter

- ◆ How the Jewish calendar differs
- ◆ Why archaeology and the Bible are not in conflict
- ◆ The sun and the moon as measurements of time
- ◆ The months and the holidays
- ◆ Six days—and then the Sabbath

Albert Einstein, perhaps the greatest mind of the twentieth century, made an important observation about the concept of time: "When you sit with a nice girl for two hours, you think it's only a minute. But when you sit on a hot stove for a minute, you think it's two hours. That's relativity."

Of course, Einstein's Theory of Relativity is a little more complicated than that. Yet in his delightfully concise illustration, Einstein got across the idea that time can be measured in different ways. Time can rush by like a roaring river or creep interminably so that every moment seems like an eternity. Time can be precious or perceived as a burden. Some adore every second and others seek nothing better than to "kill" it.

The proverb says, "Time is money." Judaism is appalled by that comparison. Time is infinitely more valuable than wealth. You can't accumulate time; you can't borrow time; you can't regain time lost. Killing time isn't murder—it's suicide. The real tragedy of life is that when people finally realize that time is golden, their hair has long since turned to silver. The Book of Psalms reminds us to ask of God, "So teach us to number our days in order that we get us a heart of wisdom." We count the days in order to make the days count.

The calendar, as the great nineteenth-century German scholar, Samson Raphael Hirsch, put it, is "the catechism of the Jew." What is the purpose of Judaism? Answer the rabbis of the Talmud: To sanctify time and turn every moment of life into the holy.

Fewer Than 6,000 Years

We measure time in years. We live with a calendar that records an annually changing number. Where we start our count tells us a great deal about what we consider most important.

The calendar we live by in America tells us we are now at the beginning of the twenty-first century. Jews have a serious Y2K problem with that. Not because of their computers, but because of their conflicting view about the event that should serve as the source of the count. The 2000+ figure stresses the birth of Jesus as the major turning point of history. It makes his appearance on Earth as the Son of God sufficient to warrant a new beginning. All dates before his birth are given as B.C. (Before Christ); all dates after his birth have appended the letters A.D. (*Anno Domini*), in the year of our Lord.

From the Mountaintop

Family names didn't come into common usage until fairly modern times. Before then, the most common way to identify a person was by his first name and the name of his father—in Hebrew *ben*, "son of." So David Ben-Gurion means David, son of Gurion.

For obvious religious reasons, Jews find it theologically impossible to use both of these abbreviations. The word *Christ* was not Jesus' family name. It was a title, from the word *Christus*, which means "the anointed one"—the very same as the Hebrew word *Mashiach*, or Messiah. Jesus is not considered Messiah by the Jews and to refer to him by that title would mean renouncing the belief that the true Messiah has not yet come. The letters A.D. are far more offensive to the Jewish faith. By referring to "the year of our Lord," they acknowledge divine status for Jesus— a belief we showed in Chapter 1 was profoundly at variance with monotheism as Judaism understands it.

Living in a world that counts "Christian time," Jews have no choice but to date their checks as their neighbors do. What religious Jews will not do, however, is use the letters B.C. and A.D. Instead of B.C., they will substitute B.C.E. (Before the Common Era); and instead of A.D., they will use the letters C.E. (Common Era). That way, there's a fine compromise between religion and reality. We won't be thousands of years off for an appointment (just a few hours late, because that's a "traditional" Jewish failing); we also won't make use of a phrase we consider blasphemous to our belief.

Jews Begin with Adam

Christianity's calendar begins with the birth of their faith. Judaism's calendar starts with a far more universalistic perspective from the birth of mankind. Jews are now in the eighth century of the sixth millennia (the year 2000 corresponded to the year 5760). Note that the calendar doesn't start from the time the Jews became a nation. Nor from the time of the birth of the greatest leader, Moses. Nor even from Abraham, the first Jew, and the time when man discovered God. More important than all of these is the moment when God created universal man, Adam, "in His image." Time gains its sanctity not from a moment solely important to Jews but from a story with significance for all mankind. The calendar itself is the most powerful declaration of Judaism's concern and respect for the entire world.

But What About All Those Billions of Years?

Jews were always careful to stress that the calendar count starts not from the "first day" of Creation but from the "sixth." What's the big deal? you ask. Why make such a to-do over less than a week? Because, Jewish philosophers long ago explained, when the Bible speaks of "days" in the story of Creation, it obviously doesn't refer to the 24-hour periods of time we speak of today based on the relationship between the earth and the sun. The Bible says the sun wasn't created until the fourth "day." Biblical "days" before man appeared on Earth weren't days as they would come to be defined by people. They were periods of time, stages in the process of the world's development.

> **Pulpit Story**
>
> The poor Jew pleaded with God: "Oh Lord, for you a thousand years are but a fleeting moment. You are the God of eternity. For you, a million dollars is no more difficult to give to someone than a penny. I ask of you, God, since I'm sure it won't be any trouble, please make me a wealthy man." To which God responded: "No problem. Just wait a minute."

From the divine perspective they were as fleeting as a "day," but we would subsequently discover they really lasted for billions of years. That's why Jews aren't troubled by the apparent contradiction between archaeologists and the Jewish calendar. The world is much older than we are—and, just like Jack Benny, we like to count birthdays in a way that reminds us that we're much younger.

Planet of the Apes

In the famous Scopes trial, when William Jennings Bryan argued to imprison a teacher who dared teach his class about evolution, rabbis would much more readily have sided with Clarence Darrow, the lawyer for the defense. They might well have quoted the first chief rabbi of Palestine, Rabbi Abraham Isaac Kook (1865–1935): "The doctrine of evolution agrees with the cosmic secrets of Kabbalah more than any other philosophic doctrine."

Darwin had it right in regard to sequence. Everything did evolve just the way he described it. In fact, the evolutionary "order" is exactly what the Bible records in the story of Creation. What Darwin didn't understand is that mutations are so miraculous, they can't possibly happen on their own. True, monkeys came before man. But even if men can make monkeys out of themselves, no monkey can become a man unless God wills that transformation. Judaism agrees that evolution happened. It denies that blind chance could ever replace the need for a divine Creator.

The Midrash teaches that before Adam there were semi-human beings "with tails like monkeys." Yet that was before God breathed "His spirit" into a living being and turned the Planet of the Apes into a home for those more holy even than the angels.

The Jewish calendar also isn't interested in commemorating the birthday of Mighty Joe Young. Apes may have appeared on earth before humans but that's about as important as their being found before "humans"—and even "God"—in the dictionary. Jews count the years from the time that years count. And only humans give meaning to history and can help make it holy.

A Monthly Honeymoon

A year on the Gregorian calendar is 365 days. That's almost how long it takes for the earth to make its annual orbit around the sun—365¼ days. The quarter day discrepancy is compensated for by making every fourth year a leap year and adding February 29. That helps everyone born on that day age much more slowly, with so many fewer birthdays, and allows everyone else to keep perfect time. And that's what we mean by a solar calendar.

Judaism, however, counts the months, as the root of the English word "month" suggests, by the moon. From the "birth" of one new moon to the next, a cycle of approximately $29^{1}/_{2}$ days, a new month begins, which is celebrated as *Rosh Chodesh*—literally "beginning of the newness." A lunar year has only 354 days instead of 365. That makes every year shorter than the one before it. Holidays that occur in the spring would soon fall in the frigid months of winter. For Muslims, who observe a pure lunar calendar, this is in fact what happens. Their month-long observance of Ramadan, requiring daily fasting, may occur during any season, as it keeps coming earlier from year to year, before the cycle is completed and starts all over again.

Judaism, however, follows a lunar-solar calendar. The moon determines the months, but the shortfall of eleven days every year is compensated for by the addition of a "leap month" seven times in a 19-year cycle. (If you're into trivia, the extra month is added in the third, sixth, eighth, eleventh, fourteenth, seventeenth, and nineteenth years of the cycle.) That keeps the discrepancy between the lunar and solar calendars at a minimum. It also ensures that Passover remains, as it is biblically required to be—a spring festival. As we'll see (in Chapter 12), what happens in nature is relevant to the proper observance of the holidays.

But I'm sure you're troubled by this peculiar way of counting the days in the year. If we know that the sun is more correct as a standard for the calendar, why use the moon and be forced to compensate for its "error" with a full extra month?

Life Isn't Always "Sunny"

The first answer a traditional Jew will give you is, "We do it this way because God said so." The lunar-solar calendar is in fact derived from the Bible. Remarkably enough, the law is considered so important that it was the *very first* commandment given to the Jewish people as they became a nation. It must have meant a lot to God if He insisted that Jewish time be identified with a monthly "honeymoon." Since God didn't explain it, it was left to the genius of the sages of the Midrash to offer a number of interpretations:

 ◆ The moon waxes and wanes. It goes from darkness to light, from appearing small and insignificant to total illumination. That is meant as a symbol of the Jewish people. Like the moon, the Jews will at times seem to disappear and then return to full glory. Jewish history will be a recurring cycle moving from adversity to glory, and then repeating the story. For that reason, at the start of every month, Jews "sanctify the moon" with special blessings. They pray not for a distant planet, but for their own symbolic representation in the heavens. To sanctify the moon is to sanctify the self. That is the way to bring the cycle to an eventual close with a Messianic age that will usher in an everlasting and unchanging light.

♦ The sun shines by day, but the moon gives light in darkness. The Jewish people have a mission to be like the moon and, in the words of Isaiah, be an *or l'Goyim*," "a light unto the nations." A world overrun by darkness—violence, cruelty, ignorance—needs a people who can inspire them "by the light of the silvery moon."

♦ When life is sunny, it's fairly easy to believe in God. The true tests of faith are the moments, as Henry Wadsworth Longfellow described them, when "darkness falls from the wings of night." Every month, Jews make a blessing as they gaze at the moon and proclaim God's mastery over time even when life is ruled by the powers of the night.

♦ The sun gives light; the moon receives it. We, too, must acknowledge our role as recipients of the blessings and beneficial rays of the Almighty Giver.

Someday, the mystics teach, the moon will no longer vary in the way it is perceived on earth. What they try to suggest is the Messianic vision that someday the varying fortunes of the Jewish people will be replaced by universal recognition and acceptance.

Twelve Months—but Sometimes Thirteen

Like the twelve children of Jacob/Israel, who became the twelve tribes into which the Jewish nation was divided, the year, too, is made up of twelve months. Their names come from the time of Jewish exile in Babylonia. Let me list them for you with the approximate time they correspond to on the secular calendar. (Remember, this will vary from year to year based on the lunar-solar discrepancy.)

Hebrew Month	Gregorian Months
Tishrei	September and October
Cheshvan	October and November
Kislev	November and December
Tevet	December and January
Shvat	January and February
Adar	February and March
Adar Sheni (second Adar) (the leap month 7 years out of 19)	February and March
Nissan	March and April
Iyar	April and May

Hebrew Month	Gregorian Months
Sivan	May and June
Tammuz	June and July
Av	July and August
Elul	August and September

A Holiday Every Month (Almost)

Every month has its own special days. Some holidays are happy, some are sad. Time forces us to remember, to commemorate, and to feast or to fast, to rejoice or to weep. Anniversaries can't be ignored; they're too important. Why events occurred when they did is the subject of much speculation and commentary. At the least, we should link months with their special days. In chapters to come, we'll explain the special significance of each of these holidays.

Hebrew Month	Holidays
Tishrei	Rosh Hashanah (New Year); Yom Kippur (Day of Atonement; Sukkot (Tabernacles)
Cheshvan	Poor, poor Cheshvan. The only month without a holiday, which is why it's sometimes called *Mar Cheshvan*, the word *mar* meaning "bitter." (Maybe it's because the month before had so many holidays—and so much eating—that Jews needed some time to recuperate!)
Kislev	Hanukkah
Tevet	The Fast of the 10th of Tevet
Shvat	Tu B'Shvat (the 15th of Shvat)
Adar	The Fast of Esther; Purim
Nissan	Passover; Yom ha-Shoa (Holocaust Memorial Day)
Iyar	Yom ha-Atzma'ut (Israel Independence Day); Yom Yerushalayim (Jerusalem Day)
Sivan	Shavuot
Tammuz	Fast of the 17th of Tammuz
Av	Tisha b'Av (the 9th of Av)
Elul	An entire month dedicated to special prayers in preparation for the coming New Year

Hooray: Two New Years

Here's one more important difference between the Jewish and the secular year: According to the secular calendar, there's only one New Year's Day. The Jewish calendar has two, but that doesn't mean Jews have hangovers twice a year. Drinking isn't the way Jews ring out the old year and bring in the new. Beginnings have much more to do with serious introspection than sipping champagne.

But why two New Years? Because when God took the Jews out of Egypt, he commanded them: "This month shall be to you the first of the months …"

The month of the exodus, the time when Passover is observed, was Nissan. It's to be commemorated as the first month to recall the birth of a nation, the Jewish people. Tishrei, however, remains the start of the year, retaining its commemoration of the birth of mankind. Two New Years because two major moments deserve annual recognition: The world and the Jew live in symbiotic relationship in real life, just as they coexist commemoratively in the calendar.

Schmoozing

The festivals are ten in number … the first is that which anyone will perhaps be astonished to hear called a festival. This festival is every day.

—Philo (20 B.C.E.–40 C.E.), Alexandria philosopher

Schmoozing

If Israel would keep two Sabbaths as they should be kept, the redemption would come at once.

—The Talmud

T.G.I.S.: Thank God It's Shabbat

Life, as Thomas LaMance—a contemporary author—observed, is what happens to us while we are making other plans. Life, unfortunately, happens too fast for most of us ever to stop and think about it. We live but we forget why. Before we realize what's happened, life is over. As someone wittily put it, life can be summed up in three words: hurry, worry, bury.

Judaism, as we've seen, is very concerned with time. So in addition to having the months focus on holidays that force us to reflect on important ideas, not a week is allowed to go by without its Sabbath, *Shabbat*. For six days our focus is physical; we tend to the needs of our body. At least once every week, every seventh day, we have to recharge ourselves spiritually and take care of our souls.

Abraham Joshua Heschel, the great twentieth-century theologian, put it beautifully: "The Temple was a sanctuary in space; the Shabbat is a sanctuary in time." For six days we live life on the level of "how"; every seventh day we change the focus of our existence to "why."

Why the Days Don't Have Names

Shabbat isn't just a day, it's a destination. It's the goal of all the other days of the week. That's why, strangely enough, Judaism doesn't have names for the days of the week. Sunday, Monday, Tuesday, and so on are secular descriptives with pagan origins. For Jews, Sunday is simply the first day to Shabbat, Monday, the second, through Friday, the sixth. The significance of every day is related to its standing in terms of the Sabbath.

Schmoozing

Every seventh day a miracle comes to pass, the resurrection of the soul, of the soul of man and of the soul of all things.

—Abraham Joshua Heschel

Schmoozing

The Sabbath and holidays are the primary reason for Jewish endurance and glory.

—Judah Halevi (1085–1140), Spanish poet and philosopher

That puts a profoundly different perspective on the whole week. Every day is viewed as a preparation for the coming Shabbat. The seventh day, which emphasizes our spiritual essence, is the goal; weekdays are merely means to a greater end. We don't rest in order to work; we work in order to have a day of rest and "resoul" ourselves and the rest of the world.

Take a Rest

"Six days shall you labor and do all your work," says the Bible in the Ten Commandments, "but the seventh day is a Sabbath to the Lord your God, you shall not do any manner of work." The Sabbath is a day of rest—but not in a passive way; rather, in a creative sense. Original Creation lasted a week and even the seventh day, when seemingly nothing new came into being, is included in the count. When an artist steps back from his painting to view it and consider whether it fulfills his expectations, that, too, is part of the process of creating a masterpiece. Our lives, if they are to be works of art, require review and evaluation. For those who don't do it on a weekly basis, there may well be a time late in life when they seek professional help to ponder the purpose of their existence on Earth. They may then be asked to "rest" and lie down on an analyst's couch. That's the kind of rest the Sabbath demands as it asks Jews to rest *from* the demands of the business world and dedicate themselves *to* the demands of our spiritual being and the meaning of our lives.

Schmoozing

The Sabbath is the day of complete harmony between man and nature. "Work" is any kind of disturbance of the man-nature equilibrium. By not working—that is to say, by not participating in the process of actual and social change—man is free from the chains of time.

—Eric Fromm (1900–1980), American psychologist

To say that the meaning of the Sabbath is not to work is like defining the purpose of Thanksgiving as having a day off from one's job. Just to refrain from doing any work without stressing the spiritual on the Sabbath is like celebrating Thanksgiving simply by not working, but without remembering to give thanks. Eric Fromm, the great American psychologist, understood it perfectly:

> Rest in the sense of the traditional Sabbath concept is quite different from "rest" being defined as not working or not making an effort. On the Sabbath, man ceases completely to be an animal whose main occupation is to fight for survival and to sustain his biological life. On the Sabbath, man is fully man, with no task other than to be human.

Pulpit Story

The Roman Emperor once asked Rabbi Joshua: "What is the special secret of the tasty meal you have just served me?" Rabbi Joshua replied, "We have a certain spice called Sabbath." The Emperor asked Rabbi Joshua to give him some of that spice for use in the palace kitchens. Rabbi Joshua explained that the spice can't be transferred; it's only effective as part of the Sabbath observance.

Light My Fire

To accomplish that goal is no small task. The work-a-day week turns us into a heel, and on Shabbat we have to get back our souls. How we accomplish this is with the help of rituals because rituals are to understanding what matches are to fire—small as they may be, they can help to light up our entire environment.

The metaphor of fire is particularly apt for Shabbat because that is the religious way in which the Sabbath is ushered in. A candle is the symbol of the soul. Two candles are lit to symbolize the mystical idea that the Sabbath grants human beings an "extra soul." The illumination the candles bring is a symbol of the divine presence. God makes Himself felt in the home because that is the most important source for Jewish continuity and survival.

It is the woman of the household who is given the honor to perform this sacred act because the home is not just her castle, it is her temple, in which she serves as high priestess. With this act, the wife and mother is acknowledged as the one who brings warmth and enlightenment to her family.

Tell Me You Love Me

The Jewish day starts not at midnight but at nightfall. This follows the biblical verses that read, "And it was evening and it was morning"—first night and then day. The Sabbath, therefore, begins Friday eve before twilight when the candles are lit. After synagogue services, the family then sits down to a festive Sabbath meal.

Before it can begin, however, Jewish husbands are obligated to sing a love song to their wives. The lyrics aren't country-western, they're more ancient Eastern. The words traditionally recited come from Proverbs 31:10–31. King Solomon extols the virtues of an *eshat chayil*, a woman of valor. Every husband is asked to make his wife feel that in his eyes she is the most wonderful of all women.

The man isn't just supposed to think it—he is required to say it. Just because men will never ask for directions when they're lost doesn't mean that they're exempt from expressing their appreciation for what they've found. And that isn't just good marital counseling. It's a mitzvah, nothing less than a religious obligation.

Ask the Rabbi

In order for the Sabbath to be a time of spiritual and physical delight, Jewish tradition recommends the following: That we eat three meals on the Sabbath, sing the special joyous family songs, wear our best clothes, spend some time in prayer in synagogue and in study of the Torah, do not converse about weekday activities, and review the direction of our own lives.

Ask the Rabbi

To greet a Jew on Shabbat, you say "Gut Shabbes" to a Jew of Eastern European origin; "Good Shabbat" to a Jew who uses modern Sephardic pronunciation; or "Shabbat Shalom" to someone who understands the Hebrew blessing for a Sabbath of peace. But no matter which one you use, you can't go wrong—good wishes are always appreciated.

A Jug of Wine, a Loaf of Challah

Wine is the traditional symbol of joy and of a festive occasion. A family meal must be happy, so before eating, the *kiddush* (sanctification) is recited over a cup of wine to acknowledge God as the Creator and the day as holy.

The family then "breaks bread" together but uses a special braided bread, *challah*, to symbolize the intertwining and connectedness that this holy day brings with it. Trust me, challah tastes nothing like white bread; there's no way to describe freshly baked, warm challah other than to repeat what Jews call it—"a taste of the world to come." Through the shared wine and challah, as well as the delicious courses that follow, Jewish ritual allows families to feel the special love, joy, and appreciation we are usually too busy to notice during the frantic pace of the week.

From the Mountaintop

Two is the minimum number of candles lit for Shabbat. Some have the custom to add an additional candle for every child. The larger the family, the more "enlightened" they are.

Shabbat allows us the time to rediscover our family and friends. Orthodox Jews won't even answer the telephone or turn on the television. It is a time to escape from the mundane and profane and choose the world of the sacred. Shabbat allows Jews to find the time to talk, to sing, to feast, to pray, to study, and even to make love—which is a mitzvah on Friday night. Can you ask for a more perfect way to spend a day?

By finding the time to do the things that really count, Judaism has discovered the way to make man the master rather than the victim of the passing years.

Friday Evening *by Isadore Kaufmann.*

(Art Resource, NY, The Jewish Museum, NY)

Pulpit Story

On Sabbath eve, a good angel and an evil angel accompany a man from the synagogue to his home. If the man finds the candles lit, the tables set, and the bed made, the good angel says, "May next Sabbath be like this!" The evil angel must answer, "Amen." If these things are not done, the evil angel says, "May the next Sabbath be like this!" and the good angel is compelled to respond, "Amen."

—The Talmud

Revive Me When It's Over

The end of Shabbat is almost traumatic. Jews have to give up the sacred and return to the secular. That transformation is marked by a beautiful ritual known as *havdalah* ("separation"). In addition to a benediction blessing God for the ability to make distinctions, the havdalah service makes use of several beautiful symbols:

- ◆ Just as Shabbat was introduced with a candle, its departure is marked with a flame, but for a totally different reason. The Midrash describes how Adam, seeing that the sun had gone down on the first day of his life, was terribly frightened. God then taught him how to light a fire that would illuminate his darkness and warm him in the cold of night. With fire, man could cook, fashion metals, and begin to control nature. The Greeks have a legend about Prometheus, who was condemned by the pagan gods because he taught people the art of making fire. Jews praise God for allowing us to share in His secrets and, in the course of the week, to become copartners with Him in the act of Creation.

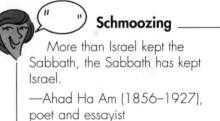

Schmoozing

More than Israel kept the Sabbath, the Sabbath has kept Israel.

—Ahad Ha Am (1856–1927), poet and essayist

- ◆ People participating in the ceremony use the light of the flame to look at their fingernails. The nails are the one part of the body that visibly grow. To look at them by the light of the candle lit immediately after the Sabbath is to challenge us by asking whether we have spiritually grown on this day as we prepare to face the secular world.

- ◆ We make a blessing over spices to dispel our sadness over the departure of Shabbat. As night brings the next day, we feel faint from the disappearance of our "extra soul" and need to be revived by the fragrant equivalence of smelling salts.

♦ A cup of wine tells us that even as we rejoice with the Sabbath, we must be happy at the opportunity to now begin the work week and contribute to society and the progress of the world.

Man Making a Havdalah
by Hermann Struck.

(Art Resource, NY, The Jewish Museum, NY)

♦ Finally, the havdalah bids us to carry forward from the Shabbat to the coming days some of what we derived from it. In the havdalah ceremony, we bring all of the five senses into play: the sense of sight as we see the light; the sense of smell as we inhale the spices; the sense of taste as we drink the wine; the sense of hearing as we listen to the benediction; and the sense of touch when, as is the custom, we extend fingers toward the light. So we leave the day that has "re-Jew-venated" us by acknowledging our indebtedness to God for our five senses as we resolve to use them wisely during the course of the coming week.

From the Mountaintop

The custom is to pour off a little of the wine from the **havdalah** cup to symbolize the hope that in the days to follow, "our cup will run over" with the blessings of prosperity, health, and joy.

The Least You Need to Know

- While the standard calendar used today makes the birth of Jesus its starting point, Jews opt for a count that is far more universal, beginning with the creation of Adam and Eve.

- The six millennia of the Jewish calendar do not include the possible billions of years of earth's existence preceding the creation of fully human beings, formed "in the image of God."

- The Jewish calendar is neither solar, like the Christian, nor lunar, like the Muslim, but a combination of lunar-solar.

- The twelve months of the Hebrew year almost all have special days of commemoration, linking major events of the past with rituals that ensure their remembrance.

- The Jewish calendar commemorates the birth of the Jewish people, as well as the beginning of mankind by way of its two New Years.

- The weekly Sabbath, Shabbat, is a sanctuary of time allowing the soul to "re-Jew-venate" on a weekly basis.

The High Holy Days

In This Chapter

- Why the Jewish High Holy Days are really the Days of Awe

- What the sounds of the *shofar* teach us

- The special laws and customs of Rosh Hashanah, the New Year, and Yom Kippur, the Day of Atonement

- How the Book of Jonah summarizes the ideas of Yom Kippur

- Why human mortality is a theme of the Day of Atonement

Here's a good bit of advice: Don't ever forget your husband's or wife's birthday or your anniversary. Not to remember is not to care and not to consider such a meaningful day important. Moments are only meaningful if we treasure them and commemorate them.

What's true for us personally is even more relevant for days that are part of our history. That's the purpose of holidays. "Holiday" is a combination of two shorter words—*holy* and *day*. A holiday is a holy day because it interrupts the daily flow of our unexamined lives with messages and reminders that we need to make life worth living. A map is a guide for people traveling in space; holidays are the signposts for people traveling through time. Without holidays we would get just as spiritually "lost" as the prover-bial male who doesn't have an inkling as to where he is and refuses to ask anyone for directions.

The Jewish year begins not with one, but with two, holi(holy)days linked by a common theme to ensure a Happy New Year.

Man, They Are Awesome

Rosh Hashanah, literally "head of the year," is New Year's Day. Ten days later is *Yom Kippur*, the "Day of Atonement." In English, they are usually called the High Holy Days. But that misses the point. (Aside from which, today, "getting high" has come to have a very different—and nonspiritual—meaning.)

A much better way to refer to these two holy days, as well as the interval between them, is the Hebrew phrase *yamim noraim*, "Days of Awe." The words capture the mood, the meaning, and the purpose of this first 10-day period of the year. These are days of awe because they are … well, really awesome. They fill us with anxiety, trepidation, humility, and soul-searching. It's always the first steps we take on any journey that set our course. How we start the year, we realize, is the key to everything else that follows. That's why we are "awed" by the potential—and the responsibility—of the first two Jewish holidays.

The Top Ten—Jewish Style

David Letterman isn't responsible for this "top 10" list. Jewish law and Jewish lore teach us the significance of the days beginning with Rosh Hashanah and concluding with Yom Kippur.

Judgment Day

Rosh Hashanah commemorates the day when God created Adam and Eve. It's the birthday of the world as far as human beings are concerned. That makes it a perfect day for God to annually judge the world and every person in it. Rosh Hashanah, therefore, has another name, as well—the "Day of Judgment."

In the zodiac, the sign that invariably corresponds with Rosh Hashanah is Libra, the scales. And one could say that this sign is a symbol of the religious meaning of this time in the Jewish year. As the rabbis of the Talmud put it, God brings out His scales in order to weigh the deeds of every person. On one side of the scale are placed a person's good deeds, the mitzvot. On the other side God places a person's sins. The way the scales tilt determines our fate for the coming year. Talk about being afraid of getting on the scales!

Tradition carries this illustration one step further: Some people will have such a super-abundance of good deeds that they will immediately be inscribed in God's Book of Life and Blessing. These are the pious who have nothing more to worry about. On the other hand, there are those who are totally wicked, for whom the scale doesn't just tip but almost topples to the side of evil. They, too, have their fate sealed immediately on Rosh Hashanah day as they are inscribed in the *Book for Death and Misfortune*.

Most people, however, don't fit into either one of these extreme categories. They are far more often in the middle. The scale swings back and forth like a seesaw of similarly weighted children without a clear-cut resolution. And so God does what any kindhearted judge might do in a comparable situation. He decides to give people one last chance to be "extra special good" before He makes His decision about the coming year. (It is almost like the last week of school when the teacher is going to be making out the report cards, and we know that final impressions can improve our marks.)

From the Mountaintop

The Talmud teaches: Because the world is judged in accordance with the majority of *its* deeds, and the individual is judged in accordance with the majority of *his* deeds, if a person performs one *mitzvah*, he can tip his own scales to the positive side, which in turn can tip the scales of the entire world toward merit and blessing. Similarly, if someone commits one sin, woe unto him, for he can tip his own scales toward a curse, and then conceivably tip the scale of the entire world to destruction. Talk about bearing the responsibility of carrying the whole world on your shoulders!

"I'll Give You One More Chance"

How long does God wait before making His final decision? Here's where the magic number 10 comes into play, just as it did when God gave the world the Ten Commandments. "I'll give you 10 days," said God, "to improve your lives by committing to the Ten Commandments. On the tenth day, the day of Yom Kippur, I'll come to a conclusion as to whether you deserve atonement." That's why the days from Rosh Hashanah through Yom Kippur are known as the *Asseret Y'mey T'shuvah*, the "10 days of repentance." Knowing this makes Jews extra careful about their behavior on these days. Sort of gives new meaning to the saying that if you're angry or about to do something you shouldn't, count to 10.

That explains the way Jews wish each other a Happy New Year. The greeting differs from Rosh Hashanah to Yom Kippur. At the beginning of the 10-day period, you wish your friends, "May you be inscribed for a good year," or "*L'shanah tovah tikatevu.*" God only "writes" but doesn't finalize your decree until He sees what you've done with this 10-day grace period. On Yom Kippur, the greeting is, "May you be sealed for good," or "*Gemar chatimah tovah.*" On Yom Kippur, the judgment is final. And that's why, of all the days of awe, Yom Kippur is the most awesome.

Come Blow Your Horn

Because Rosh Hashanah is the Day of Judgment on which God begins to decide what's in store for us, it includes an important ritual that also gives the day yet another biblical name: *Yom T'Ruah*, the day of the blowing of the horn.

No, please don't call Dizzy Gillespie to fulfill this mitzvah. It's not a traditional horn that you might see in a jazz band. It's a *shofar*—the horn of a ram. Why have "the sound of music" on a day that should more logically be devoted to words and to prayer? And why special notes not from any musical instrument but only from the horn of a ram? Although the Bible doesn't explain, the symbolism is clear to rabbinic commentators. The interpretations are limited only by the ingenuity of the people who offer them. You can add your own insights, but here are some of the most popular explanations for the shofar that have been offered:

◆ The shofar was sounded during the days when the Jews wandered in the desert from Egypt to the Promised Land whenever they were commanded to move on, to change their locations, or to go forward to their final destination. At the beginning of a new year, what more powerful message can be given than not to get stuck in our lives, but to move onward, to make progress, to "change our location" and recognize the need for improvement and growth?

◆ A shofar was used in ancient times as a call to battle. Like an air raid siren, it was meant to rouse the people to fight against their enemies. On Rosh Hashanah, the shofar also serves as a call to war, to fight against our evil nature, our inclination to remain passive in the face of injustice, our unwillingness to face up to the need to fight our tendency to choose comfort over concern for others and the easy path over the way that is right. What better day than the Day of Judgment to hear a wake-up call that reminds us to "do right."

From the Mountaintop

How do you decide who is worthy of being the person selected for blowing the shofar? The Hasidic Rabbi of Verditsch asked everyone applying for the position what his mystic thoughts were during the shofar blowing. No one's answer pleased him. Finally, one man said, "Rabbi, I am unlearned, and I know no mystic thoughts. But I have four daughters to marry off, and I have no money for their dowries. Therefore, when I blow the shofar, I think: 'O Lord of the universe, I have done my duty in obeying your command; do you also your duty and send me mates for my daughters.'" The Rabbi appointed him to blow the shofar.

♦ The shofar was heard when the Jews gathered around Mount Sinai to receive the Torah, announcing the presence of God in their midst. On Rosh Hashanah, the sound of the shofar makes us realize that even when we are away from the mountain of God, we are never far from His presence. God is always in our midst, which is why we have to live our lives with an awareness that we are always being watched by a "higher authority."

♦ The shofar was blown in biblical times to proclaim the rulership of a king. On Rosh Hashanah, Jews recommit themselves to the concept of the kingship of God and His control over the entire earth.

♦ And finally, a story that explains why it has to be the horn of a ram: Abraham was tested by God and told to take his son Isaac and offer him as a sacrifice to the Lord. Abraham felt he couldn't refuse a direct command from God. He was prepared to carry out this ungodly act in the name of God, until God Himself stopped him and taught him the real purpose of the story. Unlike pagan gods for whom human sacrifice was common, the God of Abraham made it clear that He doesn't condone killing human beings even for the sake of heaven. God told Abraham to stop as he lifted his sword to slay his son—and irrevocably altered the definition of permissible divine service.

At that very moment, while Abraham untied Isaac, he heard a noise in the bushes. A ram with beautiful horns was tangled in the thicket. Abraham sacrificed it in place of Isaac, as God had intended when He placed the ram there at that moment. The ram's horn was then selected to be the musical instrument for bringing the Jews closer to God on Rosh Hashanah. It would always serve to remind the Jews on this holy day of communion with God that it is important to be ready to sacrifice—but just as important to realize the limits of acceptable sacrifice to God.

The shofar, which has so many symbolic references to the past, is assigned one more role by Jewish tradition for the future. When Messiah is due to appear and human history will be transformed by a new age of universal peace, the sound of the shofar will be heard around the world. The notes that are meant to inspire us to a new beginning every year will be the song of redemption marking a new beginning for all of humankind.

"They're Playing Our Song"

Lyrics, it's been said, come from man and woman; music comes from God. Words speak to our minds, but melodies talk to our souls. Listen to the sound of the shofar, and you hear more than anything words can express. The shofar blasts are the word-less cries of the people of Israel speaking to God in a language that transcends rational comprehension.

We may not understand how the sounds of the shofar communicate with our subconscious, but Jewish law demands three distinct sounds in order to convey its message:

- *Tekiah*, an unbroken long sound

- *Shevarim*, three broken notes, resembling sobbing

- *Teruah*, nine staccato notes, resembling wailing

> **From the Mountaintop**
>
> In June 1967, when the old city of Jerusalem was liberated from Jordanian control by the Israel Defense Force, one of the first things that the then-chief rabbi of the IDF did was to blow the shofar at the Western Wall. The notes were carried live by radio and TV crews at the scene around the world. Could this be related to the prophecy that the Messianic Age will be ushered in with the sound of the shofar being blown and heard simultaneously around the globe?

The order in which they are to be "played" is tekiah, shevarim, teruah, followed by a final tekiah. The seventeenth-century scholar, Rabbi Isaiah Horowitz, author of *The Two Tablets of the Covenant*, offers the following beautiful interpretation: The music is the theme of Rosh Hashanah, as well as its major message. We start with a long unbroken blast, like a lengthy exclamation of joy indicating wholeness and happiness. But life doesn't let us always laugh; reality forces upon us moments of weeping and wailing. Those who are whole become broken. Pain is an inescapable portion of life.

Yet we always close with a tekiah. Those who are broken in spirit will become whole again. Those who suffer must believe that God will hear their prayers and allow them again to sing.

The music of the shofar is the melody of our lives. It plays "our song" and reminds us that optimism is more than a possibility; it's a religiously mandated mitzvah.

Sweet Dreams

Optimism is also the reason behind a famous Rosh Hashanah custom. Normally, throughout the year, salt is sprinkled on bread as a reminder of the procedure used for offerings in the Temple. On Rosh Hashanah, we want to show that we are confident of a "sweet" judgment and so we replace salt with honey. We not only dip the challah in honey, but we follow that with an apple dipped in honey as well. The apple is somewhat sour. Symbolically, we say that even if we were originally destined to endure some bitterness, may the bitter be turned to sweet and the new year filled with the pleasantness promised to a people whose land is "flowing with milk and honey."

Down by the Riverside

On the afternoon of Rosh Hashanah, it's customary for Jews to go to a flowing body of water—a river, a lake, or an ocean—and symbolically throw away our sins. The ceremony is called *tashlich*, which means "you will cast out," based on the words of the prophet Micah: "And you will cast out all of your sins into the depth of the sea."

Nobody believes it's that easy to get rid of sins, even the Jews who throw some bread crumbs into the water with a declaration that their sins be carried away. (Besides, if people's sins were really removed from them and swallowed up in the sea, there would be serious flooding in many areas!)

But tashlich does serve a purpose by allowing us to act out our disgust with improper actions. The first step in repentance is to acknowledge that we were wrong and want to rid ourselves of our imperfections.

The contemporary mystic and rabbi, Zalman Schachter-Shalomi, puts it well: Throwing away untreated sewage is polluting. Before throwing your sins in the water, neutralize them by asking, "Have I learned my lesson?" Otherwise, they will come back to you in your food and water.

The point is not to pollute the waters, but to purify yourself.

Love Is Having to Say You're Sorry

Some years ago, Eric Segal's book and movie *Love Story* popularized a phrase that swept the country. Segal claimed that "love is never having to say you're sorry." Judaism strongly disagrees with that view.

The 10 days of repentance are dedicated to *T'shuvah*—repenting. And how do you repent for sins against God as well as sins against fellow man? By admitting that you were wrong, by saying you're sorry, and by making a firm commitment never to repeat the wrong behavior.

Confession Isn't Enough

Christians confess; Jews repent. Confession goes as far as admitting a wrong. Repentance, for it to be accepted, must be accompanied by a commitment to change. To confess without changing is to accept evil as unalterable behavior. "What do you want from me?" says the sinner. "I can't be any better. I'm only human." Humanity is used as an excuse for not striving for higher responsibility.

How do we know if a person has truly repented? asks the Talmud. If a man has sinned sexually with a woman and confesses, that isn't good enough. Only if he promises never to repeat his indiscretion and then has a similar opportunity and refuses can we honestly say he is no longer the person he was before. That's when God forgives.

A 1909 chromo lithograph depicting tashlich.

(Yeshiva University Museum)

What God Can't Forgive

God can, and does, forgive people who sincerely repent for sins they committed against Him. What God can't forgive are sins committed by people against other people. After all, God isn't the injured party. Only the victim has the right to offer forgiveness.

That's why Jewish law insists that before Yom Kippur, people don't just rely on their prayers but make sure to approach every person they may have hurt by word or deed throughout the past year. One of the more beautiful sights in synagogues as Yom Kippur approaches is to see people approaching each other pleading for forgiveness. Even the most bitter of enemies have no choice but to reconcile with each other. There's no way they can be forgiven by God if they haven't made peace with their fellow man and woman.

The Day of "At-One-Ment"

Yom Kippur, the Day of Atonement, is the day Jews most want to be the day of "at-one-ment." As God's written decree for the coming year is about to be sealed, Jews want to be at one and at peace with their heavenly judge, as well as with their family, friends, and neighbors. After all, it's not just that we're supposed to feel as if our lives hang in the balance. "As if" understates it. Our lives depend on our actions on this day of "last chance" as God finalizes His judgment.

> **Schmoozing**
>
> The Day of Atonement will achieve nothing for him who says, "I will sin and the Day of Atonement will automatically atone for me."
> —Talmud, Yoma 8:9

> **Pulpit Story**
>
> Two bitter enemies have finally been brought together by the rabbi on Yom Kippur. They realize they have to speak to each other and be gracious or God will not forgive their sins. Sam finally says to Abe, "I forgive you—and I wish you whatever you wish for me." Abe, in a fury, yells out, "See, I knew it. There he goes again cursing me."

Why We're Optimistic

Yom Kippur, by "coincidence," isn't just the concluding day of the 10 days of repentance. It has a story connected with it that gives it special meaning.

When the Jews came out of Egypt, they committed a terrible crime in the desert. They made a golden calf and worshiped it. Moses had to plead with God for 40 days and 40 nights until he could gain their forgiveness. Moses started praying on the first day of Elul, the month before Rosh Hashanah. Forty days later was the tenth of Tishrei. On that day, God allowed His mercy to override His strict sense of justice, and He proclaimed that the Jews were forgiven. That day on which God first forgave His people for a major sin was selected as the Day of Atonement for all future generations. On a day when God first showed his mercy, Jews continue to believe that He will decide to deal favorably with His people, as well as with the world.

No Fast Food

Yom Kippur in the Bible is called "the Sabbath of Sabbaths." It shares with the weekly day of rest an emphasis on introspection, on self-evaluation, and on trying to figure out the meaning and purpose of life. The Day of Atonement is Sabbath squared. It's "Super Bowl Sabbath"—the most sacred day of the year. That's why pious Jews spend the entire day, from sunset on Yom Kippur eve to complete darkness on Yom Kippur night of the next day in prayer, in meditation, in confession of sin, and in reconciliation with God and with his fellow man and woman.

Pulpit Story

On Yom Kippur when the Jews were gathered in the synagogue, a humble farmer brought his son. The son, who couldn't read a word of the ritual, had a whistle with him. During the closing prayer, the *Neilah,* the boy took out his whistle and blew it. The founder of the Hasidic movement, *Ba'al Shem Tov,* jumped up and congratulated the Jews; God had opened the gates. The rabbis, with all their prayers and their learning, could not prevail with God as much as the young herdsman in his ignorance by his simple desire to serve God.

And one more thing: For 25 hours, Jews neither eat nor drink. Yom Kippur is a "festival without food." It's a day on which, hopefully, God forgives our sins—and with your fate hanging in the balance, who can possibly have the stomach to eat?

The fast for this day is biblically commanded. Commentators explain it in different ways:

◆ We express our awareness of the seriousness of this day by keeping away from the pleasure of eating and the levity that usually accompanies meals.

◆ Because we're literally praying for our lives, we don't even have a moment to spare. Our spiritual needs outweigh our physical cravings on this holy day.

◆ We give up food to express our remorse at having sinned. We not only confess our sins verbally, we also show our disgust with our own improper behavior through a concrete act of self-denial.

♦ We prove that we are higher than animals by our ability to "just say no"; we *can* look at a Dunkin Donut and leave it in the box. That's how we prove to ourselves and to God that in the coming year, we can be masters of our own destiny and control our behavior.

♦ On a day during which no food or drink passes our lips, we identify more keenly with the angels and our spiritual nature. We realize that our souls need to be nourished just as much as our bodies and on one day of the year, it's only fair for us to emphasize the former instead of the latter.

♦ Finally, by going hungry and thirsty on one day, we can empathize with those for whom deprivation is a daily condition. We can be moved by our minor discomfort on one day to do something about the suffering that millions of people have to endure all their lives. It is on Yom Kippur that the words of Isaiah are read in every congregation: "Is not this the fast that I have chosen? To loose the fetters of wickedness, to undo the bands of the yoke, and to let the oppressed go free, and that you break every yoke? Is it not to deal your bread to the hungry, and that you bring the poor that are cast out to your house? When you see the naked, that you cover him, and that you hide not yourself from your own flesh? Then shall your light break forth as the morning, and your healing shall spring forth speedily, and your righteousness shall go before you, the glory of the Lord shall be your reward." (Isaiah 58:6–8)

Schmoozing

The world of melody is near to the world of repentance. We find that sinners frequently repent on hearing the melody of *Kol Nidre*.

—Rabbi Simcha Bunam (1767–1827), Hassidic leader

All My Promises ...

Yom Kippur begins with one of the most famous passages of Jewish liturgy. People estranged from God and from faith have often spoken of the mysterious power of the *Kol Nidre* prayer to pierce the heart. Dramatically chanted by the cantor in a tune sanctified by centuries of tradition, the *Kol Nidre* begins the human dialogue with God on the most sacred day of the year.

Its special place in the service is hard to understand if you simply translate its words. The prayer, written in Aramaic, is a legal formula that asks God to consider null and void any vows and promises we may make and fail to fulfill in the

Ask the Rabbi

Want to hear the power of *Kol Nidre?* Listen to a recording on CD by one of these concert greats: Richard Tucker or Yossele Rosenflatt. I guarantee you'll understand why Jews continue to respond to this prayer even though you may not understand a word of it.

coming year. Some see in this prayer a profound concern for the importance of words. What if we can't live up to all of our promises—to God, to others, and to ourselves? The greatest of sins would be for us not to be true to our word, so we ask for forgiveness for anything that will, due to forces beyond our control, make us unable to keep our commitments.

Historians have added another possible interpretation to explain why *Kol Nidre* became so meaningful. During the Middle Ages, at the time of the Crusades and the Inquisition, Jews were often forced to reject their faith and affirm their belief in Jesus. To save their lives, many Jews verbally assented and said they renounced their God and their Torah. In their hearts, they knew they would never agree to what they were forced to state with their lips. On the holiest day of the year, Jews began their services by asking forgiveness for these promises extracted from them against their will.

A Fishy Story

As Yom Kippur slowly draws to a close, just a little while before Jews picture God placing the final seal on their decrees for the coming year, Jews read the biblical book of Jonah in their synagogues. Jonah was a prophet who was told to warn the city of Nineveh that unless the citizens repented of their evil ways, they would be destroyed. Jonah tried to flee instead of delivering the message. He boarded a ship to go to a far-away country, but during the voyage a storm broke out. Jonah understood that the storm was an expression of God's anger and that he was the cause of it. Indeed, when they threw Jonah overboard, the sea became calm and there was no more storm.

Poor Jonah, however, was swallowed by a big fish—yes, this is a whale of a story. For three days, Jonah prayed to God from the belly of the whale, and when God realized that Jonah was sorry, he made the fish throw up Jonah on dry land. Jonah finally went to Nineveh and gave them their warning from God. Remarkably enough, the people of Nineveh were moved to repentance, turned from their evil ways, and were forgiven by God.

Jonah, the prophet who succeeded, nevertheless was upset. God's mercy might cast doubt on the truth of Jonah's original prediction that the city would be destroyed. In an unpleasant mood, Jonah sat on a brutally hot day with the sun beating on his head. To protect Jonah, God made a plant with large leaves grow alongside him to provide shade. That made Jonah happy. Then, at night, while Jonah was asleep, God sent a worm to nibble and eat the whole plant. By morning, the plant had withered away. Jonah woke up, saw what happened, and again was angry.

Then Jonah heard the voice of God: "Jonah, you have pity for a plant for which you have not labored. It grew up in one night, and disappeared in one night. Yet you have no pity on the thousands of people of Nineveh and their cattle, and you are angry at me for forgiving them!"

Finally, Jonah understood.

The Essence of Yom Kippur

The story of Jonah is the quintessential Yom Kippur story. It beautifully captures all the major themes of the day:

◆ God judges the whole world—not only Jews but all the nations of the world as well.

◆ No matter how wicked people may be, there is always time for repentance. Those who change their ways will annul the decree of destruction. It's never too late—God waits until the last moment and is far more eager to show mercy than to mete out punishment.

◆ Those who follow God have an obligation to help the wicked turn from their ways. Never give up on trying to change the wicked; they may surprise you and listen to your words.

◆ No one can flee from this obligation without suffering the consequences of divine wrath. You can't hide from God no matter where you are, even hidden in the belly of a whale in the bottom of the sea.

◆ Don't be more compassionate for living things like plants and animals than for human beings.

◆ God is primarily a God of love, of mercy, and of caring for all peoples, Jews and non-Jews. On the Day of Atonement, God assures us that atonement is possible—and forgiveness is God's preference for His dealings with humankind.

The Coffin in the Synagogue

In Jerusalem, there are hundreds of little synagogues peopled by Jews who come from distant and often exotic lands. These houses of worship often maintain customs going back many centuries. In one of them, Jews of Bucharest have built into the wall of the synagogue, as their ancestors did before them, a coffin!

No, they explain, there is no dead body inside. The coffin is meant as a symbol. It is to remind us of our mortality. The Talmud teaches that every person should fully repent one day before his death. When a student asked, upon hearing this instruction,

"Yes, but how will I know when that day is?" the answer was, "Then treat every day as if it were the day before your last."

Pulpit Story

It was close to Yom Kippur, and Rabbi Sussya prayed fervently to God for some message. The innkeeper where the rabbi was staying was repairing his coat by candlelight. From the next room, the rabbi heard the innkeeper's wife calling out to her husband, "Make haste, make haste. Repair the coat quickly for the candle will soon be consumed." The rabbi thanked God for sending him this all-important message.

Death is the one decree that's even more certain than taxes. We are, all of us, eventually going to die. That needn't be morbid. Countless people who suddenly discover they have but a short time to live find those remaining months to be the most meaningful of their lives. Knowing that life will soon end is to allow us to treasure the time we have left. To realize that a coffin awaits us can make us truly appreciate every minute of love and laughter, of life and of living.

Yom Kippur, with its emphasis on introspection, has making the most of our lives here on earth as a major theme as well. There is a special garment worn by the pious on Yom Kippur called a *kittel*—a white robe that someday will serve as our shroud when we pass away. The kittel is the universal way that Jewish custom places the symbolism of the coffin into the synagogue; on the Day of Atonement we have to confront the fact that we spend most of our lives denying that we will die some day and be no more. Yom Kippur forces us to realize that we have to lead our lives more fully, that we dare not waste any moments or opportunities because there is so much to do and so little time in which to do it.

Yom Kippur is the last of the 10 days of repentance. It brings with it a sense of urgency. Its purpose is to remind us that time is running out. We keep running and running until we forget what the race is all about. The wisdom on some T-shirts proclaims, "He who dies with the most toys wins." The Day of Atonement is here to remind us that it's not about dying with toys—but living with truth. That way, even mortals can become immortal.

The Least You Need to Know

- ◆ The Jewish year begins with the "10 days of repentance," starting with Rosh Hashanah, New Year's Day, and ending with Yom Kippur, the Day of Atonement.

◆ Repentance is the focus of these days because it is now that God judges humankind, first "writing" the decree on Rosh Hashanah and then "sealing" it on Yom Kippur.

◆ The shofar, a ram's horn, serves as a wake-up call to repentance and symbolically reminds Jews of the many ideas associated with these days.

◆ Honey is a symbol for a sweet year, and tashlich, throwing bread crumbs into the sea, is a way of acting out our rejection of sin and wrongdoing.

◆ Real repentance means not just admitting past wrongs but committing yourself to improved behavior in the future; for sins against other people, it means asking for forgiveness personally.

◆ Yom Kippur, the Day of Atonement, emphasizes the spiritual over the physical, fasting over feasting, and taking advantage of the "last chance" to become reconciled with God and with fellow humans.

◆ Wearing the kittel, the white shroud eventually designated as the garb for the dead, makes us conscious of how much we have to take advantage of every single moment of life.

Chapter 12

It's Historical: The Three Feet

In This Chapter

- ◆ Passover—its names, rituals, and messages
- ◆ Shavuot commemorates the giving of the Torah
- ◆ Sukkot, The Festival of Tabernacles, when Jews leave their homes for huts
- ◆ The happiest day of the year, Simchat Torah
- ◆ Where history and nature meet

A man meets his friend, the story goes, and complains, "Whenever I have a fight with my wife, she becomes historical." The friend thinks he didn't hear right and says, "You don't mean historical, you mean hysterical." "No," says the first one, "I mean historical. The minute we have an argument, she remembers everything wrong I ever did from the minute I met her!"

Sometimes to be historical is to harp a little too much on the past. But for the Jewish people, memory is the key to survival—and history is the greatest teacher. Three festivals in particular form a unit known as the *sholosh r'golim*, literally "three feet," which commemorate three major moments of Jewish history and the ideas they are meant to teach us. In biblical times they were called "The Pilgrimage Festivals." No matter where Jews lived, they were required to make a pilgrimage to Jerusalem, to the Holy Temple, on these three holidays. Today, when the Temple no longer exists, Jews observe these three holidays wherever they are and fulfill their rituals to recall not only events of our past, but to remind us of major beliefs of our faith.

The "three feet," the three Pilgrimage Festivals, span the seasons from spring through fall. We know them as Passover, Shavuot, and Sukkot. Step by step, in three stages, they reenact the Exodus from Egypt to the Promised Land.

Don't Pass Over Passover

At the Oscar ceremonies in 1968, Bob Hope got a big laugh when he introduced the proceedings with the line, "Welcome to the Academy Awards. Or—as it's known at my house—Passover."

The Oscar may be what passed over Bob Hope's house, but because the Jews had hope, the original night of Passover was far more meaningful for them than any Academy Awards. The children of Israel had come to Egypt by invitation and were originally warmly welcomed. Almost as a preview of what would happen to the Jews in so many countries during the course of history, friendship turned to hatred, and free men suddenly found themselves persecuted, oppressed, and eventually enslaved.

It happened more than 3,000 years ago, but for Jews this story is as real as if it occurred yesterday. That's because in a certain sense it did, in the twentieth century, in the form of the Holocaust. Egypt, under Pharaoh, planned the first genocide of the Jewish people. Only through the intervention of God and His messenger Moses were the Jews saved from destruction by a series of incredible miracles.

Moses, "the Prince of Egypt" who wasn't just a cartoon figure but by all accounts the greatest Jew who ever lived, brought to Pharaoh God's message to "let my people go." God responded to Pharaoh's refusal with a highly convincing series of 10 plagues. The last plague was the most terrible one: Every firstborn Egyptian died at the stroke of midnight on the fifteenth of the month of Nissan. Jews, on the other hand, were to mark their doorposts with the blood of a sacrificed lamb so that God could "pass over" the houses in which His people lived.

At the count of 10, the Egyptians knew the fight was over. They not only let the Jews leave, they actually begged them to go. They pushed them out so quickly that the Jews didn't have time to wait for their bread dough to rise. The haste with which the Jewish people were redeemed was symbolized by their flat bread, called *matzot*, which became the ritual food used to commemorate Passover, the Festival of Freedom.

From the Mountaintop

Egypt believed in astrology and worshipped the zodiac. The first of the signs of the zodiac is Aries, the lamb or the ram. Aries coincides with Nissan, the month in which the Passover story occurred, and the Jews were told to slaughter a lamb. Is it possible that this was God's way of telling Jews they had to do away with the belief that everything is predestined, that the stars rule the future, and the zodiac decrees man's fate? Passover, or the Festival of Freedom, to make man truly free, must rid him of the erroneous belief that he has no free will.

The Five Names of the Holiday

Because there are so many important ideas to remember about this event, it's not strange that the holiday has five different names:

- *Passover,* as you read, tells us that God passed over the homes of the innocent to destroy only the wicked. It teaches us that there comes a time of reckoning, and God separates the good from the bad; He punishes the wicked and spares the righteous.

- *Pesach* refers to the Paschal lamb. The lamb was one of the Egyptian gods. In order to be saved, Jews had to "slaughter," to renounce, the way of life and the religion of those among whom they lived. Perhaps, in a more profound sense, they also had to slaughter the "lamb" of their own weakness so they'd not be guilty of going like sheep to slaughter in a society that tried to destroy them.

- *Z'man Cheiruteinu,* the time of Jewish liberation—is the third name for a holiday whose central theme is freedom. It took the United States of America until the latter part of the nineteenth century to proclaim emancipation and for Abraham Lincoln to free the slaves. The children of Abraham were shown thousands of years before that God would not tolerate people making slaves out of others: "I am the Lord your God who took you out of the land of Egypt, the house of bondage" turned the story of the Exodus from Egypt into the theme of the very first commandment. How sad that in the twentieth century, "Let my people go," and "Freedom now" are still unrealized slogans in some parts of the world.

- *Chag Ha-matzot,* the holiday of the unleavened bread—stresses how the move from slavery to freedom can be almost instantaneous. There wasn't even time for the bread to rise. So, too, should Jews remain optimistic, no matter how bleak the times appear, because change for the better can come in the blink of an eye, just as it did for the Jews who ended up eating matzo because their freedom came so quickly.

◆ *Chag Ha-aviv,* the holiday of spring—not only identifies *when* Passover occurs but also adds an additional message explaining *why* redemption occurred when it did. Spring marks the rebirth of the earth, with the bursting forth of green life. God doesn't forget the world in the cold of winter. Buried underground are the seeds of growth and rejuvenation. The spring of nature is paralleled by the spring of God's concern for His people and for the world. The key idea of the holiday, as of spring, is *rebirth*. That's why Jews believe that just as they were originally redeemed on this Festival, Messiah will in all probability reveal Himself on the Festival of Freedom, the Chag Ha-aviv.

From the Mountaintop

Mystics believe that specific days will always be marked by a constant, recurring feature. The fifteenth of Nissan, when the Jews were first redeemed from Egypt, is a night destined for redemption. In the Israeli War of Liberation in 1948, it was commonly held that whomever gained control of the port city of Haifa was assured of victory. The Jewish Army, the Haganah, gained control of Haifa on Passover night, the fifteenth of Nissan, 1948. The rest, as they say, is history, and the State of Israel was soon thereafter established.

The Jewish Last Supper

A holiday with so many names and such important messages needs a very special service. This service is too important even for the synagogue—it needs the full attention of every family. So it's observed in the holiest sanctuary of all, in the home. It involves those people most responsible for carrying on the tradition, the children. It has a fixed order, which is why it's called *seder* (literally, "order"), and it even has its own prayer book, a *haggadah*, the most widely reprinted book in Jewish history. Christians know this meal as the Last Supper. That was the meal Jesus partook of with his disciples before his execution by the Romans. For Jews, it is probably the ritual celebrated by more of its people than any other.

"May I Please Have Your Order?"

The "order" of the seder requires a good deal of preparation. Here's a list of some items you shouldn't forget:

◆ **Wine,** a lot of it, because you'll have to drink four cups. There were four stages to the process of God's liberation—and besides, wine makes you feel happy, and this is a happy holiday.

◆ *Matzot,* at least three of them, to remind us of Abraham, Isaac, and Jacob.

◆ *Karpas,* a green vegetable such as parsley, symbolizing spring and rebirth.

◆ *Haroset,* a mixture of chopped apples, nuts, wine, and spices, symbolizing the mortar that the slaves made for bricks in Egypt.

◆ *Maror,* bitter herbs, symbol of the bitterness of slavery.

◆ *Beitzah,* a roasted egg, symbol of a festival sacrifice brought in the days of the Temple.

Traditional Seder.

(Collection of Yeshiva University Museum, New York)

From the Mountaintop

During the seder, one of the rituals found in the haggadah is the recitation of the 10 plagues. Whenever we mention one of the plagues, we are required to spill a drop of wine from the cup before us. The reason? Although the Egyptians were our enemies, our "cup is not full," and we cannot totally rejoice because our freedom came at the price of the suffering of others.

◆ *Zeroah,* a roasted bone, usually a shank bone, symbol of the Paschal lamb.

◆ **Salt water,** symbol of the tears of our Jewish ancestors who cried for God's help and were answered.

Let There Be Light

Haggadah, the book used on Passover night at the seder, comes from the word "to tell." The biblical commandment is for parents to tell their children on this night what happened in our collective past. Remembering history isn't just educational, it's a mitzvah—a divine commandment.

♦ **A special cup** for Elijah because we "know" that the Prophet Elijah will appear on *this* Passover to announce the ultimate redemption and the coming of Messiah.

♦ **The *haggadah*,** so that everyone—especially the children—can take turns reading, asking questions, giving commentaries, and spending the night as required, by talking about the tragedy of slavery, reflecting on the beauty of freedom, and expressing the gratitude we owe to God for our blessings.

And, oh yes, one more thing. Don't forget to invite the entire family. After all, this is the holiday commemorating the birth of the Jewish people. And what is the most important unit of the Jewish nation if not each individual family?

From the Mountaintop

In Hebrew, there is a remarkable correspondence between the words *matzot* and *mitzvot*. Because there are no vowels in written Hebrew, both words are spelled exactly the same way. What is it that matzot and mitzvot have in common? Matzot become leavened and forbidden if we wait too long; time is their enemy. So, too, mitzvot, if they are to be done, must be done immediately. To wait too long is to have the best of our intentions become "soured."

Ask the Rabbi

The egg at the seder must be hardboiled. The reason? Almost everything else gets soft and melts when heat is applied to it. The egg is an exception. It becomes hard when put to the fire. The egg is a symbol of the Jew. Rather than melting away by adversity, Jews become tougher as a result of their suffering.

Get That Bread Out of Here!

Jews don't just eat matzot on Passover. They are forbidden to eat or even to *own* any bread, even the smallest crumb. Weeks before Passover, many Jews begin what may well be the source of "spring cleaning." According to the Bible, not a trace of the bread we eat all year round is supposed to be found in our homes during this festival. Observant Jews take this literally and not only search out closets and storage spaces, but even scrape under sinks and meticulously scrub out their stoves. The saying goes that you can tell how religiously observant people are by how exhausted they appear at the beginning of Passover!

Again, the Bible doesn't make clear why *chametz*—bread, leaven, and leavened products—should be so rejected for one week (actually, eight days) when we happily consume it 51 other weeks of the year. Perhaps, if its opposite—matzot—is the symbol of liberation, we have to show our intolerance for anything that removes us from our total dedication to freedom. Or perhaps, on the holiday that marks our becoming God's people, we should visually and literally stress that "man does not live by bread alone"—and we can reject a food staple for a spiritual symbol.

Shavuot: Seven Times Seven

The first stop for the Jews after Egypt was Mount Sinai. The Exodus was *freedom from*. Revelation and God's giving of the Ten Commandments and the Torah represented the *freedom to*. To be free isn't a divine goal unless you know what you want to do with your freedom. The holiday of Passover is followed by *Shavuot*, commemorating the day the Jews received the Law of God and were taught that true freedom means being free to be yourself—to be happy and to be holy.

The Jews were told how long it would take them to get from Egypt to Mount Sinai, and they counted the days—49 in all. To the Jewish mystics, that number is the holy number 7 (as in the Sabbath day) squared. After reaching a level of holiness of the seventh day seven times over, they were now ready for the fiftieth day, for what the Jews call Pentecost, or *Z'man Matan Torotenu*, or Shavuot—the time of the giving of the Torah.

A traditional Seder plate.

Let There Be Light

Shavuot comes from the Hebrew word for "weeks." It emphasizes that the holiday of the giving of the Torah is made possible only by the seven weeks that precede it. Without preparation, there can be no acceptance of law.

Ask the Rabbi

Why is Shavuot called the time of the giving of our Torah and not the time of our receiving the Torah? Because the Torah was given to us only once in the time of Moses, but we continue to receive the Torah all the days since then, right to the present.

Ask the Rabbi

Why was the Torah given in the desert rather than in the Holy Land of Israel? If it were given in Israel, answer the rabbis, it would seem that the law was meant only for the Jews. The desert is owned by no people; it is common land open to all. So, too, is the Bible meant for all humankind.

The Middle Man

The Talmud contains an interesting law about how people should walk together. If one person is more prominent than those who accompany him, the most important person should always walk in the middle. Students of a rabbi should walk on either side of him.

For that reason, the rabbis explain, Shavuot is the holiday in the middle of the three pilgrimage festivals. For some reason, Shavuot doesn't enjoy the same great PR as Passover and Sukkot. Some people mistakenly call it a minor holiday; others have simply never heard of it. That's peculiar when you consider that without the holiday that commemorates the giving of the Torah, there wouldn't be any other holidays in the Jewish religion—because there wouldn't be a Jewish religion!

The Annual All-Nighter

Unlike the other festivals, Shavuot has few rituals other than synagogue services. What is observed by more and more Jews today is a custom called *tikun leyl Shavuot*—staying up all night to study and read various portions of the Torah and other biblical books.

Legend has it that on the day when the Jews were to leave their tents early in the morning to gather at the foot of the mountain and receive the Torah from God, they overslept. Imagine coming late to probably the most important meeting in all of history! How can we ever make up for a lapse of that magnitude? Staying up all night is a way we express our regret for our outrageous behavior then and our delight in the Torah today, as we gladly give up a night's sleep to study its words.

Let's Decorate

There is also a tradition that Mount Sinai was covered with green vegetation at the time of Revelation. Some even think it was filled with roses—what more beautiful way could God show His love for us than with not just a dozen but thousands of roses? Because of this tradition, it is customary for synagogues and homes to be decorated with greenery and flowers. In fact, Persian Jews refer to Shavuot as the Feast of the Flowers. Italian Jews call it the Feast of the Roses. So remember, the Jewish Rose Bowl isn't in January—it's on the sixth day of Sivan, Shavuot.

Sukkot: Live in a Booth

From the mountain of Sinai, the Jews began their long trek through the desert. It would take them 40 years until they reached the Promised Land. How could anyone survive for so long in such inhospitable surroundings? From where would the Jews get food and how would they find shelter from the heat of the sun?

God had to perform one more miracle for the Jews. It would be one that would be repeated throughout the rest of Jewish history—the miracle of Divine Providence. *Sukkot* is the holiday that commemorates Jewish survival in the face of impossible odds. Jews miraculously made it through the desert because of God's special care. And Jews made it through thousands of years of subsequent wandering in countries just as unwelcoming as the desert because God continued to show His ongoing love and protection.

During those 40 years, right after the Jews had received the Torah, God fed the Jews with bread from the sky, called *manna*. (That's where we get the expression "manna from heaven.") And for protection from the harsh sun, clouds followed the Jews wherever they traveled. Jews want to remember this miracle. Instead of just talking about it, though, they go one step farther—they reenact it.

Sukkot (plural, *sukkah*) means "hut." On this holiday, observant Jews, even those who live in the most magnificent mansions, build little frail huts in which they "live" during the entire eight days of the holiday. In warmer climates, many Jews not only eat but also sleep in the sukkah. In more frigid lands, eating all one's meals there is sufficient. The point is to exchange the security of a house for a frail structure, which makes you realize that your ultimate protection comes from God.

A House Is Not a Home

Strangely enough, the very holiday in which Jews leave the luxury of their homes to "rough it" in a temporary shelter is also called *z'man simchateinu*, the time of our rejoicing. Sukkot is the holiday that represents the symbol of happiness. Why should we be happiest when we leave our possessions to sit surrounded only by our family and friends? I'll tell you why.

There is a beautiful midrash about a man who wanted more than anything else to be truly happy. He prayed fervently to God and finally was told how he could have his desire fulfilled. "Go find a truly happy man," he was told, "and put on his shirt. Then you, too, will share in his joy." For months he traveled looking for that person. Whenever he thought he finally found someone who was truly happy, he discovered after getting to know the person a little better that it wasn't so; the smile was a mask for sorrow—the apparent happiness wasn't real.

But then, at long long last, his search met with success. He found somebody whose contentment was real, whose joy in life was complete, whose laughter was a reflection of the most complete inner harmony and peace. There was only one problem. The man was so poor he didn't even own a shirt.

Ask the Rabbi

A roof of a *sukkah* must be made out of vegetation, something that grows, to make us sensitive to those things created by God rather than by man. The covering must not be so thick that we cannot look through the roof and see the heavens above, which are the true source of our protection.

Sukkoth Scene *by Solomon Joseph Solomon.*

(Art Resource, NY/The Jewish Museum, NY)

Sukkot may also be a way of reminding ourselves that possessions aren't what make us happy. A physical house is not a home. To find contentment in a frail hut with the knowledge that God is our Protector is far more meaningful than to rely on the strength of walls and a roof to make us secure and happy. On Sukkot, Jews realize that the plea "give me shelter" is not a rock song, but a conversation with God.

Four Kinds of Jews

Not only do Jews change their residence on Sukkot, when they move from house to hut, but the holiday has another important law: Jews are required to take four different plants, all species that grow in Israel, the final destination of the Jews wandering in the desert, and wave these four species in every direction.

The four species are …

- A *lulav*, the branch of a palm tree.

- An *arovot*, the branch of a willow, which grows near water.

- *Hadassim*, the branch of a myrtle bush, which has a lovely smell.

- An *etrog*, a fruit that looks like a large lemon.

Some say the lulav stands for the spine of a person, the myrtle the eyes, the willow the lips, and the etrog the heart. Through these four species, Jews express their willingness to worship God with the major parts of our body.

Pulpit Story

A Hasidic rabbi always set aside a large sum of money to buy a beautiful etrog for the Sukkot festival. Once, on his way to make his purchase, he saw a Jew who stood by the side of his fallen horse and wept. The rabbi did not deliberate long. He gave the man the money so that he might buy another horse. When he came home he was asked where his etrog was. "The whole world," he said, "may recite the blessing over the etrog, but unto me alone has been given the privilege to recite the blessing over a horse."

A more famous interpretation sees these four plants as symbols of four different types of Jews:

- The etrog has both taste and fragrance. It stands for Jews who possess learning as well as good deeds.

- The palm tree only has taste but no fragrance. It represents Jews who have learning alone but are devoid of good deeds.

◆ The myrtle has fragrance but not taste, just like Jews who possess good deeds but no learning.

◆ The willow, the least of all these, has neither taste nor fragrance. It represents Jews who are not learned and have no good deeds to their credit.

The remarkable idea that this ritual expresses is that all four have to be brought together to be blessed. None of them should be shunned; no Jew should be dismissed as unnecessary or expendable. The three that are imperfect—the lulav, willow, and myrtle—are drawn close to the etrog, just as Jews who are imperfect should be brought near those who can serve as inspiration. "All together," the four, symbolic of a unified Jewry, are then waved to all four directions of the world to show that it is the Jewish mission to be "a light unto the nations," bringing its wisdom to all of humankind.

Simchat Torah: Make a Circle

The last day of Sukkot has, in the course of time, come to have another name: *Simchat Torah*, the day of rejoicing with the Law. Because Sukkot is a holiday of joy, its concluding day was chosen as the one to be blessed with a very special distinction.

The five books of Moses, the Chumash, are divided into weekly portions, which allow it to be read and completed in the course of a year. Synagogues around the world start with Genesis and complete Deuteronomy in a twelve-month cycle. A year's project could theoretically begin any time. But custom has it that we complete the public reading on Simchat Torah—and on the same day immediately start all over again. That creates a beautiful circle of study. We symbolize it by dancing with the Torah in circles around the synagogue.

When does one finish the Torah? Never. As soon as we're done, we begin anew. Now *that's* what I call continuity!

Schmoozing

Simchat Torah means "the Torah's joy," and implies that it is not enough for a Jew to find joy in the Torah; the Torah must also be able to find joy in him.

—Rabbi Joseph Ber Solveichik of Brisk

In many places today, Simchat Torah is celebrated with such enthusiasm that synagogues arrange for their adjoining streets to be closed off so that dancing can be held outdoors. It's another way of showing that the goal of Judaism is to bring Torah "outside" to the world. It's also a magnificent way of demonstrating that we can't contain our joy, and we have to dance in the streets, literally.

A 1909 chromo lithograph depicting a Simchat Torah procession.

(Collection of Yeshiva University Museum, New York)

History and Agriculture

Thematically, we've seen that the three pilgrimage festivals each have a major theme:

◆ *Passover* represents Freedom.

◆ *Shavuot* is Revelation—the time of the giving of the Torah.

◆ *Sukkot* is Divine Providence and miraculous survival.

The Bible also stresses an agricultural dimension for each of these festivals. Passover, as the spring holiday, is connected with the time trees begin to blossom. Shavuot coincides with the season when the first fruits of the field ripen. And Sukkot is the time of the harvest.

Jewish farmers celebrated the festivals not only for their historic reminders, but for their agricultural meaning as well. Rabbis saw a profound connection between these two aspects of the holidays. Passover, as the Exodus from Egypt, was the spring of the Jewish nation, when Jews first began to blossom. On Shavuot, with the giving of the Torah to the Jewish people, God saw the first fruits of His labors. Sukkot, the time of the harvest, is a preview of the Messianic Age, when "it shall come to pass that everyone that is left of all the nations … shall go up from year to year to worship the King, the Lord of Hosts, and to keep the feast of tabernacles." (Zechariah 14:16)

The Jewish dream is a world in which monotheism will be accepted by all humankind. That, after all, is the meaning of the Messianic vision.

The Least You Need to Know

- Three holidays—Passover, Shavuot, and Sukkot—comprise the set of historic holidays known as the Pilgrimage Festivals.

- Passover, with its many names, proclaims God as liberator of Jews from slavery and emphasizes above all the ideal of freedom.

- The seder is the special Passover meal whose many symbols teach the messages of this holiday—remembering the Exodus and looking forward to final redemption.

- Shavuot, the middle Pilgrimage Festival, commemorates the central idea of Judaism: the acceptance of the Torah.

- Sukkot, in which many Jews leave their homes to live in huts, is a reminder of the time when Jews wandered in the desert and were miraculously sustained by God.

- The four plant symbols of Sukkot are a symbolic reminder of the four types of Jews and the need to achieve unity between them.

- Simchat Torah is the day when the reading of the Torah for the year is complete—and the next year's reading begins.

Feasting and Fasting

In This Chapter

- ◆ Why Purim is a different kind of miracle
- ◆ The real meaning of Hanukkah
- ◆ The saddest days of the year
- ◆ Why trees have a New Year
- ◆ The new holidays of the twentieth century

What's the difference, goes the humorous observation, between major and minor surgery? Simple. Major surgery is what happens to me and minor surgery is what happens to you. That might be the way you want to differentiate between major and minor holidays. A minor holiday is a day when *you* get off from work. A major holiday is one where *I* get a vacation. To think this way may reflect human nature, but it surely isn't a standard by which we ought to evaluate the importance of holidays.

The real distinction that's recognized by Judaism is the difference between biblical and rabbinic festivals. The days that are commanded to be observed in the five books of Moses—the two personal holy days of introspection and repentance, Rosh Hashanah and Yom Kippur, as well as the three commemorations of national historic moments, Passover, Shavuot, and Sukkot—are clearly the most meaningful. God Himself ordained them. But we have more than these five festivals.

Jews experienced events after the death of Moses that they knew had to be remembered by future generations. Some of them were happy, some were sad. They share one trait in common, however: Each of them teach Jews something so significant that we have to reflect on these lessons annually on the anniversary of their occurrence. These moments serve as a source for all the other feasts and fasts on the Jewish calendar. They are what we call the "rabbinic holidays."

Purim—Winning the Lottery

Picture Persia in the fifth century B.C.E. The King (probably Xerxes in the history books, Ahasuerus in the book of the Bible that records the story) got rid of his wife because she didn't obey him. To fill the empty slot of queen, Ahasuerus held a beauty contest. The winner proved to be a nice Jewish girl, Esther, who thus became a real Jewish Persian princess. On the advice of her uncle Mordecai, Esther decided not to reveal her Jewish identity to her new husband.

Ask the Rabbi

The custom on *Purim* is for people to put on masks and masquerade. Isn't that, after all, what Esther did when she masqueraded at first as a non-Jew before she revealed herself? And because, when we masquerade as somebody else, people laugh at our appearance, the message might well be that if we want to be taken seriously we shouldn't hide our true identity!

Every good story needs a bad villain. Purim has a real winner in the egomaniac Haman, the king's top advisor. Haman needed constant adulation. He passed a law that everybody had to bow down to him. When Mordecai refused to bow because a Jew is permitted to prostrate himself only before God, Haman became so incensed that he decreed that all Jews—men, woman, and children—would be killed on a day of his choosing. Because he was superstitious, he drew lots in order to find a day on which to carry out his "final solution" that would be propitious. Guess what the word for "lots" is in Persian? Why, of course, it's *purim*.

Haman was very happy when his drawing told him to make his plans for the month of Adar. Haman knew that that was the month in which Moses died. That must certainly be a good omen, he thought. What he unfortunately didn't know is that in Jewish tradition, great men die on their birthdays because their lives are complete and full to the very day. Moses not only died in Adar, he was also born in that month. Adar is a time not of misfortune for the Jews, but a month particularly blessed, with the greatest potential for joy.

The book of the Bible that tells the whole story is called *Megillat Esther*, or *Megillah* for short. It records how this threat of genocide was foiled when Esther revealed her identity to her husband. By a series of remarkable "coincidences," the king came to realize that Mordecai was worthy of honor and Haman deserved to be hanged. In fact, when Ahasuerus finds out that Haman had prepared a gallows for Mordecai, he orders that Haman be hanged at the very site he had set aside for the Jew—a fitting punishment in accord with the divine principle of "measure for measure."

Let There Be Light

Megillah means scroll. Without any other word after it, *megillah* invariably refers to the scroll of Esther, the biblical book that relates the Purim story.

There's No Such Thing as Coincidence

Purim commemorates the victory of the righteous over the wicked. Jews call the story a miracle. Yet there's one thing that's very peculiar about this holiday. Look at what happened, and you don't seem to be able to find anything that's particularly supernatural. The sun didn't stand still; the sea didn't split. There were no ten plagues, and God didn't suddenly appear out of nowhere to bring Haman to justice. As a matter of fact, the Megillah, which tells the whole story, is different from any other book in the Bible because God's name doesn't appear in it even once!

So what makes this story miraculous, and its tale worthy of being celebrated as a holiday?

The answer makes Purim the most relevant of holidays for our times. God's name isn't in the book because God never revealed Himself outwardly. He was active—but only behind the scenes. The coincidences of the story, beyond all statistical probability and even possibility, are what prove that this was actually a morality play directed by God, who chose to hide in the wings. Purim is a record of "hidden miracles"—the kind of miracles that are alluded to in its very name. When a lottery is drawn, the chosen name seems to be an accident, but the result is divinely predestined.

I don't know anybody who's seen water turn to blood or millions of firstborn dying at the same moment. Those are the biblical miracles of long ago. Purim miracles, however, are strange, inexplicable coincidences that some people call "synchronicity." They are all around us if we just take the trouble to notice them. And these coincidences are nothing other than God's way of choosing to remain anonymous.

Ask the Rabbi

The name of Esther, the heroine of the Purim story, in Hebrew means "hidden." How appropriate for the central character of the only book in the Bible in which God's name is hidden!

The Holiday That Keeps on Happening

That's why, throughout history, there have been many Purims celebrated by people who had their own special stories of "behind-the-scenes miracles." In Frankfurt, Germany, for example, in 1615, a local baker pronounced himself a "new Haman" and organized a tax against the Jews. Although at first successful, the Jew-hater— through a series of incredible coincidences—was himself killed, his house destroyed, and a plaque put on its site recounting the story.

Every year on the anniversary of this "Haman's" death, the Jews of Frankfurt celebrated their own special Purim and publicly read a Megillah they wrote recounting all the details. (And I bet the special food they ate to celebrate had to be frankfurters!)

The most recent—and probably most incredible—sequel to Purim had to be the events of the Nuremburg Trial, in 1946, after the Holocaust. As Julius Streicher, one of the leading Nazis, was led to the gallows, he inexplicably shouted out, *Purimfest*— Purim Festival. Streicher himself made the connection between what was happening to him, an archenemy of the Jewish people about to be hanged, and what happened to Haman a long time ago. But the connection is even more amazing than that.

> **Schmoozing**
>
> There is a saying that when other memorable days are no longer observed, Purim will still be commemorated. This means that all our festivals are demonstrations of God's miracles, but Purim is in commemoration of a natural event. Though we may not merit it that God deliver us in a miraculous supernatural manner, nevertheless we may still hope for aid in a natural way.
>
> —Rabbi Samuel Abba of Slovita

In the Purim story, the book ends with the ten sons of Haman being hanged. The judgment of Nuremburg came to a close with exactly ten Nazi leaders condemned to pay for their crimes by hanging! Was Streicher's last word also just a "coincidence" or was it one of those miracles of God acting in hiding that are the very theme of the Purim holiday?

I'll Drink to That

Wine played an important role in the Purim story. It was at a feast where wine freely flowed that the king decided to get rid of his wife, making way for Esther. And it was at parties with wine that Esther revealed she was a Jewess to her husband. It was wine that led to Haman's downfall. That's why Purim is the one holiday of the year in which heavy drinking is not only permitted but even a mitzvah. Go to a Jewish wedding, and you'll often hear guests walk up to the bar and order "a Diet Coke—straight, on the rocks." Drunks aren't common among Jews. So if you see inebriated Israelites, check your calendar, and you'll see it's almost certainly the fourteenth of Adar.

Jews also eat three-corned pastries called *hamantaschen* on Purim. As you can see, its name comes from Haman. (See Chapter 18 for more about hamantaschen.)

Hiss the Villain

One more interesting custom of Purim deserves special mention. On the festival, the *Megillah* is read twice, both on Purim night and morning. Every time Haman's name is mentioned—and as a major player, that's quite often—the entire congregation is expected to boo, make noise, and try to wipe out the memory of this villain. Some people have the custom of writing Haman's name on their shoe soles and stomping their feet until Haman is "eradicated." Others write his name on stones and bang them together. The most popular method of showing our contempt is with noisemakers, best known by their Yiddish name, *graggers*.

Schmoozing

On Purim it is man's duty to inebriate himself to the point that he is unable to distinguish between the phrases "Cursed be Haman" and "Blessed be Mordecai."

—Talmud, *Megilla* (7B)

Let There Be Light

A **gragger** is a noise-maker used during the reading of the *Megillah* whenever Haman's name is mentioned. In Israel, graggers are *rashanim*. Graggers can be anything from simple wood-turners to Rube Goldberg contraptions. They just have to make noise—the louder, the better.

Purim gragger.

(Art Resource, NY/The Jewish Museum, NY)

What's behind this unusual ritual? It's a powerful way to teach Jews from childhood that we dare never remain silent in the face of those who want to destroy us. Silence, unlike what the proverb says, isn't golden; it's sinful. The most horrible crimes of humankind have been committed not so much because of man's immorality but because of man's indifference to evil. That's why you can have the unique experience, at least on Purim, of walking into the synagogue and hearing the rabbi complain to the congregants that they just aren't making enough noise in the temple!

Hanukkah: It's Not That "Other" Holiday

No, no, no, a thousand times no. Hanukkah isn't the Jewish Christmas. True, it's usually celebrated around the same time. As a matter of fact, the day of the month is identical—Christmas is the twenty-fifth of December, and Hanukkah is the twenty-fifth of Kislev. True, too, that many Jews who live in Christian countries have made Hanukkah the most observed of all Jewish holidays; after all, we don't want our poor kids to feel deprived while everybody else is getting presents. Just like Christmas, Hanukkah also has suffered by becoming over-commercialized. But Hanukkah came before Christmas, and ironically, its major message is that Jews shouldn't assimilate or imitate the religious practices of their neighbors!

Schmoozing

In the hierarchy of Jewish holidays, Hanukkah ranks fairly low in religious significance. The socially heightened status of Hanukkah reflects its cultural or secular dimension.

—Harry A. Blackmun (b. 1908), retired (1994) U.S. Supreme Court Justice

It's Greek to Me

The Hanukkah story begins with the confrontation between the culture of the Greeks and that of the Jews. Hellenism worshipped the holiness of beauty; Judaism worshipped the beauty of holiness. The Greeks were masters of art: They idolized the body; they excelled in sports; their gymnasiums serve as models for the Olympic games. Hellenism glorified the physical; the Hebrews maintained the primacy of the spiritual.

In the second century B.C.E., the battle raged in Israel for the hearts and souls of the Jews. And the sad truth is that many Jews succumbed to the seductive lure of the Greek lifestyle. They followed the philosophy of the Epicureans, who taught that pleasure is the chief goal of life: "Eat, drink, and be merry, for tomorrow you may die." These Jews called themselves *Hellenists*. Traditional Jews referred to them as *Apikorus*, a variant of the word for Epicurean, still used to this very day to label someone a heretic.

If I Had a Hammer

Who knows what might have happened had Hellenism just remained a voluntary option. Strangely enough, anti-Semitism is sometimes a blessing in disguise. In 175 B.C.E., Antiochus Epiphanes became King of Syria. In order to unify his kingdom, he ordered all the people living in it to become Greek in religion and culture. In Israel, he was particularly tough. He outlawed the observance of the Sabbath, of kosher laws, and of circumcision, subjecting violators to death. He desecrated the Temple by sacrificing pigs on the altar and putting up a statue of Zeus. This was too much even for many Jews who had previously gone along with much of Greek culture.

That's why the Jewish priest (yes, the Jewish religious leaders at the time were known as priests) Mattathias and his five sons were able to lead a rebellion against the defilers of the Temple. "Whoever is for God, follow me," Mattathias shouted, and miraculously, he was able to draw so many followers that he defeated an empire. His family was known as the Maccabees, which in Hebrew means "hammer." The name was a tribute to the strength of the family members, especially the son who proved the most daring and courageous—Judah the Maccabee.

From the Mountaintop

The name *Maccabee* not only means "hammer," it is also an acronym for the Hebrew words, "Who is like you among the mighty, O Lord." The strength of the Maccabees came from their dedication to God.

Ask the Rabbi

The rabbis explain why a special feast is ordained for Purim but not for Hanukkah. On Purim, we celebrate the annulment of an edict to destroy our bodies. Therefore, we partake of an enjoyable meal in order to give pleasure to the body. On Hanukkah, we were rescued from a decree that would have destroyed our soul. Therefore, we chant prayers, light candles, and gratify our souls.

The First Oil Shortage

The Maccabees "hammered" away at the Syrian Greeks until, in December of 164 B.C.E., they were able to return to the Temple, remove all idols from it, and rededicate the sanctuary once more to their God. The word for dedication in Hebrew is *hanukkah*, and that's how the holiday was born.

But the story didn't end there. It closed with a clear miracle that proved God was behind the remarkable victory of the Maccabees. In the Temple was a *menorah*, a lamp whose light was a symbol of God's presence and of the holiness of His house. The ritual requirement for this menorah was kosher oil, oil prepared in a special way that made it suitable for this holy use. Unfortunately, as the Maccabees rededicated the Temple, they realized they had enough oil for only one day's supply, and it would take them eight days to get a fresh, usable batch.

Let There Be Light

The name **Hanukkah**, which means "dedication," can also be split into two shorter words. The first, *hanu*, means "they camped" or "they rested." The second word means the number 25. The name of the holiday contains the date of its observance: The Maccabees rested from their battle on the twenty-fifth day of the month of Kislev.

They lit what they had and to their amazement, found that the little cruse of oil that should have been enough only for one day lasted for eight. The first oil shortage in recorded history was solved by divine intervention!

What made this so meaningful was that they realized, here, too, just as in the Purim story, that God was behind the scenes all along. And just as the oil lasted much longer than it should have by way of miracle, so, too, did they survive and succeed against impossible odds because God was with them.

And one more thing about oil that explains why the Hanukkah story ended with it as the focus of attention. All other liquids easily blend with other liquids. Oil is unique. Try to mix it with water and it separates and rises to the top. The encounter with Hellenism in which Judaism almost perished through assimilation was beautifully brought to conclusion with a miracle appropriately involving the one liquid, oil, which refuses to "assimilate."

Menorah-mizrah with psalms.

(Collection of Yeshiva University Museum, New York)

Menorah.

(Art Resource, NY/The Jewish Museum, NY)

"Come on Baby, Light My Fire"

Jews celebrate Hanukkah by commemorating not the military battle of the Maccabees but rather the spiritual symbol of the menorah, which was enabled to "enlighten" us far longer than possible by the laws of nature. The holiday is observed for eight days because of this eight-day miracle. Every night, families stand together and light their individual menorahs. On the first night, one candle, on the second, two—until on the eighth night the maximum number is reached.

And where are these menorahs supposed to be placed? On the windowsill, facing the outside and in view—on Hanukkah, Jews proudly proclaim to the world that they are not ashamed of their religion and don't feel a need to hide or to "Hellenize" their faith.

Let There Be Light

The **menorah** was the candelabra used in the Temple of old. It had seven branches, three on each side, slightly curved toward the one in the center. Symbolically, it represented the seven days of the week, with the Sabbath in the middle as focal point of all the days surrounding it. The menorah of Hanukkah differs from the one in the ancient Temple because it requires eight places for candles or bowls of oil.

Put a Good Spin on It

We can't leave the holiday without at least making mention of the famous game that's become part of its observance. A *dreidel* is a spinning top with four sides, each of which has a Hebrew letter. The letters *nun, gimel, heh*, and *shin* stand for the Hebrew phrase, *nes gadol haya shom*, or "a great miracle happened there." In Israel, instead of the letter shin the dreidel has the letter *pey*, first letter of the Hebrew word for "here." Every letter is assigned a value, and you spin until you win, although the odds are no better than Blackjack.

Ask the Rabbi _____

Want to eat a Hanukkah meal? The food for you is *latkes*—potato pancakes fried in oil. The connection with Hanukkah? The oil, of course! And the wonderful taste that should probably only last for one day I guarantee you will miraculously last for eight.

Some people say the game started when the Greeks passed a law that the Jews couldn't study the Torah. In order not to get caught when they disregarded the decree, the Jews would keep these little spinning tops near their books and whenever government officials came by to check, they stopped studying and pretended to be in Atlantic City. With this explanation, the dreidel game reminds us of the times when it was so difficult for Jews to pursue their studies and how grateful we have to be for our religious freedom today.

Other scholars, however, put a different "spin" on this custom. Turn the top, and as you watch it spinning you'll realize, "Where it stops, nobody knows." It's what we call a game of chance. Some people might call it fate. But believing Jews know better. Just like the lottery of Purim, so, too, the dreidel of Hanukkah teaches us that nothing happens by chance. History is the story of God's hand on the draw, God's spin of the wheel. That's why history is holy, and its special moments have become holidays.

From the Mountaintop _____

The Talmud contains two conflicting recommendations for how the candles should be lit from the first through the eighth nights. One says that on the first night all eight candles should be used, with one fewer each subsequent night. The other option is to light one candle the first night, adding one each night until all eight are lit. This latter is the way we do it because symbolically we demonstrate that the light of Judaism not only survives but grows progressively lighter and brighter over time.

Remember the Sad Times

Holidays aren't always happy days. We have to remember not only the good times. Sometimes it's even more important to reflect on the bad because, as the philosopher George Santayana so perceptively put it, "Those who cannot remember the past are condemned to repeat it." Jews know how to laugh, but they also have learned how to weep.

If Jews wanted to commemorate every day of tragedy in their history, they'd probably be acknowledging every day of their year. However, Jews should be happy. Joy is a mitzvah. Therefore, only a few major moments of the past are considered so important that they require not only remembrance, but fasting:

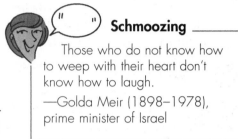

Schmoozing

Those who do not know how to weep with their heart don't know how to laugh.

—Golda Meir (1898–1978), prime minister of Israel

- ◆ The Fast of Gedaliah, *Tzom Gedaliah*, on the third day of Tishrei, commemorates an event that has a horrible contemporary parallel. Following the destruction of the First Temple (586 B.C.E.), the Babylonians appointed a Jewish governor, Gedaliah, to rule over the Jews. Gedaliah was assassinated by "zealous Jewish patriots" who were angered by his dealings with the enemy. On the day when Jews murdered a Jew, we weep in our hearts and devout Jews fast. This sad remembrance should surely have been taken to heart by the "religious" slayer of Prime Minister Yitzhak Rabin at a peace rally in Tel Aviv on November 4, 1995.

- ◆ The Fast of the Tenth of Tevet, *Asara B'Tevet*, marks the day when the walls of the city of Jerusalem were breached, leading to the destruction of the First Temple in 586 B.C.E.

- ◆ The Fast of the Seventeenth of Tammuz, *Shiva Assar B'Tammuz*, the day when Moses broke the tablets as he saw the Jewish people worshipping the golden calf "coincidentally" proved to be the same day when the Romans broke through the walls of Jerusalem to begin their destruction of the Second Temple in the year 70 C.E.

- ◆ The Fast of Esther, *Ta'anit Esther*, marks the fast that Esther proclaimed to ensure God's help in her fight against Haman. This fast day, right before Purim, presents Jews with the remarkable sequence of fast to feast. What it proves is that we can go from the depths of despair to the heights of joy literally overnight.

◆ And the most tragic day of all, the Ninth of Av, *Tisha B'Av*, commemorates a list of catastrophes so severe it's clearly a day specially cursed by God. The First Temple was destroyed on this day. Five centuries later, as the Romans drew closer to the Second Temple, ready to torch it, the Jews were shocked to realize that their Second Temple was destroyed on exactly the same day as the first.

When the Jews rebelled against Roman rule, they believed that their leader, Simon bar Kochba, would fulfill their messianic longings. But their hopes were cruelly dashed in 135 C.E. as the Jewish rebels were brutally butchered in the final battle at Betar. The date of the massacre? Of course—the Ninth of Av!

The Jews were expelled from England in 1290 C.E. on, you guessed it, Tisha B'Av. In 1492, the Golden Age of Spain came to a close when Queen Isabella and her husband Ferdinand ordered that the Jews be banished from the land "for the greater glory of the Church and the Christian religion." The edict of expulsion was signed on March 31, 1492, and the Jews were given exactly four months to put their affairs in order and leave the country. The Hebrew date on which no Jew was allowed any longer to remain in the land where he had enjoyed welcome and prosperity? Oh, by now you know it—the Ninth of Av.

Ready for just one more? World War II and the Holocaust, historians conclude, was actually the long drawn-out conclusion of World War I that began in 1914. Barbara Tuchman wrote a book about that first great world war, which she called *The Guns of August*. Had a Jewish scholar written the book, perhaps it would have been titled with a date more specific than just the month. Yes, amazingly enough, the First World War also began, on the Hebrew calendar, on the Ninth day of Av, Tisha B'Av.

What do you make of all this? Jews see this as another confirmation of the deeply held conviction that history isn't haphazard; events—even terrible ones—are part of a divine plan and have spiritual meaning. The message of time is that of rational purpose, even though we don't understand it.

Spring Has Sprung

Long before Earth Day and the movement to protect the environment, Judaism showed its concern for nature by establishing—are you ready for this?—a New Year's Day for the trees. Sounds funny? Not at all. Trees, just like human beings, are also judged by God. On the fifteenth day of Shvat, *Tu B'Shvat*, Jews observe this Day of Judgment by planting trees.

From the Mountaintop

God owes the people, say the rabbis, a way of making up for all those Tisha B'Avs of history. No day should be allowed to cause so much pain without some compensation. That's why, according to Jewish tradition, Messiah will be born on—you guessed it again—the Ninth day of Av. That's how mourning will be turned to joy and weeping to laughter. The Jewish National Fund has turned this holiday's observance into a project supported by Jews around the world. There is hardly an occasion in Jewish life that doesn't warrant someone "buying a tree in Israel" for a friend or a loved one. That's how greenbacks have turned much of the topography of Israel green.

On Tu B'Shvat, religious Jews eat foods that are characteristic of the land of Israel, specifically the seven types of fruits and grains mentioned in Deuteronomy 8:8. That way, Jews in foreign lands can identify so closely with Israel that they can almost taste it.

It's become popular today among many mystically and ecologically oriented Jews to turn Tu B'Shvat into an important holiday. Some have even written a special seder, just like for Passover, with readings that mark the significance of identifying with trees, flowers, and other plants, as well as with every living and growing thing.

Ask the Rabbi

Tu B'Shvat means literally the fifteenth day of the month of Shvat. In the Jewish calendar, the days of the month are numbered according to the Hebrew alphabet. Every letter has a numerical value. The letters making up the word "tu" have the value of 9 and 6, equaling 15. That's the only time I know of where the word "tu" (two) is really 15.

The Twentieth Century Holidays

Elie Wiesel, the Nobel Prize–winning author who's known by many as the scribe of the Holocaust, once observed, "We are the most blessed of all generations, and we are the most cursed of all generations. We are the generation of Job, but we are also the generation of Jerusalem." The twentieth century forced us to bear witness to the most terrible of all historic events: the brutal extermination of six million Jews. The twentieth century also brought about the fulfillment of a 2,000–year-old dream, when the Jews reestablished their ancient state and returned to the Promised Land, just as the prophets had long ago predicted.

Megillat Esther, Austria,
eighteenth century.

(Collection of Yeshiba University
Museum, New York)

Should contemporary events of such significance not be granted their own special days of remembrance? Yes, they should, say Jews, and so they've declared the first new Jewish holidays to come into existence in almost 2,000 years:

♦ Holocaust Memorial Day, *Yom Ha-Shoa,* on the twenty-seventh day of Nissan, commemorates the Holocaust by recalling a remarkable act of courage. Instead of dwelling on death, it honors the heroes of the Warsaw Ghetto who, in April 1943, desperately fought for life. It took the might of the German Army months to massacre most of the Jews. These Jews were sorely outnumbered and died in the end, but they put up a heroic fight—hardly "going like sheep to slaughter" during the Holocaust, as some have slanderously claimed. Suitable rituals have not yet been created for the universal observance of this day. What is clear though from the special services, gatherings, and lectures that mark Yom Ha-Shoa is that world Jewry has vowed that "never again" will genocide be met with silence and indifference.

♦ Israeli Independence Day, *Yom Ha-Atzma'Ut,* is observed on the fifth day of Iyar in the Jewish calendar. It commemorates the declaration of Israeli statehood on May 14, 1948. Jews aware of their history could not fail to be amazed by this remarkable coincidence: Abraham, the first Jew, who brought monotheism to the world, was born in the year 1948, according to the Hebrew calendar. It took thousands of years, but when the Jewish people finally fulfilled the prediction of the prophets, "and the children shall return to their borders," the year as the world marked it was once again 1948! Who says you can't clearly see the finger of God in the fortunes of His people?

◆ Jerusalem Day, *Yom Yerushalayim*, the newest Jewish holiday of all, came into being in the aftermath of the 1967 Six Day War, when Israel liberated the Old City of Jerusalem. It took almost twenty years from the time the Jews returned to their land until they could stand at the site of their ancient Temple. Although by international law the area of the Western Wall was supposed to be open to all, Jordan prevented Jews from coming to pray at their holiest place. The day when the Israelis proved their power over the armies from six Arab nations that came to destroy them and brought the war to a close was the twenty-eighth day of Iyar. In Hebrew, the words *twenty-eight* spell a word, *koach*, which means "power" or "might." Is that another coincidence?

Jewish mystics point out that when the Jews left Egypt in biblical times, their road to redemption gave them three biblical holidays: the Pilgrimage Festivals of Passover, Shavuot, and Sukkot. As the Jews have been blessed with the creation of the State of Israel, we have seen two new holidays emerge, Israel Independence Day and Yom Yerushalayim.

For the sake of parallelism, it would appear that a third and final modern-day holiday is missing. Perhaps that is the last festival of all—the one that hasn't happened yet but will be proclaimed when the end of the Jews' journey through time will be marked by the moment of Messiah's arrival.

The Least You Need to Know

◆ Purim, the holiday named after a lottery, teaches Jews that miracles can happen. Even when God isn't visible, He "pulls the strings" behind the scenes to make coincidences bring about His will.

◆ Purim, with its theme of divine intervention, is the name given to many other moments of Jewish deliverance throughout history.

◆ Hanukkah, which means "dedication," marks the victory of Judaism over Hellen-ism and the ideal of the beauty of holiness over the Greek vision of the holiness of beauty.

◆ The Hanukkah miracle of the oil lasting for eight days rather than one is a symbol of the miraculous survival of the Jews and their refusal, like oil, to assimilate.

◆ Tragedies demand remembrance just like days of joy, and the various fast days on the calendar remind Jews of the reasons for weeping.

◆ A New Year for Trees is Judaism's way of stressing ecology and its reverence for nature.

◆ After 2,000 years, the twentieth century has given rise to new holidays, which mark both the greatest tragedy (the Holocaust) as well as the greatest blessings (regaining the homeland) of Jewish history.

Part 4

From the Cradle to the Grave

We enter life, says the Talmud, as infants with our fists clenched. It is our way of saying, "I'm going to get it all." But we die with our palms out-stretched. At the end of life we acknowledge that our hands are empty and we can take nothing with us from this earth.

Life brings with it many special moments, and for Jews, every one of them has religious meaning and significance. Part 4 takes us on a spiritual journey from the cradle to the grave. We'll follow the child from the moment he or she enters this world and is named. Growing up brings with it *Bar* and *Bat Mitzvah*. This is followed in but a few short years by marriage. "Sunrise, sunset, quickly fly the years" is *Fiddler on the Roof*'s accurate description of the fleeting nature of life.

Our journey will take us from "the womb to the tomb." This part of the book ends with a discussion of the final mystery—the reality of death, as well as a peek into what lies beyond.

Chapter 14

"Mazel Tov": It's a Boy/Girl

In This Chapter

♦ Why Jewish husbands and wives have to become parents

♦ The spiritual meaning of a person's name

♦ Circumcision as a religious rite

♦ Why firstborn sons must be "redeemed"

♦ Bar Mitzvah and Bat Mitzvah and the difference between them

Groucho Marx knew how important children are in a Jewish family. "My mother loved children," he said. "She would have given anything if I had been one." Children are the way we live on even after our death. "Children," as Isaac Peretz, the nineteenth-century Yiddish novelist put it, "constitute man's eternity." And children are the key to the survival of the Jewish people. Without Jews, there is no Judaism.

Judaism gives its followers guidance from the cradle to the grave. Its laws cover all the stages of life. First and most important, however, are the laws that deal with birth and beginnings. A baby, as Carl Sandburg said, is God's opinion that the world should go on. For people for whom survival is the greatest concern, children are the secret of blessing and a viable future.

You Gotta Have 'Em

Here's a good question to test your Bible knowledge: What was the first positive commandment God gave people? Not the negative "Don't eat from the tree," but a mitzvah that God wanted Adam and Eve to fulfill? The answer: "Be fruitful and multiply."

Jewish theologians explain why this is the first law. Basic to all of our obligations is the principle of *imitatio Dei*—imitating God. And if we have to be like Him, then just as He, first and foremost, is the Creator, so must we create in order to continue the world God brought into being.

That's why Jews aren't permitted to choose to remain childless. Of course, if a married couple tries and can't successfully conceive, they are not to be blamed. But to avoid parenthood is a sin. Marriages are meant to lead to families.

Schmoozing

Every child comes with a message that God is not yet discouraged with man.

—Rabind Ranath Tagore (1861–1941), Indian poet and Nobel laureate

How many children are enough to satisfy the religious requirement? One may seem like a handful, but the minimum is two. That's so a couple at the very least can replace themselves for the future. And not just any two. Jewish law is even more demanding than that. Parents have to have at least one of each—a boy and a girl.

One more thing: Just because a family fulfills the minimum requirement and has a son and a daughter doesn't mean there's no further mitzvah to increase the tribe. Religious families are usually recognized by their numbers. Especially today, in the aftermath of the Holocaust, many people feel a personal obligation to help re-create the population of a people that almost perished. Jews realize that children may tear up a house, but they create a home.

Pulpit Story

The rabbi blessed the newlywed couple with these strange words: "May the cry of *oy* always be heard in your home." The bride and groom couldn't understand. *Oy* is a cry; it is shouted out when something goes wrong. "Why in the world would you want to hear *oy* in our home?" they asked. "You don't understand; when children are around, you're always afraid they'll break this, they'll spoil that—you don't stop saying *oy*. But that *oy*, the *oy* that accompanies having the laughter of children, is the greatest blessing you could ever experience in life," explained the rabbi.

"Mazel Tov"

Jews congratulate each other with the words *mazel tov*. The phrase is usually translated as "good luck." But *mazel* refers to a constellation, one of the signs of the zodiac. Strangely enough, congratulations are a way of praying that the stars continue to be in your favor.

Jews don't believe that astrology determines one's fate. Shakespeare can't be right that "the stars above govern our conditions" because that goes against our belief in free will.

Yet mosaic floors in ancient synagogues depict the signs of the zodiac. Jews may not believe that the stars *determine*, but they can still have some influence. (Besides, why take a chance?) One thing we all agree is that everybody needs "a little mazel." A birth of a child is surely a moment when everybody should offer this prayer. Thank your lucky stars for the baby—and say "mazel tov."

Choose a Name

Now that the baby's here, what are you going to name him or her? And, more important, does it make a difference? The Bible (1 Samuel 25:25) believes, "As is his name, so is he." A name is not only descriptive, it's also prophetic. How can that be if a mother and father are the ones choosing what they will call their child? Because, says Jewish tradition, when parents decide on a name for their offspring, they are blessed with divine inspiration.

Jewish children are given a Jewish name in addition to their secular one. Two different traditions exist to guide parents in their decision. Ashkenazim, Jews of Western European background, forbid naming a child after a living person. It's too soon, they believe, to link a child with someone whose end we still don't know, who may turn out to become wicked or who may meet a tragic death. Instead, Ashkenazim identify their newborn with someone especially beloved who has passed on. In that way, the deceased lives on in the child who serves to recall his or her memory.

Sephardic Jews, Jews from Eastern and Oriental heritage, give honor to those whom they most respect and admire by naming children after them during their lifetime. That's why if a Jew is known as a junior, you know he must be Sephardic.

> **Schmoozing**
>
> There is everything in a name. A rose by any other name would smell as sweet, but would not cost half as much during the winter months.
>
> —George Ade (1866–1944), American playwright

Schmoozing

The remembering of a man's name after his death brings renewed life to his soul in the world beyond. The name is a conduit that connects the two worlds … of the living and the dead. When the dead are buried among their people … and their names are remembered by them, it is as though they continue to participate in life upon earth.

—Yechezkel Kaufmann (1889–1963), Israeli biblical scholar and philosopher

Your Name Is Your Soul

The word for "soul" in Hebrew is *neshamah*. It's made up of four letters. The middle two letters spell the shorter word *shem*, which means "name." Your name is the essence of your soul. The Midrash adds that when a person comes to the other world, the soul is asked, "What is your name—and did you live up to its potential?"

Names are the one gift parents give to children that remains with them forever. A name stays with a person throughout a lifetime and then is put on the tombstone. Wealth doesn't follow you to the grave, but your name is for always. That's why its choice requires careful deliberation.

For a girl, her name is given at the synagogue on the Sabbath closest to birth. For a boy, it becomes part of the ceremony on the eighth day, the *brit milah*—the circumcision.

Circumcision Is a Covenant

Brit means "covenant." *Milah* is the mitzvah commanded by God to Abraham as a sign of his commitment to God, a mitzvah reenacted by Jews throughout history.

Because this law is associated with the male sexual organ, it often leads to humorous—and not so humorous—remarks. A religious ritual that first defined Abraham as a Jew and that remains the introduction of every male to his faith surely deserves more respect. Circumcision in the Bible is called "a sign in the flesh." By removing the foreskin, a Jew becomes visibly different in his very body. It is a spiritual link with God that can never be removed. Appropriately enough, it is also a declaration of Jewishness on the very organ by which future generations are created.

Schmoozing

Every man has three names: One his father and mother gave him, one others call him, and one he acquires himself.

—Midrash

Many people, in seeking a reason for this law, have opted for the hygienic. It's a good law, they say, because it encourages a cleaner genital area. More, it may even prevent a number of serious health problems. It's important to know that even if these considerations are true, they are never mentioned as reasons for the law. Circumcision is *not* given as a medical suggestion; it has a spiritual basis.

Some Jewish philosophers offer fascinating interpretation of this law as a symbol of a Jew's mission in life. If the foreskin serves no useful purpose, why did God create a man with it and then command its removal?

This comes to teach us that God purposefully left some things incomplete in creation in order to leave room for people to complete the task. The world is imperfect to allow human beings to make it better. In the words of the Talmudic rabbis, people must become partners with God. Or as George Elliot put it, God can't make a Stradivarius violin without Stradivarius. Circumcision, which is connected with the male organ of creation, teaches man he has a responsibility, together with God, to be a Creator!

From the Mountaintop

Gematria is a mystical way of analyzing words based on the numerical value of their letters. The gematria, or mathematical value of the word for name, or *shem*, is identical to the value of the word *sefer*, book. A name carries within it the book of a person's life.

From the Mountaintop

Circumcision takes place on the eighth day after birth. Medical researchers have recently made a fascinating discovery. Vitamin K, responsible for helping the blood to clot, is found to be most abundant in a child's system on precisely the eighth day after birth.

Come Join the Party

Only Jews, it's been said, could turn a surgical procedure into a party. It shouldn't seem strange, though, that a brit is a festive occasion. After all, the infant is only eight days old and already is fulfilling a mitzvah.

For this "coming off" party, here are a few things you should know:

◆ The man who performs the circumcision is known as a *mohel*. He is a specialist in this one procedure (and, no, he doesn't collect tips). It's reliably reported that when the English royal family had their children circumcised, they used a mohel rather than a surgeon because of his expertise.

◆ The person holding the infant during the circumcision is known as the *sandek*. This is considered a major honor. In mystic tradition, the sandek is rewarded by

God for his role and will be showered with blessings. Very often, he is also showered in yet another way during the ceremony!

From the Mountaintop

A *Kohen* is a descendant of Aaron, from the tribe of Levi. Every Kohen is, therefore, also a Levite, but the descendants of Levi who don't stem from Aaron aren't Kohanim (plural of Kohen). Kohanim to this day are accorded special honor at synagogue services, by being called first to the reading of the Torah.

♦ A brit is held on the eighth day even if that day coincides with the Sabbath, a holiday, or even Yom Kippur.

♦ A brit is delayed if the infant is sick, weak, or premature and medical opinion feels that a circumcision could be dangerous. Considerations of health always come first.

♦ As soon as the circumcision is completed, everyone present is required to join in a prayer of three wishes for the child: "May he grow to Torah, to *chuppah* (the wedding canopy), and to good deeds."

"Redeem" Your Firstborn

Did you know that originally every family was supposed to have at least one child who would become a rabbi? The firstborn, just like the first fruits in the field, was supposed to be dedicated to God. In the course of time, God selected a tribe—the *Kohanim*, descendants of Aaron, brother of Moses—to be God's servants in the Temple. Jews, however, are supposed to remember the original law by fulfilling a mitzvah for every firstborn son to this day.

Since the Kohanim are substituting for firstborn children, it's necessary to "redeem" the child who should have been designated for divine service. This ceremony is called *pidyon haben*. It takes place on the thirty-first day following birth. The father makes a symbolic payment of five silver coins of the basic currency of the land to a Kohen.

The ceremony is also a reminder of the last plague in Egypt. The firstborn of the Egyptians were slain; Jewish firstborn were spared. When it comes to giving thanks, Jews have long memories. To this day, Jewish firstborn are grateful for their survival.

"Today I Am a Man"

With squeaky voice and hardly a sign of hair on their chins, Jewish 13-year-old boys have for generations been standing up before congregations and declaring, "Today I am a man." To the best of my knowledge, not one of them has then gone out to earn a living, get married, or assume adult responsibilities.

At age 13, a Jewish boy becomes a man for only one reason: At this age, he is considered mature enough to be responsible for his actions. Every legal system has a time when it no longer considers someone a minor whose transgressions must be overlooked. In secular law it's 16 or 18 and in some places even 21. Judaism gives boys more credit. At 13, you are *Bar Mitzvah*—literally "son of the commandments," somebody bound by Jewish law.

Let There Be Light ___

Bar Mitzvah and Bat Mitzvah, literally "son and daughter of the commandments," implies that the young man and the young woman are now *in the category of Jewish law.* Law is their father and guide, and they are its son and daughter, its disciples.

If a Jew says, "I was never Bar Mitzvah-ed," he clearly doesn't understand the concept. Bar Mitzvah happens automatically. Responsibility is the result of coming of age, not of a party.

To commemorate a Bar Mitzvah, boys are usually asked to demonstrate some familiarity with the services. They are called to the Torah and recite the blessings or they lead the congregation in prayer. Parents express their joy at this new stage of their child's growth by throwing a party. (The sad thing about Bar Mitzvahs, though, is if the "bar" and the party that follow the service become more important than the mitzvah.)

Schmoozing ___

If one's first child is a girl, this is a good omen for future children.

—Quoted in the Talmud, Baba Batra (141a)

Girls Mature Faster

What a Bar Mitzvah is for a boy, a *Bat Mitzvah*—the word *bat* means "daughter"—is for a girl. There's only one big difference between them. Judaism recognizes that girls get smarter sooner. Girls mature at 12 and are responsible for their actions a full year before boys. (Of course, that's provided that there's no truth to the riddle, "What's the difference between men and bonds?" "Bonds mature.")

Bat Mitzvahs, like their male counterpart, should ideally emphasize the spiritual meaning of the day. Religious readings, a speech with a relevant Torah insight, and a declaration of personal commitment are the most proper. Celebrations are almost always held and are important in emphasizing that a young woman's spiritual growth is as significant as a man's.

> ### Pulpit Story
>
> When God gave Moses the Ten Commandments, He told him to speak first to the women and then to the men. Why? God said to Himself, "The first time I gave the law to mankind I started with Adam—and look how he messed up. This time I'll work with the descendants of Eve first. I'm sure I'll do better if I begin with the women."

It is an unfortunate truth that for many centuries, women were discriminated against. Bat Mitzvah, although a religious reality, was often ignored. The fault was certainly far more the result of cultural attitudes than Jewish teachings. Men and women were both created in the divine image. Holiness is to be found equally in both sexes. Happily, the contemporary Jewish world realizes this.

The Least You Need to Know

- ◆ Judaism demands that people imitate God, the Creator, by being fruitful and multiplying.

- ◆ Minimally, a traditional Jewish family must consist of at least a son and a daughter, but the greater the number of children, the greater the mitzvah.

- ◆ The name given to a Jewish child has prophetic meaning and identifies a person's character, potential, and very soul.

- ◆ Circumcision, brit milah, is a religious rite observed on the eighth day after birth through which Jewish males carry "a sign of the covenant" upon their flesh throughout their lifetimes.

- ◆ Firstborn Jewish males must be "redeemed" from their originally designated role as "priest," by the gift of five silver coins to a Kohen.

- ◆ Bar Mitzvah is automatically reached by every male at the age of 13 and demands responsibility for the fulfillment of Jewish law on the assumption that he is now mature enough to understand its meaning.

- ◆ Because girls mature earlier, their age of responsibility, Bat Mitzvah, is 12.

Chapter 15

Members of the Wedding

In This Chapter

- ◆ Why marriage in Judaism is a commandment
- ◆ How God is a matchmaker
- ◆ The Jewish wedding ceremony
- ◆ Advice for a happy home
- ◆ Divorce as a last resort

The Bible says that when God created the world, He reviewed His work every day and declared, "It is good." There is only one time when God said, "It is not good." That's when, after creating Adam, God pronounced, "It is not good that man is alone." What God meant wasn't just a divine description of loneliness. Biblical commentators take it to imply that everything else that previously had been labeled good wasn't *really* good when experienced alone. Paradise is only Paradise when it's shared with another person.

Cynics can mock the institution of marriage. As Mae West famously put it, "Marriage is a great institution, but I'm not ready for an institution yet." Judaism, however, is clear in its denunciation of the single state. The Talmud unequivocally rules that "when a man is without a wife, he lives without joy, without blessing, and without good." More, an unmarried person is considered deficient, blemished, no more than half human. It was only Eve who made Adam's day complete.

So When Are You Getting Married?

Why does every Jewish mother constantly bug her children to get married? It's not just a cultural phenomenon, it's rooted in the Jewish religion. It's the Bible that changed marriage from an option to a mitzvah: "Therefore shall a man leave his father and his mother, and shall cleave unto his wife, and they shall be one flesh." (Genesis 2:24) Non-Jews can say that a bachelor is somebody who didn't make the same mistake once. Jews insist that a bachelor is a sinner who doesn't have the good sense to realize that two are better than one.

In all the days of the Talmudic era, spanning the first 500 years of the Common Era, there was only one rabbinic scholar, the second-century teacher Ben Azzai, who remained unmarried. His reasoning was that "his soul was totally in love with the Torah," and he could find no room for any distraction from his studies. Noble as his sentiments were, he was highly criticized by his colleagues. The conclusion of Jewish sages is that although a bachelor is a man who is never "miss-taken," he is always mistaken.

"Matchmaker, Matchmaker, Make Me a Match"

The Midrash has a remarkable story about one of God's major activities:

> Once a Roman matron asked Rabbi Jose bar Halafta:
>
> "How long did it take the Holy One, blessed be He, to create the world?"
>
> He said to her, "Six days."
>
> "And from then on until now what has He been doing?"
>
> "The Holy One, blessed be He, is occupied in making marriages."
>
> "And is that His occupation?" the woman asked. "Even I can do that. I have many men slaves and women slaves and in one short hour I can marry them all off."
>
> "Though it may appear easy in your eyes," he said, "yet every marriage is as difficult for the Holy One, blessed be He, as the miracle of the dividing of the Red Sea." Then Rabbi Jose left her and went on his way.
>
> What did the matron do? She took one thousand men slaves and one thousand women slaves, placed them in two rows and said: "This one should wed that one, and this one should wed that one." In one night, she married them all off. The next day they came before her—one with a wounded head, one with a bruised eye, another with a fractured arm, and another with a broken foot.

"What is the matter with you?" she asked.

Each one said, "I do not want the one you gave me."

Immediately the woman sent for Rabbi Jose bar Halafta and said to him, "Rabbi, your Torah is true, beautiful, and praiseworthy."

"Indeed a suitable match may seem easy to make, yet God considers it as difficult a task as dividing the Red Sea," Rabbi Jose acknowledged.

—Genesis Rabbah, Midrash, 68:4

So who says being a matchmaker is easy? In Jewish thought, bringing people together is a miracle along the lines of the Passover story. That's why Judaism believes that marriages are literally made in heaven.

Finding Your Soul Mate

Women look for their ideal man; men search for their perfect woman. Too bad they can't know what has already been decreed in the Divine Book of Records. The Talmud teaches: "Forty days before the creation of a child, a heavenly voice calls forth and proclaims: So and so's daughter for so and so's son!" (Talmud, Sota, 2a) Bride and groom, in this mystic tradition, are predestined for each other. Love at first sight really means that two souls are responding to each other based on an intuitive higher knowledge.

There is a Yiddish word to describe a future mate: *bashert*. Your bashert is your intended, the one already announced as your bride or groom forty days before you were born. ("Sher" is Yiddish meaning "to cut," like "the one *cut out* for you.") Too bad it takes us so long for the information to reach us!

 Schmoozing

From every human being there rises a light that reaches straight to heaven. And when two souls destined to be together find each other, their streams of light flow together, and a single brighter light goes forth from their united being.

—Baal Shem Tov (1700–1760), founder of the Hasidic movement

Ask the Rabbi

Want to get married on a very lucky day? Try Tuesday. That's the only day, in the biblical story of Creation, for which God said "it is good," not once but twice. You'll also be lucky because caterers charge less for weddings held on weekdays!

What a Beautiful Ceremony

Once you've finally found each other, you can set the date. Jewish law asks that you remember only one thing before you send out the invitations: A wedding can't be held on the day of a festival. That's because "we must not mix one joy with another." (Talmud, Moed Katan, 8b) Don't diminish your joy by sharing it with another. Your wedding deserves your undivided attention.

For the wedding, Judaism guides the bride and groom through a number of laws and rituals meant to make the day memorable, spiritually meaningful, and the beginning of a long-lasting relationship.

The Wedding *by Leo Schutzman.*

(Art Resource, NY/The Jewish Museum, NY)

No See, No Eat

The *kallah* (bride) and *chattan* (groom) are not supposed to see each other for a small period of time before their wedding (anywhere from a day to a week). The custom is based on a simple idea: Anything constantly around us loses its uniqueness. More practically, with all the nervous tension that surrounds this time, it's a good idea for the main participants not to be in each other's way.

Observant Jews follow the law that bride and groom fast on the wedding day until after the ceremony. In this way, the holy day is compared to a private Yom Kippur—a day when we examine our past actions with a goal of self-improvement and a day on which we commit ourselves to be better human beings in the future.

The Tallit and the Veil

There's a custom that the bride give the groom a tallit, a prayer shawl (see Chapter 24), on the wedding day. One reason is that there are 32 fringes on it (eight fringes on each of the four corners), and this number is the numerical equivalent of the Hebrew word *lev*, "heart." What a romantic notion!

Before the ceremony, there is a "veiling," called the *badeken*. The groom is led to the room where the bride is seated and places a veil over her eyes. The biblical basis for the law is the story of Jacob, who wanted to marry his beloved Rachel but was tricked by his future father-in-law Laban, who gave him his other daughter, Leah, instead. Before the bride's face is hidden, for the sake of modesty, the groom has to make sure that he knows who is behind the veil. (A Jew may be fooled once, but for thousands of years to come he'll make sure not to make that mistake again!)

Another explanation for the custom is that covering is a symbol of protection. People protect those things most precious to them. The covering of someone you love is an intimate expression of caring.

The bride and groom both wear white, a symbol of purity. In very traditional weddings, the groom wears a white *kittel*, the same garb worn on Yom Kippur, to indicate the solemnity of the occasion.

> **Ask the Rabbi**
>
> Jewish parents, as you march your children down the aisle, carry two candles. The numerical value of two candles, mystics teach, is "be fruitful and multiply." Just a little hint that the couple's parents would soon like to be grandparents!

Down the Aisle

The parents of the groom march down the aisle with their son, followed by the parents of the bride with their daughter. Symbolically, this demonstrates both parents' readiness to have their relationship with their child replaced by the more intimate union of marriage. "Therefore shall a man *leave* his father and his mother"—woe to the couple where either one is still a "mama's child," more linked to parent than to mate.

> **From the Mountaintop**
>
> In ancient times, when a child was born, a tree would be planted on the fifteenth of Shvat, *Tu B'Shvat*, the holiday of the New Year of the Trees. When preparations were made for a wedding years later, the bride and groom's trees would be used as the poles holding the *chuppah*. Just as trees grow and flower, bearing seeds for the future, so too is this new couple blessed.

Under the Chuppah

The ceremony itself takes place under a canopy called a *chuppah*. A simple chuppah is a cloth held up by four poles, symbolizing the new home about to be created. Traditionally, a wedding ceremony took place outdoors, as an omen that the marriage would be blessed with as many children as "the stars of the heaven." When brought indoors, because of climate or other considerations, the covering over the heads of the bride and the groom was meant to emphasize that their union took place with the blessings of a higher power, someone "above them." A chuppah can also be created from floral arrangements, merging the beauty of nature with the sanctity of marriage.

Chuppah (wedding canopy).

(Art Resource, NY/The Jewish Museum, NY)

'Round and 'Round

In the first part of a traditional wedding, the bride circles the groom seven times. The number seven corresponds with the seven times in the Bible where it is written "when a man takes a wife." It's also the traditional number designating the holy day, as in the seventh day of the week, the Sabbath. In circling her groom, the bride mystically demonstrates that she is entering the seven spheres of her beloved's soul. She also symbolically shows that she has "captured" the heart of her beloved just as Joshua captured the city of Jericho by marching around it seven times.

The Marriage Contract

The *ketubbah*, a legal document in which the groom promises to support his wife and to provide for her if they are later divorced or if he dies before her, is then read. It is a remarkable document, hallowed by Jewish tradition, which already concerned itself with women's rights thousands of years ago. It offered financial protection to women in societies where their rights were most often nonexistent. It did not hesitate to bring up the possibility of dissolution of the marriage even under the canopy. Better to be realistic rather than romantically naive when it comes to protecting people.

The ketubbah was instituted by the Men of the Great Assembly about 300 B.C.E. All property belonging to the husband was mortgaged to pay for the financial settlement the wife was guaranteed to receive should her husband die or divorce her.

Let There Be Light

The **ketubbah** is the wedding contract obligating the husband to financially support his wife if the marriage doesn't last.

A 1733 ketubbah painted on parchment.

(Art Resource, NY/The Jewish Museum, NY)

The Ring

The round ring, with its circular shape, is a symbol of eternity. It's placed on the finger of the bride as the groom pronounces the words: "Be thou consecrated unto me with this ring according to the Law of Moses and Israel." Depending on the religious affiliation of the participants (we'll talk about the differences between Orthodox, Conservative, and Reform Judaism in Chapter 25), the bride may or may not also give a ring to the groom and make a similar declaration.

Wine and Blessings

Both the engagement, *kiddushin* (from the Hebrew word *kadosh*, or "holy"), as well the *nissu'in*, the actual wedding (from the Hebrew word "to elevate, to lift up"), are performed under the canopy. Both involve blessings over a cup of wine, symbol of joy and gladness. The kiddushin consists of two blessings, one for the wine and the second for the commitment that the bride and groom make to each other. The nissu'in consists of the recitation of seven nuptial benedictions pertaining to the creation of the world and humanity, the survival of Israel and the Jewish people, as well as the couple's happiness and future family.

The blessings put the marriage into a dynamic relationship with the beginning of time, the end of history, the Garden of Eden, and the expectation of a Messiah. The number of these blessings, seven, also contains the symbolism of the sanctity of the Sabbath. Bride and groom drink from the same cup to show that their lives will now be joined together and that they will evermore share in whatever the cup of life has to offer them.

Ask the Rabbi

For the wedding ceremony itself, the ring is placed on the right hand index finger. Mystically—just as in acupuncture—that's the finger directly linked to another part of the body: the heart. It also allows the bride to show the witnesses that she received the ring and is now married. Afterward, the bride can, of course, place the ring on whichever finger she desires.

Let's Break a Glass

The ceremony is completed with a seemingly strange custom. The groom breaks a glass by stamping on it with his foot. (Some claim this is the very last time the husband will ever get a chance to put his foot down now that he's married!) The reason for this is a beautiful way in which Judaism links our individual lives with the history of our people:

The moment of marriage is a time of supreme personal happiness. Yet the Jewish people must always remember that our joy cannot be complete as long as the Temple in Jerusalem remains destroyed. The breaking of the glass reminds us that our rejoicing must be tempered with remembrance of our people's catastrophes. In modern terms, it would be the equivalent of saying no matter how happy you may be at any time, you dare not forget the Holocaust.

As the bride and groom are ready to begin their lives together and start a Jewish family, they add an additional deeper meaning to this custom of breaking a glass. While throughout history, countless anti-Semites tried to eliminate the Jewish people, the fact that another generation has just signaled its commitment to Jewish continuity "shatters" the hopes of those who planned Jewish genocide.

Just the Two of Us

As the guests all shout "*Mazel tov!*," and the bride and groom realize they are now husband and wife, there's one last tradition followed by observant Jews. Instead of mingling with the many guests and spending the first few moments after the wedding talking to others, the mitzvah of *Yichud*—"togetherness alone"—demands that the bride and groom go off to a private room to spend some time with just each other.

Every beginning sets the tone for all that follows. "Me and you against the world" is the lyric that expresses what Judaism hopes to accomplish by ritual: Be concerned with your mate from now on more than with others.

Advice for the Couple

One of the most important words in Judaism is *shalom*. It's used both as hello and good-bye. What it really means is "peace." Peace is the greatest blessing, and *shalom* concludes every major prayer of the Jew. This is also the word that Jews use to bless marriage: *Shalom bayit*, "peace in the home." Domestic harmony is considered at least as important as peace between nations. Jews pray that all peoples of the world will eventually learn how to get along. And Jews are supposed to work at making that universal vision come true at least in the confines of their own home and their marriage.

Shalom bayit doesn't just happen. Judaism recognizes that although marriages are made in

> **Schmoozing**
>
> Great is peace, for all blessings are encompassed by it. As it is written, "May the Lord grant His people strength; may the Lord bless His people with peace."
>
> —Midrash, Psalms 19:11

heaven, they have to be preserved on earth. As it has been pointed out, "All marriages are happy ones; it's the living together afterward that is the problem."

How does Judaism help to create this ideal of shalom bayit? Here are some guidelines:

♦ In English, it has been pointed out that the word wedding has the "we" before the "i." Jewish law demands that husband and wife love each other as they love themselves and respect each other more than themselves. Selfishness and self-centeredness are the enemies of a successful marriage. The great Jewish sage Maimonides says that each partner has to place the other on a pedestal; the needs and concerns of the partner have to have a *higher* priority than one's own.

♦ The Talmud advises, "Even if your wife is short, bend down to hear her whisper." Dialogue is the ideal. Ignoring the advice of a partner leads to controversy and conflict.

♦ The law in the Torah that commands Jews to rejoice on the holidays is interpreted in the Talmud as obligating husbands to buy pretty clothes for their wives before the festivals. (In those days that's what made a woman happy. Obviously, today, any gift will do.)

♦ No partner should pressure the other to undertake expenditures beyond their means. Money should never be allowed to become more important than the marriage itself.

♦ The key to a good marriage is friendship. The prophet Malachi refers to a wife as "your friend and the wife of your covenant." The expression "friends and lovers" is part of the blessings recited under the wedding canopy. Friendship is based on honesty and openness—the traits essential for husband and wife in order to have a happy marriage.

♦ Allowing anger free reign is a sure way to break up a marriage: "Anger in the home is like a worm among sesame seeds," says the Talmud.

 Schmoozing

Whoever manages to establish peace in his home is regarded by the Bible as if he were a king who establishes peace in Israel. And whoever permits jealousy and dissention to reign in his household is regarded as if he establishes jealousy and dissention among all Israel.

—Mishna, Abot T'Rabbi Nathan 28:3

Schmoozing

Who is rich? One who rejoices in one's portion.

—*Ethics of the Fathers,* 4:1

Schmoozing

Never become angry with your wife. If you put her off with your left hand, hurry and draw her back with your right.

—Talmud, Sotah 47a

Even stronger, the Talmud explains that, "anger is tantamount to idol worship because it is evidence of the Satanic force."

♦ Compliments are much better than criticism. People who criticize others "for their own good" don't realize the more important gift they could give by offering compliments for the same reason. Criticism, the Talmud points out, is often a form of envy. Love grows best when it's watered by kindness. And it will be poisoned by condemnation.

Schmoozing

When a man makes a woman his wife, it is the highest compliment he can pay her. Unfortunately, it's also usually the last.

—Helen Rowland

10 Rules for a Successful Marriage

Rabbi Zelig Pliskin, a contemporary Jerusalem scholar and ethical teacher, has compiled a list of 10 rules for a successful marriage, culled from the basic teachings of Judaism:

1. Keep your main focus on giving rather than taking. When your goal is to give your partner pleasure, you will always find opportunities to meet your goal. You, too, will gain by doing this since people tend to reciprocate positive behavior.

2. Be careful to remain silent if your spouse insults you. By ignoring slights and insults, you will prevent many needless quarrels. The momentary unpleasantness will quickly pass.

3. Give up unrealistic expectations. People come into marriage with many expectations that are not consciously expressed. By giving up unrealistic expectations, you will prevent frustration and anger. Don't expect your spouse to be perfect and don't make comparisons.

4. Avoid labeling those things that are not to your liking as awful. Try for a more positive perspective.

5. Think of how to motivate your spouse to want to do what you want him or her to do. If your first strategy is not effective, keep trying different strategies. Remember that tactful praise is a powerful motivator.

6. In communicating with your spouse, never lose sight of your main goal—to have a happy marriage. If the response to your communication is a negative one, rethink your method of communication; in other words, change or modify your approach.

7. Be prepared to compromise. Be willing to do something you would rather not do in return for similar behavior from your spouse.

8. Don't blame or condemn your spouse for mistakes. Plan on the best method to prevent the mistakes from recurring without arousing resentment or hurting your spouse's feelings.

9. Live in the present. Whatever went wrong in the past is over. Focus on improving the current situation.

10. Keep asking yourself, "What can *I* do to create a pleasant atmosphere in my home?"

 **Schmoozing**

If a woman says, "My husband is distasteful to me; I cannot live with him," the court compels the husband to divorce her because a wife is not a captive.

—Maimonides

These might not be the Ten Commandments given on Mt. Sinai. They are 10 powerful suggestions, though, for preserving the most important unit of the Jewish people—the family.

But If It Doesn't Work Out ...

The Talmud says that "if a man divorces his wife, the very altar weeps." God is distressed by human failure. Yet divorce is far preferable to enforced perpetuation of a home filled with enmity. To stay together "for the sake of the children" represents the ultimate absurdity of maintaining a horrible marriage for the benefit of innocents who will be permanently scarred by being a part of it. When there is no better alternative, divorce is in fact a mitzvah. The legal grounds need not be adultery. They can be as simple as incompatibility.

Pulpit Story
The husband and wife fought so bitterly that the only logical option seemed to be divorce. They came before the rabbi, and the rabbi said he would grant their request on one condition. "Think carefully," he told the wife, "and tell me the one thing you want after all these years of marriage. Pick the item you love most and it is only right that you should now have it." The next day the wife returned and told the rabbi, "I have decided. What I really love most of all is my husband. I want him. It is time to put aside our foolish quarrels and to strive harder to make our marriage work."

Does Judaism take marital vows so lightly that divorce is readily permitted? Quite the reverse. Judaism reveres the matrimonial state so highly that if its demands aren't met by partners willing to live together in harmony and peace, they shouldn't continue to live a lie that besmirches the most important and holy institution of Jewish life.

The Least You Need to Know

- For Jews, marriage is more than a personal choice, it's a religious commandment.

- Jewish tradition believes that God is the matchmaker for every wedding, and the bride and groom are destined for each other from the time preceding their birth.

- The marriage ceremony—its laws, rituals, and customs—is filled with symbolic meaning emphasizing the holiness of the moment, the special nearness of God, and the seriousness of the occasion.

- The breaking of the glass at the conclusion of the ceremony links the future of the couple to Jewish history.

- Judaism offers much sage advice to the bride and groom to create shalom bayit—the ideal of household peace necessary for a lasting marriage.

- Divorce, although exceedingly painful and causing divine tears, is preferable to perpetuating a home with a climate of hatred.

Chapter 16

Death Be Not Proud

In This Chapter

- How Jews regard death
- Their belief in immortality
- Jewish burial customs
- Mourning for the dead
- Do Jews believe in reincarnation?

"Therefore choose life" is the command of the Bible. (Deuteronomy 30:19) Judaism is a religion of life that emphasizes how we are supposed to live our lives here on earth. Yet reality demands that we face the certainty of death. The thirteenth-century Hebrew poet Joseph Zabara tells of the man who, upon losing a brother, was asked, "What was the cause of his death?" He replied, "Life."

Human beings are mortal because part of us was created from the ground. "Dust returns to the earth from whence it came," said the wisest of all men, Solomon, in his Book of Ecclesiastes. But God also endowed humans with His essence, so Solomon concludes that same verse with the words, "and the spirit returns unto God who gave it." Death is the moment of separation of the soul from the body.

Judaism acknowledges the tragedy of the body's end, even as it takes note of the beginning of a new spiritual journey for the soul. Death in the Jewish view is a matter of going from one room to another, ultimately to a far more beautiful location. What Judaism teaches about the encounter with death, the way of dealing with the departed, and the proper response of the mourners reflects its outlook, not only on life, but on the life beyond.

Leaving This World

There is a remarkable tradition based on the story of how people died during the time of the Bible. At first, the story goes, when someone's time was up, he simply sneezed, and his soul departed through his nose—the place through which it originally entered when God created Adam. To this day, in almost all cultures, when someone sneezes, we say "God bless you," "*Gesundheit*" ("for health"), or another variant of the expression to remind us that this was once a moment associated with death.

As Jacob, son of Isaac and grandson of Abraham, grew old, he made a special request of God. Please don't take me without warning, he prayed. I want to have a little time to put my things in order before I depart. I want to be able to bless my children and have them accept my words with special feeling, knowing that they will be my last on Earth. I beg you to give me a final illness through which I can know that my end is near.

That's how, according to the Midrash, people stopped dying with a sneeze.

Whether we take this story literally or not, it points out a profound truth: Preparing for death, when it's possible, offers positive opportunities. Those who are terminally ill should use the time left to offer final words to friends and loved ones, to make peace with any enemies, and to recite a liturgy of confession in order to be reconciled with God.

Is This All There Is?

Judaism offers great strength to those on the doorstep of death. Faith removes fear. In the Talmud, this life is compared to the eve of the Sabbath. What follows, *olam ha-ba*, "the world to come," is compared to the Sabbath itself. This world is a vestibule, and the next is the palace.

Pulpit Story
In Israel recently, newspapers reported the story of a remarkable near-death experience: A man who had been pronounced dead returned and was able to accurately describe the people who had hovered around him and the clothing they were wearing, and could repeat what they said. The most remarkable thing about this? The man who could "see" when he was supposedly dead had been blind from birth!

There's a great deal of literature today based on "near-death" experiences. People recorded as dead, with neither heartbeat nor brain waves for a significant time, have shared their vision of rapidly moving through a long tunnel toward a strong body of light; reviewing their lives as they make this journey; and feeling an incredibly warm inner glow of contentment and serenity as they draw closer to the light to which they feel spiritually attracted. Thousands of similar experiences, as recorded in the works of Raymond Moody, Elisabeth Kübler-Ross, and others, confirm these descriptions of dying, descriptions that exactly parallel those found in ancient Jewish sources.

Schmoozing

The day of death is when two worlds meet with a kiss: This world going out, the future world coming in.

—Jerusalem Talmud, Yebamot, 15:2

Near-death experiences, of course, are recounted by those who didn't complete their journey. Judaism completes the story as it identifies the light with God and the after-death awareness with the first stage of immortality.

But How Could There Be Life After Death?

What Judaism refuses to do is fill in the details of the post-life experience. Yet for those who question the possibility of existence without a body and a life beyond the grave, the Midrash offers this fascinating parable:

> Imagine that a woman is soon to give birth to twins. Imagine further that these yet-to-be-born babies had consciousness, awareness of their surroundings, and could communicate with each other. Assume that one is an optimist, the other a pessimist. One has faith in the future, the other "realistically" only believes what she can see before her.

> The optimist says, "I can feel that we will soon be leaving this place. I don't know where we are going, but I am certain that the one who gave us life until now will not forsake us. We may be leaving the security of this sac, but I'm sure there is another, a better kind of existence awaiting us."

The pessimist replies with scorn: "There you go again, spouting your outrageous religious beliefs. Here, and here alone, we have the tube that feeds us. Here, and here alone, we are in our protected home. Leave here and we're goners. Admit it, there can't be anything after this. If you think there is, then I defy you to describe to me what it looks like."

The optimist, never having seen life on earth, knowing nothing about air or food, about life apart from her mother, cannot respond to the challenge. Yet she refuses to acknowledge defeat. "I just know I'm right, and I will continue believing," she says.

With that, the mother-to-be goes into labor. The optimist is the first to be born. The pessimist, still in the womb, strains to hear what is going on "on the other side." Suddenly she's shocked by a cry. She knows it is the scream of her sister. Sadly, she says, "I was right after all. My poor, poor sister. I have just heard her cry of death and she obviously is no more."

At that very moment, closed off to her sight, rejoicing parents are welcoming her sister, their first newborn to life, as the doctor slaps her and elicits her first cry of life.

Just as those before birth wouldn't have been able to describe life after it, so, too, we on this earth are ignorant of the details of the world to come. But our ignorance isn't reason enough to deny its validity. At the very moment when we hear the dying take their final breath on earth, it isn't hard to imagine relatives and friends who have preceded the person in death welcoming his or her soul to the world of infinite being.

 **From the Mountaintop**

The founder of the Hasidic movement, the *Ba'al Shem Tov*, explained why people are afraid to die. Shouldn't people be happy because they are returning to God? The reason, he explained, is this: In the world to come, a person gets a clear retrospect of all of his deeds on earth. When he realizes the senseless errors he has committed, he can't abide himself. His shame is the meaning of his purgatory, his personal hell. And facing that recognition is what we all intuitively fear.

Saying Good-Bye

Even as the soul moves on to its final destination, the body of the deceased must be respectfully taken care of. Survivors should know these crucial Jewish laws and customs:

◆ At the moment of death or at the funeral, the immediate relatives—son, daughter, father, mother, brother, sister, and spouse—perform the traditional act of grief and mourning by tearing their garment, or *keriah*. Some rip a ribbon, others actually rend their outer garments. The act is a symbol of the torn heart of those who grieve and a sign of respect by demonstrating the intensity of their loss. It also allows a permissible outlet for the mourners' pent-up anguish. Pagans, the Bible tells us, would make slashes in their bodies. Jews are forbidden to cause harm to themselves, so we "take it out" on our clothes.

Keriah may have a more profound meaning as well: The body is merely the garment of the soul.

Death is a rending of the garment—the suit may be torn but it doesn't affect the person. So, too, the body may be no more but the inner soul remains undamaged and unaffected.

Schmoozing

For each one of us the moment comes when the great nurse, death, takes man, the child, by the hand and quietly says, "It is time to go home. Night is coming. It is your bedtime, child of earth. Come, you're tired. Lie down at last in the quiet nursery of nature and sleep. Sleep well. The day is gone. Stars shine in the canopy of eternity.'"
—Joshua Liebman (1907–1948), American rabbi, in his best-selling book, *Peace of Mind*

◆ The dead should never be left alone. The soul hovers near the body shortly after its initial separation. It is aware of the love and respect shown to its vessel, the body. *Shomrim*, those who stay with and pray over the deceased, are assigned on a 24-hour basis so that the dead are never left alone without the soul being comforted by the recitation of holy prayers.

◆ The body is carefully prepared for burial. *Chevra Kadisha*, the Jewish Sacred Society, a group of pious volunteers usually found in every Jewish community to assist with final preparations of the deceased, performs the *taharah*, the ritual washing of the body.

Let There Be Light

Translated from the Hebrew, **keriah** means the ripping of the garment as a sign of grief. **Shomrim** (singular *shomer*) are the people who not only watch the dead, but recite prayers, usually Psalms, in the body's presence. **Chevra Kadisha** is the name of the holy Jewish burial society, responsible for the final care of the body as well as preparation for interment.

They also dress the body in shrouds, *tachrichim*—simple, handmade, perfectly white and clean, with one more important feature: Shrouds have no pockets. The final symbol of life demonstrates "you can't take it with you."

From the Mountaintop

Chevra Kadisha serves as an example of the most noble act of kindness, a kindness called *chessed shel emet*—a kindness of truth. Every other act of kindness may have in it a personal motive: I'll do something for you so that in the future you will do something for me. Showing kindness to the dead is a "true act of piety" because it cannot possibly be tinged with any hope for reciprocity.

The Talmud describes that, "formerly they used to bring out the deceased for burial, the rich on a tall state bed, ornamented and covered with rich coverlets; the poor on a plain bier; and the poor felt ashamed. Therefore, a law was instituted that all should be brought out on a plain bier." Death should not be used as a time for displays of luxury. In death, all people are equal. Jewish tradition demands a simple pine coffin. Burial follows so that the biblical decree, "to dust you shall return," can be fulfilled with the body's decay in the ground. For this reason orthodox Jews are profoundly opposed to cremation. The deceased must also be buried as quickly as possible after death, ideally no later than 24 hours, to avoid shaming the body by neglecting its required religious procedure. Orthodox Jews also forbid the viewing of loved ones after death. Memories should remain with survivors of the way they remember the deceased when alive, not as a cold and unmoving corpse. The eulogy, an important part of the funeral service together with prayers on behalf of the soul, emphasizes the ways in which the departed can continue to live in our minds and our hearts.

Ask the Rabbi

When you return from the funeral of a loved one, the custom is to eat a hard-boiled egg. Why? Life and death are a cycle. Some die so that others may be born. The egg goes round and round, as do life and death. The egg carries new birth within it. So, too, is death the way in which new life is made possible.

Mourning the Dead

"Ask not for whom the bell tolls," the poet John Donne wrote, "it tolls for thee!" The real tragedy of death is for those who must remain to mourn. For them, Judaism offers a number of ways to deal with their loss and to gain a measure of comfort and consolation.

Sitting Shiva

Shiva, literally "seven," is a time set aside for people to visit with the mourners, share meaningful stories with them about the deceased, and help them to cope by remembering all the positive memories that remain that death cannot eradicate. During the shiva, ritual law obligates the mourners to stay in one place, the mitzvah of sitting shiva, so that all those who wish to express their condolences may readily find them.

At the conclusion of shiva, the mourners are to walk around the block, symbolically making clear the need to rejoin the world in spite of their grief and not to abandon life by excessive mourning and living in the past.

Let There Be Light

Shiva is the Jewish ritual seven-day mourning period for the dead.

The Next Stages of Mourning

The *sheloshim*, the 30-day period and the following 12 months are the next two stages of mourning recognized by Jewish law. Time is a great healer, but its effects are felt only in stages. Judaism acknowledges three distinct phases in the aftermath of the death of a loved one:

- ◆ The seven-day period of grieving is the most intense. We need the help of friends and the visits of those close to us to get through this period.

- ◆ The first 30 days allow us to move on a little bit, but they still carry with them special mourning restrictions.

- ◆ The entire first year continues to recognize the mourners' grief and their inability to resume their normal lifestyles completely.

Ask the Rabbi

One of the seven days of shiva will invariably be the Sabbath. The sanctity of the Sabbath is so great that it overrides the shiva. Mourners not only may but should leave the house of mourning to attend services at the synagogue.

The Mourner's Kaddish

The *kaddish* is the most powerful and the most famous ritual for Jewish mourners. Recited for eleven months after the death of a loved one, it remarkably makes no mention at all of death or of the deceased. It is rather a statement in which the mourner affirms the justice of God and the meaningfulness of life. It expresses hope for the redemption and ultimate healing of all of suffering humankind. By extending the mourner's preoccupation with his own tragedy to a more universal concern, the kaddish elevates the mourner to a higher level of consciousness.

In yet a deeper sense, reciting the mourners' kaddish sanctifying God's name is in effect making a declaration:

> My father [or mother; it is said only for one's parents] tried to live as a Jew who brings glory to God. My parent is no longer alive, and so I will take his [her] place. By reciting the kaddish, I show my determination to live "Jewishly" and sanctify God's name in my life as my parent did. In this way I keep the memory of my loved one alive, since if it were not for him [her], I would not have been able to come into the world to make this declaration. Because I am committed to the values of my ancestor, my parent still lives in the most powerful way of all.

Ask the Rabbi

When visiting mourners, you should try as much as possible to steer the conversation to reflections about the deceased. Anecdotes that reveal positive aspects of the person's character are especially in place. On leaving, the traditional greeting to mourners is, "May the Almighty comfort you among those who mourn for Zion and Jerusalem."

Jewish tradition believes that the recitation of the kaddish serves as a source of blessing to both the mourner as well as to the soul of the deceased. As the soul is being judged after death, the heavenly scales are greatly influenced by the fact that a descendant carries on religious tradition.

Why Eleven Months?

The Jewish faith embraces the idea of heaven—although we can't describe it, we know it's a wonderful place: "One hour of spiritual bliss in the World to Come is better than the whole of this life." (*Ethics of the Fathers*, 4:17)

Hell also exists, but not in the way it's usually described, as a place of torture and burning with fire. Here, too, we're not sure of the exact nature of its suffering. The closest we can come to understanding it is that it's a place where we are estranged from God and our souls are purified from their sins.

There is one thing Jews do know, though, about hell: It doesn't have a sign on the door, as Dante described it, with the words, "Abandon hope, all ye who enter here." God would never be so cruel. The maximum time for anyone to have his or her soul "purified" in this place is 12 months. Very righteous people might possibly have "overnight cleaning service." How long the process takes depends on how much has to be done. It's only the very worst of all people who require the entire year for their purification.

So that's why kaddish is recited for 11 months. To do more would suggest that the deceased is in the category of those who require the longest time period before they get to heaven. To do less is to take a chance that prayers on behalf of the deceased might be stopped before they've accomplished their goal. Eleven months for everyone is the compromise that will serve everybody without embarrassment.

The Grave and the Stone

It's a sign of respect to visit the graves of loved ones. Souls, according to Jewish tradition, are aware of these visits and are gratified by them. They maintain a link of love, and they express what can no longer be said directly.

Approximately a year after the funeral (but in Israel observed much sooner), a stone is erected at graveside. In the simplest sense, it's a marker that serves to identify the location we will want to visit. Symbolically, it serves as a sign of permanence over the grave, reminding us that although the body is no more, there is something far more important that survives. The ceremony associated with the erection of the stone is called the *unveiling*. Words of praise capturing the essence of the person are inscribed on the stone, which is then unveiled in a religious ceremony. The kaddish is also recited then.

Let There Be Light

The **unveiling** is the ceremony associated with the erection of the gravestone.

Reincarnation?

When the opera singer finished his aria, it was clear to everyone that he was terrible. From the back of the hall came a cry, "Encore, encore." The singer, overwhelmed by this compliment, repeated the aria. Once again, the same cry of, "Encore, encore." For a third and yet a fourth time he sang the piece again. Even he began to wonder why his fan was so taken by him. Finally he understood. The person crying "Encore, encore," really meant, "Do it until you get it right!"

Are we ever asked to do an encore for our lives, to try again until we do it right? Reincarnation is a belief accepted not only by Shirley MacLaine, but also by many religions. Does Judaism share in accepting this version of a "second coming?"

Traditional sources choose—purposefully—to remain silent on the question. We ought not dwell overmuch on these issues, is the general policy. Yet mystics and the Kabbalah clearly

Ask the Rabbi

After the unveiling, whenever people go to visit a grave site, it is customary to place a little stone on top of the gravestone. By placing stone upon stone, the visitors reaffirm the concept of permanence and the belief in the survival of the soul after death.

accept the view that souls can return, not only once but several times. Is this a Jewish belief? No, it's a belief found *within* Judaism. You can accept or reject it and still be a good Jew.

What is fascinating, though, is how some mystics today apply this concept of reincarnation to explain a contemporary phenomenon. Why is it, they ask, that we find so many people in our times seeking to return to their roots? Why are there suddenly so many Jews searching for spirituality although they grew up in secular homes?

Our generation is unique in this regard. It is also the generation after the Holocaust, which witnessed the murder of six million Jews, approximately two million of whom were infants and little children who had no opportunity to live and to grow up as Jews. Perhaps, suggest the mystics, the religious seekers of our day are the reincarnated souls of Holocaust victims who are now given a second opportunity to become what they would have been in their previous existence! And who knows—there may be a kernel of truth in this amazing observation.

The Least You Need to Know

- Imminent death should not be feared but rather viewed as an opportunity to "put one's house in order."

- Death is the separation of soul from body, with the body returning to dust and the soul going back to its source, which grants it immortality.

- Judaism demands respect for the body, which served as a receptacle for the soul. It asks survivors to observe a number of laws demonstrating both grief for one's loss, as well as awareness of the soul's continued existence.

- Shiva, the seven-day mourning period, as well as the kaddish, the mourner's prayer (which doesn't even mention death), are two of the most important ways in which Judaism strives to comfort the mourners and perpetuate the memory of the deceased.

- Visiting the grave is a mitzvah and unveiling a stone on the burial site with an inscription about the deceased is a commendable custom.

- Reincarnation, while not a universal Jewish belief, is accepted by many, especially those in the mystical tradition of Kabbalah.

Part 5

All in the Family: The Home

There's a popular saying: "A man's house is his castle." For Jews, it's even more than that. A person's house is his or her temple. We visit the synagogue. We live in our homes. Here we play with our children, eat our festive family dinners, relax and find peace from our daily struggles, and make love with our mates. For Adam and Eve, Paradise was their home; for us, home is Paradise.

Part 5 is a guided tour through the various rooms of a home, highlighting their religious significance. You'll go through the front door and see that strange little box on the doorpost. Then you'll come into the kitchen and learn what the laws of kosher food are all about. You'll enter the dining room and enjoy the special menus of the different holidays and seasons. You'll even have a peek into the bedroom and talk about sex—because sex in Judaism isn't "dirty" but a God-given way to find pleasure and the most intimate union possible between two human beings. Finally, you'll go into the nursery and find out about Judaism's views on child-rearing and, hopefully, understand why Judaism believes that the most important house of God is not the synagogue, but the home.

Chapter

Welcome to My Humble Abode

In This Chapter

◆ The meaning of that little box on the doorpost

◆ The "other Hanukkah"—for the home and not the temple

◆ The modern reminders of the Temple of old

◆ Books, books, books

Here's an interesting bit of trivia: The English word *alphabet* comes from two words that are actually Hebrew. The ABCs of Hebrew begin with the letters *aleph* and *bet*—hence the *alphabet*.

These letters also mean something by themselves. *Aleph*, the first letter, represents the first cause of the universe, God the Creator. *Bet* means house, as in the more recognizable Hebrew word, *bayit*. The sequence of the letters, according to Jewish teachers, therefore, has a very important message. In order of importance, first comes God, *aleph*, and then comes the home, *bet*. These are the sources of Jewish survival.

God is all around us. "The whole world is filled with His glory," say the Psalms. Yet we're not aware of His nearness unless we sensitize ourselves to His presence. "Where is God?" the famous Hasidic rabbi of Kotsk was asked. "Wherever He is permitted to enter," was his answer. A Jewish home is not simply a place where Jews live. A Jewish home is one to which God is invited.

Some people design their homes with a view toward maximum comfort. Jews add a spiritual dimension. You can tell a Jewish home just by looking at it, from the outside as well as the inside.

Watch the Door, Please

Come to the front door. Now look at the right-hand side of the doorpost. See that little box? It can be very fancy, highly stylized, and made of silver. It can be a simple rectangular box made of wood or even plastic. It's attached with glue or hung with nails. And wherever you go around the world, you immediately know when you see it that Jews live there.

The box has a name—*mezuzah*. And it's been affixed to the doorposts of Jewish homes since biblical times: "And these words which I command you this day … you shall write them on the doorpost of your house and on your gates." (Deuteronomy 6:9)

The Talmud explains that the words aren't written on the doorpost itself but on a piece of parchment, prepared just the way the Torah itself is written. This is then rolled up and inserted into a protective container. What you see is a box. But what you really have on the doorpost of every Jewish home is a "mini-Torah" written by a scribe and containing one of the most important passages of the Bible.

Think about this for a moment. Some people brag about how whenever they come home they are greeted at the door by their dog, who joyfully acknowledges their return. Those who have a mezuzah symbolically receive an even warmer welcome. A little bit of God and His words are always waiting for us. Now that's what I call something worth coming home to!

From the Mountaintop

Very often you'll see a Hebrew letter on a mezuzah case. It looks like a horizontal base with three vertical lines coming out of it. It's called a *shin* and is the first letter of one of the names of God, *Shaddai*. As an acronym, it also stands for *shomer daltey Yisroel*—guardian of the doors of Israel.

Ask the Rabbi

If you move into a new home, you have a thirty-day grace period in which to put up a mezuzah. You can use the time to find a really nice one, but don't take any longer. A house without a mezuzah is like a house without a homeowner's policy.

The Purpose of the Mezuzah

The mezuzah, which stands at the portal of our private dwelling, the place of meeting between our personal and public worlds, can be understood on several levels:

◆ Every time we enter the place that houses our most precious gift from God, our family, we have to remember to give thanks for our blessings. The mezuzah, as a reminder of God, asks us to stop for a moment, mentally remove the impurities we've been contaminated with in our contact with the outside world, and think about our home as a place of spiritual refuge.

From the Mountaintop

The custom (optional) is to kiss the mezuzah whenever you go by it. Another custom is to kiss your wife (or husband) when you leave the house and when you come home. Jewish law does not rule on which one of these must come first.

◆ Whenever we leave our homes, we should take one last lingering look at the mezuzah on the doorpost to remember the values of our families and our homes as we go out into the world.

Fifteenth-century Italian mezuzah.

(Art Resource, NY/The Jewish Museum, NY)

◆ Jews shouldn't be embarrassed by their religion. They should proudly and publicly proclaim their identity. A mezuzah on the doorpost is a declaration that a Jew lives within—without fear, without shame, without a desire to assimilate or hide his or her faith.

◆ The mezuzah also reminds Jews of a story—a story with a message of providential care and protection. The first time Jews were commanded to perform a religious rite connected with the doorpost was on the night of the first Passover, as they were about to be redeemed from Egypt. Egyptian firstborn were slain, but God looked for a sign on the doorpost of His people so that He could "pass over" their houses. Jews smeared the blood of a lamb on the entrance to their households—in Hebrew, on their *mezuzot* (plural of *mezuzah*)—and were spared. Obedience to God's will, the mezuzah says, will grant you divine protection.

Pulpit Story

A Roman emperor gave Rabbi Judah the Prince a magnificent gift of gold and jewels. The rabbi in return sent the emperor a mezuzah. The emperor expressed his dismay. "I sent you such an expensive gift and all you send me in return is a box with a parchment?" The rabbi replied: "Your gift, because of its worth, I will have to guard carefully. It will require my constant concern. My gift to you, however, will serve as a divine blessing. You need not care for it, it will care for you. That is what makes it even more valuable."

With all this, Jewish sages were very concerned to emphasize the one thing a mezuzah is not: It is not an amulet or magical charm that frightens off demons or, as the superstitious would have it, an automatic warder-off of evil. The mezuzah works only if it reminds us to be better people, to consider our homes like a temple. If it's used like a lucky rabbit's foot, it's perverted into black magic.

Because there were people who misunderstood the mezuzah in just this way, the great Jewish sage Maimonides wrote these words in the twelfth century: "It is not enough that these fools have set a mitzvah aside but have converted a great mitzvah—the unification of God, blessed be He, and His love and worship—into an amulet for their own benefit imagining, in their stupidity, that this has an effect in terms of worldly vanities." Get the feeling that Maimonides wouldn't have approved of affixing a mezuzah to a car dashboard to protect it against accidents or of wearing a mezuzah as a lucky charm?

What's Inside the Box?

Because the parchment of the mezuzah isn't visible, many people are surprised to learn that there's something inside the box. But of course there is, and that's the essence of what we mean when we talk about a mezuzah. The name *mezuzah* itself describes the contents, not the container.

Written on the parchment are two paragraphs from the Torah. They are from Deuteronomy 6:4–9 and 11:13–21, the two first paragraphs of the *Sh'ma Yisroel* prayer—probably the most important prayer in the Jewish religion. This is the prayer Jews are obligated by law to recite twice daily, "when you go to sleep and when you get up." It's the prayer Jews recite as their last words before death. It's the prayer Jews said when they were led to their execution during the Holocaust and other times of persecution. This same prayer that defines a Jew's purpose in life is the one that stands guard at the door of his or her home!

In these two paragraphs are found these major themes: The acceptance of monotheism; the command to love God "with all your heart, with all your soul and with all your might"; the need to transmit Jewish tradition to the next generation; the obligation to review God's words constantly so that they become a part of our beings; and the realization that God is directly and constantly involved in our lives, rewarding the righteous and punishing the wicked.

True, we don't see the words of these paragraphs as we pass the mezuzah. But pious Jews are aware of their contents and think about the message whenever they walk by one.

Ask the Rabbi

Letters on parchment can fade. Be sure to check your mezuzah at least twice every seven years to make certain the writing is still legible.

Every Door Needs One

Ever hear the story of the Jewish millionaire who was almost able to afford to buy a mansion with more than 100 rooms? The purchase price was within his means. But what put it over the top was that he couldn't afford the additional 100 mezuzot!

The most important place for a mezuzah is the doorpost of the entry to the home. Yet that isn't enough. Every single room—with the exception of the bathroom where a sacred object doesn't belong—needs its own God-reminder.

Put the Right Slant on It

There are two possibilities for the correct positioning of a mezuzah. One is vertical, the other is horizontal. Which way is correct? As is so often the case, the rabbis disagreed. What normally happens in Jewish law in such a case is that we take a stand. We analyze the reasons for each opinion and declare the final law according to the one that majority opinion considers to be most logical.

The placement of the mezuzah is the only exception to this principle of Jewish law. The final law, as illustrated by the position of every mezuzah, is that it's placed on a slant. That means we know that what we're doing is definitely incorrect! It follows neither one of the possible options. Yet we do it, explain the rabbis, to demonstrate a beautiful ideal that should serve as the guiding principle for every home: The position of the mezuzah is a compromise. A family can only live happily if its members are willing to bend just a little bit, like the mezuzah.

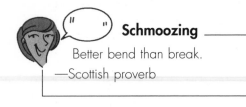

Schmoozing

Better bend than break.

—Scottish proverb

Hanukkah for a House?

You remember from Chapter 13 that Hanukkah got its name from the word for dedication. The Maccabees dedicated the Temple after it had been defiled by the Syrian Greeks. To dedicate means to declare that something is set aside for a holy purpose. When the Temple was dedicated, it meant that it would again be used in the service of God.

The Bible tells us that when the Jews had to draft men for the army, there were some people who were given automatic exemptions. Someone newly married, for example, wasn't taken away from his bride. It was more important for him to remain at home for the first year of marriage. (Jewish law not only recognized the need for a honeymoon but extended it for a full year.) Another exemption reads: "Then the officials shall address the troops as follows: 'Is there anyone who has built a new house but has not dedicated it? Let him go back to his home, lest he die in battle and another dedicate it.'" (Deuteronomy 20:5)

Schmoozing

Consecration of the Jewish home as a temple of God is the aim of the mezuzah, the sacred inscription on the doorpost.

—Samson Raphael Hirsch (1808–1888), German rabbi, scholar, and author

If you finally build your dream house, you're entitled by law to have some time to enjoy it. From this passage we see not only how much of a blessing it is to get a new home, but that we also have an obligation to have a ceremony of dedication. In Hebrew, that's called a *Hanukat habayit*. There's no fixed ritual for this ceremony. You can read Psalms or just express in your own words what this moment means to you. The one thing you can't do is take it for granted. This is a Hanukkah without candles, but still a holy day worthy of prayer and thanksgiving.

Why Didn't You Finish It?

Homes of traditional Jews have one more feature in common. They are never completely finished. That's not because of laziness or lack of funds. It's because of a remarkable custom.

Beginning with the exile of the Jewish people from Jerusalem and Israel in the year 70 C.E., Jews instituted various rituals of mourning. Wherever we are, we're supposed to temper our joy in recognition that the Temple is still destroyed. You read in Chapter 13 about the days of fasting to commemorate this tragedy. Our homes offer us another way to express our feelings of incompleteness.

One small corner of the homes of devout Jews is left free of decoration and unpainted, *zecher l'hurban*, as a reminder of the destruction of the Temple. Looking at that spot may jar the sensitivities of someone seeking perfection. What a good way, though, to remind ourselves that life isn't perfect, that we still have dreams unfulfilled.

Ask the Rabbi

A proper gift to bring for *Hanukat habayit* is a basket of bread, candles, and salt. The bread represents the hope that there will always be enough to eat, the candles symbolize the light and joy that will hopefully pervade the house, and the salt serves as a reminder of the Temple sacrifices.

Schmoozing

We have preserved the Book, and the Book has preserved us.
—David Ben-Gurion (1886–1973), first Israeli prime minister

Which Way Is East?

Wherever Jews are, they have to pray facing Jerusalem. That's one more way to demonstrate on a daily basis how important the Holy City is to us. For Jews in the Western world, that means facing east. To help us remember the direction, many Jewish homes have a *mizrach*, Hebrew for east, which is a plaque, watercolor, embroidered cloth, drawing, collage or wall hanging placed on an eastern wall of the home with the word *mizrach* painted on it. A compass points north so you can always orient yourself. A mizrach helps your soul find its way home by pointing east.

A book is the most delightful companion. An inanimate thing, yet it talks. There is in the world no friend more faithful and attentive, no teacher more proficient. It will join you in solitude, accompany you in exile, serve as a candle in the dark, and entertain you in your loneliness. It will do you good and ask no favor in return. It gives and does not take.

—Moses Ibn Ezra (1055–1135), Spanish-Hebrew poet

And the *Very* Best Way to Tell a Jewish Home

A mezuzah by the door, a mizrach on the wall, and just one more thing and you can be sure you're in a Jewish home. There must be shelves filled with books. For Jews, books are holy. The law is, "If a drop of ink falls at the same time on your book and on your coat, clean first the book and then the garment." When Mohammed needed a short description for the Jews, he called them "the People of the Book." So don't be surprised if you find that a Jewish home may be missing fancy furniture. But what you'll almost certainly be sure to see is an overflowing bookcase (hopefully with this book on it!).

The Least You Need to Know

- ◆ Most Jewish homes have a small box on the doorpost called a mezuzah, which serves as a reminder of God at the place of meeting between one's public and private worlds.

- ◆ The mezuzah contains within it a parchment, like a mini-Torah, with perhaps the most important of Jewish prayers written on it.

- ◆ The mezuzah is placed on a slant to emphasize the importance of compromise in family relationships.

- ◆ Every home should be dedicated, just as the Temple was on the first Hanukkah, in a ceremony similarly named *Hanukat habayit*.

- ◆ The unfinished part of every Jewish home is a reminder of exile and the tragedy of the Temple's destruction.

- ◆ Jews in the West face east, toward Jerusalem, during their prayers and place a reminder of some sort on an eastern wall of the home, called a mizrach.

- ◆ Jews are known as "the People of the Book" and Jewish homes almost invariably demonstrate their occupants' veneration of books by their number as well as the prominent place assigned to them.

Chapter 18

The Kitchen

In This Chapter

- ◆ The purpose of the kosher laws
- ◆ What is and what isn't kosher
- ◆ How kindness to animals is incorporated into Jewish law
- ◆ The rule that forbids mixing meat and milk
- ◆ The history of vegetarianism in Judaism
- ◆ The religious importance of health

Owen Meredith, the nineteenth-century English statesman and poet, had it right:

> We may live without poetry, music and art;
> We may live without conscience, and live without heart;
> We may live without friends; we may live without books;
> But civilized man cannot live without cooks.

That's why the kitchen might very well be the most important room in the house. From it comes our food, the basic staple of our lives. We all have our memories of the delicious smells from the stove, the aromas of freshly baked cakes and cookies that we couldn't wait to devour. The kitchen, we always realized, is the source of our daily bread.

Judaism comes to remind us, as the Bible says, that "man does not live by bread alone." So that's why the Jewish kitchen is spiritualized. What comes out of it is supposed to be kosher. Too bad that most people don't know what kosher really means.

Kosher Is More Than Clean

No, kosher food isn't food that's blessed by a rabbi. That's probably the first misconception people have. The second is that *kashrut* (the laws of kosher food) refers to cleanliness. Kosher food, people think, is super-clean. (Sometimes I can only say I wish it were so!)

Actually, the word *kosher* in Hebrew means "fit", or "suitable." It doesn't have to be applied to food; it can refer to almost anything else as well. Do you think that someone wearing an Ally McBeal mini-skirt is wearing a kosher dress? Or that a man who steals from his employer is doing something that's kosher? What's kosher is legal and proper. In the realm of food, it's what's accepted by Jewish law as permissible. Hopefully, it's also clean, but what makes it kosher is that it's approved by the Highest Authority.

It's Not Health Food—It's Holy Food

Here's one more misconception about kosher food: The laws of kashrut are based on matters of health and are meant to prevent disease and sickness. That's not true. Nowhere in the Bible are medical considerations mentioned as the reason for these laws. Instead, the Bible explicitly says they should be followed so that "you sanctify yourselves and be holy." (Leviticus 11:44) We are to be concerned with what we eat, not for the sake of our bodies, but for the sake of our souls. So that makes Jews the first people on earth to discover the joys of soul food!

How can observing dietary laws make you more holy? How does the way you eat affect the spirituality of your soul? Jewish philosophers give several answers:

 **Schmoozing**

A physician restricts the diet of only those patients whom he expects to recover. So God prescribed dietary laws for those who have hope for a future life. Others may eat anything.

—Midrash, Leviticus Rabbah 13:2

◆ The laws of kashrut impose the need for self-discipline. We all know how hard it is for people to stick to a diet. The dietary laws are even more demanding. To learn to control cravings, to say, "This I can eat and this I can't because God said so," is to become "master of your own domain" for one of the most powerful needs of human beings (and, sorry Seinfeld, I'm not talking about sex). Accomplish this, and you become holy—because holiness means to learn how to conquer your own passions so that you control them and they don't control you.

◆ Learning self-control with regard to food allows us to then transfer this religious discipline to other areas. If I can resist shrimp and a nonkosher sizzling steak, I can also find the inner strength to "just say no" to other temptations.

◆ Holiness is the ability to elevate basic urges we share with beasts to a higher spiritual level. Animals share our need for food. If we, however, can elevate this mundane act by investing it with the fulfillment of religious law, we turn a moment of physical satisfaction into a spiritual act.

◆ The very first law God ever gave humankind had to do with food: "From all the trees of the Garden you may surely eat, but from the Tree of Knowledge of Good and Evil you shall not eat of it." God didn't give Adam and Eve a reason. Maybe that was the very meaning of the commandment. Do it even though you don't understand it to prove you acknowledge that God has more knowledge than you. That's why disobeying meant they ate of the "Tree of Knowledge"—they felt they knew better. To refrain from eating something just because God commanded it is to demonstrate that we will accept what He says, even if we don't know the reason. And that, too, makes us holy.

> **Schmoozing**
>
> Dietary laws train us to master our appetites and not to consider eating and drinking the end of man's existence.
>
> —Moses Maimonides, *Guide for the Perplexed*

> **Schmoozing**
>
> One should eat to live, not live to eat.
>
> —Benjamin Franklin

You Are What You Eat

The great Jewish philosopher, Maimonides, suggests one more possible explanation. To appreciate it, we have to know something about which animals are forbidden and which are permissible under the laws of kashrut.

The permissible animals under Jewish law, Maimonides points out, are all herbivorous—they eat plants. The animals that are forbidden to be consumed by Jews, interestingly enough, are carnivorous—they eat other animals. Their survival depends upon their capturing and devouring their prey.

Isn't it possible, says Maimonides, that we really are what we eat? Foods can affect us more than physically. Liquor changes the way we look at the world and loosens our inhibitions. We now know that the smallest drop of LSD can totally distort our personalities and alter our behavior. Who knows? Maybe the kosher laws keep us healthy not in a medical sense but in a moral one: By not ingesting the meat of cruel animals we may be preserving our own kindness and compassion!

Schmoozing

The laws of kashrut come to teach us that a Jew's first preference should be a vegetarian meal. If, however, one cannot control a craving for meat, it should be kosher meat, which would serve as a reminder that the animal being eaten is a creature of God, that the death of such a creature cannot be taken lightly, that hunting for sport is forbidden.

—Pinchas Peli, contemporary Israeli scholar, author

What's In and What's Out

Pigs could really have used much better PR. People seem to think that they are the prime example of nonkosher food. Actually, eating bacon or ham is no worse than consuming any of the other nonkosher foods listed in the Bible. They include a number of animals, birds, seafood, and creeping things. Here's a short list just to give you some idea:

Let There Be Light

The word *treif,* used as the opposite of kosher, comes from the Hebrew word for "torn." Literally, it refers to animals torn by wild beasts and dying without the benefit of proper slaughter. Traditionally, treif is extended to apply to anything that is unfit to be eaten by religious law.

◆ Kosher animals have to chew their cud and have a split hoof. Examples are cattle, sheep, goats, and deer. Animals that don't meet these qualifications are *treif*—the Hebrew word that designates things that aren't kosher. They include horses, donkeys, camels, and, yes, pigs.

Here's a fascinating sidelight: Pigs do have one of the signs of kosher animals, split hooves. You'd think that they would be considered less treif than animals missing both kosher signs. The Midrash explains why the pig nevertheless became the greatest symbol of foods that are rejected by pious Jews.

The pig puts out his foot as if to say, "Look at me, I'm kosher." It's trying to fool you. What you can't see is that it doesn't chew its cud. A pig is kosher on the outside, but treif on the inside—just like a con artist who shows you his good side and hides his real essence. That's why he's more "dangerous" than another animal whose defect is obvious. And that's why the pig became the ultimate symbol of treif food.

♦ For fish to be kosher they have to have both fins and scales. Here's a list of fish you can offer your rabbi: anchovies, halibut, bass, herring, shad, bluefish, mackerel, smelt, sole, butterfish, pike, trout, carp, cod, red snapper, tuna, fluke, salmon, haddock, sardines, whitefish— and even porgy, although its first three letters make you think of something else. With all these good kosher choices, you don't need eels, catfish, shark, porpoise, or whale, all of which are on the no-no list.

From the Mountaintop

The Talmud rules that boorish people with no morals or learning are forbidden to eat meat. If your lifestyle makes you no better than an animal, what right do you have to take an animal's life to feed yourself?

♦ Sorry, but shellfish, scavengers, and bottom-dwellers are out. On the forbidden list are (boo-hoo) shrimp, lobster, oyster, turtle, scallops, crab, clam, frog, and octopus (yes, every one of its eight legs). You might be interested to know, though, that thanks to the miracle of modern food engineering, those who keep kosher can still enjoy "mock shrimp" because it's only an imitation made from tofu.

♦ Thankfully, most domestic birds are kosher—they're what we call fowl-weather friends. They include turkeys, chickens, pigeons, capons, ducks, geese, and doves—the ones you're most likely to find on menus. It's the wild birds and birds of prey that are treif, and the Bible lists 24 varieties. Among them are such interesting species as eagle, ostrich, vulture, hawk, kite, and the cuckoo. (And if Maimonides's reason is correct, the English name would be a great reason to explain why it's treif—who wants to be cuckoo?)

Ask the Rabbi

If you want to know whether a packaged product is kosher, look for a U in a circle on the label. That's the symbol used by the Union of Orthodox Jewish Congregations of America to identify kosher items. It's sort of like a spiritual Good Housekeeping Seal of Approval.

♦ The last category of treif are all living creatures that crawl or creep on their belly (snakes, for example); what the Bible calls "winged swarming things"; and rodents and lizards. These forbidden foods include gourmet delicacies such as eel, snails, rattlesnakes, ants, and other assorted insects (which are eaten by some people). Although all fruits and vegetables are automatically kosher, they should still be checked to make sure insects haven't gotten into them. An apple a day is fine as long as you're not an early bird who gets the worm.

Be Kind to Animals

Follow this carefully because it gets a little tricky. Even kosher animals can end up not being kosher. It isn't enough for an animal to be on the "approved" list. It must also be killed in a particular way to make it permissible for eating.

Ask the Rabbi

Don't even think about hunting for sport. First of all, it's forbidden by Jewish law because it's cruel. Second, if you kill the animal in a way other than *shechitah*, you won't be allowed to eat it anyway.

At the beginning of the twentieth century, Upton Sinclair caused a sensation when his muckraking novel, *The Jungle*, described the barbaric conditions of the Chicago stockyards. The way animals are slaughtered may have improved some since those days, but they're still far from humane. Kosher food has an extra bonus. You can rest assured that the animal was put to death in the most painless way possible.

Merciful Killing

For a kosher animal to be eaten, it must be slaughtered by the method known as *shechitah*. This is a procedure designed to cause the least suffering to the animal. It

Let There Be Light

A *shochet* is the name of the man designated to perform ritual slaughter, **shechitah**. In addition to his necessary qualification of skill, he must also be pious and God-fearing. Only those who understand the holiness of life are permitted to prepare an animal for human consumption.

requires a perfectly sharpened blade, free from the slightest nick or unevenness. The knife swiftly moves over the wind and food pipes in a fraction of a second, severing the trachea, the esophagus, and the two vagus nerves, as well as both carotid arteries and the jugular veins.

Research has shown that this method results in instant loss of consciousness; that the cut itself is painless (just as when you cut yourself with a razor, and you're only aware of what happened when you see the blood); and there is no pain during the fraction of time before consciousness is completely lost.

Long before there were any societies for the prevention of cruelty to animals, Jewish law insisted on a humane death for all living things. The penalty for not obeying? You can't eat the animal, it just isn't kosher.

Do unto Others ...

Think about this a moment: No Jewish child has ever seen a parent wring the neck of a chicken or cruelly put it to death and then serve it for supper. When violence is outlawed as a way of preparing our food, it gets to be viewed as unacceptable in our human relationships as well.

Please Salt It First

Bet you think that after you've taken a kosher animal and slaughtered it in the kosher way, then that's it; you needn't do anything else. Not true, for there is still one more way in which meat can be considered nonkosher. The Torah forbids the eating of the blood that courses through the body, in any form. Before meat can be eaten, it has to be soaked and salted—soaked to loosen it and allow it to properly absorb, and salted to cause the blood to exude and be drained off.

From the Mountaintop

What does it mean when it says on the box "kosher salt" if all salt by definition is kosher? It's just a way of saying that this salt is thick enough to be used for "koshering" meat; thin salt tends to melt away and become absorbed into the meat instead of acting to absorb the blood from the meat and to drain off.

Blood Libel? No Way

Jewish law is so fearful of anyone consuming even a drop of blood that not only meat has to go through this procedure, but even eggs have to be thoroughly checked for blood spots. If even the tiniest speck is found, the egg has to be discarded. Knowing this, you can see how incredible it is to discover that a popular accusation against Jews throughout much of the Middle Ages and even into the twentieth century was the "blood libel."

Anti-Semites spread the lie that *matzo*, the Passover staple, had to be baked together with the blood of Christian infants. The wine at the seder meal wasn't wine, they argued, but blood that Jews required for their religious rituals. Here's a perfect example of how even the most outrageous lies, when repeated often enough, can end up being believed.

Schmoozing

The Jews have what they call their Easter feast (Passover), the feast of the unleavened bread, which is celebrated by bleeding a non-Jew. Then they take a piece of flesh and mix it with the *matzah*. The rabbi himself does the butcher's work. This is the nature of our enemy.

—Anis Mansour, contemporary Egyptian intellectual and journalist, from a 1972 article in a Cairo daily

The truth is, Jews are so revolted by the thought of consuming blood that even a drop of the nonhuman variety in an egg or animal meat makes it nonkosher!

A Cheeseburger—Yecchhh!

So you finally have your kosher hamburger, and you think there can't possibly be any more restrictions. Guess again. The Bible forbids mixing meat and milk. So there goes your cheeseburger—and your milkshake with your meat as well.

According to strict religious law, meat and dairy products can't be eaten together, cooked together, or even served in the same vessels. Orthodox Jews have two sets of dishes—one for meat products (in Yiddish, *fleishig*—recognize the similar English word, *flesh?*) and the other for dairy foods (in Yiddish, *milchig*—catch the connection with *milk?*). Now you know what Jews mean when they say they just bought a "service for two," even though there are at least a dozen people in the family. It's for both kinds of meals they will be serving.

What's wrong with eating meat and milk together? And what does God have against cheeseburgers? Okay, I'll grant you that's one of the mysteries of life. This law is a perfect example of a chok—a law whose reason is simply beyond our comprehension. Some have tried to explain that milk is the life-giving element of an animal (with which it nurses its young) and meat is the death element (the flesh destined for decay). And so we symbolically separate these two realms by not eating milk and meat together—it's the recognition of the need for reverence for life and the

Let There Be Light

Pareve describes any food product that is neither meat nor dairy; it's a neutral food like fruits and vegetables. In Yiddish, the word has come to be used to describe people who are neutral—they don't have too much personality, and they're neither here nor there. If anyone calls you pareve, don't take it as a compliment.

refusal to diminish its sacredness by commingling it with death. For some, this explanation has meaning. For others, it's sufficient to observe it because … well, because the Bible says so.

Adam and Eve Were Vegetarians

Even though we've just seen that animal meat can be kosher, there are some Jews who prefer to be vegetarians and not feed themselves at the expense of another living thing. Interestingly enough, these people are following in the footsteps of a famous couple. Did you know that Adam and Eve, the first human beings, were also vegetarians? And this was because they were following divine instructions.

"From all the trees in the garden, you may surely eat," was what God told the inhabitants of Paradise. What grows on trees was to be their diet. Meat wasn't permitted to human beings until the time of Noah. Was it then a concession to people who like meat or need the nutrients it provides, or a new Godly policy? Jewish scholars have been arguing that one for centuries.

> **Ask the Rabbi**
>
> Are any rabbis vegetarians? Yes, including two chief rabbis of Israel! What's clear is that a good steak is permitted by Jewish law today. But whether the permissible is the same thing as the ideal remains a fascinating question. Sometimes Judaism, with all of its laws, lets you make your own decision.

> **Schmoozing**
>
> For animals, every day is Treblinka [the infamous Nazi concentration camp]. One day, in 1962, I decided: no meat, no fish. I just think it's the wrong thing to kill animals.
>
> —Isaac Bashevis Singer (1904–1991), Polish-born novelist and Nobel Prize winner

Not Healthy, Not Kosher

One last consideration can make even the most kosher food be off-limits. What's not healthy is not kosher—and no amount of rabbinic supervision can ever get around that problem. Some people may argue that their own health is their business. If I choose to do harm to my body, they'll say, who is anyone to tell me I can't? Yet the claim is fundamentally flawed because of a major religious principle: The human body is given to a person in trust by God. You have an obligation to take care of it. Health isn't an option, it's a religious commandment.

Foods that endanger health, the rabbis declare, are to be avoided even more than food forbidden by religious law. If there's a recall of an item because of fear it may be

Ask the Rabbi _____

Because unhealthy foods are forbidden and, thus, not kosher, many rabbis today teach that cigarettes are also treif. For Jews, the Surgeon General's warning is just as relevant as a biblical law.

tainted with salmonella, then no matter how small the possibility, it's more nonkosher than bacon or ham.

What follows from this is a rule: If your doctor gives you strict instructions on medical grounds to stay away from certain food items, then you've just added some personal extras to your biblical list of nonkosher products. Strange but true: French fries and ice cream might be kosher for everyone else—but not for you!

The Least You Need to Know

◆ Kosher food doesn't mean food that's blessed by a rabbi or that's especially clean; it's food that's fit to be eaten in accord with Jewish law.

◆ The reason for kosher laws is not medical but spiritual: eating kosher is supposed to make you holy, not healthy.

◆ Pigs aren't the only nonkosher food; there's a long list of animals, birds, seafood, and insects that are forbidden, or treif.

◆ Kosher laws are also concerned with pain to animals, and the only meat permitted is that from an animal slaughtered by shechitah, a ritual of instantaneous and painless death.

◆ Blood is forbidden as food and for that reason meat must be salted and eggs with blood spots discarded.

◆ Meat and milk are forbidden to be consumed together, and this law is a prime example of chok, statutes for which we were not given a reasonable explanation.

◆ Vegetarianism goes back to Adam and Eve and remains a viable option for Jews.

◆ What is dangerous to health is not kosher, and Jews don't have the right to eat foods that are harmful to their physical well-being on religious grounds.

Chapter 19

The Dining Room

In This Chapter

- ◆ The miracle of our daily bread
- ◆ Blessings before and after the meal
- ◆ The secret of chicken soup and the special menus for all of the holidays

Here's a short summary of a joyous Jewish holiday: They tried to destroy us. We won. Let's eat!

There isn't an important Jewish occasion, be it a festival or a family time of rejoicing, that doesn't revolve around a special meal.

Maybe it all goes back to the time when the Jewish people became a nation. God said, "I'm going to take you out of your bondage. You're going to leave tonight right after I slay the firstborn of the Egyptians. But first, sit down and enjoy a *seder*—that way you'll always remember the exodus with special joy." A meal allows for the family to be together. It encourages conversation between those who truly love each other. It's more than a coffee break—it's a time out at home to enjoy God's blessings of food, as well as the warmth of family.

So let me bring you into the dining room. And like a typical Jewish mother always says, "Enjoy, enjoy."

Wait—Don't Start Eating Yet!

I don't care how starved you are or how delectable the food looks, you can't just dig in without doing something very important first. In Jewish law, you're not permitted to take a bite of anything unless you recite a blessing. If not, the Talmud says you're guilty of stealing. That's because God gives us His gifts but demands as payment not only our gratitude but also our acknowledgement of the wonders of the universe. Blessings are meant to remind us that we live in a world of miracles.

Don't Take Miracles for Granted

The Midrash describes how the blessing for bread, "Blessed are You O Lord our God, King of the Universe, who brings forth bread from the ground," first came to be said:

> The Jews who left Egypt wandered in the desert, despondent over their lack of food. God assured them that He would answer their prayers with a miracle. Sure enough, the next day the Jews awoke to find bread, which had fallen from the sky, all around their camp. (I guess this was the first "wonder bread" in history.) The Jews called it manna—manna from heaven.

> You can imagine how impressed they were with this miracle. The next day it was repeated, and they were equally astonished. Days turned to weeks, weeks to months, and the manna became part of their daily lives, expected and accepted as a routine phenomenon. For 40 years the Jews enjoyed their manna and then it was time for them to enter the Promised Land. A new generation had replaced the old and they no longer remembered how they had eaten regular bread a long time before. When Moses told them that in Israel the bread from the sky would fall no more, they were perplexed. "How will we eat? From where will we get our bread?"

> Moses carefully explained to them what they must do. "Plant seeds in the ground," he said, "to grow wheat." "Seeds in the ground?" they replied in amazement. "If we put anything in the ground it will rot. How could you possibly tell us to do that?"

> Moses continued to describe the entire agricultural procedure for growing wheat, getting grain, making flour, and baking bread. At every point, the Jews were incredulous. It seemed impossible that something as delicious as bread could come from the ground itself.

But when they entered the land, they did as they were told
Moses had said. The seeds didn't spoil. Edible grains actually
ground. The new generation stared in amazement and said, "W
nessed a true miracle. Any fool knows that bread comes from the
have now witnessed bread made from something that came out of th

Spontaneously, to acknowledge the miracle of this "unnatural" occurren
yelled out in unison, "Blessed are you O Lord our God, King of the univer
who brings forth bread from the ground."

The only reason we fail to see that food that comes from the earth is a great miracle
is because we are so accustomed to it that we take it for granted; we see it simply as
a part of nature. A blessing is meant to instill within us a sense of wonder, as well
as a sense of appreciation. Look at the world and all its blessings, and you'll be overwhelmed with the joy of knowing that God makes miracles for you every day.

 Schmoozing

The most important discipline of Judaism involves the blessing. When a blessing is
recited before eating, then the act itself becomes a spiritual undertaking. Through the
blessing, the act of eating becomes a contemplated exercise. Just as one can contemplate a flower or a melody, one can contemplate the act of eating.
—Aryeh Kaplan, contemporary American rabbi and author

In *Fiddler on the Roof*, you find out that there is a blessing for a sewing machine and
even for the czar. More relevant for the dining room, there's a blessing for every kind
of food. Fruits and vegetables, meats and fish, desserts and pastries—an observant Jew
has to learn the right blessing for every one. Hard to remember so many different
blessings? So what? It's worth it. Say the right blessing—and now you can start eating!

Jewish Penicillin

Everyone has his or her own favorite food, but somehow almost all Jews—who usually
do not agree on anything—admit that chicken soup is the cure for everything. It's the
Jewish penicillin and probably helps to explain why the Jews are the only people who
have survived from the time of Abraham!

What's the secret of this "medicine" traditionally served at every Jewish Sabbath
meal? Nobody has as yet discovered it, even though most recent scientific findings—

Behold, it was as
came from the
e have just wit-
heavens. Yet we
e earth."
e, they
se

iously—confirm its efficacy. Call it a placebo if
 want to. I personally wish to be numbered
ong the true believers, almost as assuredly as I'm
 inced of the existence of God.

make sure you get your money's worth out of
ook, I'm going to add a recipe for chicken soup
ere. Okay, I admit I myself am a disaster in the
. My wife, Elaine, however, is a culinary
and what I offer you next is what has gar-
mpliments from hundreds of people
throughout the years.

Homemade Chicken Soup

Here's what you'll need:

> 1 pullet chicken, cut up
>
> 1 bunch parsley
>
> 3 stalks celery
>
> 3 carrots
>
> 12 cups water
>
> 1 parsnip
>
> 2 large onions
>
> 4 cloves garlic
>
> Salt and pepper to taste

Boil chicken and skim off fat floating on top of stock. Add remaining ingredients, partially cover (so steam can escape), and simmer until chicken is soft, about 2½ to 3 hours. Remove and discard onion, parsley, and parsnip.

Pulpit Story

The packed theater is stunned as an actor collapses on stage. The play is halted, and the stage manager announces that the rest of the performance must be cancelled because the actor has died. From the balcony comes a cry, "Give him chicken soup." "Chicken soup? Didn't you hear? I said he was dead. What good is chicken soup?" From the balcony comes the same voice, "Well, it wouldn't hurt."

Matzo Balls

And if you want a preview of the delights of the world to come, let me also share with you a secret for feathery light matzo balls.

Gather together:

4 eggs

1 tsp. salt

4 TB. oil

4 TB. water

Dash pepper

1 cup matzo meal

Beat eggs. Add remaining ingredients and refrigerate for half-hour. With wet hands, form into balls and drop into boiling salt water. Cook for one hour. Drain and transfer to soup.

After you've transferred the matzo balls to soup, be prepared to be transported yourself—to the celestial spheres!

Ask the Rabbi

Schmaltz is the Yiddish word for melted chicken fat. For those who aren't worried about cholesterol, collect the fat you usually throw away when cleaning a chicken and defatting chicken soup and freeze it. When you've collected a sufficient amount, cut it into small pieces while still frozen. Then when you need them, use them for making *matzo* balls, chopped chicken liver, and meat *kreplach*.

Special Foods for All Seasons

You'll need a Jewish cookbook if you want to crack the code for all the other delicacies that have made Jewish cooking famous. I'm sure some day there'll be a *Complete Idiot's Guide* for that. Until then, let me give you an overview of the foods that are identified with special days on the Jewish calendar. They usually have a good reason to be on the menu on the occasions when they're served. Not simply because they're good—in some way, what they look like, what they taste like, and what they remind us of have a connection with that special day in history.

Shabbat

Foods for the Sabbath meal:

◆ **Challah,** twisted, braided bread, illustrates that the holiness of the Sabbath must be intertwined with the secular week.

From the Mountaintop

Every day God sent manna from the sky to feed the Jews. There was always enough for one day except on Friday when a "double portion" of manna fell so that the Jews would have sufficient bread for the Sabbath. For that reason, to this very day, two loaves of *challah* are placed on the Sabbath table to commemorate the double portion God provides for the day of rest.

◆ *Cholent* is an ideal dish for the Shabbat midday meal, because cooking is prohibited on the Sabbath. It takes 18 to 24 hours to cook, and its flavor improves with time. Generations of Jews have cooked it for Shabbat in countries from North Africa to those in Eastern Europe. It combines meat, potatoes, beans, onions, barley, and other "secret ingredients" that Jewish housewives add to give it their own personal flavor. To die without ever having tasted cholent is clearly to have led a wasted life.

Let There Be Light

Cholent, the special Sabbath food left on the stove for many hours, probably derives its name from two French words, *chaud lent,* meaning "to warm slowly."

◆ **Gefilte fish** is served on Friday night because fish are a symbol of fertility, and on this night sexual relations are encouraged. Hopefully, Friday night activities of husband and wife will lead to a larger Shabbat table.

The Holidays

Foods for the Jewish holidays:

◆ On Rosh Hashanah, honey cake is the cake *du jour* because honey is sweet, and we pray for a sweet year. Similarly, a good main dish is honeyed chicken with almonds. On the side, try *teiglach*—dough balls made of eggs, margarine, sugar, flour, baking powder, and chopped nuts, mixed together with honey syrup. (You'll thank me doubly for this one.) And a great side dish is sweet potato and carrot tzimmes. *Tzimmes* is a Yiddish word for "fuss" or "excitement." But surprisingly enough, tzimmes dishes don't require much fussing (but you'll probably make a joyful fuss when you taste them).

♦ Yom Kippur, when Jews fast, obviously doesn't have any food dishes—there's no such thing as Jewish "fast" food. But the meal before Yom Kippur, when we have to fill up before the long fast, tradition-ally features *kreplach*. They're pretty close to what Chinese restaurants call wontons, but they have more dough and more filling. They're linked with the idea of atonement in a mystical way, and their three corners are meant to remind us of the three fathers of the Jewish people, Abraham, Isaac, and Jacob.

♦ As the Festival of the Harvest, Sukkot features fruits and vegetables. Because Simchat Torah, the day when Jews rejoice with the Torah, is an important part of the Sukkot holiday, pomegran-ates are popular. That's because the two finials on top of the wooden staves on which the Torah scrolls are rolled are called *rimonim*, which is also Hebrew for "pomegranates." Originally, these dec-orations must have been created in the shape of pomegranates and therefore acquired that name. In Israel, it is custom-ary not only to eat pomegranates but also to decorate the Sukkot with them.

From the Mountaintop

On Rosh Hashanah, one custom is to bake the chal-lah in the shape of a lad-der or with a ladder on top to remind everybody that God decides who will ascend or descend life's ladder. Others make a round challah to symbol-ize the cycle of the year and to pray that our lives, like a circle, don't come to an end in the coming year. Many also add raisins for an extra touch of sweetness.

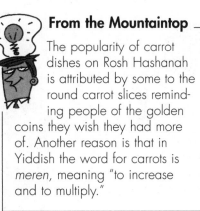

From the Mountaintop

The popularity of carrot dishes on Rosh Hashanah is attributed by some to the round carrot slices remind-ing people of the golden coins they wish they had more of. Another reason is that in Yiddish the word for carrots is *meren*, meaning "to increase and to multiply."

♦ Hanukkah highlights foods that, for obvious reasons, are fried in oil. (Remember the miracle of the oil? If not, see Chapter 13.) In most European countries, as well as in the United States, potato *latkes* are the menu highlight. In Israel, it's *sufganiyot*, doughnuts dropped into hot oil without being shaped that then come out in different odd forms, the funnier the better. (The variety of odd types, the saying goes, is meant to symbolize Israelis.)

♦ Tu B'Shvat, the New Year of the Trees, features any foods that come from Israel. Ironically enough, an Israeli-grown product is one of the most universally popular items—a fruit known in English as St. John's bread, or carob pod. (So *that's* how a saint made it into the Jewish holidays!)

♦ Purim has *hamantaschen*, and if you look at the first part of the name of this delicacy, you'll recognize the connection. Hamantaschen are pastries with three corners, in the shape of Haman's hat. They are filled with prune or apricot preserves, and by consuming them, we're eradicating Haman in yet one more way. Because the best part—the filling inside—is hidden, it's also a perfect symbol for this Holiday of Hidden Miracles.

Let There Be Light

Hamantaschen, the name of the Purim pastry, is Yiddish for Haman's pockets. According to one interpretation, it reminds us of the story that Haman's pockets were full of bribe money, which he used to convince the king to approve his plan to kill all the Jews.

♦ Passover has all the items mentioned as part of the seder, together with a heavy emphasis on foods made out of matzo. For those who aren't culinary disadvantaged, you will surely recognize matzo brie, matzo balls, and maybe even *knaidlach*, which are matzo balls stuffed with matzo meal.

Woman preparing Matzoh Knaidlach *by Alphonse Levy.*

(Art Resource, NY/The Jewish Museum, NY)

♦ Israel Independence Day allows Western palates to re-experience the delights of Middle Eastern foods. *Falafel* (fried balls of spicy mashed chick peas), *tahina* (a sauce made from sesame paste), and *hummus* are probably more popular in Israel than pizza.

♦ Shavuot is known for its dairy dishes, especially those made with cheese. Among the reasons given is that after the Jews witnessed the Revelation on Mount Sinai, they were too hungry to take the time to slaughter an animal, prepare it ritually, and cook its meat, which they now had to do after they received all these laws. Furthermore, on returning to their tents after spending all day receiving the Torah, they found their milk had gone sour, and therefore they had to turn it into cheese. The most popular Shavuot dishes are *blintzes* (crepes filled with sweetened cottage cheese), cheese-filled *kreplach* (dumplings), cheesecakes, and other cheese-filled pastries.

♦ Tisha B'Av, which has no special food item on the day itself because it is a fast day, is preceded with a meal that requires the eating of an egg. An egg symbolizes rebirth. Its shape reminds us that the reality of life, like the oval, goes round and round. As we face a day of tragedy, we remind ourselves that bad times turn into good, that the same prophets who preached destruction also promised rebirth and resurrection.

From the Mountaintop

You've surely heard of seven-layer cake. In Sephardic communities, Jews bake a "seven-heaven" cake for Shavuot. Each layer of the cake is intended to form a step. The top of the cake is decorated with replicas of Mount Sinai and the tablets of the Ten Commandments.

Enjoy all these foods throughout the course of the year, and your heart will overflow with gratitude so complete you may even forget your heartburn!

Graceland—for Jews

For pious Jews, every meal has to end the same way it began—with a blessing. The grace after meals, Judaism teaches, is far more important than the blessings recited before we eat. It's not hard to bless God for the food you're about to eat when you're hungry. The true test of a person comes when he or she is fully sated. "And you shall eat, and you shall be satisfied, and you shall bless the Lord your God." (Deuteronomy 8:10) Gratitude should move a person spiritually even more than great need.

Schmoozing

If you pick up a starving dog and make him prosperous, he will not bite you. This is the difference between a man and a dog.
—Mark Twain

But before some Jews say grace at the conclusion of a meal, they fulfill a fascinating law. All knives are removed from the table because knives, like swords, are symbols of war and violence. When God gave instructions for building the altar in the Temple, he insisted that no knives or swords be used to cut the stones for this holy object that serves to bring peace between people.

The table we eat on is like an altar of God, and the food we consume from it is considered similar to a sacrifice. We eat not like animals but in order to feed the receptacles of our souls. That's why the dining room isn't just a restaurant. It's more like a mini-Temple, where Jews worship God, even in the way they consume their food and drink.

The Least You Need to Know

- ◆ Blessings recited before eating food serve to restore the sense of wonder we ought to feel at the miracle of our daily bread.

- ◆ The Shabbat, the weekly Sabbath, as well as all the holidays of the year, have their own special foods that serve to emphasize the spiritual message of the day in a culinary manner.

- ◆ Jews say grace after meals because prayer should not only be said by those who are hungry and in need, but also by those who have been the recipients of God's blessing.

Chapter 20

The Bedroom

In This Chapter

- Why sex is kosher
- What Judaism teaches about the sex drive and its fulfillment
- Some advice about good sex—as well as frequency
- When sex is a no-no and why
- The bath that's about more than cleanliness

Judaism recognizes that sexual desire stems from the same divine source as a person's spirituality. It acknowledges the body as God's handiwork, which must be respected and is perceived as no less holy than the soul. Body and soul together can be harmoniously fused, and even the most mundane actions on earth can be invested with meaning and spirituality.

Why is the sexual drive so strong? Judaism responds, precisely because it is so holy. Without sex, the world would not reproduce itself. Without sex, God's creation of the world could not endure. Without sex, God's presence on Earth would be diminished with no more human beings in His image. That's why God made sex so much fun. And that's why God said sex isn't just permissible, it's a divine commandment.

Sex Is Kosher

Puritans didn't just give us the word *puritanical*. Their most harmful legacy is the linking of their sexual attitudes with the supposed intent of the Bible. In Jewish thought, nothing could be farther from the truth. The chief figures of the Bible don't shy away from love and sex. As the great tenth-century Babylonian philosopher Saadya Gaon pointed out, "How could there be anything reprehensible about such relations if God's holy men engaged in them with His approval? These men engaged in the act as a natural part of their lives, a part that in no way detracted from their singular relationship to God."

Schmoozing

Of all sexual aberrations, chastity is the strangest.

—Anatole France (1844–1924), French author and Nobel Prize winner

Even more striking is the fact that the prophets Hosea, Isaiah, Jeremiah, Ezekiel, and Malachi all didn't hesitate to use vivid sexual imagery to describe the relationship between God and the Jewish people. God gave us eyes because He wants us to see. God blessed us with ears so that we can hear the sounds that surround us. So, too, God gave us sensual desires and sexual organs—and their gratification is as just, as legitimate, and as necessary as the fulfillment of any other human task or need.

Sex—You Can't Do Without It

Jewish law says that a man commits himself to three major obligations in marriage: He owes his wife food, clothing, and sex. To refuse any one of these three is tantamount to annulling the marriage. To say, "We're married—but no sex," is an illegal contradiction.

From the Mountaintop

The *Ba'al Shem Tov*, the founder of the Hasidic movement, was once asked how a person could differentiate a real religious leader from a phony. He answered: "Ask him if he knows a way to prevent impure sexual thoughts. If he says he does, he's a charlatan."

The Talmud has an interesting dispute between two major rabbinic schools of thought. In a case where a man forbids himself from having intercourse with his wife by taking a vow, the school of Shammai says that the wife has to go along with the vow for up to two weeks. If it lasts any longer, the court can then compel the husband to divorce her. The school of Hillel, however, disagrees and says the longest she can be compelled to accept this deprivation is for only one week. The final decision, accepted into Jewish Law, is in accord with the school of Hillel.

What's even more remarkable about this ruling is that its intent was to safeguard the *woman's* sexual needs. Strangely enough, in talmudic times, the rabbis were more concerned that the husband not say, "I have a headache," than his wife. Since women require the protection of the law in greater measure than men, the emphasis was on their rights in marriage—and it's noteworthy that Judaism acknowledged, long before Spike Lee, that "She's Gotta Have It."

How Often?

Because marital relations are a mitzvah, the fulfillment of a religious obligation, Jewish law has to be precise with its details. Obviously, the first requirement for making sweet music Jewish style is "high fidelity." Let's not forget, though, that "high frequency" in this case is also commendable.

In the Talmud, the rabbis prescribe a minimum schedule for sexual relations based on a man's profession:

> For men of independent means, every day. For laborers, twice weekly. For donkey drivers, once a week. For camel drivers, once every thirty days. For sailors, once every six months.
>
> —Talmud, Mishna, Ketubot 5:6

Your guess is as good as mine how a corporate lawyer fits into this picture—and if a teacher should be put in the same category as a camel driver or a laborer!

Travel for Business?

I can't leave this sexual catalog of job descriptions without sharing with you one more remarkable law appended by the legal codes to this discussion:

If somebody originally worked in a trade near his home, which put him in the category of those expected to have greater frequency of sexual relations, and he wanted to change to a trade where he would have to travel far from home, his wife could have legally prevented him from changing jobs. She was permitted to insist

---

Pulpit Story

Moses comes down from Mount Sinai and tells the people, "I have good news and bad news." "What's the good news?" the people ask expectantly. Moses replies, "I got God down to Ten Commandments." "What's the bad news?" the Jews continue. "Adultery is still in."

 Schmoozing

Jewish thought never identified 'the flesh' with the evil impulse, nor regarded flesh and spirit as hostile to one another.

—Robert Travers Herford (1860–1950), Christian scholar and author

that she didn't want her sexual rights diminished. (Of course, there must have been wives who would have given anything for their husbands to become sailors!)

Always on Shabbat

Some years ago there was a movie called *Never on Sunday*. The theme revolved around what is euphemistically called "a house of ill repute" in a religious Catholic country that closed its doors on Sunday. The prostitutes might have offered sex for money, but they weren't going so far as to do it on "the day of the Lord." That's a far cry from the advice given by Jewish law: "The ideal time for sexual relations is on Friday night, the time of the holy Sabbath. Let the holy act be performed on the holy day."

The opposite of "Never on a Sunday" is the Jewish commandment "Always on Shabbat."

Only because sex is elevated to the sublime level of holiness can we understand this incredible linkage between the most spiritual day of the week and the fulfillment of our sexuality. This is how Rabbi Jacob Emden, the great eighteenth-century German Talmudist and *halachik* (Jewish legal) authority, explained it:

> The wise men of the other nations teach there is shame in the sense of physical feeling. This is not the opinion of the Torah and of our Sages. We understand marital relations to be good, elevated, and beneficial for the body and the soul ... and absolutely holy. If marital relations were not holy and pure but shameful, how could the Holy One, blessed be He, be involved? Undoubtedly, therefore, when the act is performed with the proper attitude and intent, there is no human activity which is on a higher level of holiness.

Ask the Rabbi

The Ten Commandments teach that we may not lust after another man's wife. The implication seems clear to me: You should certainly lust after your own wife.

Getting to Know You

If sex is holy, though, it's because the Bible identifies it with another word. It's extremely important that the four-letter word for sex in the Torah is *know*. There's almost no one who hasn't heard the leering question, "How well do you know her? Did you get to know her in the biblical sense?" It seems that even those with the slightest background in Bible know that the phrase "and Adam knew his wife Eve" is the way intercourse is indicated. But they probably don't think about the profound implication of the expression.

By describing ideal sex as "knowing," the Torah elevates a physical act to the level of an intimate and meaningful relationship. Without really "knowing" another, the meeting of genitalia doesn't even deserve to be described as sex. If sex is to count for anything, it has to include two people's profound visceral knowledge of the very essence of each other. Two people have to become, as the Bible puts it, "one flesh." The physical closeness is to mirror the emotional unity and mutual awareness.

Some years ago there was a song with the lyric, "Hello, I love you, won't you tell me your name?" We just had sex, is the implication, and now it might be time for me to know a little bit more about you. That is what Judaism, with its idealization of sex, cannot accept. Sex without "knowledge" can at most produce orgasms. Sex, in which two caring and sharing people meet in the most intimate knowledge of each other, is capable of producing for its participants not only ecstasy but the exalted state of holiness.

Have an Affair with Your Wife

There's an incredible story in the Talmud about a student who sneaked into his teacher's bedroom and hid under the bed. Hours later, he was rewarded by being able to eavesdrop on what he wanted to hear. He listened intently as his rabbi passionately engaged in sex with his wife. What he could not see he tried to imagine as he heard the moans from above his hiding place. Suddenly, because of an inadvertent movement, he was discovered. The rabbi, in shock and amazement, demanded to know what his prize pupil was doing under the bed. The student's answer has to stand as an all-time classic response: "This, too, is Torah, and I need to learn!"

There's no record of the rabbi's reaction. The Talmud implies that the student surely went too far in his love of study. But his mistake, however, was only in his insistence on first-hand observation. Jewish texts make clear that his major assumption was in fact correct. "This, too, is Torah."

Judaism is a religion of life, and its laws cover every possible situation. Something as important—and as we've shown even holy—as sex is not surprisingly the subject of a great deal of rabbinic discussion, guidance, and law. They don't go so far as to write how-to manuals for better sex, but rabbis do try to teach ways in which marriage can capture the passion of an affair and how to banish boredom from the bedroom.

 From the Mountaintop

The mitzvah of sexual relations is not dependent upon the possibility of conception. Those who are sterile, beyond child-bearing age, or pregnant are all still obligated by Jewish law to engage in sexual relations. Sex isn't just to have a family; it's also for fun.

Men are cautioned about the need to engage in foreplay and be sensitive to women's slower time for sexual arousal. The Talmud advises that, "Those who restrain themselves during intercourse to enable their wives to have orgasms first, their children shall be male." (Babylonian Talmud, Niddah 31b) Commentators suggest that in a society where fathers wanted sons, this was a most powerful inducement to ensure that husbands be concerned not only with their own sexual release but also with that of their wives.

With Love and Mutual Consent

Whereas marital rape has only fairly recently been acknowledged as a crime, the thirteenth-century Biblical scholar Moses Nachmanides wrote: "A man should never force himself upon his wife and never overpower her, for the Divine Spirit never rests upon one whose sexual relations occur in the absence of desire, love, and free will. The Talmud tells us that just as a lion peers at his prey and eats it shamelessly, so does an ignorant man shamelessly strike and sleep with his wife." (Babylonian Talmud, Pesachim 49b) Rather, "act so that you will warm her heart by speaking to her charming and seductive words."

Schmoozing

Part of my being able to talk about issues of sexuality has to do with my being so Jewish. Because for us Jews there has never been a question of sex being a sin, but of sex being a mitzvah and an obligation.

—Ruth Westheimer, sex therapist "Dr. Ruth"

Caresses, caring words, tenderness, and modesty, combined with passion—all these are ideals for which Judaism found biblical support and legal expression. Sometimes it's hard to think of all those long-bearded and saintly looking scholars being so knowledgeable about, and so interested in, sexual matters. Then again, they always seemed to have large families and radiated a sense of inner joy and contentment, so maybe they did know something after all!

But Sometimes It's a No-No

With all of its "user-friendly" advice about sex, Jewish law seems extremely strict in one way. And for Jews who obey biblical commandments, this particular law has become the cornerstone of Jewish marital relations. In Hebrew, it's called *Taharat Ha Mishpachah*, meaning "family purity."

"Family purity" limits sexual activity between husband and wife. Every month, there is a time when married people can be friends, but not lovers. Sex, according to biblical law, follows an on-again, off-again cycle. The specifics of the law are fairly complicated. The gist of it, though, is this: Sex is forbidden from the onset of the wife's menstrual period until the end of seven days without any sign of blood following the wife's period—a time of about twelve days.

Unfortunately, a great deal of confusion has arisen about this law because of an awkward mistranslation of a Hebrew word in the Bible. To express the idea that one's wife was sexually off-limits, the Torah calls her "TA-MEY." Because it refers to a religious category, it has no really accurate English equivalent. The word "impure" is probably the best we can do if we remember it stresses a legal/spiritual idea rather than a value judgment of status. Sadly, a number of translations use a far more negative term. They translate "TA-MEY" as "unclean." Of course, that is insulting and it explains why so many women and men have been put off by a seemingly offensive biblical attitude to a very natural biological function. But the Bible never calls a woman unclean. The errors of translators shouldn't be held against God.

While this is another example of a chok, a law for which no reason is given, a number of attempts have been made to understand the Divine motive:

- Abstinence—just like absence—does make the heart grow fonder. The most universal and perilous enemy of marital bliss is boredom. Even sex can become routinized. Steak every day loses its glamour. Jewish law deals with the problem by creating an enforced monthly honeymoon. Those who must separate sexually rediscover each other with renewed passion. The Jewish law of family purity is based not on a desire to diminish sex but to improve it. "Less sex for better sex" is seen by the Talmud as its slogan.

- True love should be more than just physical contact. To force a married couple to base their relationship on conversation, on friendship, and on a meeting of the minds for half of every month is an ideal that hasn't been explored outside of the Jewish legal system, but it may help to explain the far lower rate of divorce among observant Jews.

Schmoozing

Sex has become one of the most discussed subjects of modern times. The Victorians pretended it didn't exist; the moderns pretend that nothing else exists.

—Bishop Fulton John Sheen

Schmoozing

… Not every peak emotion may be expressed through sex; nor can every newly married spat be settled in bed. One also learns quickly that sex cannot be used as a reward or punishment. If sex is being regulated by a force "out there," it becomes less a matter of one or the other controlling or manipulating.

—Blu Greenberg, contemporary Jewish writer

◆ Sometimes one or perhaps both spouses need to rest up without being made to feel guilty or sexually inferior. In our society, where we so often talk about sexual performance, it can be a gift to know there are times we're not expected to perform.

◆ There could even be something said for the ideal of self-discipline applied to the strongest urge that seeks to control us. Freud made us aware that creativity comes from our ability to redirect sexual energy. Sublimation isn't denial; it's positive redirection. Freud understood the benefit of channeling the sex drive into other areas. Judaism, centuries before, legislated it into family life. Who knows if Jewish genius and creativity aren't in some way related to the laws of family purity?

The Jewish Bathhouse

Would you believe that the Jews are the original "baptists"? Baptism, the belief in the holiness of immersion in water, goes back to a Jewish practice most commonly related to sex. As part of the laws of family purity, according to biblical law, a ceremonial ritual has to be performed by the wife every month before spouses can resume normal marital relations. Just as during the time of the Temple, priests had to undergo immersion before being permitted to enter upon their sacred duties, women require the same rite once a month before engaging in sex. The striking comparison between these two sacred duties was meant to impress upon couples the holiness of their sexual activity.

> **Schmoozing**
>
> When Judaism demanded that all sexual activity be channeled into marriage, it changed the world.
>
> —Dennis Prager, contemporary American editor, author, and radio talk show host

One other situation has this requirement of immersion. Converts to Judaism, as the final act of their conversion, undergo this symbolic spiritual purification that makes them be considered reborn. The wife who rejoins her husband sexually is just like a new person, spiritually pure and hopefully as appealing as a newlywed bride.

Place of Purification

The place where this immersion is performed is in Hebrew called a *mikvah*. It is specially constructed according to religious specifications. Many people make the mistake of thinking that its purpose is cleanliness. That would make a home shower or bath just as suitable. A mikvah isn't concerned with dirt. It removes spiritual impurity in a religious as well as a mystical sense.

Remnants of mikvahs can be found going back thousands of years. At Masada, near the Dead Sea, where Jews committed suicide in the days of the Romans rather than allow themselves to be taken captive as slaves, we can still see the mikvah they built and used.

Jewish law decrees that if a community is strapped for funds and they lack both a synagogue and a mikvah, the mikvah takes priority. Jews can make do without a place for communal prayer, but they can't survive without the facility needed for the purity of family life. A mikvah is one of the lesser known sites for contemporary secular Jews. For the observant, it's one of the most important. It's what makes sex kosher.

Let There Be Light

Mikvah, the place for ritual immersion, comes from the Hebrew word for "gathering." It is a gathering of rainwater, water from the heavens, which is then used to wash away human sin and impurity.

The Least You Need to Know

◆ Sex in Judaism isn't a concession or an un-Godly activity, but a mitzvah, a divine commandment.

◆ The sexual drive was created by God so that we might enjoy creating and is considered a legally protected need for both men and women.

◆ Judaism is concerned not only with the quality of sex, but also with its frequency, recommending optimal times per week for the sex act and especially encouraging relations on Shabbat.

◆ The Bible refers to intercourse as "knowing" to emphasize that more than a meeting of body parts, there must be a meeting of minds and souls.

◆ Jewish law offers guidance for sexual happiness and fulfillment for both partners because sex is a major component of a happy marriage.

◆ Judaism forbids sex at certain times every month, probably because "abstinence makes the heart grow fonder."

◆ A mikvah, the ritual bath used by a wife before resuming sex and by converts before becoming Jews, is not concerned with cleanliness so much as it is with spiritual purification.

The Child's Room

In This Chapter

◆ The challenge of parenthood

◆ When to begin parenting

◆ How to be a good parent

◆ What children owe parents

The Roman historian Tacitus condemned the Jews for "their contemptible prejudice that it is a crime among them to kill any child." To a world that considered children expendable, Judaism proclaimed the biblical view that a child is the highest of human treasures. When the first Jew, Abraham, realized that his wife, Sarah, was barren, he cried out, "O Lord God, what will You give me seeing that I go childless?" Children may be a burden, but they are also the greatest blessing.

In the last chapter, you read about what Judaism has to say about sex. Now let's see what it has to tell us about parent-child relationships.

Everybody knows raising children isn't easy. We all sympathize with the seventeenth-century Earl of Rochester, John Wilmot, who admitted, "Before I got married, I had six theories about bringing up children; now

I have six children and no theories." No one has all the answers, and one of the main reasons there are no perfect children is because there are no perfect parents. The least we can do, though, is try to be the best parents possible. And one of the best ways to do this is to learn from the past. The oldest of all religions must surely have some valuable insights.

Bringing Up Baby

Judaism couldn't agree more with the English language, when it tells us that the word *parent* is both a noun and a verb. It's not enough to be responsible for the biological birth of a child. To parent also means to train, to educate, to teach—to take responsibility for the development of a human being as a worthy member of society. King Solomon, considered by Jewish tradition to be the wisest of all men, said it all: "Train a child in the way he should go and when he grows old he will not depart from it." (Proverbs 22:6)

Schmoozing

There are only two lasting bequests we can hope to give our children. One of these is roots; the other, wings.

—Hodding Carter, Pulitzer Prize–winning contemporary author

Schmoozing

'Tis education forms the common mind / Just as the twig is bent the tree's inclined.

—Alexander Pope (1688–1744), English poet

Children are like clay, waiting to be shaped and formed. And parents are the sculptors, who in great measure determine the destiny of their offspring. That's what the Bible means when it teaches, as part of the Ten Commandments, that God "visits the sins of the parents unto the children, unto the third and fourth generation." The mistakes we make can have lasting consequences. The flip side of this is that we can also positively influence our children in enduring ways.

"Give me half a dozen healthy infants and my own world to bring them up in," Professor John B. Watson, an American psychologist (1878–1958), wrote, "and I will guarantee to turn each one of them into any kind of man that you please." Over-confident and unrealistic? For sure.

Judaism doesn't guarantee success—after all, the child's free will can undo our best efforts—but our faith demands that we try. "And you shall teach your children. ..." Every teacher isn't necessarily a parent, but every parent is a teacher.

When Do You Start?

A mother of a child of five, goes the apocryphal story, came to see Sigmund Freud. She heard of his expertise in the field of child development. "Please tell me," she asked, "when is the best time to begin my child's education." "Hurry home quickly," Freud answered, "you've wasted the best five years already!"

I can't be sure that Freud's answer was influenced in any way by his Jewishness. But whether he realized it or not, Freud expressed an idea that has its source in Jewish tradition.

The Talmud tells how the mother of the Talmudic sage, Rabbi Joshua ben Hananya, would carry him to the house of study in his cradle to accustom him to the words of Torah. The rabbis agreed that this must have played an important role in turning the child into one of the giants of Israel.

The Bible itself expresses a similar idea. Once every seven years, the Book of Deuteronomy tells us, the king would read the entire Torah in front of all the people. It was a mitzvah to attend. The law demanded that "men, women, and children, even infants" be a part of this religious ritual.

What significance could it possibly have for a child who still lacked the ability to understand the Torah? Mystics respond that the ceremony makes its impact, not on the mind, but on the soul. Freudian psychologists might speak of its effect on the subconscious. Other commentators simply say that this is the Bible's way of teaching that when it comes to the spiritual training of children, it's never too early.

Learn the Letters with Honey

How do you begin to teach your child the *aleph-bet*, the Hebrew letters of the alphabet? There is a beautiful custom that goes back many years, which, to my knowledge, has no secular counterpart. The letters are carefully formed of honey on a sheet. The child is taught

Ask the Rabbi

The Talmud says a parent also has to teach a child how to swim. Swimming in the days of the Talmud was a necessary survival skill. Today, I think it means you've got to teach them how to drive a car safely, to stay away from drugs, the danger of AIDS, and everything else we have to know to make it in this crazy world.

Schmoozing

I re-emerged to Judaism, I would say, through the birth of my children and through a decision I had to make about how I was going to raise them. I think that's what led me, that and events around the world, very naturally—to the decision to make *Schindler's List*.

—Steven Spielberg

how to read each letter in turn and then allowed to lick it off the page. "See, my child," the instructor says, "how sweet are the letters. They will always give you joy as you continue to taste the sweetness of the words they form." That's how Jews figured out a way to literally make Torah sweet to their children.

Can't you just picture the incredible scene of little kids pleading, "Please let me do some more homework, I'm hungry,"?

How to Be a Good Parent

From the Bible, the Talmud, and the major works of Jewish scholars, some parenting principles stand out as crucial concepts of Judaism. Though far from all-inclusive, the following are a good start:

◆ Children need lots of love, but they also need discipline. King David is criticized in the Bible for his failure to be strict with his son Absalom. The son who was never taught any limits ended up rebelling against his own father and attempting to kill him. Really loving a child means saying "no" sometimes. "The thing that impresses me most about America," the Duke of Windsor once said after a visit, "is the way parents obey their children." That's reversing the biblical commandment and a sure prescription for trouble. Discipline without love is cruel, and love without discipline is counterproductive.

◆ "A man should never impose an overpowering fear upon his children and household," the Babylonian Talmud teaches. It records the story of a little boy who broke a bottle on the Sabbath. His father, in great anger, warned him that he would soon receive a beating. The boy committed suicide. The rabbis then passed a law: No parent should threaten a child with physical punishment.

◆ Discipline, if it is to have any meaning, must follow the bad behavior immediately. It is illegal in Jewish law for a mother, for example, to say to a child who has misbehaved, "Just wait until daddy gets home." (*Shulkhan Arukh*) When you put your hand on a hot stove and it immediately hurts, you learn not to do it again. The pain is indelibly associated with the action. Wait five hours until the child is punished, and there is no link between the deed and the discipline. You have accomplished absolutely nothing.

◆ Favoring one child over another is such a terrible thing to do that it was actually responsible for Jewish exile. Do you remember the biblical story of Joseph and his brothers? The brothers hated Joseph for a reason; their father Jacob had given Joseph a coat of many colors (yes, that was the Technicolor Dreamcoat). How would you feel if you were being dissed by your own father? Parental favoritism produced envy, and that envy led to the brothers ganging up on Joseph and selling him down the river. The Jews finally ended up in Egypt as slaves. Whose fault? Rabbis don't hesitate to give Jacob part of the blame.

◆ Show-and-Tell is good parenting. All tell and no show is more than hypocritical— it's just plain stupid. You can't tell your children they must always speak the truth, and then let them hear you tell the ticket seller at the movies that they're under the age of 12 when they're not. Your words coupled with your actions are what's required in order to guide them.

Schmoozing

Children need love, especially when they do not deserve it.
—Harold S. Hulbert

◆ The Midrash describes Moses pleading with God not to destroy the Jews after they sinned by worshipping the golden calf. It's true, he says, the Jews built a golden calf—but it was You, God, who caused it to happen because You allowed them to have too much gold. Imagine, Moses continued, a father who gave his son unlimited gold, jewelry, and precious gems (translated in modern terms, that's unlimited use of a credit card) and allowed him to go to a place filled with houses of immorality. "What shall the son do so that he not sin?" Moses said. God, according to the Midrash, agreed that it was partly His own fault and He forgave the Jews! To give to your children is good. To give excessively is to be guilty of forcing your child to face too much temptation.

◆ Children are people—only littler. Judaism forbids insulting others publicly, and this includes children. Judaism demands you respect other's opinions and not put them down, and this, too, includes children. Judaism demands that you not destroy other people's self-esteem, no matter how old or young. A person's age is never sufficient grounds for disrespect.

Schmoozing

If a child lives with approval, he learns to live with himself.
—Dorothy Law Nolte, contemporary author

◆ There is a section in the Bible that deals with "the rebellious child." He is punished for the sin of "not listening to the voice of his father and his mother." The

Talmud says the Bible emphasizes "to the voice" because the child is guilty only if the parents spoke to him with *one* voice. If parents contradict each other, and the child gets mixed messages, it isn't his fault if he disobeys. Parents who demand respect should deserve respect—first and foremost by respecting each other. "What's the most important thing a father can do for his children?" a Hasidic master was asked. His answer: "To love and respect their mother."

God Never Said It'd Be Easy

Schmoozing

Insanity is hereditary; you can get it from your children.

—Sam Levenson (1914–1980), American comedian

The rules aren't easy. What makes it even harder, as many psychologists have pointed out, is that most of us become parents long before we have stopped being children. Yet as difficult as parenting is, so, too, are its potential rewards great and without measure. Judaism adds one more comforting message to its words of guidance: Try, and with God's help you will succeed.

Honor Mom and Dad

Here's a shocking thought: Children aren't the only ones with rights. Parents have them, too. As a matter of fact, the Ten Commandments chose to emphasize the obligations of a child to a parent rather than the reverse. The reason is probably simple. Parents don't have to be commanded to take care of their children. It's natural and intuitive. Children, though, need to be reminded every so often that honoring father and mother isn't just divine for the parents—it's a divine obligation.

Rabbis long ago noted that the Torah doesn't command children to love their parents. It's hard to command a feeling. What it asks for is a way of acting toward those who gave you life and took care of you before you could take care of yourself.

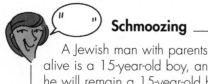

Schmoozing

A Jewish man with parents alive is a 15-year-old boy, and he will remain a 15-year-old boy until they die!

—Philip Roth, *Portnoy's Complaint*

Sadly, there often comes a time when the tables are turned and parents need children to take care of them. That's when the Yiddish proverb says it best: "One mother, ten children is easy; ten children, one mother is impossible." Mothers can readily take care of their children but children find it too difficult to take care of aged mothers. Honor and respect demand more than just the words, "I love you." In an age of entitlement, it's important to stress, as Judaism does, that parents are also entitled.

Love First, Money Second

Jewish law says that, "Honor consists of providing parents with food, drink, and clothing; covering them; and aiding them to enter and to leave the house (i.e., providing them with opportunities for social contact)." (Babylonian Talmud, Kidushin, 31b) The Talmud makes clear, though, that honor means more than financial support. Listen to this remarkable passage from the Palestinian Talmud:

> One man may feed his father fattened chickens and inherit hell, and another can put his father to work treading a mill and inherit the Garden of Eden.
>
> How is it possible for a man to feed his father fattened chicken and inherit hell? There was once a man who used to feed his father fattened chickens. Once his father said to him, "My son, where did you get these?" He answered, "Old man, old man, shut up and eat, just as dogs shut up when they eat." Such a man feeds his father on fattened chickens but inherits hell.
>
> How is it possible for a man to put his father to work in a mill and still inherit the Garden of Eden? There was a man who worked in a mill. The king ordered that millers be brought to work for him. Said the man to his father, "Father, you stay here and work in the mill in my place and I will go to work for the king. If insults come to the workers, I would prefer that they fall on me and not on you. Should floggings come, let them beat me and not you." Such a man puts his father to work in a mill, yet inherits the Garden of Eden.
>
> —Kidushin, 1:7

It's not only what you do for your parents but how you do it. Pay for the nursing home costs, but speak to them with disrespect, and whatever you do is worthless. Treat them with kindness and show them reverence, even though you can't afford to give them material goods, and you fulfill the Fifth Commandment.

You'll Get Your Reward

Did you ever notice that only one of the Ten Commandments has a reward mentioned in the Bible? "Honor your father and your mother," it says, "so that your days on earth be lengthened." Length of life is the gift promised to those who keep *this* law, not for any other. "What makes this so special?" the commentators ask.

Perhaps, they answer, the Torah isn't telling us here about a divine reward but rather a natural consequence. What happens in heaven is never mentioned. We'll find out about that after we leave this Earth. But one thing you can be sure of. If you honor your parents, your children will see it and use it as a model for their own behavior. When you get old, they'll understand that they have to treat you the way they watched you treat your elders. In doing that, you will be blessed with a long life—because your kids will see to it.

Pulpit Story

The Eskimo father was intrigued as he watched his son building a wooden sled. "Why are you building that so large?" he asked. "Oh," said the boy, "I'm building it for you. I saw you take your father up to the mountain top and leave him there when he became very old. I know that the time will come for you, too, eventually. I want to be prepared to do for you what you did for your father."

The Least You Need to Know

- Being a good Jewish parent demands training, educating, and inspiring a child.

- Judaism offers many important parenting guidelines, including the need for discipline and ways to it; and the evils of excessive anger, favoritism, and of giving too many material things.

- Parent-child is a reciprocal relationship that imposes obligations on both.

- Honoring parents, one of the Ten Commandments, stresses deed over feeling, and reverence and respect over love.

- For honoring parents, the Bible promises the reward of long life.

Part 6

The Synagogue

Christians, if they're religious, go to church on Sunday mornings. The most devout Orthodox Jews attend synagogue three times a day. And on Saturdays and holidays, they spend hours at a stretch praying, reading from the Torah, listening to a sermon, and—to be honest—talking and socializing. The synagogue is a very important part of an observant Jew's spiritual life.

Part 6 takes you on a tour first of the building, its architecture, its important accessories, and its religious leaders. You'll learn why people pray and the different reasons for Jewish prayer. You'll become familiar with the *siddur*, the Jewish prayer book, and discover why its words speak not only to God but to the hearts of all those who use it.

Finally, you'll learn about "designer fashions" for the synagogue—the shawl with the fringes, the boxes on the hand and the head, and the reason why some Jews feel they always have to have their heads covered.

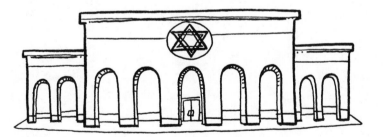

Chapter 22

Let's Take a Tour

In This Chapter

- ◆ The three functions of a synagogue
- ◆ Synagogue architecture
- ◆ What's inside a synagogue
- ◆ Who are the people who keep the synagogue functioning?

"There must be another way," the Jews in Babylonia said to themselves long ago. They had seen their holy Temple, built by Solomon, burned to the ground in 586 B.C.E. Now they found themselves exiled in a foreign land, without an opportunity to worship in a way they had done for centuries. How could they get along without the House of God, they wondered.

Inspiration came with an insight for which we are grateful to this day. It was revolutionary and had never been thought of by worshippers of any other religion. If there were no longer a Temple in Jerusalem, Jews reasoned, they would have to create mini-Temples where they were. Surely "God's glory fills the whole world," as the Psalmist had assured them. God's presence can't be restricted to one location. And so Jews created the synagogue, a place of religious service that would later be imitated both by the church and the mosque.

The synagogue universalized God. He could be encountered everywhere. Exile no longer deprived the Jewish people of their ability to communicate with their Lord. Without the possibility of bringing sacrifices, which could only be offered in the Temple of Jerusalem, prayer became the recognized substitute for animal offerings. Priests were no longer crucial for worship; every Jew became a religious functionary, everyone stood as an equal before God.

Every tragedy, goes the saying, carries within it the seed of greater blessing. Even as the Babylonians destroyed a national religious center, they paved the way for the Jews to create a far more democratic and universal way of worshipping God.

What's the Name on the Door?

"I'm going to shul," says one Jew.

"I'm going to the synagogue," says another.

Ask the Rabbi

This suggestion is really a law: When you go to the synagogue, it's a mitzvah to walk quickly or run; when you leave, you should depart very slowly. Your walk should illustrate that you're eager to get there and sorry to leave.

From the Mountaintop

Part of the name *Beit Ha-Knesset*, the word *Knesset*, is today the official name of the Israeli Parliament. That's because it, too, is a place of gathering—and also because as an Israeli politician, you have to learn how to pray in order to survive!

"I'm on my way to the temple," says a third.

Guess what? They're all headed to the same place.

Shul, synagogue, and *temple* are different descriptions for an institution of Jewish life that fulfills so many different functions it needs at least three different names.

In Hebrew, the place we most often refer to as the synagogue has three different names as well:

- *Beit Ha-Knesset*, literally, House of Gathering. That became the word synagogue, from the Greek *synagoge*, congregation.

- *Beit T'filah*, House of Prayer

- *Beit Midrash*, House of Study

Which one of these three descriptions would you put on the front door? It probably depends on which of the three functions of a synagogue you consider most important.

The House of Gathering

Beit Ha-Knesset emphasizes the synagogue's social role. It brings people together, it allows for communal activities, it permits people to gather regularly and maintain bonds of friendship and support. It's the "meetin' and greetin' place" and, if you stop and think about it, that, too, makes it a religious and even a holy place. After all, "love your neighbor as yourself" may be the most important verse in the entire Bible.

In its social role as *Beit Ha-Knesset*, synagogues often assumed the role of Jewish centers, even affixing those words to their names. A Jewish center sponsors social gatherings, has sisterhood meetings and teas, men's club activities, such as bowling leagues, even—if it's wealthy enough—builds a shul with a pool. What in the world do all these activities have to do with a House of God? They bring Jews together, and whatever unifies the people may be considered holy, goes the response.

> **Schmoozing**
>
> In all their long history, the Jewish people have done anything scarcely more wonderful than to create the synagogue. No institution has a longer continuous history, and none has done more for the uplifting of the human race.
>
> —Robert Travers Herford (1860–1950), scholar and author

The House of Prayer

Did you know that you don't need a synagogue in order to pray? Do you realize that the vast majority of the prayers in the Bible are those offered by individuals in private, sacred moments? Prayer is a meeting of man and woman with God and can take place anywhere. Yet a second major function of the synagogue is to be a Beit T'filah, a House of Prayer.

What's so special about communal prayers? The early rabbis were certain that praying as part of a group is far more effective than praying alone. As a matter of fact, some of the holiest prayers are only permitted to be recited when there is a *minyan* present—a quorum of 10 people, which is the minimum necessary, according to Jewish Law, to establish a congregation. A group experience, the rabbis explain, creates a more spiritual climate than when we are by ourselves. Imagine the difference between reading a play from a book in

> **Schmoozing**
>
> My beloved friend Dudya Silverberg goes to shul to talk to God, and I go to shul to talk to Dudya.
>
> —Leib Goldhirsch (1860–1942), American journalist, quoting from his father's autobiography, *The Right Time*

your own home and seeing it performed in a crowded theater. The emotion of prayer comes from sharing it with others.

Public prayers are also less selfish than private ones. As part of a congregation, we ask God to help not only us but the entire community. We feel the pain of other people, we know that we are not alone in our suffering, and we remove ourselves from the pettiness of our own concerns to gain a larger perspective. Jewish prayer always uses the plural "we," rather than the singular "I." Never do we say grant *me* long life, health, and strength—it's always grant *us*.

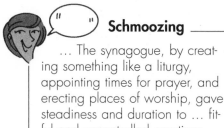

Schmoozing

… The synagogue, by creating something like a liturgy, appointing times for prayer, and erecting places of worship, gave steadiness and duration to … fitful and uncontrolled emotions, and raised them to the dignity of a proper institution.

—Solomon Schechter (1847–1915), scholar

Awareness of communal responsibility is created by standing together with others. "In the multitude of people is the King's glory," said King Solomon in his Book of Proverbs. (14:28) The more people, the better. That's why we need a synagogue as a house of prayer. You'll never do it as well or as effectively by yourself.

The House of Study

The synagogue, for centuries, was a place where Jews went, not only to pray, but to study. Prayer, the early rabbis said, was man and woman talking to God. Study, on the other hand, is God talking to man and woman. If we want God to hear our requests, we've got to listen faithfully to what He wants from us.

Facing the Ark in the interior of a Florence, Italy, synagogue.

(Art Resource, NY/Alinari)

The synagogue always had copies of the holy books needed for study. Jewish Law decreed:

> Dwellers of a city may compel each other to buy a scroll of the Torah and the Books of the Prophets and the Writings, so that whoever of the public wishes to read in them may do so. And in our days when books are printed … one may compel the purchase of necessary printed books, such as the entire Hebrew Bible with a *Rashi* commentary, the Mishna, the entire Talmud, the *Shulkhan Arukh*, so that whoever desires to do so, can come and study from them.

—Mishna B'ruhrah, a major commentary on the Shulkhan Arukh

The community-owned books were kept in the synagogue, the *Beit Midrash*. That meant that the synagogue was really the first open library in history.

Since that's where the books were, the synagogue for many centuries also served as a center for the formal education of children. Jewish Law was the first to make universal education compulsory. The Talmud tells us that "there were 480 synagogues in Jerusalem and each and every one of them had an elementary school and a secondary school." These were most often found in the same building that served for prayer and communal gatherings.

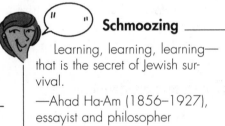

Schmoozing

Learning, learning, learning—that is the secret of Jewish survival.

—Ahad Ha-Am (1856–1927), essayist and philosopher

So Which One Do *You* Belong To?

Now you can see why the name by which you refer to the synagogue is so important. If you say "shul," the Yiddish word for "school," you're stressing the educational focus. If you say "center," or "synagogue," you're emphasizing the social component. The name "temple" is most specifically identified with the role of prayer. The bottom line? Whichever one makes you happy. Just be pleased to know that every one of them is a mitzvah!

Is That the Lost Ark?

Let's walk into the shul now (okay, I'll admit it, I'm most comfortable with this name) and look around. There, in the very front, is the most imposing and important area. Of course, it's the Ark—in Hebrew, *Aron.*

Synagogue architects all have different ways to make this the focus of the sanctuary. The fact is, there are hardly any rules on exactly how a synagogue should be built. Yet if you're in Bangkok or Bombay, New York or Jerusalem, there is the Ark either directly before the front wall or built into it. It contains the Scrolls of the Law, the five books of Moses written on parchment attached to two rollers that allow for easy reading.

The Ark in the days of the First Temple was originally a golden box in which the two tablets of stone—given by God to Moses with the Ten Commandments inscribed—were kept. The Ark was made of gold, both outside and inside. The rabbis explained that this was a symbol to teach that those who house Torah within themselves—the scholars—must be completely golden. In other words, outer signs of piety must be accompanied by inner goodness.

On the Ark of the Temple there were two winged figures, the *cherubim*. They were angels with the faces of children. The symbol reminds us that only when children are trained in the way of the Torah can Judaism survive. Children represent the future and preservers of Torah, of Jewish teachings.

From the Mountaintop

The Ark was built with two staves, or poles, on each of its sides, placed in rings, which were never to be removed. That was so the Ark could always be readily transported. Symbolically, it told the Jews that wherever they would go around the world, they must carry the Torah with them.

When the Jews wandered in the desert and had a portable temple, or tabernacle, they placed the Ark in the most prominent position. Then they hung a beautiful curtain, the *parochet*, in front of it to separate it from the items of lesser holiness.

Today, you know that that Ark is lost (and even Harrison Ford wasn't able to bring it back). Every synagogue in the world remembers it, though, with a pretty good replica. We don't have the tablets of stone with the Ten Commandments, but we do have a copy of the Torah. We put it into our arks, place a parochet in front of it, and show our respect and devotion.

Who knows, maybe some day we'll finally live to see some Raiders of the Lost Ark succeed where others failed, and we'll have a chance to pay homage to the original. Until then, as the rabbi keeps saying, please rise as we open the ark—and acknowledge that the Torah is the holiest item in the synagogue.

East Is East and West Is West

Please don't forget that since the congregation has to face the ark during prayer, its ideal place is in the east. Jews must pray toward Jerusalem, the Holy City, which for us in the western world is in an easterly direction. Sometimes the synagogue's location prevents placing the ark just where it should be. In that case, so as not to shame the Torah within it, the congregation faces the ark, even though they're not "pointing" their prayers in the right direction. Somehow we're sure they'll find their way just the same. But if at all possible, remember that where the sun rises is the way we ideally want to face as we pray.

From the Mountaintop

Where is the lost Ark? No one knows for sure. According to one story, it was buried in a spot on the Temple Mount when the Temple was destroyed. Another says it was carried off into Babylon and is still there somewhere to this day. Yet another version has it that the Ark is buried in a cave near the River Jordan. All agree, though, that we'll see it again when Messiah comes.

Look at the "Furniture"

Now look around the synagogue some more. There are other things that should catch your eye:

- The eternal light, called in Hebrew the *ner tamid*, hangs right in front of the ark. One of the things Jews pray for is that there not be a power outage because the eternal light should always be on as a symbol of God's constant guiding light and protection. In the Bible, the Jews were told "to cause a lamp to burn continually" (Exodus 27:20–21) in the Tabernacle. The light also stands for the light of the Torah, which the Jewish people must always keep burning brightly.

- The *bimah* is an elevated platform from which the Torah is read. In many congregations, according to ancient tradition, it is placed in the middle of the synagogue. That demonstrates that the Torah must be at the center of Jewish life and that it is the heart of the Jewish people. More practically, it makes it easier to hear the Torah reader—an important consideration when you know that synagogue decorum isn't always what it's supposed to be!

- *Yizkor* tablets, tablets of remembrance of the dead, often appear on at least one of the walls of a synagogue. This is a plaque that bears the names of people who've passed away, with the dates of their death. Lights attached to this plaque are lit on the days commemorating the time of death as well as on the holidays when the prayer of Yizkor is recited. It is a mark of respect and a way to remember loved ones who have passed on but whose lights still continue to shine in the lives of their survivors.

◆ One more feature of synagogue architecture has special symbolic significance. A shul must have windows, ideally twelve of them corresponding to the twelve tribes of Israel. Windows teach us to look out to the world around us. They remind us that self-centeredness goes against the meaning of real prayer. Only when we care about others will God listen to our personal requests.

◆ Orthodox synagogues also have one more special feature. A *mechitzah*, a divider, separates men from women during prayer. This tradition goes back to the time of the Temple when there was an *ezrat nashim*, "the court of the women," to keep the sexes apart. Orthodox Jews believe that commingling men and women serves as a distraction when we're supposed to concentrate on God. Conservative and Reform Jews have done away with this synagogue architecture. (This is one of the many differences between the major branches of Judaism that you'll read about at greater length in Chapter 25.)

From the Mountaintop

A beautiful interpretation of the twelve windows required for a synagogue, corresponding to the twelve tribes, is that they are there to teach that there's more than one way to God. Every "tribe" is encouraged to have its own window to heaven.

From the Mountaintop

Unlike a priest, a rabbi is invested with no special holiness and has no greater link to God than any of the congregants. A rabbi's claim to leadership is based solely on superior knowledge of the Torah, Talmud, and other Jewish texts. If a rabbi doesn't know, he's no rabbi.

Schmoozing

The life of a rabbi is essentially a life of pathos … for he is isolated at the very center of the community he "leads" and serves as the spokesman of a group tradition at a time when the group has become all but traditionless.

—Morris Adler (1906–1996), American rabbi and author

Who Are These People?

Now that you've familiarized yourself with some of the synagogue's physical features, it's time to meet the cast of characters. These are the people who make the synagogue function.

Meet the Rabbi

So what does the rabbi do? Ask a disgruntled congregant—and there are always a few of those in every congregation—and he'll tell you, "My rabbi is invisible six days a week and incomprehensible on the seventh." For some strange reason, Jews often have a love-hate relationship with their rabbis. They respect the profession but delight in tearing down its practitioners. (Some people claim it's a defense mechanism so that no other rabbi should ever again think himself so great that he claims to be God!)

Yet a rabbi probably has one of the most difficult jobs of all because he has to do so many things well and please almost everybody while doing them.

A rabbi is supposed to teach and preach. And provide religious guidance and direction. And offer leadership to a community. And be an executive director. He has to be a fundraiser and a pastor. A rabbi has to be a friend to all, but not too friendly or else he's in danger of becoming "just one of the boys." A rabbi has to speak at every occasion and say just the right thing, which, of course, everyone believes is something different!

In spite of all this, Jews realize that the rabbi is the true heart of the synagogue. He defines it, publicizes its presence, and creates its climate of spirituality. If successful, the rabbi builds not only a synagogue but a Jewish community. And that's why there are still Jewish young men who are inspired by the challenge and want more than anything else to grow up to be a rabbi.

 Schmoozing

A rabbi who they don't want to drive out of town isn't a rabbi, and a rabbi who they actually drive out isn't a man.

—Israel Salanter Lipkin (1810–1883), Lithuanian rabbi

Let There Be Light

The word *rabbi* comes from the shorter Hebrew word *rav*, or "teacher." Adding the *i* at the end makes its meaning "my teacher." Saying "my rabbi" is redundant—"rabbi" by definition is "my teacher."

Listen to the Cantor

The cantor, in Hebrew, *chazan*, has an awesome role. He is the messenger of the congregation for their prayers. In fact, in Talmudic times, a cantor was called the *sheliach tzibur,* the "deputy of the congregation." He leads the congregation in prayer and chooses the melodies to inspire them. Very often the cantor will also have duties in the synagogue relating to choral programs, a choir, and the preparation of Bar and Bat Mitzvah students.

According to Jewish law, cantors must meet a number of rigid qualifications. They have to be pious and God-fearing, so that their prayers have merit. They cannot be too young or else

 Let There Be Light

The Hebrew word for cantor, *chazan,* comes from a root meaning "to see." The cantor must see the needs of the community and then pray for them.

they lack sufficient maturity for the seriousness of the task. They ought to be married (some say so that they can empathize with those who suffer), so that their prayers come from the heart of someone who needs to support a family. Ideally, cantors should have children so that they understand the foibles of others and have developed patience and compassion.

Oh, and one other thing. If possible, it wouldn't be a bad thing if they also have a good voice!

What's a Sexton?

No, no, no. We'd better not call him by the English name, or you'll get the wrong idea about the job description. The Hebrew name is *shammash*, just like the word *shemesh*, which means "sun." The shammash takes care of the practical aspects of synagogue life. He supervises the daily services, takes care of the ritual items of the synagogue, and usually serves as the Torah reader and even as a substitute for the cantor. He's what we might call the religious "handyman," ready to tackle almost any of a synagogue's duties.

In most communities, the *shammashim* (plural of *shammash*) also serve another major role: They are usually the scapegoats who take the blame when people are upset about not receiving their "well-deserved honor"! (What do I mean by "honor"? Turn to "Stop the Services" in Chapter 23 to find out.)

The Lay Leaders

Congregations, it's been humorously said, are democracies *and* dictatorships. They're democracies before its leaders are elected, and dictatorships afterward. Synagogues are run as independents. There's no central body controlling their activities. There is usually a board of directors, as well as officers, headed by a president. The president works with the rabbi (and sometimes against him) to direct the congregation's activities.

When serving the congregation with dedication and commitment, lay leadership can make an extremely positive contribution to a community. It is one of the blessings of Jewish life that those without special religious credentials can, if they're willing to give of their time and effort, play an important role in their communities—a role comparable even to that of their spiritual leaders.

Why Is Everybody Talking?

So you've seen the physical building and you've met the important people. There's one more thing I should tell you. It's something that almost always strikes people who come into a synagogue for the first time and observe the services. Okay, granted, it doesn't happen everywhere, but it's frequent enough to warrant a little warning.

> **Pulpit Story**
>
> Jake went looking for his old friend Abe, who he heard had just become president of his local synagogue. "Do you know where I can find Abe Cohen?" he asked one passerby. "That miserable no-goodnick," the man replied, "he's two blocks from here." The more people he asked, the more he received the same type of answer—complaints about Abe, the shul president. When he finally saw Abe, Jake asked him, "Tell me, why did you become president of a synagogue?" "To tell you the truth, Jake, it's a lot of work," Abe replied, "but I do it for the honor."

You'd expect a synagogue to be as quiet as … well … as a church. Most often, it isn't. Children are often running around. People turn to their neighbors and talk. The decorum is far from perfect. I've asked Jews in my travels around the world to try to help me understand why this is so. Invariably they answer me in a way that's helped me to understand the role of a synagogue much more profoundly: "Rabbi, what do you mean, why do I talk here? You know why I don't sit rigidly in my seat without speaking to anyone? It's simple. It's because here I feel at home."

The Least You Need to Know

◆ A synagogue has three names, corresponding to its three functions: a house of prayer, a house of study, and a house of assembly.

◆ The Jewish House of God brings people together socially, is a library and place for communal study, and is the ideal setting for praying with others.

◆ The ark containing the Torah, the most important place in the synagogue, reminds us of the original Ark in the Temple, which contained the Ten Commandments.

◆ The architecture of the synagogue has few requirements other than the position of the ark (which faces east in western countries), the need for windows, an eternal light, a bimah and—in Orthodox synagogues—a divider separating men from women.

◆ The synagogue is staffed by several people, headed by the rabbi and including lay leadership.

23

Let Us Pray

In This Chapter

- ◆ The reasons for prayer
- ◆ The different kinds of prayer and how prayer works
- ◆ When prayer is inappropriate
- ◆ How often Jews pray and why it is so
- ◆ Important passages from the Jewish prayer book
- ◆ Pray from the heart

Nobody can explain it. Scientists are stumped. But newspapers around the world reported the amazing finding: Prayer works. People who pray get better faster. Not only that. People for whom others pray, even when they don't know about it, recover at a far greater rate. Imagine—not even a placebo, just a prayer, and the effect is powerful!

Prayer, for many people, accomplishes miracles. For others, it remains a mystery. The Ba'al Shem Tov, founder of the Hasidic movement, offered a parable: A deaf man walks by a window with people dancing inside. He can only see them gyrating peculiarly, making weird motions. He thinks they are insane. That's because he doesn't hear the music. If you're deaf to the melody, the motions of prayer seem absurd. If you believe that conversation between man and God is possible, prayer not only makes sense, it lets you dance to celestial music.

But Why Should I Pray?

Logically, though, prayer just doesn't seem right. Jewish philosophers, like those of many other faiths, ask a number of obvious questions:

Is God such an egotist that He has to hear us praise Him?

Why should I waste my time asking God for anything? If He wanted to give it to me, I would already have it.

Am I bringing my problem to God's attention by praying? Does that mean He wouldn't realize what I'm going through or be sensitive to my suffering if I didn't remind Him? What kind of God could He possibly be if He needs mortals to fill in His work list?

Is God, in the words of the famous Protestant clergyman Harry Emerson Fosdick, a "cosmic bellhop" who waits for us to place our orders so that He can fill them in accord with our instructions?

And finally, if we believe that God is smart enough to run the world according to His will, isn't prayer the ultimate act of arrogance—asking Him to change His mind?

> **Pulpit Story**
>
> A Hasidic rabbi spoke about the importance of a radiant countenance. A very plain-looking woman asked, "But what would you do if you had a face like mine?" Without a moment's hesitation, the rabbi replied, "I would pray. If you light it up from within, any face will shine on the outside."

Judaism answers all these questions by explaining that prayer isn't meant to change God; it's meant to change us. Prayer is not supposed to save us, it's supposed to make us worth saving. Prayer is a way of looking at our lives with an awareness that God exists. It's a self-preached sermon for which we are the audience.

In English, the word *prayer* comes from a Greek root, *precare*, which means "to beg." That, Judaism believes, would be pointless. To pray in Hebrew is *L'hitpallel*, which means "to stand in self-judgment." As I pray, I heighten my awareness of God. Standing in His presence, I feel more spiritual and become a better person. That better person hopefully then deserves more from God. And that's how I can have my prayers answered.

Rabbi Herbert Goldstein put it beautifully in his *Letter on Prayer:*

> Prayer serves not only as a petition to God, but as an influence upon ourselves. Our sages, centuries ago, voiced the thought echoed by the great poet, George Meredith, who declared, "He who rises from his worship a better man, his prayer is answered." Prayer has the double charm of bringing God down to man and lifting man upward to God.

That's why the Hebrew words *Da Lifney Mi Atoh Omed*, "Know Before Whom You Stand," are prominently displayed at the front of almost every synagogue.

Praying is not so much *asking from* as it is *being with*. People who pray a lot spend a lot of time with God. Isn't it true that you're known by your friends and influenced by your peers? Hang out with God a lot, and you'll not only feel like a new person—you'll be one!

 Schmoozing

Prayer is a vehicle for self-transformation. It is not begun with the hope of changing God's mind to give us things we haven't received. It is cultivating our own will power to establish a direct connection to God so that we can change ourselves and become capable of receiving what has been waiting for us all along.

—Rabbi David Aaron, Director of the Israelight Institute, in *Endless Light*

The Three Kinds of Prayer

It's a shame that the English language has only one word for what Judaism recognizes as three different kinds of conversations with God. Each one has its own purpose, is illustrated by different prayers, and expresses a unique idea about our relationship with God. There are prayers of praise—*shevach*. There are prayers of request—*bakashah*. There are also prayers of thanksgiving—*ho-da'ah*. If you haven't expressed all three, you haven't fulfilled the Jewish obligation of prayer.

Praising God

Of course God doesn't need our praise. *We* need to awaken within ourselves a sense of awe at His work. Abraham Joshua Heschel, one of the most outstanding Jewish theologians of the past century, pointed out that the real problem of religious thinking today is not whether God is dead or alive, but whether we are dead or alive to His realness. "A search for God," he said, "involves a search of our own measure, a test of our own spiritual potential." If we don't praise God, *our* souls become deadened to the holiness all around us.

Praising God for His qualities, such as compassion, righteousness, and mercy, has a second benefit. To praise the Divine One is to acknowledge what is divine. He gives us goals to which we can aspire. Prayers of praise teach us what we should strive to be.

Schmoozing

Blessings intensify life by increasing our awareness of the present even while awakening our connections to the past.

—Marcia Falk, *The Book of Blessings*

Prayers of Request

Jews pray, "Please fulfill the requests of our heart *for good*." Not simply "Give us what we want," but "Give us only that which is good for us." Who knows, I may be asking for things that, if granted, would make my life a living hell. George Bernard Shaw was right: "There are two tragedies in life. One is not getting what we ask for. The other is getting it."

We ask, but in Jewish prayers we also qualify by acknowledging that, "You know best—so do what You see fit." That's why, even when we don't get what we want, we can still feel that our prayers are answered. Judaism assures those who pray that "God hears all our prayers." That means He listens and then does what He thinks is best.

That's surely what the author of this anonymous observation had in mind: He asked for strength that he might achieve; he was made weak that he might obey. He asked for health that he might do greater things; he was given infirmity that he might do better things. He asked for riches that he might be happy; he was given poverty that he might be wise. He asked for power that he might have the praise of men; he was given weakness that he might feel the need of God. He asked for all things that he might enjoy life; he was given life that he might enjoy all things.

Schmoozing

I have lived to thank God that all my prayers have not been answered.

—Jean Ingelow (1820–1897), English poet and author

Pulpit Story

A victim of the Holocaust who had lost a leg prayed to God. An atheist standing nearby couldn't help commenting, "How foolish! Do you really think God will give you back your leg just because you pray?" The survivor calmly replied, "Of course I don't expect God to give me back my leg. I'm praying to God to help me to live without it."

Prayers of Thanks

God doesn't really need to hear a "thank you." Yet we need to become people who never fail to be grateful. How shameful to go through life without expressing thanks to God for His gifts. Get into the habit of taking divine blessings for granted, and you'll be just as ungracious to your parents, to your husband or wife, or to your friends. Who wants to have a relationship with someone like that? All of us ought to share the sentiment of the Hasidic rabbi who regularly prayed, "O God, You have given so much to me, I dare to ask You to give me one thing more—a grateful heart."

From the Mountaintop

Would you believe that even God prays? According to the Talmud, God's prayer is this: "May it be My will that My mercy overcome My anger, and My loving qualities overcome My strict traits; that I treat My children with a quality of mercy and that I always deal with them beyond the letter of the law." Surely we can say "Amen" to that!

God, Am I Bothering You Too Much?

A classic Yiddish story has it that a very pious man kept on praying all day, every day. His neighbors who were not so devout seemed to be blessed more than he was. He couldn't understand why his prayers, repeated so often, weren't answered while those of others were. He went to his rabbi for help. The rabbi, as only he was able to do, went directly to God for a response. "All day my disciple turns to you for help. Why don't you hear him and grant him his wishes?" the rabbi prayed. "Because," responded God, "he's a *nudnik*—he just doesn't stop bothering me!"

Don't take that little story too literally. God obviously doesn't resent people who want to talk to Him—even if it is full-time. Yet there's a profound truth in the story because Judaism does recognize there's a time when people pray too much. That's when they put all of their trust in God and use it as an excuse for their own inaction.

Basic to Jewish thought is an idea that the Midrash makes part of a famous story: When the Jews left Egypt, the Egyptian army chased them and caught up with them at the Red Sea. The Jews didn't know what to do, so they started praying. God turned to Moses and said, "Why are you crying out to me? Speak to the Jewish people and tell them to *move!*"

The Midrash clarifies: This is not a time for lengthy prayer. The Jews have to learn that when they're in trouble, they shouldn't count on God to do everything for them. God only helps those who help themselves. Prayer can't be a substitute for human effort.

I'm sure Napoleon never heard the words of these sages, but somehow he was smart enough to come to the same conclusion. "When you fight," he told his men, "fight as if everything depended on you. When you pray, pray as if everything depended on God."

Take It Three Times a Day with Meals

How many times a day should a person pray? Judaism says the answer is three. The soul must be fed as often as the body. Jews pray in the morning, afternoon, and evening: *shacharit, minchah,* and *ma'ariv.*

The three prayers in Jewish tradition were initiated by the three founders of the Jewish religion, Abraham, Isaac, and Jacob. Each one of them decreed a special time for prayer. In accord with their practice, Jews to this day recite the morning prayer of Abraham, the afternoon prayer of Isaac, and the nighttime service of Jacob.

Rabbis recognize in this series of three services an important idea about the meaning of prayer:

- ◆ Abraham prayed in the morning because his life, like the morning, was filled with brightness and joy. He taught us that prayer is proper as it pours out of a mood of gratitude for all that we enjoy on Earth.

- ◆ Isaac's life, although at first sunny, became progressively darker. He was forced to endure personal hardships and watch one of his children, Esau, go astray. His biography could be summed up as the setting of the sun. No coincidence then that his prayer is the afternoon prayer, teaching us that even as things start to go wrong we should not lose contact with God.

- ◆ Jacob had a life filled with pain almost all of his days. He could have called his life story *Night,* just as Elie Wiesel did. Yet Jacob prayed. Darkness doesn't have to lead us to total despair or renunciation of our belief in a just and compassionate God.

To pray three times a day is to acknowledge, as Abraham, Isaac, and Jacob did, that prayer is appropriate in every circumstance of our lives.

Schmoozing

When she prayed, an exuberant calmness, a glow, would come over my mother that I never saw at any other time. Her eyes would be glazing; her cheeks would seem fuller, and she had full cheeks. It was as if she had a direct link to God.

—Herb Kalisman, quoted in *Growing Up Jewish in America: An Oral History*

But Why Not Only When I Feel Like It?

There have always been those who argued that prayer should only be spontaneous. To set fixed times for it is to turn it into something like a dreaded piano practice. Why shouldn't we only pray when and if we feel like it? For the same reason, the rabbis answer, that those who aren't forced to practice will never truly learn how to play the piano.

The famous line, "How do you get to Carnegie Hall? Practice, practice," is just as valid for a far more important question: How do you learn to speak to God? Practice, practice.

Take a Prayer Book, Please

The Jewish prayer book is called the *siddur*. That's because it's arranged in a logical "order," and the Hebrew word for order is *seder* (just like the Passover seder, with its fixed order; see Chapter 12). The Torah is God's gift to us; the siddur is our gift to God. God wrote the Bible to share with us His essence. Man wrote the prayer book to verbalize his innermost thoughts and to confide his profoundest feelings. If either a Bible or a siddur falls to the ground, a Jew is obligated to quickly pick it up and kiss it. That's how Jewish law teaches us that we consider both of them holy.

Don't be confused if you see people turning the pages of a siddur backward. That's because more Jewish prayer books are written in Hebrew, which is written from right to left. You'll have to get used to the fact that the cover is what you normally think of as the back of the book.

Schmoozing

Jews commonly assume that, like breathing, one should be able to pray automatically. When they find that they cannot do this, they are disconcerted and annoyed. Prayer, however, is a skill; it does not usually come spontaneously to people ... most of us require extensive training and practice to master the skill of prayer.

—Elliot Dorff, *Knowing God: Jewish Journeys to the Unknowable*

Of course, *siddurim* (plural of siddur) usually have English translations as well. We'll be talking later (Chapter 25) about the different denominations in Judaism—Orthodox, Conservative, Reform, and Reconstructionist—and every one of them has a different emphasis, not only on kinds of prayer but on language as well. Orthodox Jews pray almost entirely, if not exclusively, in Hebrew. They feel the holiness of the language in which God wrote the Bible means it's the most fitting vehicle for our prayers as well. We should speak to Him as He spoke to us. Other Jews, while accepting the sacred stature of Hebrew in the main, opt—in different degrees—for comprehension by the congregants over the traditional sanctity of the language of our ancestors. Rest assured that whichever siddur you choose and whatever your words, be they as strange as Swahili, will be understood by the One whom you are addressing.

Ask the Rabbi

Entering a synagogue? Then repeat the words of Balaam, whom the Bible tells us came to curse the Jews but ended up blessing them: "How goodly are your tents, O Jacob, your dwelling places, O Israel." (Numbers 24:5)

The siddur begins with a blessing that Jews have to memorize. It has to be said every morning as soon as we open our eyes:

> I gratefully thank you, O living and eternal King, because you have returned my soul within me with compassion—abundant is your faithfulness.

The first words out of the mouth of every pious Jew every single day are an expression of thanks. Hopefully, that sets the tone for the rest of our waking hours.

The siddur continues with a list of blessings thanking God for giving us the Torah; for giving us sight; for clothing the naked; for allowing us to stand; for providing us with our needs. And yes, there's even a blessing to be said after using the toilet:

> Blessed are you our God, King of the universe who fashioned man with wisdom and created within him many openings and many cavities.

> It is obvious and known before Your throne of glory that if but one of them were to be ruptured or if but one of them were to be blocked it would be impossible to survive and to stand before you. Blessed are you O Lord who heals all flesh and acts wondrously.

Even relieving your body of its natural wastes presents an opportunity for a sense of wonder and thanksgiving for the genius of human anatomy!

The siddur has the order of the three daily services, as well as those for the Sabbath and every holiday. There is a special section with a list of blessings for unusual or special moments. There's a blessing for seeing lightning, hearing thunder, spotting a rainbow in the sky. There's a blessing upon experiencing an earthquake, or seeing a comet or an exceptionally

Ask the Rabbi

Whenever you hear a blessing recited, you are supposed to answer "amen," which literally means "I believe." You can't just listen to someone uttering something so true without affirming that you agree.

beautiful mountain. There's a blessing for meeting an outstanding Torah scholar and another for getting together with a genius in any secular field.

And—I'm serious about this—there's even a blessing for seeing an exceptionally beautiful woman. I have memorized it because I still hope the day will come when I run into Sharon Stone—and I want to be religiously prepared!

From the Mountaintop

Is there really a blessing for the czar like Tevye says in *Fiddler on the Roof?* You bet there is. It should even be said if you chance to meet with the president of the United States, a king, prime minister, or any ruler of a country. It is, "Blessed are You O Lord our God, King of the universe, who has given of His glory to human beings."

Some Favorite Prayer Book Passages

"Which one of your children do you love the best?" is a question I can never answer. My children are all equally beloved, as I'm sure yours are, too. That's pretty much the way I feel about prayers in the siddur as well. When they asked Michelangelo to name his favorite work, he replied, "My next one." It's almost impossible to pick from so much perfection. Yet some prayers—because of their special meaning, their message, or their prominence in the service—have to be mentioned.

The Sh'ma

The *Sh'ma Yisroel* is comprised of three paragraphs that come from the Torah. The Bible commands that they must be read twice a day, "when you lie down to sleep and when you arise." The opening line, "Hear O Israel, the Lord is our God, the Lord is one," is the most succinct expression of the faith of a Jew.

That's why, as I've already indicated, it's the verse Jews are to recite as their last words on earth. It's the sentence uttered by martyrs to explain why they choose death over an ungodly life. Its words, according to mystics, have the power to spiritually transform a person just by being recited, almost like a religious mantra.

Ask the Rabbi

Before you begin the *Shemoneh Esrei* prayer, take three steps backward and then three steps forward— as if you were entering the presence of a king. When you finish, repeat the same procedure to indicate you're going back to the world after your private encounter with God.

Stand Up and Be Heard

The *Amidah*—literally, "the standing," because it must be recited in standing position with feet together like the angels—is also known as the *Shemoneh Esrei*. The term *Shemoneh Esrei* means "eighteen" because this prayer originally consisted of eighteen blessings. It contains all three types of prayer: praise, request, and thanksgiving.

Ask the Rabbi

Don't kneel when you pray. That's a Christian, not a Jewish, mode of worship. The Shemoneh Esrei is called the *Amidah*, "standing," because Jews in prayer don't beg on their knees, but in standing straight hope to change themselves to be worthy of having their prayers answered.

In it, Jews ask not only for what they need but are reminded of what their true needs really are. The first of these, even before the request for help and prosperity, is for knowledge and insight.

In response to a historical event, a nineteenth blessing was added to the Amidah sometime after the destruction of the Second Temple (70 C.E.). A heretical sect of Jews slandered fellow Jews to the anti-Semitic Roman government and caused them much harm. That's why, to this very day, Jews include this additional prayer, "And for slanderers, let there be no hope."

Although there are now nineteen blessings in this major prayer, Jews most often still refer to it by its older name, "the eighteen."

The concluding prayer of the Shemoneh Esrei has always been especially moving for me. After a Jew finishes praying for almost everything, almost as an aside, he adds these words:

> My God, guard my tongue from evil and my lips from speaking deceitfully. To those who curse me, let my soul be silent, and let my soul be like dust to everyone. Open my heart to Your Torah, then my soul will pursue Your commandments. As for all those who designed evil against me, speedily nullify their council and disrupt their design. Act for your name's sake, act for your right hand's sake, act for your sanctity's sake, act for your Torah's sake. That your beloved ones may be given rest; let your right hand save, and respond to me.

With a prayer like that, who can go wrong?

And in Closing ...

The *Aleinu* is the prayer that closes every prayer service. It expresses the idea that upon us there rests a special obligation to make God's greatness known to the rest of the world. It concludes with the hope that "You will reign for all eternity in glory, as it is written in Your Torah: The Lord shall reign for all eternity." (Exodus 15:18) And as it is said: "The Lord will be King over all the world, on that day the Lord will be one and His name will be one." (Zechariah 14:9)

A Jew can say he's finished his prayers only after he acknowledges his mission to bring the entire world closer to God.

Stop the Services

Every Sabbath, every holiday, and several times during the week, Jews literally interrupt the service in order to have a Torah reading. It's a way of saying that we can't just talk to God without also listening to Him. The Torah reading is what turns the prayer service into a dialogue.

A Torah is taken from the ark and brought to the *bimah*, the raised platform (see Chapter 22 if you forgot what that is). A selection from the Torah is read aloud by a reader, who is called the *Ba'al Kore*. The Torah, written on parchment, has no vowels or punctuation. The reader is expected to have memorized the correct reading, as well as its special melody. Believe me—that's not easy.

People are called up to the Torah (in many synagogues, seven of them on the Sabbath) to recite blessings, and this is considered one of the greatest honors a synagogue has to offer. The honor is called an *aliyah*. A section is read every week to complete the entire five books of Moses in the course of a year. (As I explained in Chapter 12, the completion of the entire reading and the new beginning take place on Simchat Torah.)

The honor of being called to the Torah is especially reserved for people commemorating special moments. A person reaching the age of religious maturity, a bridegroom on the Sabbath before his wedding, a parent celebrating the birth of a child, someone who has completed a period of mourning—all reaffirm their link with God's law by this public demonstration of love for the Torah.

From the Mountaintop

The Torah is read on three days of the week: Monday, Thursday, and *Shabbat*, the Sabbath. The Torah is compared to water and no one can live without water for three days. That's why the maximum time without a public reading is from Monday to Thursday. More than two days, and Jews would expire from spiritual thirst!

Ask the Rabbi

Be very, very careful if you are given the honor of lifting up the Torah (called *hagbah*). If you were to drop it—God forbid—everyone witness to this scene would have to fast and give charity.

Let There Be Light

An **aliyah,** from the word meaning "going up," refers either to the honor of being called up to the Torah or to taking up residence in the Land of Israel. To a Jew, either one "elevates" one's existence.

"Feelings ..."

When the Torah portion for the day is completed and the scroll is placed back into the ark, the prayer service continues. Synagogue services are known for their length. On Sabbath morning in some Orthodox and Conservative synagogues, they can run for three to four hours, on holidays even longer. So many prayers, so much to tell God! Yet with all the words, Jewish tradition is still sensitive enough to the real meaning of prayer to refer to it in Hebrew as *avodah sh'belev*, the worship of the heart. The lips verbalize, but the heart is the real source of the message. Words without feeling are less effective than feelings without words.

The Hasidim, the disciples of the Ba'al Shem Tov in the eighteenth century, realized how far people had strayed from a proper understanding of this mitzvah. They told stories that had a profound impact on their listeners and that slowly reintroduced fervor to mechanical prayer and feeling to what had become almost meaningless ritual. We, too, can learn a great deal from some of these classic tales.

Here are a few of them:

◆ A little boy was left orphaned and had no one to teach him how to read Hebrew. Standing in the synagogue on Yom Kippur, he cried because he did not know how to pray. All he had learned was the names of the letters. Tearfully, he repeated them over and over and said, "O God, I do not know how to turn these letters into words, but I offer them to you with all my heart. Please make of them beautiful prayers to express how much I love you." At that moment, the rabbi of the congregation saw the heavens open and heard God say, "Because of the prayers of the orphan who gave me his gift of heartfelt letters, I will save the Jewish people."

◆ The Ba'al Shem Tov was able to see what occurred in the heavens on New Year's Eve. The prosecuting angel had placed the sins of the Jewish people on one side of the scale. The angel for the defense had put all of the good deeds the Jews performed during the entire year on the other side. The scale weighed far more heavily toward the side of sin. It appeared the Jews were doomed. The angel for the defense made one last appeal: "You have only placed on the scale the actual prayers offered by Jews. You failed to include the fervor and the enthusiasm with which they were offered. I ask that you note how much more the words weigh when there is added to them the feelings of the supplicants." It was so ordered. The scales turned to the side of merit. And the Ba'al Shem Tov forever after told his disciples that how they prayed was far more important than what they prayed.

◆ On a frigid winter day, the Ba'al Shem Tov walked with his disciples and noticed an idol that had been fashioned out of ice by some non-Jewish villagers. "Behold," the rabbi said, "how remarkable. We use water to purify ourselves. We immerse in the mikvah, and it makes us holy. Yet, you see, when it freezes, water can be turned into an idol. So too, when the heart becomes cold, even its prayers are no more than pagan worship. Without warmth and feeling, holiness disappears."

◆ A Hasidic rabbi suffered from an injured right foot. Yet during his prayers, he kept stomping on it in his fervor. After his prayers, a disciple asked him, "But why, Rabbi, did you stomp on the foot that hurts you so?" The rabbi responded, "Had I realized while I was doing so that it was the foot that was hurting, I certainly would not have continued."

◆ A disciple of the Ba'al Shem Tov complained that after praying he was afflicted with headaches. The rabbi chided him severely, "What has worship to do with the head? Worship is service from the heart, not a labor of the mind."

◆ A Hasidic rabbi entered the synagogue and visibly drew back in shock. "Why is the rabbi so disturbed? Why does the rabbi not enter and walk toward his accustomed place near the ark?" his students asked. The rabbi told them, "I cannot move because the synagogue is so filled with prayers that I am unable to get past them." His disciples took it as a compliment. But the rabbi continued, "Your prayers were said without any feeling. They were uttered merely as an act of obligation, without sincerity. As you spoke them, your thoughts were profane, you were concentrating on your business and on private matters. That is why your prayers didn't ascend to the heavens but remained here, in the synagogue, lifeless and unavailing. That is why I could not move past them. They block my way, and I cannot go to my place until you direct them properly to God above."

◆ And finally, the advice of Rabbi Mendel of Kotsk, the renowned nineteenth-century Hasidic master: "He who is about to pray should learn from a common laborer, who sometimes takes a whole day to prepare for a job. A woodcutter, who spends most of the day sharpening the saw and only the last hour cutting the wood, has earned his day's wage."

So if we sometimes wonder why our prayers seem so lifeless and ineffective, maybe it's because we keep forgetting the rabbinic teaching of Joseph Ibn Pakuda that "Prayer without the heart is like a body without the spirit."

The Least You Need to Know

◆ Prayer is meant not to change God's mind as much as it is to alter ourselves through the act of communion with Him.

◆ The three kinds of prayer—prayers of praise, of request, and of thanks—serve different purposes but share in sensitizing us to the importance of God's role in our lives.

◆ Prayers aren't a substitute for action and human initiative, but must complement our efforts because, as tired as the old cliché is, it's true that "God helps those who help themselves."

◆ Jews pray three times a day, reflecting three different moods and motivations for speaking to God.

◆ Although spontaneous prayer may seem preferable, fixed times are necessary to ensure that we practice often enough to be able to pray properly when we really need to.

◆ The prayer book has blessings for every important occasion of life, and passages from the siddur represent some of the most beautiful expressions of humankind's spiritual creativity.

◆ The key to prayer is "service of the heart," and its effectiveness is predicated primarily on its sincerity and fervor.

Chapter 24

Synagogue Fashion

In This Chapter

- ◆ The law of fringes on four-cornered garments
- ◆ The meaning of the *tallit*, the prayer shawl
- ◆ The symbolism of the *tefillin*, the phylacteries on the hand and the head
- ◆ Why some Jews keep their heads covered at all times

Fashion, Oscar Wilde said, is a form of ugliness so intolerable that we have to alter it every six months. The good news for Jews is that synagogue fashion hasn't changed in thousands of years. If there were such a thing as a time machine that could take us back many centuries, we would search in vain for Calvin Klein clothes, but we'd immediately relate to the "designer-wear" items we'd see in the synagogue.

Clothes serve as our uniforms. They separate us from animals. That's why Judaism insists that our garb say something about our dedication to God. Long before someone thought of an alligator logo, Judaism insisted we add a reminder of our "designer" to what we wear.

Fringe Benefits

In the days of the Bible, people wore four-cornered garments that looked just like ponchos. God told Moses: "Speak to the Jewish people and instruct them to make for themselves fringes on the corners of their garments throughout the ages ... thus you shall be reminded to observe all of my Commandments and to be holy to your God." (Numbers 15:37–41)

The fringes, called *tzitzit* in Hebrew, were God's way of getting us to put the equivalent of a string around our finger so as not to forget something important. The strings attached to our clothing would be visible at all times. "Look at them," God says, "and recall all the Commandments of the Lord and observe them so that you do not follow your heart and eyes and your lustful urges."

How, you ask, can a few little strings accomplish so much? A string around the finger can help you remember to pick up a bottle of milk on the way home—but fringes to help you recall *all* the Commandments? The rabbis offer some ingenious answers:

From the Mountaintop

The *tzitzit* no longer have the required thread of blue because the required color could only be obtained from a certain marine animal called *hellizon*, which we can no longer identify. Rather than use a color that's even slightly off, we keep all the fringes basic white.

From the Mountaintop

It was David Wolffsohn, the famous philosopher and historian, who suggested that the Israeli flag be blue and white, based on the tallit. He felt that the ritual "with which we wrap ourselves when we pray" should be our national symbol of pride.

◆ Precisely because clothing is what distinguishes us from beasts and reminds us that we have a sense of shame, a spiritual "string" is a perpetual reminder to act like a human being and obey God's law.

◆ *Tzitzit* turn simple clothing into a uniform with a special insignia, like soldiers in the army who know they owe allegiance to a higher authority.

◆ One of the fringes had to be blue—the color of the sky and the heavens. The blue and white color combination, later adopted as the colors of the flag of Israel from this biblical source, symbolizes the need for people to incorporate the sacred into the profane, to bring the holy into everyday activities.

◆ This one's a bit of a stretch but the mystics love it: In gematria (the mystical process of analyzing words by the numerical value of their letters), the word *tzitzit* adds up to 600. By tradition, there are eight strands plus five knots for the fringes. 600 + 8 + 5, of course, adds up to 613, the exact number of Commandments in the

Torah. Just to look at the tzitzit, therefore, is to remember all the mitzvot—if you can quickly do the math every time you have a look at them!

And if you still don't understand, there's nothing like a story to prove a point:

The Talmud, which doesn't hesitate to share with us the foibles of even great men, tells of a rabbi who couldn't resist an encounter with one of the most beautiful harlots in the world. (Just who was proficient enough to make this judgment is not clearly indicated in the text!) Although the woman charged an astronomical fee, the rabbi was not deterred.

Inflamed by passion, he entered the room where the harlot lay naked and was overtaken by a frenzy of desire. Quickly, he started to undress. As he removed his four-cornered garment with the tzitzit, the fringes flew up and slapped him in the face. He was suddenly reminded of his religious commitment. Instantly he knew he couldn't go through with this act of sin.

I guess you could say he was saved by a thread. And that's what Jews call a real fringe benefit.

But We Don't Wear Ponchos

The law in the Bible is pretty clear. The tzitzit are put on garments that have four corners. What do we do when our clothes aren't made that way? The simple answer might be that then we don't have to wear fringes. But that would deprive us of a mitzvah and risk the chance that a biblical law might just disappear.

Of course, there has to be a solution. As a matter of fact, Jews found not only one but two ways to resolve the problem. There's the "long form" and the "short form" and both help preserve an ancient law in our contemporary world.

> **Schmoozing**
>
> Although one is not obligated to buy a garment and wrap himself in it just so as to provide it with fringes, it is not proper for a devout or pious person to exempt himself from observing this precept. He should strive to wear a garment that requires fringes so as to perform this precept.
>
> —Moses Maimonides

The Long Form

A tallit is the special prayer shawl worn at services. Actually, it's simply a four-cornered garment put over our clothing that, because of its shape, can legally have tzitzit attached. It's usually large enough for the person wearing it to wrap it around the body. A kabbalistic prayer some people recite as they perform this mitzvah makes a profound connection:

> As I wrap myself in this tallit, so should my soul and my 248 limbs and my 365 veins be wrapped in the light of the tzitzit, which is 613.

My limbs and veins, just like the tzitzit, have a numerical correspondence with the laws of the Torah. Many people have told me that fulfilling the mitzvah of tzitzit this way makes them feel "en-wrap-tured."

This "long form" of the four-cornered garment is most often identified with the synagogue and prayer. Among the pious, it serves yet another purpose: After death, there is a tradition to be buried wrapped in the tallit that one wore during one's lifetime. It's a way of demonstrating that we go to the other world dressed for our meeting with God in the same way we always encountered Him here on Earth.

Ask the Rabbi

There's a great way to tell who is single and available among the men in the synagogue. Because the law of tzitzit is right alongside the law of marriage in the Torah, the custom has developed that only married men wear a tallit at services. That's why, instead of saying, "All the good ones are taken," Jewish women often complain, "Look how the nicest men are all wearing a tallit."

The Short Form

A tallit doesn't really accomplish the intent of the original biblical law. The "string around our garment" was meant to be with us all the time, not just when we pray in the synagogue. It would probably be fair to say that its role as a reminder of God and the Commandments is needed far more when we're involved in the secular world than when we stand in the sacred.

The substitute for a tallit is a smaller item of clothing known, appropriately enough, as *tallit kattan*—a little tallit. Usually worn by traditional Jews under their shirts, the tallit kattan also has four corners and fringes and is worn throughout the day. (Because the Bible says, "And you shall *see* them," Jewish law rules that tzitzit are not necessary at night when they are only visible by artificial light.)

Some Orthodox Jews take the tzitzit out from under their shirts so that they can literally see them. Others feel they fulfill the law just by wearing them. In either case, you probably wouldn't notice as you walk by them that these Jews, just like their ancestors thousands of years ago, are still pulling strings to make sure they get into heaven!

Put a Box on Your Head and Your Hand

Clothing with fringes may not seem so unusual. Walking around wearing boxes surely looks much stranger. Yet that's another biblical law God commanded known as *tefillin*. The English translation, phylacteries, hardly explains it. Etymologically related to the word *amulet*, it almost makes tefillin seem like black magic. Tefillin in the Bible was another part of Jewish dress code meant to remind its wearers of important spiritual messages.

What Are the Tefillin?

What the mezuzah is to the Jewish home, the tefillin are to the Jew himself. Just like the mezuzah contains a parchment inside with a passage from the Torah written by a scribe, the two small black boxes of the *tefillin* contain small scrolls of parchment upon which are written four biblical passages. Every one of these selections mentions this mitzvah—the Commandment to put on tefillin as a sign, as a symbol of faith, and as a reminder of God's ongoing presence in history.

In describing the tefillin, the Bible says, "Bind them as a sign on your hand and as a symbol between your eyes …" That implies two different boxes, one for the hand and the other for the head. (Between your eyes is not literal but, as the rabbis explain, at the beginning of the hair line, positioned in the center, midway between one's eyes.)

Clearly, the major symbols of tefillin revolve around where the boxes rest on the body. The head is the seat of human intellect. The hand is the source of power and human activity. By placing over both a reminder of God and His law, we make our intellect and our actions subservient to God.

Schmoozing

Lord of the Universe! I saw an ordinary Jew pick up his tefillin from the floor and kiss them; and You have let your tefillin, the Jewish people, lie on the ground for more than two thousand years, trampled by their enemies. Why do you not pick them up? Why do you not act as a plain Jew acts? Why?

—Prayer of Rabbi Levi Yitzhok of Berdichev

From the Mountaintop

The tefillin box placed on the head is divided into four sections. The one for the arm is a single box. Some see in this a symbolic teaching that Jews may differ intellectually and divide into different groups (as you'll read in Chapter 25), as long as they unite when it comes to action.

The Other Hand, Please

The box for the hand is put on the fleshy part of the hand, right over the muscle. Which hand? Strangely enough, Jewish law stresses that it's to be the weaker hand. Notice I didn't say the left hand, because that wouldn't be true for everyone. Right-handed people are to put it on the left hand; lefties on the right. The reason for this is to teach another important idea.

God says put it on your weaker hand because "with a *strong hand*, I took you out of the Land of Egypt." Man's hand is weaker than God's. The box reminds us that it is God who controls human history. We acknowledge our "weaker" role. Some people think they do it all. Jews are taught to recognize that a stronger power determines the destiny of the world.

What If You're Ambidextrous?

Here's an interesting question: What if a person is equally strong in both hands? Which is his "weaker hand" for the purpose of tefillin? The Talmud answers, "We check which hand he uses for various activities. If, for example, he uses his left hand for his sword and his right hand to write, he is considered right-handed." Why? Jewish law, long before Bulwer Lytton, decreed that "the pen is mightier than the sword."

Getting Married to God

The tefillin box on the arm has a black strap that is wound seven times around the forearm below the elbow. The length of strap remaining is then wrapped around the palm of the hand in such a way that it spells out one of the names of God. When the strap is wound around the ring finger, these words, from the prophet Hosea, are recited: "I will betroth you to myself forever; I will betroth you to myself in right-eousness and in justice, in kindness and in mercy. I will betroth you to myself in faith-fulness; and you shall know the Lord."

Schmoozing

The symbol language of Judaism is alive now, as it was ages ago, still ruling the behavior of millions of people. It is the hieroglyph of the master ideas of the Bible carved on daily life. A Jew can hardly live Judaism without his ancient sacred short-hand anymore than a financier can conduct modern finance without its symbols. True symbol is not make-believe for mummery; it is reality distilled.
—Herman Wouk

A metaphorical ring around the finger together with words of betrothal make the wearer "married" to God. That's as daring as the imagery of the Song of Songs (remember Chapter 7?). What a feeling to know that we're just like a beautiful bride who has the good fortune to be blessed with God as a groom.

Jews Really Don't Have Horns

For the longest time, there were many people who believed that Jews have horns growing out of their heads. Some people think this misconception came about because of a famous statue by Michelangelo. Michelangelo put horns on his representation of Moses because of a faulty translation of a verse in the Bible. The word *keren* in Hebrew can mean horn or beam of light. The Bible says that when Moses descended Mount Sinai, a beam of light emanated from him. One translator took this to imply that a horn grew out of his head. Unfortunately, that was the text Michelangelo had, so Moses, of all people, became "horny!"

That may very well be the reason so many thought all Jews shared this trait. However, there could be a far simpler explanation. Jews originally wore tefillin all day, wherever they went. That means they did have something on their heads—a little black box that, from a distance, could very well be confused with a horn (as on unicorns). So maybe we shouldn't blame Michelangelo after all. Instead of a statue, it could have been a religious statute that confused the gentiles.

To this day there are still lots of people who don't know what to make of a Jew when they see him with a box on his head. My favorite true story is about the time someone watched me put on tefillin on a plane and asked admiringly if I was able to get good reception with that special antenna on my head!

Take It Off

There's one major difference, though, between how the law of tefillin is observed today and the way it was practiced a long time ago. Very pious Jews used to wear tefillin the entire day. They walked in the street wearing them, they worked with them. Tefillin were as much part of Jewish dress as shirts and shoes. Later generations decided that there were too many times when the proper reverence and respect for tefillin couldn't be maintained in daily surroundings. The accepted compromise was to wear tefillin only during moments associated with sanctity.

Tefillin today are part of synagogue attire. They are worn only when praying.

One other thing may surprise you. Go to synagogue on Sabbath or Jewish festivals and no one will be wearing tefillin. That's because Jewish law considers tefillin a reminder needed only on days that aren't themselves sacred. Weekdays require portable mini-Torahs worn on our bodies, but because holy days surround us with their special aura of spirituality, other symbols then would only be overkill.

Take Off Your Hat—Not!

Let's make one thing clear: Tzitzit and tefillin come from the Bible. Wearing a hat is a much later custom. For Orthodox Jews, it nevertheless remains an important religious statement. It's a visible way of identifying oneself as an observant Jew. For Conservative Jews, it's most often required as synagogue wear. For Reform Jews, it depends on the temple—some demand it, some forbid it, and some have a *laissez-faire* policy. (In Chapter 25 I'll explain the differences between these denominations in greater detail.)

Head coverings come in all shapes and sizes. They can be regular hats or cloth, velvet, or satin *kippot*—the Hebrew word for small round headgear. You may have heard them also referred to by their Yiddish name, *yarmulke*. Jews usually end up with large collections because they're invariably given out as "favors" at special occasions like weddings and Bar or Bat Mitzvahs.

Let There Be Light

Yarmulke is the Yiddish word for *kippot,* or "head covering." An interesting etymological explanation for the word is that it may come from the Aramaic *yeru,* "fear of," and *malka,* "the king."

Showing Respect

How did a custom that originated long after the close of the Bible gain such acceptance? For one thing, its symbolic meaning appeals to many. It's a way of acknowledging that there is someone "above us." The *kippah* (singular of kippot), as a symbol of God, also implies by its position that God is smarter than we are. Finally, in the absence of tefillin, which used to be worn all the time on the head and identified the wearer as Jew, the kippah is a substitute symbol for a biblical law we no longer consider ourselves worthy of fulfilling.

Ask the Rabbi

What does the pope have in common with Orthodox rabbis? They all wear skullcaps, of course. Some customs are obviously so strong they break the religion barrier.

It's unfortunate that in western culture removing one's hat is considered a sign of respect. Traditional Jews sometimes appear to be lacking in manners when they insist on keeping their heads covered. So please try to be understanding next time you see an Orthodox Jew who doesn't take his hat off when a woman enters an elevator. He really means "hats off to you" as he shows his respect by keeping his headgear firmly planted on his head.

The Least You Need to Know

- Tzitzit are fringes placed on four-cornered garments to remind Jews of God and His Commandments.

- Today, the two religious substitutes for tzitzit are the tallit, the prayer shawl worn at synagogue, and the tallit kattan worn by traditional Jews as part of daily attire.

- The two boxes of the tefillin symbolize subservience of man's intellect and man's actions to God.

- The tefillin on the hand are worn on the weaker arm and the straps are wound around the ring finger to demonstrate symbolic marriage with God.

- Head covering, while not a biblical law, is considered an important custom by Orthodox Jews to symbolize the acceptance of a "higher power" over their heads.

Part 7

The Crucial Questions

Until now, I've talked about Judaism as if it only had one voice. The truth is that since the eighteenth century, different denominations have come to the fore, each one claiming its views best represent the real essence of Judaism. You need to hear what they all have to say—and judge for yourselves the merits of each.

Can we boil Judaism down to a basic message, idea, or principle? Is it possible to summarize a religion that has so much to say? Let's see how some have tried—and let's decide whether they merely dreamed the impossible dream.

Finally, let's imagine that after a lengthy lecture, we open up the discussion for questions from the floor. Of course that's impossible, literally, in the context of a book. But from my many years of teaching Judaism I have gathered a list of the most frequently asked and the most interesting questions and their answers. It's only right that after the main course you should have an opportunity to enjoy a "Viennese table" of assorted delights and desserts.

Chapter **25**

What Kind of Judaism?

In This Chapter

- ◆ Comparing and contrasting the different types of Judaism
- ◆ Orthodox, Reform, Conservative, and Reconstructionist
- ◆ "Who is a Jew?"
- ◆ The difference between Hasidim and Orthodox Jews
- ◆ Why secular Jews are also religious

A Jew was shipwrecked on a desert island. Ten years later, rescuers finally found him. In amazement, they saw that he had built himself two synagogues. "We understand," they said, "why you needed a synagogue. But why two? You're here all alone." "What's so hard to understand? One synagogue is the one I pray in. The other one—that's the one I'll never set foot into!"

Sure, it's just a story. But it reflects a reality that's all too common in Jewish life. Jews love to argue. Two Jews, three opinions, goes the saying.

So do all Jews agree with a single definition of Judaism? You might as well ask if all politicians are Democrats, if all ice cream lovers choose chocolate, or if all baseball fans root for the New York Yankees.

People are different. The Talmud observes that just as no two human beings have the same physical features, they are also not alike in their mental capacities and their views of the world. There may be only one God, but today there are 13 million Jews. Every one of them has an opinion. That's why we shouldn't be surprised that there are different kinds of Judaism with different emphases and different interpretations. The truly amazing thing is not that there are so many denominations of Judaism but that there are so few!

Orthodox Judaism

Let's start with Orthodox Judaism, not because it's the largest movement—it isn't by far—but because it's the oldest. Many people don't realize that until the eighteenth century there was no organized difference of opinion within Judaism. Judaism was Judaism, and it was basically Orthodox Judaism. There were some differences in practices and customs between the Ashkenazic Jews of Eastern Europe and the Sephardic Jews of Spain and the Middle East, but these differences were not significant. They revolved around customs and rituals. There was no controversy about fundamental concepts. Jews viewed their beliefs and their practices as one long chain of tradition. Their ancestors were Abraham, Isaac, and Jacob. Their defining religious moment was the Revelation at Mount Sinai. Their texts were the Bible, the Talmud, and the later commentators.

Let There Be Light

Orthodox comes from two words, *ortho* ("correct") and *dox* ("faith"). Guess they got the most complimentary name of all denominations because they came first!

Judaism, just as the famous *Fiddler on the Roof* put it, could be summed up in one word: Tradition.

The Past Is Holy

Orthodox Judaism is committed to keeping its contract with the past. It stresses commitment to *halacha*, Jewish law, and observance of all of the mitzvot. Orthodox Jews share these fundamental beliefs:

- God gave Moses the entire Torah at Mount Sinai. Every letter of the five books we have today is exactly as it was dictated.

- The Torah passed down throughout the generations includes not only the written text but also the Oral Law, the Torah's traditional interpretation, which eventually became codified as the Talmud.

♦ The 613 mitzvot of the Bible, together with later rabbinic legislation meant to safeguard the observance of the mitzvot, are all equally binding upon Jews, no matter where they live or how much contemporary culture may have changed.

♦ Technology, scientific advances, and modern-day medicine must all be evaluated by Judaic teachings and legal principles. Jewish Law never changes with the times, but the times can be changed by the Law, whose ethical and moral concepts remain relevant throughout the ages.

♦ Orthodox Judaism stresses Torah study as the key to Jewish survival. With Torah, we *will* survive, Orthodox Jews say, and without Torah, *why* survive?

From the Mountaintop

Some people have suggested a new word, *Orthoprax*, to describe Jews who practice the teachings of Orthodoxy. That's to distinguish them from people who only identify themselves as Orthodox because, "If I would ever attend a synagogue, it would be an Orthodox one."

The Future of Grandchildren

As the oldest denomination in Judaism, Orthodoxy stakes its greatest claim for acceptance on its proven ability to assure Jewish continuity. As Rabbi Jonathan Sacks, Chief Rabbi of Great Britain put it: "The great question that Jews in the *Diaspora* must ask themselves today is, will we have Jewish grandchildren? And only Orthodox Jews answer in the affirmative with any degree of certainty." (Italics added.)

Statistically, Orthodox Jews suffer far fewer losses from their ranks as a result of assimilation and intermarriage than do the other contemporary movements. In light of their commitment to mitzvot and their adherence to the Commandment to be fruitful and multiply, Orthodox Jews are also the only segment of the Jewish population experiencing natural growth through a high birth rate.

Let There Be Light

Diaspora is a term that refers to Jewish communities outside the land of Israel. Because such communities are scattered round the world, the term used to describe them is from the Greek for "dispersion."

Modern Orthodox Jews tend to have twice as many children as Conservative and Reform Jews; "ultra-Orthodox" types have roughly four times as many children as their non-Orthodox counterparts. (I'll explain these distinctions between Orthodox Jews shortly.)

In Hasidic families, it's not unusual to have anywhere from ten to twelve children. While non-Orthodox Jews are barely replacing themselves and their rate of intermarriage tends to be over fifty percent, Orthodoxy, despite its emphasis on the past, seems to be the one movement most confident of its future.

But Even Orthodox Jews Can Disagree

Orthodoxy prides itself on its authenticity. It speaks in the name of the traditions and the texts of the past. Yet even it finds itself represented by different views. While equally reverential of ancient teachings, there is sufficient room for conflicting interpretation to allow for diverse sects within this seemingly monolithic movement.

- The "Modern Orthodox," following the orientation of nineteenth-century Neo-Orthodoxy popularized by Samson Raphael Hirsch, believe in the concept of synthesis. Western learning and Torah study are compatible. Secular universities, the professions, art, literature, and culture can all be comfortably incorporated into a Jewish way of life. In fact, they feel that synthesizing the sacred and secular is Judaism's goal. Modern Orthodoxy believes religion doesn't want us to flee from the world or to fear it. Instead, it asks us to hallow it.

From the Mountaintop

Modern Orthodoxy is best represented by Yeshiva University in Manhattan, New York, whose slogan is *Tora u'madda*—Torah and secular knowledge. Its most outstanding spokesman was Rabbi Joseph Soloveitchik, a rabbinic scholar considered by many to be the greatest of his generation, who also earned a doctorate in philosophy in Berlin during the 1930s.

- On the other end of Orthodoxy's spectrum are the *charedim*, literally "those who tremble"—that is to say, who live their lives in constant fear of God and His Law. Sometimes known as "ultra-Orthodox," they condemn secular study, reject participation in modern Western culture, and try to avoid as much as possible any contact with the "impurities" of contemporary society. Their ideal lifestyle is dedication to Torah study. Financial support will somehow be taken care of by God, fellow Jews, or charitable organizations.

- Between these two extremes can be found many degrees of middle ground. Orthodoxy includes under its broad wings those who, on religious principle, refuse to own a television set, as well as those who write scripts for some of the most popular TV series; those who dress as if they stepped out of the pages of *Vogue* and those who look like they never made it out of the nineteenth-century *shtetl* in Poland; those who can beat anybody in a game of Trivial Pursuit and those who won't bother to learn the English language because it's part of a "non-Jewish world."

All groups suffer from stereotypes. Like the Chinese Jew who came to America and met his first bearded rabbi said, "That's funny, you don't look Jewish." Orthodox Jews also come in so many different versions, it's often very hard to recognize them. (In the interest of full disclosure, I think before I go any farther I should reveal that I am modern Orthodox but hopefully fair to all other viewpoints.)

Ask the Rabbi

Here's a tip: Every kippah tells a story about its wearer. A small knitted kippah, kippah s'rugah, identifies its wearer as being modern orthodox. A large kippah s'rugah, especially in blue and white colors, is an expression of identification with the state of Israel. A velvet kippah or black hat is the headwear of the haredi or right-wing faction of orthodoxy, many of whom are opposed to the state of Israel as a secular country that does not fulfill the Messianic vision of the prophets.

Reform Judaism

The 1990 National Jewish Population Study found that the greatest percentage of Jews in the United States—38 percent—identified with Reform Judaism. That's quite a success story for a movement that is only a little more than 100 years old. It established its first American Rabbinical seminary, the Hebrew Union College of Cincinnati, Ohio, in 1875.

Reform Judaism began as a radical rebel. At the lavish dinner honoring the first graduates of the new rabbinical seminary, the menu featured shrimp as the main course, a nonkosher food. It was as clear a statement of belief as the Pittsburgh platform of 1885, which shortly followed.

In it, Judaism was redefined and biblical law was no longer considered binding. In fact, Reform's founders stressed that "rituals impede the mission of Israel to bring about a universal morality." Together with the denigration of ritual as a practice that needlessly isolates Jews from their neighbors, Reform Judaism, for the same reason, also opposed Zionism for many decades.

In its efforts to respond to a free and open society, the allure of modernity and the desire for greater acceptance, Reform Judaism went through many stages. As Mark Twain pointed out for the teenager whose parents were the stupidest people on earth until he grew a little older and was "amazed to see how much they had learned in those few years," Reform Judaism readopted many of the practices it first condemned, changed its mind about support for Israel, and has come to express a much greater respect for tradition.

A Modern Code of Belief

What do Reform Jews believe today? How do Reform Jews observe Jewish religion? Leaders of Reform Jewry gave this answer in the Spring 1997 issue of *Reform Judaism* magazine:

> If anyone were to attempt to answer these two questions authoritatively for all Reform Jews, that person's answers would have to be false. Why? Because one of the guiding principles of Reform Judaism is the autonomy of the individual. A Reform Jew has the right to decide whether to subscribe to this particular belief or to that particular practice.
>
> But there is a historic body of beliefs and practices that is recognized as Jewish. We Jews have survived centuries of exile and persecution as well as centuries of unparalleled spiritual and intellectual creativity because we have always thought of ourselves as a people created in the image of God, dedicated to *Tikkun Olam*—the improvement of the world …
>
> We Reform Jews are heirs to a vast body of beliefs and practices embodied in Torah and the other Jewish sacred writings. We differ from more ritually observant Jews because we recognize that our sacred heritage has evolved and adapted over the centuries and that it must continue to do so …
>
> Reform Judaism accepts and encourages pluralism. Judaism has never demanded uniformity of belief or practice. But we must never forget that whether we are Reform, Conservative, Reconstructionist, or Orthodox, we are all an essential part of *K'lal Yisroel*—the worldwide community of Jewry.

Schmoozing

… I envisage it [Judaism] as a sort of tree, with Orthodoxy as the strong, gnarled trunk … whose roots are deep in the earth … Conservatism as the branches that come out of the trunk. And I envisage Reform Judaism as the beautiful leaves, flowers and fruits at the end of it; all three are necessary for the health of the tree of Judaism.

—Solomon Liptzin, (1901]–1995) American-born professor and author

Reform Judaism's readiness to "reform" Judaism and to alter it stems from its belief that the Torah was not written by God. The movement accepts the critical theory of authorship—that the Bible was written by separate sources and redacted together. "Commandments" that were not commanded literally by God have little claim on Jews unless Jews voluntarily choose to observe them.

A New Breed Emerging?

Interestingly enough, though, studies show that a large percentage of newly ordained Reform rabbis keep kosher, and twice as many Reform Jews today light Sabbath and Hanukkah candles, as well as attend the Passover seder, than did a generation ago. More recently, a movement within Reform Judaism has spoken out for acceptance of the laws of kashrut, Shabbat, and family purity, as well as belief in the divinity of Torah. What this means for the future of Reform Judaism is something we will discuss in Part 8. But one thing we can say for sure: If Orthodoxy and Reform end up meeting on common ground, Messiah will surely come!

But Still Miles Apart

Two issues, however, make for an almost unbridgeable rift between Orthodox and Reform Judaism. And these two issues are critical because they go to the very heart of what it means to be a Jew. In Israel today, the issue threatens the stability of the government. Around the world, its ramifications are so profound they cannot yet be fully measured. What's at stake is nothing less than the future of the Jewish people.

Conversion

The first deals with conversion. It determines the answer to the question brought before the Israeli Supreme Court: "Who is a Jew?" Judaism happily accepts converts. One of the most famous, the Moabite Ruth, has a biblical book named after her, recounting her story. Although not genetically Jewish, conversion allowed her to become worthy of becoming the ancestress of King David. Clearly, worth in God's eyes is determined by faith and not family.

> **Schmoozing**
>
> Some people dislike the term "conversion," preferring to call those who enter the Jewish family other than by birth "Jews by choice." Well, I am a Jew by choice, and if I had to choose again I'd choose Jewishness with all my heart, and without a second's hesitation—only this time I'd choose it forty years sooner.
>
> —Louise Kehoe, journalist, in the American Jewish Committee series on "What Being Jewish Means to Me"

Acceptance into the Jewish fold, however, is predicated on commitment. Clubs have their rules for joining. Becoming an American citizen must follow a prescribed procedure. You can't just say you're an American and be one. So, too, to join a people defined by shared values and obligations, you must comply with their entrance requirements.

Orthodox Judaism insists that male converts to Judaism be circumcised and that both male and female converts go through a process of immersion in a mikvah, a ritual bath (see Chapter 20). Prospective converts must go through a lengthy course of study to make sure they know the full extent of their new faith commitment and then must pledge to observe Jewish law. This procedure, part of ancient Jewish tradition, is considered immutable.

Schmoozing

All vestiges of negative or quizzical attitudes toward converts must be totally eradicated. Not only are these attitudes counterproductive to the future of the Jewish community but, much more important, they are in opposition to Jewish law.

—Deborah E. Lipstadt

Schmoozing

If your son or daughter is married to someone who has converted to Judaism, then there is no intermarriage. An intermarriage means a marriage between someone born Jewish and someone born non-Jewish who has not converted.

—Lawrence J. Epstein

Reform Judaism, however, has adopted a far more liberal approach. Circumcision and immersion are considered unnecessary and commitment to Jewish practice is not mandatory. For that reason, Reform conversions are considered invalid by the Orthodox, as well as by almost all Conservative religious leaders.

This means that there are people considered Jews by some and not by others. As the number of Reform conversions grows, there will be more and more people in this category. With added uncertainty as to who's "in the family" (important, for example, for finding a marriage partner), it will take the genius of an Einstein to discover an acceptable theory of "relative"-ity. The realization that Jews and Christians long ago also started as family until religious differences that prevented them from marrying each other forced them to go their separate ways is truly frightening.

By Mother ... or Father?

The second issue erupted when the Reform movement passed its patrilineal descent ruling, declaring that children of Jewish fathers and non-Jewish mothers could be considered as Jews without conversion. That goes against Jewish law that for thousands of years has defined a Jew by the religion of his or her mother. (Thus, an Orthodox Jew might respond to the news that actress Gwyneth Paltrow is Jewish on her father's side, by noting, "We don't go by Paltrow-lineal descent.")

With one change, Reform told the rest of world Jewry that your gentile is our Jew. That means people who care are going to have to keep genealogical charts of their ancestry. That also means unless we can find a way to resolve issues that alter the definition of a Jew, Judaism will branch off into different streams that will no longer be able to share bonds of kinship.

Conservative Judaism

A scholar from Cambridge University in England, Rabbi Solomon Schechter, Ph.D., came to the United States in 1902 and, more than anyone else, was the major force behind the rise of *Conservative Judaism*. Schechter was a traditionalist who believed in change, a believer who was willing to question, an observant Jew who felt there was still room for some adjustment of ancient laws to modern-day realities.

Schmoozing

Reform declared that Judaism has changed throughout time and that Jewish law is no longer binding. Orthodoxy denies both propositions, insisting upon the binding character of Jewish law and negating the view that Judaism has evolved. Conservative Judaism agrees with Orthodoxy in maintaining the authority of Jewish law and with Reform that Judaism has grown and evolved through time.

—Rabbi Robert Gordis (1908–1992), American Conservative Rabbi and author

Let's Compromise

The founders of the Jewish Theological Seminary, Manhattan, training ground for Conservative Rabbis, were motivated by rejection of the extreme measures of early Reform Judaism. They felt very strongly that serving bacon and studying the Bible were incompatible.

To the claim of Reform leaders that if not for their liberal reinterpretation of Judaism there would be a mass exodus of Jews from their faith, Schechter responded with these words: "Reform Jewry's tampering with Torah in order to hold onto its followers reminds me of the

Let There Be Light

Conservative Judaism is conservative from the perspective of the left. Orthodox Jews, who are far more conservative in their approach to Torah, would call Conservative Jews liberal. The name "Conservative" makes sense because as a movement it responded to Reform's excesses by stressing a more conservative approach.

man who proclaimed, 'I would give up part, or if necessary, all of the Constitution in order to preserve the remainder.'"

Unlike Reform Judaism, Conservative theology believes itself bound by almost all Torah precepts. The truths found in Jewish Scriptures and in the Oral Law come from God. Unlike Orthodox Judaism, however, Conservative rabbis consider themselves free to introduce innovations in *halacha*, Jewish law. The basic tenets of halacha are binding, but law can accept changes and absorb aspects of the predominant culture while remaining true to Judaism's values.

Conservative Judaism is generally considered to be the middle road between Reform and Orthodox Judaism. It seeks compromise and accommodation.

It stresses the beauty of both tradition and innovation, continuity and creativity. It quarrels with Orthodoxy by permitting its members to drive to the synagogue on the Sabbath, by doing away with the *mechitzah* (the divider between men and women), and permitting mixed seating at the synagogue, as well as considerably expanding the permitted roles of women in congregational ritual.

Yet Conservative Judaism is deeply disturbed by Reform Judaism's rejection of biblical authority, its liberal attitude to conversion, and its acceptance of patrilineal descent as definition of a Jew.

Finding itself between two far more extreme positions on both the left and the right, Conservative Judaism is either complimented for its moderation or criticized for its permissiveness.

From the Mountaintop

Solomon Schechter really wanted a different name to describe the Conservative movement. He loved the phrase, "Catholic Israel." By that he meant that Jewish traditions were important not just because they were given by God but because they became hallowed through centuries of observance by Jews. (*Catholic* beginning with a small *c* means universal.) Can you guess why the name never caught on?

Reconstructionist Judaism

The founder of *Reconstructionist Judaism*, Rabbi Mordecai Kaplan, grew up in an Orthodox home, lived most of his life as a Conservative Jew, and created a denomination that for some people deserves only to be called Reconstructionist but not Judaism. The Reconstructionist label doesn't fit neatly into either the traditional/

liberal or the observant/nonobservant contin-
uum that most people use to classify movements of Judaism.

Reconstructionist Judaism isn't so much concerned with God as it is with Jews. It doesn't
care so much for Commandments as it does
for culture. It considers Judaism not so much a
religion as a civilization.

> **Let There Be Light**
>
> **Reconstructionist Juda-**
> **ism,** founded by Rabbi Mordecai
> Kaplan in the twentieth century,
> views Judaism primarily as a cul-
> ture, not as a religion, and treats
> its laws and customs as an
> "evolving religious civilization."

Culture Is Holy

Reconstructionists believe that Judaism is an "evolving religious civilization." They
don't accept a personal deity who is active in history. You might think that places
them to the left of Reform, with complete disregard for ritual and religious observance. Yet interestingly enough, Reconstructionism places much greater emphasis on
observance than Reform—not because it's the Law but because it's a valuable cultural
remnant.

Kaplan may not have been as successful as the other movements in terms of numbers.
Yet he had a profound influence on the three major movements—Orthodox, Reform,
and Conservative—with his emphasis on the idea of a synagogue as a Jewish center.
While rejecting the idea that Judaism is not a religion but a civilization, a strong feeling developed among all branches of Judaism that the Jews have created a unique civilization by way of their religious values. What Reconstructionism thought of as a
replacement for religion became viewed instead as a valued partner.

Hasidic Judaism

Here's a simple truth they teach you in Philosophy 101: Just because all Fords are cars
doesn't mean all cars are Fords. Don't be surprised then to learn that all Hasidic Jews
are Orthodox, but not all Orthodox Jews are Hasidim.

In the 1700s, the movement known as Hasidism was founded by Israel ben Eliezer,
who was more commonly known as the Ba'al Shem Tov, or the *Besht*. Until then,
Judaism had placed major emphasis on study. The scholar was the one to be admired.
Religious experience was the province of the mind; serious scholarship was the sole
legitimate service of God.

The Ba'al Shem Tov and his disciples chose the way of the heart over the head, feelings and fervor over fixed hours of study, and the joy in the performance of mitzvot

over fear that one may have overlooked a minor point of law. Hasidism embraced mysticism and danced its way into the hearts of common Jews who knew they could never be scholars but who were certain they could be faithful servants of God.

Let There Be Light

Herem, a ban of excommunication, forbade Jews from having any contact with the person placed under excommunication. The procedure is to be used only in extreme circumstances and is almost unknown in practice today.

Because some of these ideas were so radical, Hasidim were originally placed in *herem*, a ban of excommunication, by prominent rabbis of their day. With the passage of time, it became clear that Hasidism, with its teachings, wasn't a threat to tradition but rather a long-needed corrective to some improper excesses. Hasidism reinvigorated Judaism. It brought back to the forefront spirituality, respect for the simple Jew, the primacy of ethics and compassion for others, and the conviction that true religion and happiness must be synonymous.

My "Rebbe" Is Holy

The founder of Hasidism was revered as a holy man. His disciples in turn were regarded as having special powers because of their saintliness and their closeness to God. They were called *Tzaddik*—righteous one—or *Rebbe*, the "Yiddishized" variant of the word *Rav*, which in English would later become Rabbi. The Rebbe would be asked to pray for his followers. His word was law. His advice was godly.

For those opposed to Hasidim, called *Mitnagdim* ("opponents"), this seemed too close to idolization of a human being to be permissible. It was another reason why the Hasidic movement at first was greeted by a great deal of antagonism. Yet the Hasidic Rebbes almost always preserved their integrity and didn't misuse their power. Their teachings, by word and by example, remain a magnificent legacy of the Hasidic movement for our generation. One of the more recent Hasidic leaders, Rabbi Menachem Mendel Schneersohn, commonly referred to as the Lubavitcher (after the town Lubavitch in Russia where this revised Hasidic dynasty began), created a movement that literally spread around the world, helping Jews no matter what their level of religiosity and bringing tens of thousands back to their ancestral roots.

Schmoozing

When I would see the [Lubavitcher] *Rebbe*, he touched the depth in me, and that was true of everyone who came to see him. Somehow, when people left, they felt that they lived deeper and higher, on a higher level and with a deeper sense of life, a quest for life and meaning.

—Elie Wiesel

Secular Judaism

With all of the denominations we've discussed, the truth is that most Jews still remain secular and unaffiliated. They are part of the mainstream for whom Judaism is an accident of birth, not a blessing. Are they still Jews? Judaism is quite clear about defining the status of those who reject it: "A Jew, although he may sin, is still considered a Jew."

Judaism, just like circumcision, stays with you for life. It may be hard to get into the "club," but once you're in you can never get out. That's because Judaism never gives up on anybody. As the Rebbe of Lubavitch put it so beautifully, "There are only two kinds of Jews: Religious Jews and not-yet-religious Jews."

Is "Secular Judaism" an Oxymoron?

Secular Jews say they're not religious—and then give more charity than anyone else other than religious Jews. Secular Jews claim they're not religious—and then serve on the boards of hospitals, involve themselves in communal activities, protest against injustices around the world, and take up the causes of the oppressed and the persecuted. Secular Jews help orphans and widows, love learning and education, spend much of their free time in Tikkun Olam—projects to improve the world.

Somehow secular Jews are affiliated with Judaism without even realizing it. Secular Judaism is probably also a religious denomination. Its members just don't realize that the adjective shouldn't be taken too seriously.

 Schmoozing

Today we do not deem the non-Orthodox and the secularists as heretics. Even the Orthodox must love them as Jews who share the same fate, if not the same faith. To help them back one must understand them.

—Rabbi Emanuel Rackman

The Least You Need to Know

♦ Orthodox Judaism, which until the eighteenth century was the only form of Judaism, maintains all of the teachings and traditions of the past as immutable and unchanging for every age.

♦ Orthodox Judaism embraces under its wing a fairly wide diversity of views—from a willing acceptance of modern culture to complete rejection of the secular world.

◆ Reform Judaism, while believing in the religious autonomy of the individual, has gone through several stages since its inception and today, while rejecting the divinity of Torah, is far more accepting of ritual practices and supportive of the State of Israel.

◆ Disagreements about conversion and patrilineal descent, with Orthodox and Conservative on one side and Reform on the other, are the issues that most threaten Jewish unity for the future.

◆ Conservative Judaism has found its niche as a middle-of-the-road approach to Judaism, rejecting the extremes of both right and left.

◆ Reconstructionist Judaism views Judaism as a civilization rather than as a religion and has had its greatest impact by way of its influence in fostering the development of synagogues as community centers.

◆ Hasidic Judaism revolutionized Jewry in the eighteenth century by emphasizing the heart over the head, and prayer over study as the ideal forms of worship of God.

◆ The Hasidic movement, while originally viewed as a threat to those who stressed the primacy of Torah study, has today become a powerful partner of traditional Orthodoxy and has to its credit great achievements in spreading Judaism to many who found themselves far removed from their faith.

◆ Secular Judaism, while rejecting a religious basis, clearly manifests expressions of Jewish compassion, Jewish values, and Jewish concern.

Chapter 26

What's Most Important?

In This Chapter

- Looking for the essence of Judaism
- Defining holiness
- The obligation to help others grow spiritually
- The relationship between the Law and the Promised Land
- Choosing one mitzvah above all others
- The last word

A Chinese delegate to the United Nations was besieged by reporters when he arrived in New York. One of the questions they asked him was, "What strikes you as the oddest thing about Americans?" He thought for a moment, then smiled and said, "I think it is the peculiar slant of their eyes."

That just goes to show that perspective is everything. What you see depends a lot on the point of view you bring with you.

Judaism, as you now realize, has many different faces. There are laws and customs, concepts and principles, values and viewpoints on all the major issues of life. That's why the bottom line for this chapter is: How can we summarize the essence of Judaism? What's *most* important? What's *the* message of this most ancient religion?

You'd think after all these years there might be some kind of consensus. The truth is that even when it comes to eternal truths, there are "different strokes for different folks." Just as Chapter 25 explained how the various denominations within Judaism differ with regard to its teachings, you'll find in this chapter that major Jewish movements disagree on what we ought to consider the most important mitzvot, or holy commandments. Let's discuss some of these views and see if we can come to any conclusions.

Be Holy

"You shall be holy for I the Lord your God am holy," says the Bible in the Book of Leviticus. Holy is the opposite of profane. Holy means to be spiritual. Holy means to be saintly. Isn't *that* what the Jewish religion is all about?

> ### Let There Be Light
>
> The **Musar** movement, founded by Rabbi Israel Lipkin in the nineteenth century, from the word *musar*, "reproof," stresses improvement of permanent character, ethical perfection and holiness as the more important ideals of Judaism.

> ### Pulpit Story
>
> Rabbi Moses Sofer, a rabbinic giant of the nineteenth century, once heard a man protesting his complete unworthiness, stating that he was unlearned and unworthy of respect. The rabbi looked at the man and said, "You are not so great that you can afford to be so small."

The *Musar* movement, founded in the nineteenth century in Lithuania by Rabbi Israel Lipkin (who lived in the town of Salant and is therefore known as Israel Salanter) would say that, yes, to be holy is indeed the core teaching of Judaism. The word *musar* means "instruction," "reproof," or "calling attention to the need for a better life." It's a call to improve character and behavior so that we come closer to being like God. That's the ultimate goal of a Jew. To be holy like our Creator.

Holy Moses—I'm Not Moses

Holiness is so hard to achieve that for most of us it has to remain a dream rather than a destination. We have to chase after it, but we know that its achievement will always elude us. Yet our task is to try. Judaism judges us more for our effort than for our successes. To seek the holiness of someone like Moses is to stress virtues such as his in our daily lives.

Humility is the trait the Torah singles out as the key to the greatness of Moses: "Now the man Moses was very meek, above all the men that were on the face of the earth." When Abraham spoke to God, he humbly said, "Who am I but dust and ashes?" When Saul was chosen as the first King of Israel, he was discovered "hidden … among the baggage." When God appointed Moses to be the Jewish leader, his response was, "Who am I?" because he didn't consider himself worthy. Humility is man's awareness of his real worth in the presence of God.

Truly wise people have always known what the saintly Rabbi Nahman of Bratzlav taught: "Before man attains greatness he must descend to lowliness." It's only humility that makes a big man bigger and a little man big.

Holiness and humbleness go hand in hand. Even if a person knows his true worth, it doesn't allow him to be arrogant. Because he was given superior talents, God demands more of him. Modesty comes from an awareness that you're not living up to your potential.

Schmoozing

Only when thinking becomes quite humble can it set its feet upon the way that leads to knowledge.

—Albert Schweitzer

"God's seal is truth," say the rabbis. To be holy is to be honest. In Hebrew, the word for truth is *emet*. Remarkably, the three letters that form the words *aleph*, *mem*, and *tof* are, in order, the first, the middle, and the last letters of the Hebrew alphabet. If something is true it has to be true "from A to Z"—including the middle.

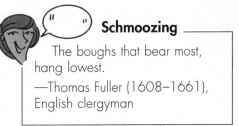

Schmoozing

The boughs that bear most, hang lowest.

—Thomas Fuller (1608–1661), English clergyman

Anger is such a terrible vice that when Moses lost his temper the Bible tells us his wisdom departed from him. The Talmud teaches that someone who's quick to anger has a life that's not worth living. He is always upset and miserable, and God Himself refuses to come into his presence. There are two things, the rabbis teach, that a man should never get angry about: What he can help, and what he cannot help. Anger is not only a sin but also stupidity. It's clear that the person who often flies off the handle usually has a screw loose.

Envy is called an "evil eye" by the Talmud. Someone with a "good eye" is happy at other people's successes. An envious person can't even enjoy his own good fortune because there is always someone else whose happiness makes him despair. "Oh God," is the prayer of an envious person, "don't just make me successful. Make my friends fail." Because that's not the kind of prayer God will answer, envious people are doomed to sorrow.

Pulpit Story

The wife of Rabbi Pinchas of Koretz once bought a gilded *kiddush* goblet. On Friday evening, when he saw the goblet, he called to his wife indignantly: "Since when do we have golden utensils in our house?" His wife sought to justify herself, saying, "See, it is not genuine, but only a gilded goblet." "Then," said the rabbi, "you have not only brought arrogance but also deceit and falsehood into the house," and he refused to use the goblet for the sacred ceremony.

Malicious talk and slanderous gossip, in Hebrew called *lashon ha-ra*, are considered by the Musar movement to be on the highest rung of sinful actions. The tongue is what separates man from beast; the power of speech is what makes us closest to God. To debase that is to destroy our greatest potential for holiness. A Spanish philosopher and rabbinic scholar pointed out that "God doesn't love tale-bearers, even when they are right. The tale-bearer is a cannibal." That's why the laws of slander and gossip appear in the Bible right next to the laws listing nonkosher foods. God is just as concerned with what comes out of our mouth as what goes into it.

From the Mountaintop

The rabbis taught that the Bible says, "Death and life are in the power of the tongue." See how, they observed, when a doctor wants to determine if a person is sick he tells the patient, "Stick out your tongue." From the tongue we can, medically and morally, tell the condition of a human being.

Schmoozing

A person cannot be religious and indifferent to other human beings' plight and suffering.

—Rabbi Abraham Joshua Heschel (1907–1972), American Rabbi, theologian, and author

Compassion, according to the Talmud, is one of the three signs by which a Jew may be recognized: "Jews are modest, merciful, and doers of kindness." A Hasidic master showed how all three traits could be combined in one example: A rabbi gave a coin to a beggar who had a bad reputation. His disciples asked him, "How can you give a coin to such a bad man?" The rabbi replied, "Is he worse than I, to whom God gave it in the first place?" Judaism understands that man is honored for his wisdom but loved for his kindness. And kindness, as the rabbis point out, consists of loving people more than they deserve.

Respect for others (in Hebrew, *kovod ha-beriot*), "respect for God's creations," is the natural consequence of our recognition that human beings are created in the image of God. All people, of whatever race, religion, age, or intelligence, are entitled to dignity. We will be judged, says the Talmud, more by how we treat others in word than in deed. Blows only hurt the flesh; cruel comments harm the soul.

When his disciples asked Rabbi Israel Salanter how they could best make the necessary preparations on Friday for the coming of the Sabbath, he replied, "Help your wives with the housework and speak especially gently to them, showing them the respect they deserve."

Make these character traits part of your nature, said the masters of the Musar movement, and you will become the holy person that is the highest goal of Judaism.

Be a Blessing

No sooner did Abram discover God than God told him, "It's time to change your name." Your name (as was explained in Chapter 14) defines your mission in life. Abram implies that he is "the father of Aram," leader of a small locale. The name change told Abram that now he had to become *Avrahom*, the Hebrew of Abraham, meaning "father of many nations." Now that you know the truth, it imposes upon you a mission: Spread the word to the world.

The Midrash says that the Jews can be compared to someone who finds a magnificent jewel, so brilliant and beautiful that whoever looks at it is overwhelmed. To keep it hidden would be a sin. Whoever possesses a gift that can bring incredible joy to others is obligated to let them enjoy it as well. That's why Abraham and all of his descendants have a mission.

From the Mountaintop

The Bible calls the Jews "a kingdom of priests and a holy nation." The rabbis ask: "But not all Jews are priests, descendants of Aaron." They answer, what the priests are to the rest of the Jewish people, the Jewish people as a whole are supposed to be to the rest of the world.

Like the saying goes, "If you've got it, flaunt it." That's also why God commanded Abraham, "Be a blessing." God didn't bless Abraham as much as He imposed upon him what is perhaps the major responsibility of the Jewish people: To *be* a blessing to the entire world.

The Donkey and the Diamond

Love is a hard thing to explain. "How do I love thee? Let me count the ways," wrote Elizabeth Barrett Browning. Judaism was faced with the need to clarify the real meaning of love because of a biblical verse: "And you shall love the Lord your God with all your heart, with all your soul, and with all your might." What does that really mean?, asked the sages of the Talmud. What am I supposed to do to fulfill this Commandment?

As rabbis so often do, they answer with a story:

> Rabbi Simeon ben Shetach lived in poverty most of his life. His students bought a donkey from an Ishmaelite to present to their master as a gift. When the rabbi brought his donkey home, he found a little bag tied around the animal's neck with a costly diamond inside. He called his students and asked, "Did you buy a donkey with a diamond and pay for both?" The students told their rabbi they knew nothing about the precious stone. Rabbi Simeon immediately returned the diamond to the Ishmaelite. The Arab was so overwhelmed by the rabbi's honesty that he exclaimed, "Praised be Simeon ben Shetach and praised be the God of Simeon ben Shetach."

That, the rabbis declared, is the very *best* way to fulfill "You shall love the Lord your God." Act in such a way that God's name becomes beloved by the world because of you.

"Sanctify God's Name"

To act as Rabbi Simeon did is known as *kidush ha-shem*, sanctifying God's name. The concept is so important that Jews are prepared to die for it. It demands that we act honorably so that people recognize God's greatness because of the deeds of His disciples. If a Jew commits a crime, it brings shame not only to him as a person but also to the One whom he represents. A Jewish pornographer, criminal, or murderer has committed a *chilul ha-shem*—a desecration of God's name. That sin, some say, can never be forgiven.

 Schmoozing

Israel has a mission still: Truth-seeking in the world of thought, and right-doing in the world of action.

—Steven Wise

During the Holocaust, the Nazis offered to spare the lives of Jews—at least for the moment—if, for their amusement, they would perform an act of bestiality or commit some other gross immoral act. Most often, Jews preferred death to dishonoring God. To do otherwise would have been a chilul ha-shem.

One Yom Kippur night in the concentration camp of Auschwitz, the Nazis laid out a huge buffet table with the most tempting morsels of food. Knowing that it was religiously forbidden for Jews to eat, they commanded the Jews to break their fast. Starving, with the smells of food they could only fantasize about wafting around them, not one person stepped forward to partake. That was a kidush ha-shem.

Bring Them Back

To spread God's word is the chief goal of a contemporary movement whose ideal is to bring back to the fold those who have lost their way. The *Ba'al Teshuva* Movement—the "Movement of Return"—is concerned with Jews who never had an opportunity to learn about Judaism, Jews who were estranged from their past, not by choice but by ignorance. Today, there are hundreds of organizations and thousands of people involved in *kiruv* programs, helping to draw "near" those who, through no fault of their own, are unaware of the beauty of their own tradition.

Scholars say that never in all of Jewish history has there been a comparable phenomenon of so many Jews returning to their roots as today. Reaction to the Holocaust and the world's indifference, as well as pride in the birth of the State of Israel, help in some measure to explain it.

Mystics believe it's messianic. The end of days, in Jewish tradition, marks a time when everyone will thirst for the word of God as people thirst for water. Maybe that's why, some people have pointed out, the most recognized words around the world today are *Coca Cola* and *Lubavitch.* The first one is "the pause that refreshes"; the second, the powerful movement that restores the souls of those who have strayed to the faith of their ancestors.

Ask the Rabbi

Did you know that when you influence someone else to perform mitzvot and good deeds you get a share of that person's reward as well? Help others spiritually, and you could be paving your own road into heaven!

From the Mountaintop

The Lubavitcher Rebbe was once asked, "Why do we call those who accept Judaism later in life Ba'al Teshuva? They are breaking with their past, so why call them returnees as if they are returning to something?" The rebbe answered, "It is because they are returning—returning to their inner essence and to what their own souls really want them to be."

Be an Israeli

Zionism is the name of the movement that puts major emphasis on another aspect of Judaism. From the word *Zion,* another name for Israel and Jerusalem, Zionism stresses the Promised Land as the most important component of being a Jew. Religion and nationalism are seen as inseparable.

When Abraham accepted God, the first thing he was told was to leave his land, his birthplace, and his father's house to go "to the land which I will show you." That land, then Canaan, would become home to the prophets and kings, to the temple of God, and to the sages of the Talmud. No place would be holier. It was, as the Bible said, "a land flowing with milk and honey." Its milk nursed the Jewish people from infancy; its honey sweetened their lives until the tragedy of exile. "Whoever is privileged to walk four steps in the Holy Land," taught the Talmud, "is assured of a place in the world to come."

> ### Schmoozing
>
> *Eretz Yisrael* [Israel] is not something apart from the soul of the Jewish people ... [it] is part of the very essence of our nationhood; it is bound organically to its very time and inner being. Human reason, even at its most sublime, cannot begin to understand its unique holiness.
>
> —Rabbi Abraham Isaac Kook, (1865–1935) first Chief Rabbi of Israel

The attachment of Jews to the land never faltered, even when they were forcibly exiled from it. Three times a day they prayed, "And to Jerusalem, Your city, return us speedily in mercy." Every meal was concluded with the recitation of grace, not only thanking God for His food, but begging Him to "rebuild Jerusalem, the Holy City, speedily in our days," so that they might be not only physically sated but spiritually fulfilled.

The holiest day of the year, Yom Kippur, as well as the seder meal on Passover, highlight the cry, "Next year in Jerusalem." Jews believe that God, just as any loving parent, wants His children to have a place they can call home.

"If You Will It, It Is No Dream"

Known as the father of political Zionism, Theodore Herzl lived for only 44 years, but he proved the power of his personal motto: "If you will it, it is no dream." In September 1897, while attending the First Zionist Congress he called together in Basel, Switzerland, he wrote in his diary: "If I could sum up the Basel Congress in a word, which I shall guard against pronouncing publicly—it would be this: At Basel, I founded a Jewish state. If I said this out loud today, I would be answered by universal laughter. Perhaps in five years, and certainly in fifty, everyone will know it."

> ### Ask the Rabbi
>
> It's considered a great mitzvah for Jews to be buried in Israel. But take a tip from me: Don't wait until you're dead to visit the Holy Land. You'll enjoy it much more when you can see it with your eyes wide open.

His prediction was off by only one year. The State of Israel was founded in 1948.

Herzl's followers felt—and feel—that the land is the ultimate fulfillment of the Jewish dream. Zionists were, in the main, not "religious" in the ritual sense. Yet Rabbi Abraham Isaac Kook, Chief Rabbi of Palestine after 1919, declared, "Those who rebuild the land are as favored in the sight of God as the ritually observant."

Today, unfortunately, conflict is all too often the prevailing attitude between the religiously observant and secular Zionists. Extremists of both camps make it appear that Judaism is an "either/or" proposition: Land no longer requires religion, or religion is independent of land for its proper fulfillment. The truth in all certainty rests in the lesson of Jewish history. Jews can survive even in exile because of their faith. It is their faith, however, that always assured them that someday they would again be a people who could dwell safely and securely in their Promised Land.

> **Schmoozing**
>
> Palestine is the center of the world, Jerusalem the center of Palestine, and the Temple the center of Jerusalem. In the Holy of Holies there was a stone, which is the foundation of the world.
>
> —Midrash

The Prisoner's Problem

A story that took place in the Middle Ages offers us an opportunity to find the answer to the question: Which is the greatest mitzvah? A rabbi had to give a legal response in a fascinating case that required just this kind of decision.

A Jew who had been imprisoned by the feudal baron was unexpectedly shown some mercy. "Because it is my birthday, I have decided to show you kindness," said the baron. "Although you must remain my prisoner forever, I will allow you one day of freedom per year. On that day, you may return to your family and your community, and you may freely practice your religion. Furthermore, I don't care which day you choose. But remember, you only have one day a year. Only then can you be free to practice your faith. You have a day to be a Jew. Decide for yourself which one it will be."

If the prisoner chooses Passover for his one day, he'll be able to observe the seder, eat matzot, and drink the four cups of wine. If he selects Rosh Hashanah, he'll have a chance to hear the shofar and pray in the synagogue. If his decision is Sukkot, he'll be able to eat in the "hut" together with his family as the Bible commands. But maybe it should be Shabbat? Or Shavuot, the day the Torah was given? So many mitzvot. To pick one day meant to exclude the possibility of observing the laws connected with another. What a terribly difficult decision!

The Jew was allowed time before he gave his answer. He was able to send a messenger to Rabbi David ben Abi Zimra, the greatest rabbi of the sixteenth century. Anxiously, he awaited a response. He projected all kinds of possible answers but he was totally unprepared for the reply he received: "The day you must choose is the very first day available, be it a Shabbat, a weekday, or any holiday."

Why? The rabbi made clear that he was to choose the very first day precisely so that he would not be forced to choose between mitzvot. To choose one law above another is not just to say that it is more important, but that the other is less important. And how dare we say that any law given by God is less than another?

The rabbi explained that he based his ruling on a Mishna in *Ethics of the Fathers*: "Be as scrupulous in performing a 'minor' mitzvah as you are a 'major' one, for you do not know the rewards given for mitzvot."

God didn't tell us how much we're rewarded for mitzvot just so that we should not weigh them on a scale before we decide which one we'd most like to do. Selectivity is a sin because it permits us to base our observance on personal preference. Religion then becomes nothing more than a moral code to follow when one agrees with it. Judaism can only have meaning if it's approached with a sense of reverence and humility. As someone wittily said, Judaism teaches, an "I" for an "I": To replace the egotism of my "I" with the wisdom of the greater "I"—"I am the Lord your God."

The Sentence That Says It All

Judaism is an organic whole. It's a total philosophy of life. It's a way of living that encompasses every moment. It's a commitment to a value system rooted in a belief that this is God's will. Its "system," as we've seen, is a manual of 613 "instructions." We just discovered we aren't permitted to choose between them. Yet a famous Talmudic passage dares to seek out the DNA, so to speak, of Divine Law. There's no more fitting way to close this chapter than to quote it (Babylonian Talmud, *Makkot* 23b–24a):

> Rabbi Simlai taught: 613 commandments were revealed to Moses; 365 negative commandments and 248 positive commandments. When David came, he summed up the 613 commandments in 11 ethical principles: Lord who may sojourn in Your tent, who may dwell on Your holy mountain?
>
> 1. He who lives without blame
>
> 2. Who does righteous acts
>
> 3. Who speaks the truth in his heart

4. Whose tongue speaks no deceit

5. Who has not done harm to his fellow

6. Or borne reproach for his acts toward his neighbor

7. For whom a contemptible person is abhorrent

8. Who honors those who fear the Lord

9. Who stands by his oath even when it is to his disadvantage

10. Who has never lent money for interest

11. Or accepted a bribe against the innocent

When Isaiah came, he summed up the 613 commandments in six ethical principles:

1. He who walks in righteousness

2. Who speaks honestly

3. Who spurns profit from fraudulent dealings

4. Who waives away a bribe instead of taking it

5. Who closes his ears and doesn't listen to malicious words

6. Who shuts his eyes against looking at evil

The prophet Micah then came and reduced them to three principles: It has been told to you, O man, what is good and what the Lord requires of you:

1. Only to do justly

2. To love mercy

3. To walk humbly before your God

Again, Isaiah came and reduced them to two principles: Thus says the Lord,

1. Keep justice

2. Do righteousness

But finally, Habakkuk came and based them all on one principle:

But the righteous shall live by his faith.

No, the Talmud doesn't mean that this verse replaces all of Jewish Law. What it teaches is that this is the underlying principle of Judaism:

"The righteous"—Judaism will let you know right from wrong and bring you the joy that comes from doing the right thing.

"shall live"—Judaism will replace existential angst with the spiritual bliss that accompanies days filled with meaning and purpose.

"by his faith"—because without faith we're like stained-glass windows in the dark, but with faith the light of God can shine through, illuminating our lives and bringing us blessings.

The Least You Need to Know

◆ The Musar movement identifies the essence of Judaism as holiness—the character traits of humility, truth, honesty, compassion, human dignity, and proper speech.

◆ Jews, just like Abraham, whose name implies a mission to spread the word of God to others, must serve as an example for the world and sanctify God's name by their actions.

◆ The Ba'al Teshuva Movement of our times is an unparalleled historic phenomenon, and those who engage in bringing people closer to God are fulfilling another major tenet of Judaism.

◆ Zionism stresses the significance of the Land of Israel in Judaism.

◆ "All mitzvot are created equal," say the ancient rabbis, and selecting one above another only creates a system of morality based on personal preference.

◆ The Talmud chooses a verse from Habakkuk, "And the righteous shall live by his faith," as the most succinct summary of the principles found in all of Jewish Law.

Chapter 27

Any Questions from the Floor?

In This Chapter

- Twenty questions—from astronauts and adoption to the secret of happiness

- Those other things you've always wanted to know about Judaism but were afraid to ask

Rudyard Kipling could have been Jewish when he wrote these words:

> I keep six honest serving men
> They taught me all I knew:
> Their names are What and Why and When
> And How and Where and Who.

One of the beautiful things about Judaism is that it encourages questions. The youngest child is introduced to ritual by being told to ask the Four Questions at the Passover seder. Jews take seriously the advice of Voltaire "to judge a man by his questions rather than by his answers." That's why I've often had the experience, as a lecturer, to have a program chairman tell me, "We've allotted a half hour for your talk and an hour for the question-and-answer period that follows."

Unfortunately, a book doesn't permit that kind of personal give-and-take. Yet as I bring this section on *The Crucial Questions* to a close, I can't think of a more fitting way to conclude than with a question-and-answer "session." I'll have to imagine what you might ask (by using a sampler of questions I've been asked throughout the years when speaking about Judaism) and hope that if there's something I don't cover, we'll get a chance to meet personally to discuss it some day.

Is Heaven Only for Jews?

Does Judaism believe that only Jews can go to heaven?

The good news is you don't have to be Jewish to get into heaven. The bad news is you still have to deserve it.

The Talmud teaches, "The righteous of the nations of the world have a portion in the World to Come." So who's righteous? God expects the Jews to observe the Commandments He revealed to them at Mount Sinai. But that's only relevant for the people who agreed to accept the Torah. Jews have a covenant defined by 613 Commandments. Non-Jews are obviously not bound by that.

From the Mountaintop

The name of Ruth, the convert revered as ancestress of King David, has a numerical value in gematria of 606. What's so special about that number? Simple: In accepting Judaism, she actually added precisely 606 of the 613 Mitzvot upon herself, because 7 of the 613, the "7 universal laws," she was already responsible for even before she became a Jewess.

Judaism, however, believes that there are seven "universal laws." In the language of the Constitution, "We hold these truths to be self-evident." People are required to obey these laws, not because they're Jewish, but because they're human. They are binding not just on the descendants of Abraham but of Adam—because man was created "in the image of God." Here's a short version of the laws meant for all mankind:

> To refrain from murder, sexual immorality, idolatry, tearing limbs from live animals and consuming them, cursing God, and theft, and to abide by the requirement to set up a system of law.

Waiting for Messiah

Is the belief in Messiah really very important in Judaism? Why? What is supposed to happen when Messiah comes?

Maimonides, as we've learned, lists the belief in Messiah as part of the 13 major principles. Although never explicitly mentioned in the five books of Moses, the Messianic vision became an important part of the message of many prophets. Throughout the centuries, it gave the Jews hope and may help to account for their survival in the face of the most horrible times of persecution.

The rabbis believe that the messianic concept is implicit in the story of Creation. God wanted a world like the Garden of Eden. Mankind was supposed to live in a literal Paradise. Human sin demanded expulsion. "Paradise Lost" became our lot ever since. Yet the Bible makes clear God didn't destroy Paradise. He, just like we, anxiously awaits a time when we will be worthy to return. The Messianic Age in Judaism is "Paradise Found"—bringing us back to the kind of world God originally intended.

The specifics of this vision have been the subject of much speculation. Some see the Messianic Age in highly supernatural terms. Others stress its blessings of universal peace and monotheism. As Maimonides put it, "At that time, there will be neither hunger nor war, neither envy nor competition, for the good will be found in great abundance and all delicacies as accessible as the dust of the earth. The whole world will have no other occupation than to know the Lord."

The smartest thing, he added, is not to dwell too much on the details. You'll know it when you see it—and for now our mission remains to make ourselves worthy of Messiah's coming.

From the Mountaintop

Jewish folktales delight in filling in details of the Messianic Age. That includes even the menu of meals to be served. Banquets will feature meat of the Leviathan and the Wild Ox, two legendary creatures, and wine that has been stored in the vat from the six days of Creation will be the liquid refreshment. (Tradition has it that was a very good year.) The entertainment will be Moses delivering a Torah lecture, the dancer will be Miriam, and King David will play the harp. All I can say is if that isn't true, a lot of people will be *very* disappointed!

Does Adoption Make It My Child?

Judaism demands, "Be fruitful and multiply," but what if we can't have any children? If we adopt, have we fulfilled the mitzvah? Is the child considered our son or daughter?

The Talmudic rabbis rule that whoever adopts an orphan is considered as if giving birth to that child. Rearing a child also makes you a parent. An adopted child is a member of the family in every respect.

From the Mountaintop

What was the name Moses' mother gave him? The Midrash says it was *Tov*—good. Just imagine if that would have remained his name; we'd have to be shouting "Holy Good" instead of "Holy Moses."

The most famous adopted child was, of course, Moses. Found in a basket by the daughter of Pharaoh, he was raised by her in the palace, and the Bible says, "And he was to her for a son." Not only that, it was the daughter of Pharaoh, not Moses' biological mother, who gave him his name Moses, "because from the water I drew him." To this day, Jews call their greatest leader by the name she gave him to acknowledge gratitude for the kindness of an adoptive mother.

The Chosen People?

Do Jews believe they are the "Chosen People"? And if that's what Judaism teaches, doesn't it make it a racist religion?

The four-line poem says it best:

> How odd of God
> To choose the Jews.
> It's not so odd
> The Jews chose God.

Jews aren't the chosen people as much as they are the choosing people. Jews accepted God's law, and Judaism prays that the rest of mankind will soon follow. We are, all of us, God's children. Some of us just don't realize it yet! That doesn't make Jews superior. Anyone who wants to convert is welcome to become part of a people with greater responsibility, more stringent obligations, and a heavier burden of serving as "a light unto the nations."

An Eye for an Eye—Ouch!

If God is kind and compassionate, how can he put a law as cruel as "an eye for an eye" in the Torah? We teach our kids two wrongs don't make a right—should we commit a barbaric act just because someone else did?

No, of course we shouldn't, and put your mind at ease—the Torah doesn't want us to either. Here's a perfect example of the need to understand the Written Law as interpreted by the Oral Law. The Talmud makes clear that the intent is to fine a person who put out another's eye, to exact monetary retribution, not physical vengeance.

Why then does the text say, "an eye for an eye?" For a simple reason: The Torah couldn't possibly use the words "money for an eye" because that would suggest there is parity between them. Just imagine a very wealthy man who hates his neighbor. He looks at the Bible and sees "money for an eye." He says to himself, "I can afford it," and knocks out the other guy's eye.

Pulpit Story

A man finds a bottle, a genie pops out, and … you know the rest. Only this genie offers its finder only one wish and attaches a peculiar condition. "You can ask me for anything you want, but whatever you get, your biggest enemy gets double. If you ask for a million dollars, he'll get two; you want a mansion, he'll have two. This is your big chance to get your heart's desire, but you've got to tell me right now, what is your greatest wish?" It takes only a moment for the response: "Okay, if that's the condition, I want you to make me blind in one of my eyes."

The Written Law says "an eye for an eye" because as far as God is concerned, that's what *should* be. If God based law on strict justice, when you take out somebody's eye, you ought to lose your own. But God won't stoop to your level. The Oral Law teaches us how God tempers justice with mercy. Together the Written and Oral Law manage to convey the duality of God's response: the harsh sentence that *should* be carried out and the merciful judgment that *is* in fact the law.

Kill the Bum?

Civilized societies are moving away from imposing capital punishment. Yet the Bible quite often says, "Die he shall die." Does Judaism want us to carry out executions for all the crimes it considers capital offenses?

Here's another example of how we can't take the words of the Torah literally until we add to them the commentary of the Oral Law. The Talmud tells us that a *Sanhedrin*— Supreme Court—that put someone to death once in seventy years was considered bloodthirsty. Seventy years is, of course, a generation. That's the equivalent of saying a Sanhedrin that *ever* carried out a capital punishment was considered barbaric.

How could they possibly condemn a Supreme Court that was just following the instructions of the Bible? But the court wasn't if it actually put somebody to death. The Oral Law explains that "Die he shall die" is God's way of saying, "If you do that, you *ought* to be killed."

There's all the difference in the world between a threat and actual punishment. If I want to impress upon my child how serious a misdeed it is if he runs into the street without looking, I tell him, "Next time you do that, I'll kill you." We both know that's not what I mean. I'm only saying it in the strongest language possible because I don't want him to get hurt. That's just how God writes the laws of the Bible. They're preventative rather than punitive. They're meant to scare you and stop you from committing a host of crimes. After the fact, if a warning didn't work, the court must find ways to ensure that capital punishment is never carried out.

So does Judaism believe in capital punishment? Only to the same extent that someone who really loves you will caution you, "Don't you dare—or you're dead."

From the Mountaintop

Though the laws of capital punishment weren't carried out in the time of the Sanhedrin (the Time of the Temple), the details of a "possible execution" were given. One of them required that before anyone was to be put to death, he had to be given a very strong drink, sort of like an anesthetic. That's the reason why, to this day, when you offer someone a drink, you say *L'chaim*, "to life." This drink, you're pointing out, has nothing to do with the executioner's potion.

Can I Lie Just a Little?

Is truth an absolute value in Judaism? Can I ever tell a little white lie?

Let's answer your question with a question: Suppose you're at a wedding. You go over to the bride to wish her *mazel tov* and she asks, "How do I look?" To put it bluntly, she couldn't place last in the Miss America contest. What do you say?

One rabbi in the Talmud, Shammai, felt you've got to tell the truth at all cost—no matter how much it hurts the person. After all, Shammai said, doesn't the Bible teach, "And from a false word you shall keep far"? But Hillel strongly disagreed. Lie in the interest of peace, he taught, because peace is a greater value than truth. And it is his view that became accepted as final law!

To prove the point, the Talmud illustrates with a remarkable biblical story. The angels told Sarah that she would give birth in a year's time. She couldn't believe it and exclaimed, "It's impossible, seeing that my husband is old." (This was before Viagra, and she knew the reality of her sex life.) God then repeated the conversation to Abraham but didn't do it verbatim. He told Abraham that his wife couldn't believe the prediction because she said she was too old. How's that for making an old man feel good by not impugning his virility! God was sensitive to Abraham's feelings but in the process the Almighty Himself told a lie.

So the next time your wife asks you, "Tell me the truth, honey, how do I look in this dress?" make sure you give her a Godly response.

Schmoozing

A truth that's told with bad intent, / Beats all the lies you can invent.
—William Blake

My Son, the Astronaut?

Is there any problem with a nice Jewish boy becoming an astronaut? Are there any good reasons why the Jewish religion would tell him not to go?

Glad you asked. Dr. Gerald Wittenstein, a 20-year veteran of NASA and currently CEO of International Space Systems, Inc., researched this question some time before the Israeli astronaut Ilan Ramon went up in space and came up with the following points:

1. Science and seeking answers to ultimate questions about the universe are encouraged by Judaism. We are partners with God in making this a better world. A mission that can be of benefit to mankind is a mitzvah.

2. Praying is a problem if services are determined by light and dark for the astronaut. There is a rabbinic ruling, though, that the astronaut should pray according to the time in Mission Control.

3. Dr. Wittenstein spoke to a dietitian in Space Lab who assured him that kosher food could be provided for a religious astronaut.

4. The big problem is that the Torah commands, "Be very careful to guard your life." Taking dangerous chances that are life-threatening is forbidden. As we know all too well from *Apollo 13*, the *Challenger*, and the most recent ill-fated *Columbia* mission, failure is possible. It might be a good idea, therefore, to wait until manned space flight has a record as good as the domestic airlines!

Bottom line? Although not encouraged, it's probably all right for a Jewish mother to say, "So go around the world, but don't forget your scarf and your galoshes."

> **Pulpit Story**
>
> A man returning from the world's first Bar Mitzvah on Pluto seemed disappointed. "What's wrong?" asked his friend, "the band was no good?" "The band was very good," he answered. "The food was no good?" asked his friend. "Out of this world!" "*Nu*, so what was the problem?" asked his friend. "There was no atmosphere."

Life on Mars?

What does Judaism teach about the possibility of life on other planets?

Rabbi Chasdai Crescas, way back in the fourteenth century, wrote that nothing in the Torah outlook precludes the existence of life on other planets. As a matter of fact, the verse in the Book of Psalms (145:13), "Your kingdom is one which encompasses all worlds," implies the existence of more than one world. The Talmud suggests that there are at least 18,000 other universes! The fact that they have to rely on Divine Providence makes it reasonable, in the eyes of many commentators, to assume that life does exist there.

What aliens look like, we can't possibly know. God must, of course, have given them laws in accord with *their* natures. The only thing we can be sure of is that all of them undoubtedly get fundraising appeals from their local synagogues.

Is *Star Trek*'s Mr. Spock Jewish?

I'm a Star Trek *groupie, and I have a question about a greeting in the series. Mr. Spock from the planet Vulcan greets people with, "Live long and prosper," while holding his hand toward them with a gap between his thumb and first finger, and a gap between his middle and third finger, something like the letter "W." I know that Leonard Nimoy, the actor who plays Mr. Spock, has Jewish parents. I've also seen this hand symbol on souvenirs in Israel. Around it was a Hebrew blessing. Is Mr. Spock really sending out a Jewish message?*

For all you "Trekkies," here's a fascinating bit of trivia: The "Vulcan" hand gestures of Mr. Spock, alias Jewish Leonard Nimoy, originate from the Torah.

The Kohanim, the descendants of Aaron, are commanded to bless the Jewish people by raising their hands in a specially prescribed way. The hands are to be held together, palms down, fingers split so that there are five spaces, one space between the thumbs, a space between the thumb and first finger of each hand, and a space between the second and third finger of each hand. The five spaces are an allusion to the verse in the Song of Songs (2:8), which says that God "peeks through the cracks in the wall."

The idea is that God's protection is strong even when He appears to be hidden. In this case, even if God's law is hidden in a *Star Trek* custom, you should be proud that you were able to find it.

Are Bacteria Kosher?

I know that bugs aren't kosher. Then how come yogurt, with live acidophilus and bifidus cultures, can be eaten? Or can they?

Okay, let's do it one more time—answer a question with a question. Are we allowed to breathe, since zillions of microorganisms are floating around in the air and we swallow some with every breath? Of course—that's rhetorical. Jewish law is concerned only with bugs that can be seen by the naked eye. Organisms that are visible only with the aid of a microscope are all kosher. The logic behind this is that the Torah was given to human beings, not to angels. Its laws are determined by normal human experience. Only "real-life" bugs are forbidden; invisible ones can be disregarded.

> **Pulpit Story**
>
> When strong microscopes were invented, a Jew rushed to a prominent rabbi and suggested that we should filter our water to avoid consuming the organisms we now know are present. The rabbi responded, "If you give a dime to charity by holding it under a magnifying glass, do you now get credit for giving a quarter?" It's what you see that counts.

Now You See It, Now You Don't

Judaism strongly forbids occult practices and "turning to magicians and soothsayers." Does that mean I can't hire a magician to entertain at my child's birthday party?

The problem with magicians, biblical commentators explain, is that people might take them seriously and ascribe to them divine powers. Magic that could lead to idolatry is prohibited. A Jewish magician should ideally tell the people that the "rabbit out of the hat" is just a trick. Penn and Teller, when they did their Refrigerator Tour show on Broadway, demonstrated one "magic box trick" so that the audience knew how the trick was done. (They must have consulted with a rabbi about how to get around biblical law.) The bottom line here is that as long as it's clear to everyone that it's just a show, it's kosher.

 **From the Mountaintop**

The stock phrase of magicians, *abracadabra*, comes from an Aramaic expression, *abra*, "I will create," and *k'dabra*, "as I speak."

A Six-Pointed Question

Why is a six-pointed star a symbol of Judaism? And why is it called the Star of David? Does it go back that far in history?

In southern Italy, a tombstone dating back to 300 C.E. was found with a six-pointed star on it. In the year 1354, King Carl IV insisted that the Jews of Prague make a flag for themselves that would feature this six-pointed star, as well as the five-pointed star of King Solomon. The words *Magen Dovid* literally mean "shield of David." Some say that the soldiers of King David's army wielded shields in the shape of a six-pointed star. King David's personal seal was not a star, but rather a shepherd's staff and a bag. His son, King Solomon, used a five-pointed star for his personal seal.

The significance of the Magen Dovid, according to the Jewish mysticism of the Kabbalah, is that the number 6 represents the heavens and the earth and the four directions (north, south, east, west). That suggests the idea of God's omnipresence. Interestingly, the words *Magen Dovid* in Hebrew are made up of six letters. The Magen Dovid also has 12 sides. David, as King, unified the twelve tribes. Later scholars, such as Franz Rosenzweig, suggest that the top triangle strives upward toward God, while the lower triangle strives downward toward the real world. The intertwining makes the triangles inseparable and pictorially captures a major ideal of Judaism.

"I Changed My Name"

I've heard that some people change the names given to them at birth. Is this permissible? Is there a religious reason for doing this?

Changing your name for a frivolous reason is frowned upon. Your name isn't like the color of your hair—hair today, dye tomorrow. You don't mess with something that defines your soul. Yet for a life-threatening situation, it's not only legal, it's suggested.

We know that Abram had his name changed to Abraham and Jacob to Israel. Once their names were changed, their lives were altered. Someone extremely ill can also assume the new name Chayim (for a male) and Chayah (for a female) both meaning life. Hopefully, the new name is more successful than medicine. At worst, it's a placebo; at best, it's a mystical miracle worker.

"Love Your Eyes—Can I Have Them, Please?"

Organ transplants obviously weren't possible in the days of the Bible. Does Judaism have anything to say about whether this life-saving measure is permissible?

To save another person's life, you can violate almost any law. As you've learned elsewhere in this book, only idolatry, adultery, and murder are exceptions to this rule. The Torah may not have explicitly mentioned organ transplants, but it did say this:

"Do not stand idly by as the blood of your neighbor is being spilled." In other words, you're obligated to help save another person and to refuse to do so is inhumane.

Does this apply even after death? Almost all modern religious authorities believe it does. To save someone else's life is so important it even supersedes the law that requires us not to "mutilate" the dead. There's no greater dignity that can be given to the deceased than to allow the departed to save another person's life.

That's not meant to say that organ transplants can readily be done without rabbinic consultation. Every case is different and requires analysis. A heart transplant is the most difficult of all cases because if the heart still works—which it obviously has to if it is to be donated—then the first person is still legally alive according to Jewish law. We can't "kill" one person to save another, no matter how much longer the second will live. But eyes and other organs can live on after death. Can't you just picture the angelic smile on the spirit of someone who passed away and knows that part of him is still regularly going to shul?

Two to One

Why is it that my friends in Israel celebrate a holiday for only one day and here in the United States it's observed for two? How can Judaism have different laws for different Jews?

Before the middle of the fourth century C.E., Jews didn't have a fixed calendar. Instead, the new moon was declared on the basis of testimony by witnesses in front of the Sanhedrin, the Supreme Court. The information about the day declared as the first of the month was transmitted by torch signals from community to community throughout all of Israel. Jews in distant places had to be informed by messenger. Travel was difficult and uncertain, and communities in the Diaspora, outside of Israel, were often not sure of the proper day for observing the holiday. Out of doubt, they added a day to the observance of all the major festivals. Then these far-away communities could be sure they had "both bases covered." This second day of observance became known as the Second Day Festival of the Diaspora.

So, you ask, what does that have to do with today, when we no longer have to wonder which is the correct day? The calendar tells us, and besides, even if we use witnesses, we could immediately flash the news around the world.

The answer is one word sacred to Judaism: tradition. We got so used to doing it one way, we just couldn't stop. Besides, as the philosopher Yehudah HaLevy suggests, maybe Jews who live outside of Israel need twice as much of a holiday to capture its spirituality as do Jews who live in the Holy Land!

Just Like the Amish

Does Judaism demand that observant Jews wear beards and sidelocks? And if it does, how come there are religious Jews who remain clean shaven?

Jewish Law teaches, "You shall not mar the corner of your beard" (Leviticus 19:27), which was a practice of the idolatrous nations of the times. The Law specifically forbids the use of a knife or razorblade. Scissors, clippers, and electric shavers are not included in this ban. Some Jews prefer to stick to the letter of the Law and not "cut" at all. Others make use of the permitted methods and shave. Don't be fooled by external appearances, though. As a wise observer of the Jewish scene once said, "I've seen rabbis without beards, and I've also seen beards without rabbis. Of the two, in all honesty, I prefer the first."

Mirror, Mirror on the Wall

Why do Jews cover their mirrors in a house of mourning?

We look into mirrors to make sure that we look good. In the midst of mourning, our appearance should be unimportant. Another reason is that a mourner may see how much grief has affected his appearance. That can make him feel even worse and add to his pain. Covering mirrors is to express concern for the mourner's feelings even as it stresses proper priorities for grieving.

Bet I Can Go to Vegas

What are the odds that Judaism says gambling is a no-no? The casino in Las Vegas is willing to "comp" me for a week's stay—can I go?

I would have said, "No problem," until I heard the second part of your question. The Talmud discusses whether gamblers can serve as "kosher witnesses." One opinion is that anyone who gambles is suspect. Gamblers can never be trusted. The second view, the opinion accepted as law, declares that only professional gamblers are rejected as witnesses. People who don't work for a living but rely on games of chance contribute nothing to the world and are called "wicked"—the category that isn't believed for testimony.

Now tell me why the casino is willing to treat you so well that it will give you complimentary passes? If it's because you're a full-time professional, you can count on two things: You'll never be a witness according to Jewish Law—and you'll never be rich.

> **Pulpit Story**
>
> A man once asked the saintly Chafetz Chaim, one of the greatest rabbis of the last century, to bless him so that he'd win the lottery. The rabbi refused. "But you give blessings to people who gamble on stocks; why not when they gamble on lotteries?" the man asked. The Chafetz Chaim answered that he gives blessings to stock investors because if the stock goes up, no one loses money. Blessing one lottery ticket, though, is a "curse" upon all the other tickets. That he said he wasn't willing to do.

Don't "Take It Easy"

Does Judaism have a simple formula for happiness?

Yes, and interestingly enough, it's a bit of advice that goes against a popular American saying. When people say goodbye to each other, they often offer the "blessing" of "take it easy." That's because it's commonly assumed that happiness is the by-product of inactivity. The fantasy is lying on the beach, a drink in your hand, with nothing to do. Judaism says that Adam and Eve were put into a place where they had a job, to work it and guard it, and God called it Paradise.

To have nothing to do is a curse. Life gains its joy from a sense of purpose. You only feel good when you accomplish something. Happiness comes from doing; depression is often the result of dying piecemeal of stagnation and boredom.

When Jews leave each other they don't say, "take it easy." The word is *shalom*. It means not only peace, but also whole, complete. The best prayer you can give a friend is the prayer that I want to offer you as I bring this section to a close:

> May you replace ease with effort; may you find joy in always scaling new mountains; may you never rest from your pursuit of knowledge; may you desire to always be a little bit better than yesterday and a little bit less than tomorrow. That's what will make you a *whole* human being and bring you true happiness.

The Least You Need to Know

- Judaism encourages questions—and its religious and ethical teachings are applicable to many contemporary areas, from space travel to organ transplants.

- Judaism is unique among religions in teaching that "You don't have to be Jewish to get to heaven."

◆ Jews don't believe they are "the chosen people"; they are rather "the choosing people" who were ready to accept God's laws before other people.

◆ The Jewish secret for happiness is to endow life with purpose.

◆ Instead of saying "good-bye," Jews take leave of each other with the word *shalom*, which means not only "peace" but also "complete" or "whole"—a prayer for spiritual harmony and completeness.

Part 8

Welcome to the Twenty-First Century

We're now in the twenty-first century, and we'd have to be deaf, dumb, and blind to be unaware of the dramatic differences between the world of our parents and the one we've inherited. Historians point out that in just the past few decades we've witnessed more changes in almost every area of life than in many previous centuries. Every part of our way of life has been affected.

Religion may deal with ancient truths but it, too, has to contend with modern times. Solomon, considered the wisest of men in Jewish tradition, begged God, "Renew our days as of old." What he prayed for was the right balance between the old and the new, between tradition and modernity. So do we also hope to create a new and better future building on the irreplaceable foundations of our ancestors.

This last part is devoted to the challenges Jews and Judaism confront in this new century. What are the most significant changes affecting us and how have the different branches of Judaism responded? What are the key problems that threaten our survival? And—most important of all—can we be optimistic about our future?

Chapter 28

The Times They Are A-Changin'

In This Chapter

◆ How Jews are accepted, envied, and even imitated in contemporary culture

◆ How Judaism made it to outer space

◆ Reform Judaism: turning back to tradition

◆ Conservative Judaism: looking for the right balance

◆ Orthodox Judaism: guardians of the faith

Five centuries before the Common Era, the pre-Socratic Greek philosopher Periclitus taught his students: "There is nothing permanent, except change." In our times, Bob Dylan (born Robert Zimmerman) expressed it in the form of a song that became the battle cry for an entire generation: "The Times They Are A-Changin'."

The Torah preceded both of them. In Moses' final speech to the Jewish people, he commands them, "Remember the days of old, consider the years of generation to generation." (Deuteronomy 32:7) The commentators point out that the Hebrew word (*shnot*), which Moses uses for "the years," also means "the changes." Remember the past, he advised, but always take into account the ways in which the world is no longer what it once was. What was wise in one generation may not be appropriate for another. Here's one instance where the Bible clearly agrees with Darwin: "It is not the strongest of the species that survive, nor the most intelligent, but the one most responsive to change."

Judaism may emphasize preserving the past, but it just as strongly preaches the need to change the world in order to bring about a more perfect future. It's what Alfred North Whitehead called the key to progress, "To preserve order amid change and to preserve change amid order."

Judaism, as we have seen, began with the profound discovery by Abraham of monotheism. It seeks to safeguard the divine truths revealed to the Jewish people at Mount Sinai. As we now move forward in the twenty-first century, Jews—and Judaism—take to heart the mandate of the late President John F. Kennedy: "Change is the law of life. And those who look only to the past or present are certain to miss the future."

It's "in" to Be Jewish

If a Jewish Rip Van Winkle were suddenly to awaken today after a sleep of no more than half a century, there's one thing that would probably amaze him more than anything else: Madonna wearing tefillin! No, of course I don't mean Madonna, the mother of Jesus. I am talking about the modern-day "Material Girl" idolized by tens of millions of adoring fans for her singing, her dancing, and her sensuality. It's this Madonna who, in the music video for *Die Another Day*, transforms herself from "the Material girl" to "the Kabbalah girl," winding the leather straps of the tefillin around her left arm in the exact same way this holy mitzvah is performed by religious Jews.

We can rightly question—as many people have—the appropriateness of a religious symbol in a secular blend of music and sex. But what should certainly strike us as an amazing commentary on our times is that Madonna assumed that her many millions of non-Jewish fans would recognize an object sacred to less than two percent of the American population and would not harbor any negative feelings toward a distinctly Jewish practice!

Ask the Rabbi

Jewish tradition teaches that Kabbalah should only be studied toward the end of one's life, after becoming fully conversant with the major texts of Judaism. It should only be a dessert after you've completed the main meal.

Jews above a certain age can easily remember a time when wearing a yarmulke, putting on a tallit, or wearing tefillin were things you just didn't do in public. Living in a gentile society carried with it a certain sense of shame about actions that marked you as different. But surely, if Madonna, who isn't even Jewish, isn't embarrassed by tefillin, well—"we've come a long way, baby."

Pulpit Story

The sophisticated suburban socialite sends her son to Hebrew school. The little boy becomes inspired when his teacher tells him all about the *mezuzah* that Jews affix to the doorpost of their homes. The boys begs his mother to get one for their house as well. The mother finally gives in, goes to a Judaica store, asks to buy a *mezuzah*, but begs the owner, "Please, don't let it look too Jewish."

A few decades ago, American Jews blessed their good fortune for living in a land where they were tolerated. Today Jews are amazed to see that even more than being tolerated, they are often imitated. And as we all know, imitation is the sincerest form of flattery.

Theater critic Walter Kerr recognized this remarkable trend a number of years ago. "What has happened since World War II," he wrote, "is that American sensibility itself has become part Jewish, perhaps nearly as much Jewish as it is anything else." The famous Madison Avenue slogan, "Dress British, think Yiddish," has become more than a funny tag line; it describes a contemporary American reality.

In the middle of the twentieth century, Jews who survived the Holocaust wondered whether their fate, their culture, their religion, and their people would also survive. In a remarkable and truly miraculous rebirth, corresponding to the vision of Ezekiel in which the dead dry bones came back to life, Jews in the twenty-first century find themselves not only alive, but admired, respected, and in many ways imitated.

From the Mountaintop

Professor Sylvia Barack Fishman of Brandeis University titled a famous November 1966 article, "US Culture Has Been Judaized and Vice Versa." She calls this process a "coalescence of two cultures."

"The Gift of the Jews"

Probably at no other time in history could a book titled *The Gifts of the Jews: How a Tribe of Desert Nomads Changed the Way Everyone Thinks and Feels* have made it to the bestseller list—and stayed there for more than two years.

The author, Thomas Cahill, had previously written a book that sold fairly well, *How the Irish Saved Civilization: The Untold Story of Ireland's Heroic Role from the Fall of Rome to the Rise of Medieval Europe*. Sure and begorrah, there must be a lot of Irish people willing to drink to that, and it's not surprising that this book enjoyed a fairly large readership. But who would have guessed that a popular account of ancient Jewish culture that glorifies its contributions to the Western world and modern civilization would so capture the interest of millions of Americans.

Cahill credits the Jews not only for monotheism and the idea of a personal relationship with God; it is these concepts, he reminds us, that led us to the understanding that we have a personal responsibility for ourselves and our relations with our neighbors, as well as to our respect for history itself. The roots for what we consider Western individuality, personal responsibility, conscience, and culpability for ourselves and the world—all these can be traced to the monotheism of the Jews.

And one more thing, perhaps the most important gift of all: Jews and Judaism gave to the world the idea of progress. Prior to the rise of Judaism, Cahill explains, men believed in life as a "circularity." We're born. We die. The next generation comes along and repeats the process. Life has no direction but merely keeps reiterating itself. Only with Abraham and God's command to "Go forth from your land, from your birthplace and from your father's home, to the land that I will show you," do we recognize the idea of life as a journey of discovery. Abraham, Cahill makes clear, is not only the first Jew. He is our first explorer, the first human to intentionally set out for the unknown. This notion of life as a process or a progression created the very idea of history, of a present different from the past. From it stems the belief that the future can become poles apart from the world we live in at present.

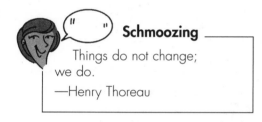

Schmoozing

Things do not change; we do.

—Henry Thoreau

Albert Einstein, the man *Time* magazine chose as its Man of the Millennium, gave the world the insight that time is relative. Cahill makes it clear that it was the Jewish people, almost four millennia ago, who gave the world the understanding that time is linear instead of cyclical. That concept, with its profound implications for progress, proved as significant as Einstein's theory. And Einstein himself, verbalizing this age-old Jewish perspective, would couch the idea in a way that makes it even more relevant: "The world we have created is a product of our thinking; it cannot be changed without changing our thinking." And that truth isn't relative. It's the unalterable principle of life that Jews discovered, transmitted to the world, and for which today they are at last being acknowledged and thanked.

Like the "Stars in the Heavens"

In our contemporary culture, it isn't just Cahill who loves the Jews. Superstars from the world of sports and song, among others, keep making it clear that being Jewish, far from being a pejorative, is now a significant source of pride.

Consider former Toronto Orioles baseball great, Shawn Green. When his contract came up for renewal, he told his bosses that salary wasn't his main consideration. Although raised with minimal exposure to his Jewish heritage, Green said he'd been so moved by the cheers of Jewish fans around the league that he wanted to learn more about the Jewish people to have an opportunity to contribute to his heritage. He would only sign to play in a city with a large Jewish community. And sure enough, he signed with the Los Angeles Dodgers, where he proceeded to set some incredible records in his new hometown, a city with one of the largest Jewish populations in the country. On May 23, 2002, Green became only the fourteenth player in major league history to hit four home runs in one game. He set a major league single game record with 19 total bases. He went six for six with a double and single against the last-place Milwaukee Brewers. He drove in seven runs, scored six. Green set franchise single-game records for the most home runs, most runs scored, and most total bases. And how far did his home runs soar? Some spectators said they seemed to travel "to the stars in the heavens"—the very phrase God used to predict to Abraham the greatness of his descendants!

I am sure that Shawn Green was as happy on that day as pop star Michael Jackson says he was when he attended Sabbath services at the Carlebach Synagogue in New York City. This time Jackson wasn't on stage but merely an onlooker. Yet he said it was one of the most moving experiences of his life.

The very first synagogue in the United States, in Newport, Rhode Island, had a tunnel built under the bimah through which the congregants could flee if it ever became too dangerous to be caught praying in a synagogue. Today the only reason that might necessitate a tunnel in a Jewish House of God would be to save a rock star from crazed fans coming to mob him when they learn he is in the synagogue!

From the Mountaintop

The Touro Synagogue, the oldest one in the United States, was officially designated a national historic site in 1946.

"My Son, the President"

To really understand how far Jews have come from the turn of the century, we need only to recall the quip of Jules Farber from not too long ago: "The time is at hand when the wearing of prayer shawl and skull cap would not bar a man from the White House—unless, of course, the man is Jewish!"

Pulpit Story

The first Jewish president invites his mother to come visit the White House. He promises to have her picked up in front of her house by the presidential limo. A neighbor, seeing the fancy car, asks her where she's going. She answers, "You know my son, the doctor? Well, I'm going to visit his brother!"

Thanks to Joe Lieberman, the joke has lost its relevance. As Al Gore's running mate for vice president of the United States, Lieberman would have been a heartbeat away from the presidency. His religious affiliation didn't prevent Lieberman and Gore from winning the popular vote in 2000, if not the presidency. And polls showed that Lieberman's commitment to Judaism, Orthodox Judaism at that, wasn't a negative. Americans appreciated Lieberman's commitment to spirituality, even as they jokingly said they knew that if he won he would dedicate himself totally to his duties as vice president, "24/6." In a stunning expression of the present-day feelings toward Jews and Judaism, Americans clearly proclaimed their unflinching readiness to accept "the gifts of the Jews" for the highest position of leadership.

... And Even in Outer Space

In January 2003, Judaism observed another milestone. For the first time in the history of mankind, the laws of Shabbat, the seventh day of rest, as well as Kashrut, the eating of Kosher food, were observed in outer space.

From the Mountaintop

Ilan Ramon sent a message to Israel's president, Moshe Katsav: "This morning we flew over Israel. From space I could clearly see Jerusalem. When I looked at our capital, I said one small prayer: "Hear O Israel, the Lord is our God, the Lord is One"—Judaism's most fundamental affirmation of faith.

The space shuttle crew of the ill-fated *Columbia* mission included the first Israeli astronaut. Colonel Ilan Ramon, a combat pilot in the Israeli Air Force, identified himself as a secular Jew. But that didn't stop him from making the commitment to observe the laws of his people while in outer space. "This is symbolic," Ramon said. "I thought it would be nice to represent all kinds of Jews, including religious ones." He joked about affixing a mezuzah to the shuttle's door, but said it was up to the commander. And he took with him a few items of very special spiritual significance. These artifacts, he explained, would "emphasize the unity of the people of Israel and the Jewish communities abroad."

One was a kiddush cup. Another was a picture of the earth as it might be seen from the moon, drawn by a Jewish boy in the Theresienstadt concentration camp—a dream of the skies imagined by someone who was denied his place on earth. Together with these was a Torah scroll with an incredible story. Dr. Joachim Josef, a researcher at Tel Aviv University responsible for one of the experiments to be performed in space, had shared with Ramon the story of the small Torah scroll used at his Bar Mitzvah almost sixty years ago, while he was in a concentration camp in Germany. The elderly rabbi performing the ceremony gave the Torah he had smuggled in to the death camp to the Bar Mitzvah boy, with instructions to tell people in the future what had happened there. Colonel Ramon—himself the son and grandson of Holocaust survivors—asked Dr. Josef if he might take it into space with him as a tribute. During the mission, Ramon held up this very Torah several times so that a picture of God's words in outer space might be beamed back to the world.

Colonel Ramon, as we all know, did not make it back. For reasons we will never understand, the Torah that survived the Holocaust perished with him. But we can at least derive some measure of comfort from the knowledge that almost 4,000 years from the time that Moses brought the Torah down from the heavens, a true Jewish hero once again elevated it to the heights from where it had come. Like Moses of old who didn't succeed in reaching the Promised Land, the first Israeli astronaut wasn't fortunate enough to complete his mission. But he will nevertheless be remembered forever for his *kiddush ha-Shem*, his sanctification of the name of God, in the heavens themselves.

Ask the Rabbi

Prime Minister Ariel Sharon asked Ilan Ramon in a televised conversation to space, "What do you see from there that you can't see from here?" Ramon answered: "Our earth is beautiful, really, and the atmosphere which makes it possible for us to live and breathe is really thin. We've got to take care of it like the apple of our eye." That's not only good advice, it's a *mitzvah* as well.

What Do We Do Now?

So how are we Jews supposed to react to this change of fortune? We are no longer pariahs. We are respected personalities.

To welcome the year 2000, *Time* magazine listed the hundred most influential people of the twentieth century—and the list included fifteen Jews. Isaiah's prediction that we were meant to be "a light unto the nations" is becoming ever more a reality. If it's "in" to be Jewish, how should that affect us?

The philosopher Henri Bergson said, "To exist is to change; to change is to mature; to mature is to create oneself endlessly." The world around us has changed. It's matured. So we have to change and mature as well. And that means we have a responsibility to create ourselves anew, taking advantage of the countless possibilities that present themselves to bring the world that much closer to its messianic ideal.

The major movements of contemporary Judaism each have shown, in their own ways, the desire to live up to this task—to adjust to changing times but to still cling to unchanging principles.

Reform Judaism: "Back to the Yarmulke"

With the greater interest and respect of the world for all things Jewish, the movement for greater identification with Jewish ritual and practice couldn't help but make inroads into the Reform movement.

1998 for many Jews became known as "The year of the Oreo." The largest-selling cookie in America received kosher certification, a sure sign that Jews, like the rest of Americans, loved "the cookie with a hat"—but also proof beyond doubt that there were enough consumers concerned about kashrut to prompt Nabisco to pay for kosher certification. Shea Stadium, home of the baseball New York Mets, opened a "Glatt Kosher" food stand serving hot dogs, knishes, and falafels. And the Reform Union of American Hebrew Congregations decided it would serve only kosher food for its new summer camp in Ontario, Canada—the very first time that any camp in North America sponsored by Reform Judaism had gone kosher.

In 1885, when Reform Judaism made its official appearance on the American scene, the first graduates of the Reform Rabbinical Seminary celebrated with a banquet featuring shrimp as the first course. By one of the ironies of fate (or perhaps as a sign of God's sense of humor) the CCAR, the Central Conference of American Rabbis (the Reform Rabbinic Body) at its annual convention in the very same city of Pittsburgh on May 26, 1999, made official its desire to return to observance of many of the rituals the founders of classical Reform had rejected.

From the Mountaintop

Today there are more than 45,000 products certified as kosher, up from just 1,750 about 20 years ago.

Reform Rabbis had taken note of the fact that ritual practice was on the upswing within the movement, due in no small part to the greater interest in spirituality among younger Reform Jews. Not only were such practices as praying in Hebrew with a head covering and prayer shawl and celebrating Rosh Hashanah for two days on the rise, but the kosher laws were also being taken more seriously than ever. The then president of the CCAR, Rabbi Richard Levy, proposed a draft known as "The Ten Principles" which sought to reorient the movement toward greater Jewish traditionalism. In its original version, the platform not only asserted that the "*mitzvot* of the Torah," not modern values, were at the center of Judaism, but actually spelled out some of those mitzvot as viable options for Reform Jews. These included the kosher laws, Sabbath observance, and immersion in the *mikvah* (ritual bath).

Levy's proposal was met with far from unanimous acceptance. Many of those raised in the tradition of classical Reform, which stressed ethics rather than ritual, felt that their brand of Judaism was being replaced by an orthodoxy that had long since been considered outdated. Yet after numerous revisions that moderated its emphasis on tradition, a sixth version of the text was approved. It acknowledged that "God, Torah and Israel" are the central tenets of Judaism, balancing this affirmation with the recognition of "the diversity of Reform Jewish beliefs and practices."

Nevertheless, Torah was identified as "the foundation of Jewish life." Jews were called upon to study the mitzvot which, it was agreed, "demand renewed attention." Still, the platform reaffirmed the traditional reform concern with ethics, social action, and world peace. It also reaffirmed the Reform movement's liberal stance by welcoming the intermarried and those of any sexual orientation.

The *New York Times* portrayed the statement of principles as a turning point "for encouraging the observance of rituals that Reform's founders had discarded." *Time* magazine headlined its story, "Back to the *yarmulke*." *New York* magazine quipped that the Reform movement finally passed the bold new principle that "attendance at Woody Allen films no longer qualifies as religious observance."

For some rabbinic leaders, the change of emphasis had gone too far. Reform with a yarmulke, they felt, lost its reason for being. For others, Reform's shift to the right hadn't gone far enough. Judaism, they said, could be—well, a little more Jewish. But no matter what one thought of the compromise of the new Pittsburgh platform, it was clear that today's Reform Judaism recognizes that a changing world requires a change of direction.

> **Schmoozing**
>
> The old reformed Judaism is dead; a new post-reformed is struggling to be born.
>
> —Rabbi Arnold Jacob Wolf

Conservative Judaism: Finding the Right Balance

Conservative Judaism, like its Reform counterpart, also found itself pulled in two directions. It couldn't escape the insistence of many of its younger rabbinical graduates with stricter standards, in line with the Conservative commitment to the discipline of Jewish law. As the new millennium approached, the Committee of Law and Standards of Conservative Judaism declared that intermarried Jews couldn't hold professional positions that might make them religious role models, such as Hebrew school principals, teachers, and youth group leaders. The United Synagogue of Conservative Judaism, the movement's congregational arm, decided to elevate the standards for lay leaders as well. Moving strongly to the ideal of greater observance, they established "eight behavioral expectations" for those who wanted to serve on its governing boards. Included were items such as a commitment to praying, if at all possible with a minyan; studying Torah at least one hour a week; adding the performance of three new mitzvot every year; helping to repair the world through charitable activity; strengthening ties with Israel; and learning Hebrew.

What made this so remarkable was not the specific content of the suggestions as much as the implicit assumption that Jewish leadership requires people who can speak in the language not of "do as I say" but rather "do as I do."

Schmoozing

The synagogue is not simply a Jewish organization. It is not merely a club to which people belong for Jewish identification. The synagogue is mandated to challenge its members toward Jewish growth.

—Rabbi Jerome Epstein, executive vice president, United Synagogue

Sensitive as well to the new emphasis on Torah study and the desire for more knowledge on the part of most American Jews, the Conservative movement also took a leaf from the highly successful *daf yomi* program started by the Orthodox—a program where a *daf* (a page) of the Talmud was studied by Jews every day of the year so as to complete the entire Talmud in a little over seven years. The Conservative movement initiated a *perek yomi*, the study of a chapter a day of the Bible. The United Synagogue provides study guides and, in today's age of the Internet, of course set up a website to facilitate the project.

"The Tree of Life"

To reach out even more to the tens of thousands of Jews thirsting for Torah, the Conservative movement, in September 2001, came out with a ground-breaking new translation of Torah and commentary, *Etz Hayim* (literally, "Tree of Life"). Billed as the first new Torah commentary for Conservative Judaism in over seventy years, *Etz Hayim* boasts an all-star cast of writers, including Harold Kushner (of *When Bad Things Happen to Good People* fame), Chaim Potok (author of best-selling *The Chosen*, as well as *My Name is Asher Lev*), in addition to a number of other famous scholars. What makes this commentary a monumental achievement, its authors are quick to note, is not only the breadth of its commentaries (making this a 1,516-page work) but also the fact that it incorporates recent archeological findings, textural interpretations, and—for the first time—the opinions of female rabbis.

What has caused a great deal of controversy though—especially from Orthodox readers—is the willingness of the editors to accept views that are far from traditional. The Conservative version of the Torah doesn't shirk from declaring that there is today a consensus that there never was an actual historical person called Abraham, and that the exodus from Egypt never really happened. Moving to the more traditional direction in terms of observance, the Conservative movement appears to be swaying more to the left in its theology.

That's probably both the attraction as well as the potential turn-off of the denomination that seeks to find its rightful place between Reform and Orthodoxy.

Orthodox Judaism: Protecting the Fort

As the oldest branch of Judaism, Orthodoxy sees its strength deriving from its direct link with its roots. It perceives its smaller numbers not as a sign of weakness but as a necessary—almost predictable—condition resulting from its being the most difficult and demanding denomination of Judaism. Like the Jewish people themselves, who were biblically consigned to the role of a "small nation," chosen "not because of your numbers" (Deuteronomy 7:7), Orthodoxy is prepared to exchange popularity for what it considers total allegiance to truth.

Even as Conservative and Reform Judaism flourish, Orthodoxy considers its efforts rewarded by the very existence of its sister movements. All too often, Conservative and Reform Jews are the "trickled-down" remnants coming from Orthodox backgrounds. Claim the Orthodox, "And where would these Jews with minimal links to their faith come from if there didn't exist a hard core of fully committed observers of Torah law?"

Orthodox Judaism views the contemporary concern with ritual, tradition, and spirituality, even when they appear in diminished form in Reform and Conservative Judaism, as derivative blessings stemming from the orthodoxy of Jews committed to not diluting their Judaism.

With the shift to the right and an increased receptivity to religious practice, Orthodoxy today is witness to two divergent and seemingly contradictory movements. On the one hand, the success of the *Ba'al T'shuvah* movement, attracting countless Jews who have strayed back to religious observance, as well as the greater respect afforded Orthodox Jews as "Guardians of the Faith" has led some rabbinic leaders to feel confident, and therefore more accepting of others. As Rabbi Yaakov Perlow, head of the ultra-orthodox *Agudath Israel*,

> ### Schmoozing
>
> My Orthodox parents have come to expect that their children will reject at least certain aspects of their own outlook on life, and cannot even be certain that they will choose to attend a secular university or pursue careers requiring advanced study.
> —Historian Jack Wertheimer, *Commentary* magazine

> ### From the Mountaintop
>
> In 1996, a new organization, *Edah*, was founded under the slogan, "The courage to be modern and orthodox." Its purpose, according to Director Rabbi Saul Berman, is "to deal with the challenge of orthodoxy confronting a changing world."

observed, "We're no longer poor and shaky"—and that's why he feels "Orthodoxy is now secure enough to relax its fortress mentality and project love and friendship toward those outside the group."

But the very same forces that make for greater understanding also lead to a sense of triumphalism, a sense that "we were right all along," and a sometimes disturbing willingness to write off all those who disagree in the slightest way as "unredeemable heretics."

As I've already shared with you, I'm an Orthodox rabbi, so it's hard to maintain total objectivity. I love the fact that the focus of my faith is Torah, doing the will of God, performing mitzvot, and "fixing the world" by adhering strictly to the will and the wisdom of God's guidance. I am troubled by extremism of any kind and the ability of some of God's committed followers to sometimes forget that the most important injunction of the entire Torah is to "love your neighbor as yourself."

But then again, to fulfill this law properly, I better not criticize anybody else.

And After the Changes

We've come to see that Judaism in the twenty-first century has come quite a long way. In the world at large, we used to be confronted with prejudice. Today we can be filled with pride. In a little more than 50 years, being Jewish has gone from a yellow badge of shame to a respected—and sometimes even envied—mark of honor. Being religious no longer carries the stigma of simplistic and foolish faith. It defines someone who seeks greater meaning in life than a hedonistic pursuit of pleasure, fame, and fortune.

Every branch of Judaism has in some way responded to this new reality. Even those who profess to be secular Jews, like Ilan Ramon, of blessed memory, want to connect with their past, forge a link with their people, and search for the serenity of spiritual meaning to their lives.

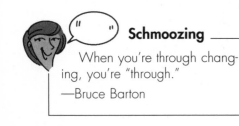

Schmoozing

When you're through changing, you're "through."

—Bruce Barton

Jews can't help but look back at this little more than 50-year jubilee since the Holocaust, and reflect on the miracle. What has happened to us since those days when we stood on the brink of annihilation vividly demonstrates what Richard Bach said so beautifully: "What the caterpillar calls the end of the world, the master calls a butterfly."

The Least You Need to Know

♦ Jews—and Judaism—have gone from being tolerated to being respected, envied, and even imitated.

♦ *The Gift of the Jews*, a national best-seller, made Americans conscious of the great debt they owe to this small but extremely influential people.

♦ America has been in the forefront of religious tolerance, and today even the election of a Jewish president doesn't seem out of the realm of possibility.

♦ In response to the general shift back to tradition, Reform Judaism underwent major theological changes with the adoption of a new set of principles at its convention in Pittsburgh in 1999.

♦ Conservative Judaism is making much greater demands for religious commitment by its lay leadership, is placing renewed emphasis on study of Torah by all of its congregational members, and has produced a ground-breaking new translation of Torah and commentary, *Etz Hayim.*

♦ Orthodox Judaism sees its strength not in numbers but in unwavering commitment to Torah and tradition and feels its approach vindicated by the Ba'al Teshuva movement as well as by the continued survival of Judaism.

Chapter 29

Problems, Problems, Problems

In This Chapter

- ◆ The sin of religious extremism and the contemporary threat of fanaticism

- ◆ What September 11 taught the world

- ◆ The reasons for anti-Semitism

- ◆ Anti-Zionism as the code word for hatred of the Jews

- ◆ The turning point in Catholic-Jewish relations

- ◆ Acceptance and the danger of assimilation

Tell the truth, did you ever hear anybody say, "I have good news and good news"? Of course not. An imperfect world is always going to confront us with difficulties. John Cleese had it right: "Having a problem is no problem. It's denying you have it that creates the difficulty."

God teaches us pretty much the same thing, according to Jewish mystics, by way of the very first letter of the Torah. The Torah begins with the letter bet. That's the second letter of the alphabet, and numerically it stands for two. Why not begin with the *first* letter of the alphabet, the aleph? Because, the Rabbis respond, the world that God created is defined by the number two. Everything in it has a dual quality, good and bad.

Human beings are destined to struggle, to confront the world's problems, to constantly be faced with good news and bad news. In all probability, the reason, as Charles Kettering put it, is that "Problems are the price of progress." Human beings grow only as a result of being forced to face up to challenges and to find the strength to master them. That's why it's important for us to not only be aware of the positive changes in Jewish life that I shared with you in the previous chapter, but also to acknowledge the very real and the very tough issues that still have to be overcome.

So let's talk about some of the most significant problems confronting contemporary Jewry. And let's always remember the wise words of Piet Hein:

> Problems worthy
> Of attack
> Prove their worth
> By hitting back.

"In the Name of God"

Most people think that the third of the Ten Commandments, "Thou shalt not take the name of the Lord thy God in vain," warns us about the sin of using God's name for no reason. It's concerned, they believe, with people who curse and use the word *God* before they say *damn*. But that seems like a pretty minor offense to be worthy of inclusion in a list that has in it such crimes as idolatry, stealing, and murder. Look closely at the wording in Hebrew and you'll understand the real meaning as explained in Jewish tradition. The text actually says, "Don't take God's name *to something that is vain*." Don't use God to justify doing evil. Don't commit crimes and claim they are not only permitted, but even commanded. Don't rationalize evil by claiming it has a divine purpose.

Schmoozing

Beware of ever lightly cloaking political views, no matter how much you believe in them, in the mantle of *Halachah*.

—Rabbi Dr. Norman Lamm, president, Yeshiva University

Years ago, the comedian Flip Wilson popularized the phrase, "The devil made me do it." The only thing worse than that Flip-pant justification is claiming, "God made me do it."

That was probably one of the most disturbing parts of the horrific attack on September 11. Nineteen terrorists brought down the twin towers of the World Trade

Center and brought about the deaths of more than 3,000 innocent people. Incredibly, they had the temerity to claim they were acting in the name of God.

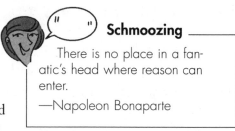

Their act has a name. It's called *fanaticism*. It takes the holy and profanes it. It takes God and demeans Him. It takes the sacred and sullies it beyond recognition.

"A fanatic," Finley Peter Dunne brilliantly pointed out, "is a man who does what he thinks the Lord would do if only He knew the facts of the case." There is an egotistical side to fanaticism that believes no one else is as wise or as capable of coming to truth. Fanatics, simply put, deify themselves because they believe only their vision is the correct version of truth—even though it defies every moral and ethical principle that God clearly taught to the world.

Religious extremism is the most dangerous of all forms of fanaticism. Its power rests in its supposed partnership with God. And history is strewn with the victims of religious persecution in numbers that perhaps exceed any other form of barbarity.

Until the twenty-first century, it was Jews who most often felt the effects of this kind of persecution—as victims of Crusades, inquisitions, blood libels, and tortures intended to convert them to "the true faith." September 11, 2001, forces Western civilization as a whole to recognize the threat to its very survival of a religious fundamentalism that justifies mass murder in order to destroy "all the infidels."

In a headline that appeared in hundreds of newspapers around the country after September 11, journalists expressed their feelings with the words: "Now we are all Israelis." Americans learned that Islamic fanatics don't distinguish between Christian or Jew; "infidels" include anyone who doesn't agree with their mindset. The fanatics of September 11 made clear that what they want to destroy is Western civilization and the values it upholds: democracy, secularity, modernity, individual rights, and the basic freedoms that define us.

That's why Americans of all faiths may well say today, "Now we are all Jews." The problem of confronting, challenging, and overcoming religious extremism is, as prominent historian Bernard Lewis put it, "The single most important issue that the world has to face today—or pay the price of global destruction."

"Blessed Are You Oh Lord Our God ..."

In the last decade, we witnessed two unspeakable acts of savagery committed in the name of God that share a remarkable connection. Both will go down in history as ultimate acts of evil. One was committed by a Jew. His name was Baruch Goldstein. He murdered 29 Arabs at prayer in the cave of *Machpelah*, the holy burial site of the Jewish patriarchs and matriarchs, in Hebron. The other was committed by Mohammed Atta, ring leader of the al Qaeda terrorists responsible for the events of September 11.

Ironic, isn't it, that in the name of God these vicious crimes were committed by "Baruch" and "Atta"—the same two words that begin every Jewish blessing. Perhaps that's our ultimate warning that fanatics, too, can speak in God's name. And that must be why the rabbis of the Talmud teach that when God proclaimed the words of the third commandment, "The entire earth trembled."

From the Mountaintop

Orthodox rabbi Shlomo Riskin, after the assassination of Israel's Prime Minister Yitzhak Rabin by a religious fanatic, publicly declared that "such a desecration of God's name emanating from an individual who purports to speak in God's name as well as any fundamentalist who entertains the blind conviction that he alone possesses the truth must be sternly rebuked by religious leaders."

Let There Be Light

Machpelah is the Hebrew word for "couples." It refers to the four couples—Adam and Eve, Abraham and Sarah, Isaac and Rebecca, and Jacob and Leah—buried together in the cave in Hebron.

Ask the Rabbi

Would there still be anti-Semitism if there were no Jews? Strange as it sounds, the answer is yes. Polish anti-Semitism is notorious for its presence in the absence of a Jewish population in Poland.

Oy Vey, They Hate Us

On Passover night, when Jews celebrate their redemption from Egypt at the traditional seder, they read these words from the Haggadah:

> In every generation they rise up against us to destroy us.

It's a Jewish way of teaching our children that anti-Semitism is an age-old problem that just won't go away. Does that make us paranoid? Well, as Henry Kissinger famously quipped, "Even paranoids have enemies."

Thousands of years of history gave proof to this unpleasant truth. For reasons that go beyond reason, Jews have always been victims of hatred.

So Why Do They Hate Us?

You might almost believe that Jews are collectively guilty of some unspeakable crime. What else could explain the animosity that has for centuries been directed towards them? Most often, though, the sin of the Jews could probably best be illustrated by an incident recorded in the Talmud:

> A certain Jew happened to be walking in the street when the Emperor rode by. The Jew greeted him.
>
> "Who are you?" asked Hadrian.
>
> "I am a Jew," answered the man.
>
> The Emperor flew into a rage. "How dare a Jew greet me! Let him be executed for his impudence."
>
> The next day another Jew chanced to be walking as the Emperor went by. The man had learned of the previous day's incident and did not dare greet the Emperor. Hadrian again showed his anger. "Who are you?" he demanded.
>
> The man did not answer.
>
> Hadrian then shouted: "What impudence of this fellow to walk past me and not acknowledge me. Let him be executed for his disrespect."
>
> His counselors then said: "Sire, we do not understand your policy. Yesterday a man was executed for greeting you and today another man is executed for not greeting you."
>
> Hadrian replied, "Why do you try to teach me how to behave toward the Jews? Whatever they do is wrong."

So Jews are too liberal or too conservative, too cheap or too spendthrift, too passive or too pushy, too charitable or too selfish, too religious or too secular—pick any characteristic and Jews have been blamed either for possessing too much of it or not having it at all.

What it probably boils down to is what Hitler so clearly understood: "If there were no Jews, we would have to invent them." Jews are the scapegoats for the sins of every political system. Max Nordau, the great Zionist leader, had it right: "The Jews are not hated because they have evil qualities; evil qualities are sought for in them, because they are hated." Perhaps even more pointedly, as Theodore Dreiser explained it, "The world's quarrel with the Jew is not that he is inferior, but that he is superior." It's not the Jews' failings that are so troubling to the rest of mankind; it's the Jews' accomplishments that drives the world crazy with envy.

"To Bigotry No Sanction"

The United States of America is the one country in the world that's made Jewish fears seem almost unfounded. Going all the way back to the days of the first presidency, George Washington wrote a letter to the Jews of Newport, Rhode Island, in which he expressed an ideal that's become the official policy of America towards the Jewish people: "For happily the government of the United States, which gives to bigotry no sanction, to persecution no assistance, requires only that they who live under its protection should demean themselves as good citizens. May the children of the stock of Abraham who dwell in this land continue to merit and enjoy the good will of the other inhabitants, while every one shall sit under his own vine and figtree, and there shall be none to make him afraid."

> **Pulpit Story**
>
> Cohen wants to get into a club that doesn't allow Jews. He changes his name and converts. When the membership committee asks him his name he answers, "Kane"; when they ask which college he graduated from, he responds, "Yale"; when they ask him his religion, he answers, "Goy," of course.

> **Pulpit Story**
>
> Sam Goldberg is deeply upset. He complains to his friend, "Those d-d-d-dirty anti-s-s-s-Semites. They wouldn't g-g-g-give me the job, just because I'm J-J-J-Jewish." "What job were you trying out for?" asks his friend. "R-r-r-radio a-a-a-announcer," Goldberg answers.

That doesn't mean that America didn't have its share of bigotry, cruelly expressed all too often by signs with the words, "No Jews Allowed." Anti-Semitism as a personal prejudice couldn't be legislated out of existence. But by Constitutional principle, Jews were equal under the law of the land and, as we saw in the last chapter, the twentieth century came to a close with a common cultural understanding that even the slightest appearance of anti-Semitism was considered politically incorrect.

But the Whole World Still Doesn't Get It

For the rest of the world, unfortunately, the Passover Seder's warning about anti-Semitism is still relevant in the twenty-first century. What's changed is that now it most often makes its appearance masked by a different name. True, it's no longer "in" to attack Jews as Jews or to revile any other religion. That's why the contemporary threat to Judaism is packaged as anti-Zionism or anti-Israel instead of what it really is: anti-Semitism.

Dr. Martin Luther King Jr. was prescient in recognizing this even during his lifetime. Like all true prophets, he was also fearless in speaking out and "telling it the way it is":

Do you declare, my friend, that you do not hate the Jews, you are merely anti-Zionist? And I say, let the truth ring forth from the high mountaintops, let it echo through the valley of God's green earth: When people criticize Zionism, they mean Jews—this is God's own truth.

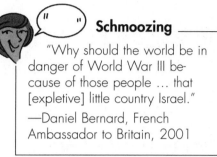

Schmoozing

"Why should the world be in danger of World War III because of those people ... that [expletive] little country Israel."

—Daniel Bernard, French Ambassador to Britain, 2001

As recently as 2002, Egypt aired a television miniseries, *Horsemen Without a Horse*, based on the century-old anti-Semitic tract, *The Protocols of the Elders of Zion*, a proven forgery that places all the blame of the world's woes on an international Jewish conspiracy.

Muslim fanatics continue to preach their hatred of Jews not only to their Arab followers but insidiously carry it to countries around the globe—very often with remarkable success. "Classical anti-Semitism," Bernard Lewis writes, "is an essential part of Arab (and I would add, Moslem) intellectual life at the present time and that classical anti-Semitism has found a home in European universities, among scholars as well as the media." The UN World Conference against Racism in Durbin, South Africa, in 2001 was a glaring example of a gathering ostensibly convened to protest the sin of racism, hypocritically lifting their voices almost as one to promote racism against the Jewish people.

The delegates at Durbin once again concluded, "Zionism is racism." We desperately could have used Dr. King to once again remind us what they really had in mind. And too bad that even after the Holocaust, there are still people who, incredibly enough, believe that the Jews are paranoid!

From the Mountaintop

In 1993, a Russian court pronounced *The Protocols of the Elders of Zion* an anti-Semitic forgery, the first such verdict in the land where the fraud originated ninety years ago. "The ruling today under Russian law destroys any veneer of respectability that hate-mongers around the globe have tried to bestow on this hateful work."

—Rabbi Abraham Cooper, Simon Wiesenthal Center, after the verdict

> **Schmoozing**
>
> The venal hatred of Jews that has taken the form of anti-Zionism, and which has surfaced at this [Durban] conference, is different in one crucial way from the anti-Semitism of the past. Today it is being deliberately propagated and manipulated for political ends.
>
> —Mordechai Yedid, Israeli representative to the Durban Conference prior to his departure, together with the American delegation

Thank God for the Pope

There is one ray of sunshine in this bleak picture that's truly historic. For many centuries, a chief source of Jew hatred, unfortunately, was the Catholic Church. Jews were condemned for the heinous crime of deicide, the charge that they were Christ-killers. Pogroms were the norm in Christian countries stirred up by Sunday and Easter sermons. For almost 20 centuries, anti-Semitism was religiously based and Christian sponsored.

In light of this, the words of Pope John Paul II were clearly a historic turning point in the relationship between Christians and Jews. The Pope officially declared anti-Semitism to be "a great sin against humanity." In a document called *Memory and Reconciliation*, the Vatican reviewed wrongdoings dating back centuries, including the Crusades, the Inquisition, and more recently, the Holocaust. It "recognized Christian responsibility for past wrongs against Jews throughout history" and, using the Hebrew word *t'shuvah*, "repentance," asked for forgiveness.

Small-minded people might ask, "Why did it have to take them 2,000 years to finally get it?" But when the Pope does t'shuvah, Jews throughout the world should exult—and pray that what's good enough for the Pope may soon be acknowledged by all of mankind.

Oy Vey, They Love Us

No, that isn't a misprint. You read it correctly. When they hate us, that's a serious problem; and when they love us, that's a serious problem, too—and, believe it or not, maybe even more dangerous for our survival.

Theodore Herzl, the founder of political Zionism, certainly thought so. "Our enemies have made us one," he said. "It is only pressure that forces us back to the parent stem. If Christian hosts were to leave us in peace for two generations, the Jewish people would merge entirely into surrounding races."

Think the theory is off the wall? A generation later, Albert Einstein came to the same conclusion as Herzl: "It may be thanks to anti-Semitism that we are able to preserve our existence as a race; that at any rate is my belief."

The idea can be traced back to an ancient midrash:

> The sun and the wind had an argument. Each one claimed it was more powerful.
>
> As they debated, a Jew was walking along the road, carrying his Siddur and sefer in his hands, a tallit around his shoulders, and tefillin on his head.
>
> Let me show you what I can do, boasted the wind to the sun. Watch, he said, as I remove every religious item precious to the Jew from his body. I'll blow the tallit and tefillin right off. I'll force the holy books out of his hands.
>
> And so the wind began to blow with great force. With galelike velocity, the Jew felt his precious Jewish possessions endangered.

Schmoozing

The sole tie that binds the Jewish people together is the hostility and disdain of the societies which surround them. It is the anti-Semite who makes the Jew.

—Jean-Paul Sartre

> But the Jew wouldn't allow it to happen. The stronger the wind, the more the Jew held on to his heritage. Confronted by danger, the Jew simply wouldn't let go.
>
> Now came the sun's turn. Let me take over, he said, and show you how it really should be done.
>
> The sun shone with great warmth. The day became more than pleasant; it made the Jew forget all his recent troubles.
>
> It was so nice in fact that the Jew felt the tallit was no more than a burden. The tefillin weren't necessary. And the books? Who had time for study on such a glorious day!
>
> With a broad smile of victory, the sun turned to the wind and said, See, what you couldn't do to the Jew by force, I easily accomplished by friendship.

The twentieth-century problem the Jew faced was the wind. The challenge of the twenty-first century is the one posed by the sun. Judaism has proven it can withstand enemies who want to destroy it from without. The tougher question is, can Jews survive when the challenge is from within? The first threat is called genocide; the second is spiritual suicide.

Emil Fackenheim, the prominent Jewish theologian, has popularized what he calls "the 614th commandment." "A Jew of today," he says, "is forbidden to hand Hitler yet another posthumous victory." Hitler tried to physically destroy us. For contemporary Jews to voluntarily give up their Judaism by assimilating would achieve what Hitler could not accomplish even by way of his "final solution."

Assimilation has been called "a spiritual Holocaust." It is self-inflicted destruction. Jews lost six million at the hands of a monster whose goal was the elimination of the Jewish people. Assimilation accomplishes the very same goal, albeit in a far less painful manner.

 Schmoozing

I do not want my house to be walled in on all sides and my windows to be stuffed. I want the cultures of all the lands to be blown about my house as freely as possible. But I refuse to be blown off my feet by any.
—Mahatma Gandhi

Does that mean that Jews should look longingly back to "the good old days" when they were persecuted? Of course not. There are much better reasons to be Jewish than as an "I'll show them" response to oppression. Being Jewish shouldn't be based on fear; it should be rooted in faith. Holding on to tradition doesn't have to be an act of revenge; it can be an expression of sincere religious commitment. Continuing beautiful traditions of the past needn't be a response to those who want to destroy your roots; it can be a voluntary choice to bring to fruition the great potential and blessing of your family tree.

Now that the sun is finally shining for so many Jews, we're going to have to face the challenge of being Jewish without the wind. It's easy for Jews today to be accepted. That makes it almost effortless to give up a culture, a faith, and a heritage that's thousands of years old. But the bottom line is what Isaac Ber Levinsohn said so clearly: "There is no greater sin than to cause one's nation to disappear from the world." And after reading this book, you've got to admit what a loss it would be if there were no more Jews—and no more Judaism.

The Least You Need to Know

◆ The third commandment is concerned not with the unnecessary use of God's name but with the far greater sin of appropriating His name to rationalize the doing of evil.

◆ Fanatics deify themselves because they believe only their vision is the correct version of truth.

- After September 11, Western civilization is most threatened by religious fundamentalism, which justifies homicide bombings in order to destroy "all the infidels."

- Anti-Semitism is still a powerful threat to Jews under the guise of anti-Zionism.

- Anti-Semitism has many causes, all of which say a great deal more about the people who hate than about the Jews who are hated.

- The Catholic Church, in a dramatic act of repentance, has asked forgiveness from the Jews for centuries of sinful behavior.

- Being loved can sometimes be even more dangerous for Jewish survival than being hated.

- Anti-Semitism and assimilation, each in their own way, present major threats to Judaism.

Chapter 30

The Crystal Ball: So What's in the Future?

In This Chapter

◆ The future of Jews without Judaism

◆ The secret of Jewish survival

◆ The problem of Judaism without Jews

◆ The optimists versus the pessimists

◆ Why Judaism and the Jews will survive

Niels Bohr, a Nobel Laureate in physics, dryly observed: "Prediction is very difficult, especially if it's about the future."

As we come to the close of this book on Judaism, it's only appropriate that we devote this final chapter to thinking about what lies ahead. From the days of Abraham until now, Judaism has brought a great deal of blessing to the world. As the mother religion of both Christianity and Islam, Judaism is really responsible for the religious faith of most of the people on earth, as Maimonides correctly pointed out. The ideas and the ideals of the Bible still remain the core values of modern civilization. And after thousands of years of persecution and attempts to wipe out Jews as well as Judaism, both have somehow miraculously survived.

Is there any way we can predict what lies in store for the future? Of course, it would be much easier to do what Winston Churchill suggested when he said, "I always avoid prophesizing beforehand because it is much better to prophesize after the event has already taken place."

But there is a purpose to predicting. It lets us diagnose what we are doing wrong and what we are doing right. It permits us to plan. And, done correctly, it allows us to have hope. So for the final chapter in this book, I'm going to accept Shakespeare's challenge: "If you can look into the seeds of time, and say which grain will grow and which will not, speak then unto me." Let me try, because what's at stake is Judaism's very survival.

Can Jews Survive Without Judaism?

Jews are a people. Judaism is a religion. For most of history, they bonded together just like "love and marriage" and "horse and carriage."

Sometimes, though, we've seen that even love and marriage aren't synonymous. And so there are also those who question the relationship between Jews and Judaism. Thinking about the future, there are those who believe that Jews don't need Judaism to survive. They think that even if secularism and assimilation prevail, even if no one continues to believe in the Jewish idea of God, even if all of Judaism's holy books are left to gather dust on the shelves, Jews will nevertheless remain on this earth, identifiable as descendants of the original children of Israel.

It is a vision that defies current statistics as well as ancient insights. Jews without Judaism is like … well, like chicken soup without chicken. You don't have to be a prophet to guess what *will* happen; we already have the proof from what *has* happened, time after time.

It usually takes only three generations. As Arthur Hertzberg noted, "A generational clock has ticked away over and over again in the open society. Whether in Paris and Bordeaux in the 1850s, in Budapest around the turn of the century, in Berlin and Vienna in the 1920s, and now in the United States, it tells the same frightening time. The third generation of the open society intermarries and erodes out of Judaism at a rate of one in three."

A famous chart that was published a few years ago in *Moment* magazine came as a harsh wake-up call to tens of thousands of Jews. It showed, based on projections from most recent studies, that by the fourth generation, 200 secular Jews will have produced all of 10 Jewish great-grandchildren. The same number of ultra-orthodox Jews will have produced more than 5,000 Jewish great-grandchildren. There's just no escaping the truth of Ahad Ha'am's observation that, "More than the Jews have kept the Sabbath, the Sabbath has kept the Jews." Jews without Judaism not only doesn't make sense, it's almost an impossibility.

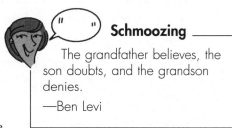

Schmoozing

The grandfather believes, the son doubts, and the grandson denies.

—Ben Levi

So What *Is* the Secret of Jewish Survival?

If Jews need Judaism to exist, which part of Judaism is its most vital life-giving source? What one thing above all others has to be treasured, nurtured, and emphasized so that Jews don't just die out? Has Judaism ever defined its insurance policy for survival?

The response may seem a little "fishy," but it was given almost 2,000 years ago by one of the greatest rabbis in Jewish history. It's part of a fascinating story that appears in the Talmud, as I've already shared with you:

Long ago, the land of Israel was ruled by Romans, who enacted cruel and barbaric laws against the Jewish people.

Once, the government of Rome issued an edict forbidding Jews to study and practice the Torah.

Pappus, son of Judah, found Rabbi Akiva sitting in a public place, with students all about him, teaching and studying Torah in defiance of the Roman law. This was an enormously dangerous thing to do, because the penalty for violating a Roman edict was death.

Pappus was shocked that Rabbi Akiva was taking such a risk. In amazement he asked, "Akiva, aren't you afraid of the Roman government?"

Rabbi Akiva replied with a parable:

Once, a fox was walking alongside a river. He could see fish swimming in schools in the water. It appeared to him that they were swimming to and fro, as if trying to escape something or someone. The fox was very hungry and thought that a nice, fat fish would surely make a delicious lunch for a hungry fox.

The fox called out to the fish, "What are you fleeing from?" The fish replied, "We are trying to avoid the nets that fishermen cast to catch us."

Slyly, the fox said, "Would you like to come up onto the dry land so that you will be safe from the fishermen's nets?"

The fish weren't fooled by the sly fox. They replied, "Are you the one that is known as the cleverest of all the animals? You are not clever! You are foolish. If we are in danger here in the water, which is our home, how much more would we be in danger on land!"

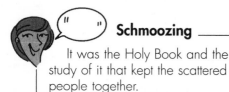

Schmoozing

It was the Holy Book and the study of it that kept the scattered people together.

—Sigmund Freud, *Moses and Monotheism*

"So it is with us," Rabbi Akiva explained. "If we are in great danger when we sit and study, teach and practice Torah, of which it is written, 'For this is your life and the length of your days,' (Deuteronomy 30:20) how much worse off would we be if we neglect the Torah? It is the Torah that is our natural habitat, the only medium in which we can survive. Take us out of the waters of Torah and we will perish just as surely as fish out of water."

And with that, Rabbi Akiva returned to his studies.

Rabbi Akiva's insight has been repeated in many different forms throughout the centuries. Like the famous ad of some years ago with the tagline, "You don't have to be Jewish to love Levy's rye bread," you don't have to be religious to recognize that without study, the story of the Jewish people is over. Many of the scholars, historians, and sociologists who have acknowledged this truth were not observant Jews. Ahad Ha'am, who is one of the greatest nonreligious Jewish thinkers of modern history, made it his mantra: "The secret of Jewish survival is learning, learning, learning."

That's why the daily morning service begins with the following prayer:

These are the precepts whose fruits a person enjoys in this world but whose principal remains intact for him and the world to come. They are the honor due to father and mother, acts of kindness, early attendance at the house of study morning and evening, hospitality to guests, visiting the sick, providing for a bride, escorting the dead, absorption in prayer, bringing peace between man and his fellow man—*but the study of Torah is equivalent to all of them.*

Ask the Rabbi

Who is obligated to study? Jewish law is clear: Every Jew, rich or poor, even a beggar, healthy or not, young or old, until the day of death.

All the mitzvot mentioned are important. All of them receive divine reward in this world as well as in the world to come. But study has a primary place, the position of greatest honor, because study doesn't simply elevate a person: It helps to preserve a people.

And I hope you realize as you're reading this and learning more about Judaism that you're fulfilling the greatest commandment that Judaism requires of its adherents.

Can Judaism Survive Without Jews?

The prognosis for Jews without Judaism, we've concluded, is pretty dismal. Judaism without Jews, however, is a far more certain disaster. A religion without a people is like a soul without a body. Small wonder that the commandment to "be fruitful and multiply" appears at the very beginning of the Bible.

For the longest time, Jews took this commandment very seriously. Large families were a staple of Jewish life. For the philosopher Ernest van den Haag, that's the explanation for an otherwise incomprehensible fact. If you were to be asked, he pointed out in *The Jewish Mystique*, to make a list of men who have dominated the thinking of the modern world, most educated people would name Freud, Einstein, Marx, and Darwin. Of these four, only Darwin wasn't Jewish. In a world where Jews comprise one-quarter of 1 percent of its population, Jews consistently make contributions far disproportionate to their numbers. Since 1901, out of 720 Nobel Prize awards, more than 130 Laureates were Jews!

What can possibly account for this statistical abnormality? What is it about the Jews that makes them so smart? Van den Haag thinks it's genetic. There's a simple reason to explain the intellectual gap between Jews and Christians. Historically, the smartest Christians were urged to become priests. That meant the best genes were owned by people who took an oath of celibacy. So here's what happened: "The most intelligent portion of the population did not have offspring; their genes were siphoned off, generation after generation, into the church, and not returned into the world's genetic supply. The result was a reduction of the average intelligence level of the non-Jewish western population to a level considerably below that which would have been achieved otherwise."

 **Schmoozing**

He who brings no children into the world is like a murderer. —Babylonian Talmud

 From the Mountaintop

How many children are required for a husband and wife to fulfill the mitzvah of "Be fruitful and multiply"? According to Jewish law, the minimum is a boy and a girl—to "replace" the parents—but the more children, the greater the mitzvah!

Jews encouraged their brightest to become rabbis. And rabbis believed God when He said that everything that He created was "very good"—including sex. For religious Jews, the noise of many children was nothing less than the sound of music. And that music is what brought the Jewish people the blessings of superior creativity and achievement.

"The Vanishing American Jew"

The Holocaust effectively eliminated more than one-third of the Jewish people. In its aftermath, there were many who felt a special obligation to ensure Jewish survival by having even more children than they normally would have had. (The apocryphal story has it that when a rabbi urged one of his congregants to help make up the loss of the six million, the man begged the rabbi not to count on him personally for the whole task.) In religious communities, it was common to see countless families try to prove that "cheaper by the dozen" isn't an exaggeration.

But for the most part, the majority of Jews chose personal preference over people-hood. In fact, studies bore out the terrifying conclusion that as the twentieth century came to a close, Jews had the lowest birth rate of any religious or ethnic community in the United States. The average American Jewish woman today bears 1.1 children—and if you think that's a problem for the Jewish people, just imagine how tough it is for the .1 child!

One frightening Harvard study predicts that if things continue as they are now, the American Jewish community will probably number fewer than a million and perhaps even as few as 10,000 by the time the United States celebrates its tricentennial in 2076. With the Jewish population in America today approximately six million, consider the terrible irony of the loss of a comparable number of Jews to those who perished in the Holocaust as a result of a voluntary decision to limit reproduction! Some contemporary scholars have even gone so far as to say we have reached the time to say *kaddish*—the memorial prayer—for the American Jewish community.

The Cry of the Pessimists

In his book, *The Sacred Chain*, historian Norman Cantor echoes this depressing forecast. "Jewish history as we have known it is approaching its end. The sacred chain is running through its last links."

Cantor not only says kaddish for the Jews and Judaism, but offers a disturbing eulogy. The way he sees it, Judaism accomplished all of its goals. "The Jews served their own purpose, and God's purpose, and mankind's purpose. Pragmatically, they are no longer very much needed as a distinct race. The Jewish heritage would endure if the Jews disappeared as a major group in the world in the 21st century."

According to Cantor, it's all over for the Jews, but not to worry: There isn't much more we could have accomplished anyway. Tell you the truth, that isn't a Cantor I'd like to listen to in my synagogue.

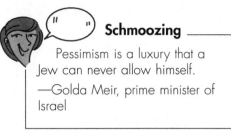

Schmoozing

Pessimism is a luxury that a Jew can never allow himself.

—Golda Meir, prime minister of Israel

The Faith of the Optimist

Helen Keller, who surely had more than enough good reasons to be a pessimist, observed that: "No pessimist ever discovered the secret of the stars, or sailed to an uncharted land, or opened a new doorway for the human spirit." She might have added that no prophesier of doom for the Jewish people ever proved to be an accurate prophet.

In 1964, a *Look* magazine cover story featured "The Vanishing American Jew." The then-popular weekly set forth a list of seemingly irrefutable reasons for the demise of the Jewish people by the turn of the century. Guess what? *Look* magazine is long gone and forgotten, but the Jewish people, like Mark Twain, who read an obituary about himself, continue to smilingly prove that the "report of my death was greatly exaggerated."

Schmoozing

An optimist stays up until midnight to see the New Year in. A pessimist stays up to make sure the old year leaves.

—Bill Vaughan

But don't blame *Look* for its inability to understand the *Life* of the Jewish people. The historian Simon Rawidowicz calls the Jews "the ever-dying people." He notes, "There was hardly a generation in the *diaspora* who did not consider itself the final link in Israel's chain." Reviewing centuries of history that had Jews seemingly on their deathbeds, Rawidowicz comes to the conclusion, "There is no people more dying than Israel, yet none better equipped to resist disaster, to fight alone, always alone."

Jews are the one people on earth who persistently defy every fatal diagnosis. For them it seems the fat lady will never sing. For them Yogi Berra seems the only prophet worth taking seriously: "It ain't over till it's over."

So What's the Secret?

So how come pessimists never seem to get it right when it comes to the Jews?

Maybe the answer is found in the words of William Arthur Ward:

> The pessimist complains about the wind
> The optimist expects it to change
> The realist adjusts its sails.

Change the word *realist* to *Jew* and you've got the answer. Jews long ago learned that they couldn't just allow themselves to be buffeted by the winds of the world's hatred. They remembered the lesson made clear to Moses when the Jews stood at the shore of the Red Sea. Watching in fright as their Egyptian enemies fiercely rushed towards them, Moses began to pray. "Why do you cry out to me," said God to Moses. "Tell the Jewish people to move." "Don't just stand there, do something" is more than a maxim—it's a divine commandment.

There is a telling joke that makes this point very well:

God announced that He changed His mind and decided to flood the world in seven days, as He did in the days of Noah, but this time without allowing anyone to build an ark. Catholics were aghast, and the Pope called on everyone to confess their sins during the coming week. Protestant leaders asked their followers to engage in seven days of prayer. The chief rabbi told the Jews, "We only have one week to figure out how to live under water."

For Jews today that means finding ways to overcome all of our contemporary problems. We have to discover solutions that will permit us to survive in the face of both of our challenges: being too hated and being too loved.

Pulpit Story

An Italian, a Frenchman, and a Jew were condemned to be shot. Their captors offered them a final meal before their execution. They asked the Frenchman what he wanted. "Give me some good French wine and some French bread." So they gave it to him, he ate it, and then they executed him. Next it was the Italian's turn. "Give me a big plate of pasta." So they brought it to him, he ate it, and they executed him. Then came the Jew. "I want a big bowl of strawberries," he said. "Strawberries? They aren't even in season." "*Nu*," replied the Jew, "so I'll wait."

If history has shown us anything, it is that no matter how tough the battle, the Jewish people will prevail.

The Bible's Prediction

In the sixth century B.C.E., the Chinese poet Lao Tzu said, "Those who have knowledge, don't predict. Those who predict, don't have knowledge."

Sorry, but that's not true. There is Someone with knowledge who did make a prediction. In His very first meeting with Moses, God weighed in on the future of the Jewish people. And He did so by way of a striking—and unforgettable—visual image.

You all know the story. Moses was tending his sheep in the desert of Sinai when he suddenly saw a bush that was engulfed in flames. Yet strangely enough, although the bush was burning, it was not consumed. That defied the laws of nature. Fire *always* destroys. At this very moment, as Moses stood transfixed by the miracle before his eyes, God revealed Himself and proclaimed, "I am the God of your fathers."

Superficially, the story seems simply to tell us that God performed this wondrous act to impress Moses before asking him to assume the mantle of leadership. God chose this sign so that Moses grasped the meaning of divine power. But that begs the question. Couldn't God have performed another miracle even more striking, more convincing, more indicative of His control over the entire world rather than just a single bush in the desert?

Rabbinic commentators supply us with a beautiful answer. God wasn't simply performing a miracle. He was sending a message. God knew what was uppermost in the mind of Moses. From the time he fled from Egypt and watched his brothers suffering under Pharaoh's brutal oppression, Moses worried and wondered: Are my people still alive? And so the very first thing God did was to reassure Moses—not only for the present but for all the days of the future as well.

The bush was a symbol of the Jewish people. The bush was burning but, against all laws of nature, it was not consumed. So, too, the Jewish people, against all laws of history, will never perish!

When Arnold Toynbee completed his classic 10-volume analysis of the rise and fall of human civilizations, *The Study of History*, he was troubled by one seeming refutation of his universal rules governing the inexorable decline of every people on earth. Only the Jews survived in defiance of Toynbee's carefully reasoned analysis. So Toynbee proclaimed the Jews nothing more than "a vestigial remnant," a people destined to shortly expire.

But somehow, in spite of all those brutal attempts to destroy the children of Israel, Jews have demonstrated the ongoing miracle of the burning bush.

Jewish history, simply put, defies explanation. Jewish survival is nothing short of a miracle. But it is a miracle long ago predicted by God. And it is a miracle which, God assured Moses, will never cease to repeat itself until the end of time.

Let's close this book with the words of a famous author who understood this message of the burning bush although he wasn't Jewish. Leo Nikolayevich Tolstoy, an Orthodox Christian best known for penning *War and Peace*, wrote this in 1908:

> A Jew is the emblem of eternity. He who neither slaughter nor torture of thousands of years could destroy, he who neither fire, nor sword, nor inquisition was able to wipe off the face of the earth. He who was the first to produce the Oracles of God. He who has been for so long the Guardian of Prophesy and has transmitted to the rest of the world. Such a nation cannot be destroyed. The Jew is as everlasting as Eternity itself.

The Least You Need to Know

- Jews without Judaism are usually lost to the Jewish people in three generations.

- The secret of Jewish survival has always been study of Torah.

- "Be fruitful and multiply" must be observed by Jews in accord with Jewish law or the Jewish people will not survive.

- Jewish concern with reproduction as opposed to Christianity's adoption of celibacy for their best and brightest may account for the statistically skewed percentage of Jewish Nobel Prize winners.

- "The Vanishing American Jew" has been predicted for many years, just as kaddish has been recited for the Jews throughout the centuries.

- Pessimistic scholars believe Jews have "fulfilled their mission" and are doomed to near-term extinction.

- Jews have managed to survive against all odds, fulfilling the prediction God revealed to Moses at their very first meeting when He showed him the miraculous bush that "was burning, but was not consumed."

Glossary

Adar   The twelfth month of the Jewish year, occurring in February/March.

Afikomen   From Greek, meaning "dessert." A half piece of matzo set aside during the Passover seder, which is later hidden by children and then ransomed by parents. It is eaten as the last part of the meal.

Al Cheit (*AHL CHAYT*)   Lit. for the sin. A confession of community sins recited repeatedly on Yom Kippur.

alef-bet (*AH-lef-bet*)   The Hebrew alphabet. The name is derived from the first two letters of the alef-bet.

aliyah (*uh-LEE-uh*; *ah-lee-AH*)   Lit. ascension. (1) Reading from the Torah; (or reciting a blessing over the reading) during services, which is considered an honor (generally referred to in English as having or getting an aliyah and pronounced *uh-LEE-uh*). *See also* Bar Mitzvah. (2) Emigrating to Israel (generally referred to in English as making aliyah and pronounced *ah-lee-AH*).

Amidah (*uh-MEE-duh*)   Lit. standing. A prayer that is the center of any Jewish religious service. Also known as the Shemoneh Esrei or the T'filah.

Aninut   The period of mourning between the time of death and the time of burial.

Arbah Minim   Lit. four species. Fruit and branches used to fulfill the commandment to "rejoice before the Lord" during Sukkot.

Aron Kodesh (*AH-rohn KOH-desh*)   Lit. holy chest. The cabinet where the Torah scrolls are kept.

Ashkenazic Jews (*ahsh-ken-AH-zik*)   Jews from eastern France, Germany, and Eastern Europe and their descendants.

Av   The fifth month of the Jewish year, occurring in July/August.

Avelut   The year of mourning after the burial of a parent.

Ba'al Shem Tov (*bahl shem tohv*)   Lit. master of the good name. Rabbi Israel ben Eliezer. The founder of Hasidism.

Bar Mitzvah (*BAHR MITS-vuh*)   Lit. son of the commandment. A boy who has achieved the age of 13 and is consequently obligated to observe the commandments. Also, a ceremony marking the fact that a boy has achieved this age.

Bat Mitzvah (*BAHT MITS-vuh*)   Lit. daughter of the commandment. A girl who has achieved the age of 12 and is consequently obligated to observe the commandments. Also, a ceremony marking the fact that a girl has achieved this age.

B.C.E.   Before the Common (or Christian) Era. (*See also* C.E.)

beginning of day   A day on the Jewish calendar begins at sunset. When a date is given for a Jewish holiday, the holiday actually begins at sundown on the preceding day.

Beit Din (*BAYT DIN*)   Lit. house of judgment. A rabbinical court made up of three rabbis who resolve business disputes under Jewish law and determine whether a prospective convert is ready for conversion.

Beit Knesset (*BAYT K'NESS-et*)   Lit. house of assembly. A Hebrew term for a synagogue.

Beit Midrash (*BAYT MID-rahsh*)   Lit. house of study. A place set aside for study of sacred texts, such as the Torah and the Talmud, generally a part of the synagogue or attached to it, and another name for the synagogue as well.

bentsch (*BENTSCH*)   Yiddish: bless. To recite a blessing. Usually refers to the recitation of the *birkat ha-mazon* (grace after meals).

Berakhah (*B'RUHKH-khah*; *b'ruhkh-KHAH*); pl: Berakhot (*b'ruhkh-KHOHT*)   A blessing. A prayer beginning with the phrase *barukh atah* (blessed art Thou).

Bimah (*BEE-muh*)   The pedestal on which the Torah scrolls are placed when they are being read in the synagogue—that is, the pulpit.

Birkat-Ha-Mazon (*BEER-kaht bah mah-ZOHN*)   Lit. blessing of the food. Grace after meals. The recitation of *birkat ha-mazon* is commonly referred to as *bentsching*.

Brit Milah (*BRIT MEE-lah*)   Lit. covenant of circumcision. The ritual circumcision of a male Jewish child on the eighth day of his life or of a male convert to Judaism. Frequently referred to as a *bris*.

C.E.   Common Era. Used instead of A.D., because A.D. means "the Year of our Lord," and Jews do not believe that Christ is our Lord.

Chai (*KHAHY, rhymes with hi*)   Lit. living or life. The word is often used as a design on jewelry and other ornaments. Donations to charity are often made in multiples of 18, the numerical value of the word.

challah (*KHAH-luh*)   A sweet, eggy, yellow bread, usually braided, which is served on Sabbaths and holidays.

Chevra Kadisha (*KHEV-ruh kah-DEESH-uh*)   Lit. holy society. An organization devoted to caring for the dead.

children of Israel   The most common designation of the Jewish people used in Jewish literature. It signifies the fact that we are descended from Jacob, who was also known as Israel.

Chilul Ha-Shem (*khil-LOOL bah SHEM*)   Lit. profanation of the Name. Causing God or Judaism to come into disrespect or causing a person to violate a commandment.

Chol Ha-Mo'ed (*KHOHL bah MOH-ed; KHOHL bah moh-AYD*)   The intermediate days of Passover and Sukkot, when work is permitted.

cholent (*TSCHUH-lent*)   A slow-cooked stew of beef, beans, and barley, which is served on Sabbaths.

chuppah (*KHU-puh*)   The wedding canopy, symbolic of the groom's house, under which the nissu'in portion of the wedding ceremony is performed.

Dati (*DAH-tee*)   Orthodox Jews in Israel.

Days of Awe   The ten days from Rosh Hashanah to Yom Kippur, a time for introspection and consideration of the sins of the previous year.

dreidel   A toplike toy used to play a traditional Hanukkah game.

etrog (*ET-rohg*)   A citrus fruit native to Israel, used to fulfill the commandments to "rejoice before the Lord" during Sukkot.

Family Purity   Laws relating to the separation of husband and wife during the woman's menstrual period. Also referred to as the laws of niddah or *taharat hamishpachah*.

fleishig (*FLAHYSH-ig*)   Yiddish: meat. Used to describe kosher foods that contain meat and therefore cannot be eaten with dairy.

Four Questions   A set of questions about Passover, designed to encourage participation in the seder. Also known as *Mah Nishtanah* (Why is it different?), which are the first words of the Four Questions.

G-d   A way of avoiding having to write a name of God, to avoid the risk of the sin of erasing or defacing the Name.

Gefilte fish (*g'-FIL-tuh*)   Yiddish: lit. stuffed fish. A traditional Jewish dish consisting of a ball or cake of ground fish.

Gehinnom (*g'hee-NOHM*); **Gehenna** (*g'HEHN-uh*)   A place of spiritual punishment and/or purification for a period of up to 12 months after death. *Gehinnom* is the Hebrew name; *Gehenna* is Yiddish.

Gemara (*g'-MAHR-uh*)   Commentaries on the Mishna. The Mishna and Gemara together are the Talmud.

Gematria (*g'-MAH-tree-uh*)   A field of Jewish mysticism that finds hidden meanings in the numerical value of words.

get (*GET*)   A writ of divorce. Also called a *sefer k'ritut*.

grager (*GREG-er; GRAG-er*)   A noisemaker used to blot out the name of Haman during the reading of the Megillah on Purim.

Haphtarah (*hahf-TOH-ruh*)   Lit. conclusion. A reading from the Prophets, read along with the weekly Torah portion.

Haggadah (*huh-GAH-duh*)   The book read during the Passover Seder, telling the story of the holiday.

halacha (*huh-LUHKH-khuh***)** Lit. the path that one walks. Jewish law. The complete body of rules and practices that Jews are bound to follow, including biblical commandments, commandments instituted by the rabbis, and binding customs.

Hallel Lit. praise God. Psalms 113–118, in praise of God, which are recited on certain holidays.

Haman (*HAY-men***)** The villain of the story of Purim.

Hamantaschen (*HAH-men-TAH-shen***)** Lit. Haman's pockets. Triangular, fruit-filled cookies traditionally served or given as gifts during Purim.

hametz (*KHUH-mitz***)** Lit. leaven. Leavened grain products, which may not be owned or consumed during Passover.

Hanukkah (*KHAH-nik-uh***; ***KHAH-noo-kah***)** Lit. dedication. An eight-day holiday celebrating the rededication of the Temple in Jerusalem after it was defiled by the Seleucid Greeks.

Hanukkahiah (*KHAH-noo-KEE-ah***)** A name sometimes used for a Hanukkah menorah.

Hanukat Habayit (*KHAH-noo-KAHT hah BAHY-eet***)** Lit. dedication of the house. A brief ceremony dedicating a Jewish household, during which the mezuzah is affixed to the doorposts.

Haredi Ultra-Orthodox Jews in Israel.

haroset (*khah-ROH-set***; ***khah-ROH-ses***)** A mixture of fruit, wine, and nuts eaten at the Passover seder to symbolize mortar used by the Jewish slaves in Egypt.

ha-Shem (*hah SHEM***)** Lit. The Name. The Name of God, which is not pronounced. The phrase *ha-Shem* is often used as a substitute for God's Name.

Hasidism (*KHAH-sid-ism***); Hasidic (***khah-SID-ic***)** From the word *hasid*, meaning "pious." A branch of Orthodox Judaism that maintains a lifestyle separate from the non-Jewish world.

Hatafat Dam Brit (*hah-tah-FAHT DAHM BRIT***)** A symbolic circumcision of a person who has already been circumcised or who was born without a foreskin. It involves taking a pinprick of blood from the tip of the penis.

Havdalah (*hahv-DAH-luh***)** Lit. separation, division. A ritual marking the end of the Sabbath or a holiday.

Hazzan (*KHAH-zen***)** Cantor. The person who leads the congregation in prayer. May be a professional or a member of the congregation.

Iyar The second month of the Jewish year, occurring in April/May.

Jacob (Israel) Son of Isaac. Father of twelve sons, who represent the twelve tribes of Judaism. One of the three patriarchs of Judaism.

Jew A person whose mother was a Jew or who has converted to Judaism. According to the Reform movement, a person whose father is a Jew, is a Jew.

Jewish star The six-pointed star emblem commonly associated with Judaism, also known as the Magen David, the Shield of David, or the Star of David.

Judah (1) Son of Jacob (Israel). Ancestor of one of the tribes of Israel; (2) the tribe that bears his name.

Judah Ha-Nasi (*JOO-duh hah NAH-see*) Compiler of the Mishna.

Kabbalah (*kuh-BAH-luh*) Lit. tradition. Jewish mystical tradition.

Kaddish (*KAH-dish*) Aramaic: holy. A prayer in Aramaic praising God, commonly associated with mourning practices.

Kashrut (*KAHSH-rut; KAHSH-root; kahsh-ROOT*) From a root meaning fit, proper, or correct. Jewish dietary laws.

kavanah (*kuh-VAH-nuh; kah-vah-NAH*) Concentration, intent. The frame of mind required for prayer or performance of a mitzvah.

keriah (*KREE-yuh*) Lit. tearing. The tearing of one's clothes upon hearing of the death of a close relative.

Ketubbah (*KTOO-buh*) Lit. writing. The Jewish marriage contract.

Kiddush (*Ki-DOOSH*) Lit. sanctification. A prayer recited over wine sanctifying the Sabbath or a holiday.

Kiddush Ha-Shem (*ki-DOOSH ha SHEM*) Lit. sanctification of The Name. Any deed that increases the respect accorded to God or Judaism, especially martyrdom.

Kiddushin Lit. sanctification. The first part of the two-part process of Jewish marriage, which creates the legal relationship without the mutual obligations.

kippah (*KEY-puh*) The skullcap head covering worn by Jews during services, and by some Jews at all times, more commonly known as a *yarmulke*.

Kislev The ninth month of the Jewish year, occurring in November/December.

Kittel (*KIT-'l, rhymes with little, but the *t* is pronounced distinctly*) The white robes in which the dead are buried, worn by some during Yom Kippur services.

Kohen (*KOH-hayn*); pl: Kohanim (*koh-HAHN-eem*) Priest. A descendant of Aaron, charged with performing various rites in the Temple. This is not the same thing as a rabbi.

Kol Nidre (*KOHL NID-ray*) Lit. all vows. The evening service of Yom Kippur or the prayer that begins that service.

kosher (*KOH-sher*) Lit. fit, proper, or correct. Describes food that is permissible to eat under Jewish dietary laws. Can also describe any other ritual object that is fit for use according to Jewish law.

kugel (*KOO-gul; KI-gul*) Yiddish: pudding. A casserole of potatoes, eggs, and onion, or a dessert of noodles, fruits, and nuts in an egg-based pudding.

Ladino (*Luh-DEE-noh*) The "international language" of Sephardic Jews, based primarily on Spanish, with words taken from Hebrew, Arabic, and other languages, and written in the Hebrew alphabet.

latkes (*LAHT-kuh; LAHT-kees*) Potato pancakes traditionally eaten during Hanukkah.

L'Chayim (*l'-KHAHY-eem*) Lit. to life. A common Jewish toast.

leap year A year with an extra month, to realign the Jewish lunar calendar with the solar year.

Levi (*LAY-vee*); Levite (*LEE-vahyt*)   (1) A descendant of the tribe of Levi, which was set aside to perform certain duties in connection with the Temple; (2) Son of Jacob (Israel). Ancestor of the tribe of Levi.

L'shanah Tovah (*li-SHAH-nuh TOH-vuh*; *li-shah-NAH toh-VAH*)   Lit. for a good year. A common greeting during Rosh Hashanah and Days of Awe.

lulav   Lit. palm branch. A collection of palm, myrtle, and willow branches, used to fulfill the commandment to "rejoice before the Lord" during Sukkot.

Ma'ariv (*MAH-reev*)   Evening prayer services.

Magen David (*mah-GAYN dah-VEED*; *MAH-gen DAH-vid*; *MOH-gen DAY-vid*)   Lit. shield of David. The six-pointed star emblem commonly associated with Judaism.

Mah Nishtanah   Lit. Why is it different? A set of questions about Passover, designed to encourage participation in the seder. Also known as the Four Questions.

Maimonides (*mahy-MAH-ni-dees*)   Rabbi Moshe ben Maimon, one of the greatest medieval Jewish scholars. Commonly referred to by the acronym "Rambam."

mamzer (*MAHM-zer*)   Lit. bastard. The child of a marriage that is prohibited and invalid under Jewish law, such as an incestuous union.

Mashgiach   A person who certifies that food is kosher.

Matzo (*MAHTZ-uh*)   Unleavened bread traditionally served during Passover.

mechitzah (*m'-KHEETZ-uh*)   The wall or curtain separating men from women during religious services.

Megillah (*m'-GILL-uh*)   Lit. scroll. One of five books of the Bible (Esther, Ruth, Song of Songs, Lamentations, and Ecclesiastes). Usually refers to the book of Esther.

Melachah (*m'-LUH-khuh*)   Lit. work. Work involving creation or exercise of control over the environment, which is prohibited on Shabbat and certain holidays.

menorah (*m'NAW-ruh*; *me-NOH-ruh*)   A candelabrum. Usually refers to the nine-branched candelabrum used to hold the Hanukkah candles. Can also refer to the seven-branched candelabrum used in the Temple.

Messiah   Anglicization of the Hebrew, *Mashiach* (anointed). A man who will be chosen by God to put an end to all evil in the world, rebuild the Temple, bring the exiles back to Israel, and usher in the world to come.

Messianic Age   A period of global peace and prosperity that will be brought about by the Messiah when He comes.

mezuzah (*m'-ZOO-zuh*; *m'-ZU-zuh*)   Lit. doorpost. A case attached to the doorposts of houses, containing a scroll with passages of scripture written on it. The procedure and prayers for affixing the mezuzah is available.

Midrash (*MID-rash*)   From a root meaning "to study," "to seek out," or "to investi-gate." Stories elaborating on incidents in the Bible, to derive a principle of Jewish law or pro-vide a moral lesson.

mikvah (*MIK-vuh*)   Lit. gathering. A ritual bath used for spiritual purification. It is used primarily in conversion rituals and after the period of sexual separation during a woman's menstrual cycles, but many Chasidim immerse themselves in the mikvah regularly for general spiritual purification.

milchig (*MIL-khig*)   Yiddish: dairy. Used to describe kosher foods that contain dairy products and therefore cannot be eaten with meat.

Minchah (*MIN-khuh*)   Afternoon prayer services.

minhag (*MIN-hahg*)   Lit. custom. A custom that evolved for worthy religious reasons and has continued long enough to become a binding religious practice. The word is also used more loosely to describe any customary religious practice.

minyan (*MIN-yahn*; *MIN-yin*)   The quorum necessary to recite certain prayers, consisting of ten adult Jewish men.

Mishna (*MISH-nuh*)   An early written compilation of Jewish oral tradition, the basis of the Talmud.

Mitnagdim (*mit-NAG-deem*)   Lit. opponents. Orthodox Jews who are not Hasidic.

mitzvah (*MITS-vuh*); pl: Mitzvot (*mits-VOHT*)   Lit. commandment. Any of the 613 commandments that Jews are obligated to observe. It can also refer to any Jewish religious obligation or, more generally, to any good deed.

Mohel (*Maw-y'l*, rhymes with oil)   Lit. circumciser. One who performs the ritual circumcision of an eight-day-old male Jewish child or of a convert to Judaism.

Mordecai (*MOR-duh-khahy*)   One of the heroes of the story of Purim.

Musaf (*MOO-sahf*; *MU-sahf*)   An additional prayer service for Sabbaths and holidays.

Neilah (*n'-EE-luh*)   Lit. closing. The closing service of Yom Kippur.

Ner Tamid (*NAYR tah-MEED*)   Lit. continual lamp. Usually translated "eternal flame." A candelabrum or lamp near the ark in the synagogue that symbolizes the commandment to keep a light burning in the Tabernacle outside of the curtain surrounding the Ark of the Covenant.

Niddah (*nee-DAH*)   The separation of husband and wife during the woman's menstrual period. Also refers to a woman so separated. Also referred to as *taharat hamishpachah*, or "family purity."

Nihum Avelim   Lit. comforting mourners. One of the purposes of Jewish practices relating to death and mourning.

Nissan   The first month of the Jewish year, occurring in March/April.

nissu'in   Lit. elevation. The second part of the two-part Jewish marriage process, after which the bride and groom begin to live together as husband and wife.

Noahic Commandments   Seven commandments given to Noah after the flood, which are binding on both non-Jews and Jews.

Olam Ha-Ba (*oh-LAHM hah-BAH*)   Lit. The World To Come. (1) The Messianic Age; (2) The spiritual world that souls go to after death.

oral Torah (*TOH-ruh*)   Jewish teachings explaining and elaborating on the Written Torah, handed down orally until the second century C.E.

pareve (*PAHR-ev*)   Yiddish: neutral. Used to describe kosher foods that contain neither meat nor dairy and therefore can be eaten with either.

Parokhet   The curtain inside the Ark (cabinet where the Torah scrolls are kept).

Parsha (*PAHR-shah*)   A weekly Torah portion read in synagogue.

Passover   Holiday commemorating the Exodus from Egypt.

Patriarchs   Abraham, Isaac, and Jacob. The forefathers of Judaism.

Pentecost   A festival commemorating the giving of the Torah and the harvest of the first fruits, known to Jews as Shavuot.

Pesach (*PEH-sahkh*; *PAY-sahkh*)   (1) Holiday commemorating the Exodus from Egypt, known in English as Passover. (2) The paschal lamb that, in Temple times, was sacrificed on this holiday.

phylacteries   *See* Tefillin.

Pidyon Ha-Ben (*Peed-YOHN hah-BEHN*)   Lit. redemption of the son. A ritual redeeming the firstborn son from his obligation to serve in the Temple.

Pirkei Avot (*PEER-kay ah-VOHT*)   Lit. *Ethics of the Fathers.* A tractate of the Mishna devoted to ethical advice from many of the greatest rabbis of the early Talmudic period.

Purim (*PAWR-im*)   Lit. lots (as in "lottery"). A holiday celebrating the rescue of the Jews from extermination at the hands of the chief minister to the King of Persia.

pushke (*PUSH-kuh*)   A box in the home or the synagogue used to collect money for donation to charity.

rabbi (*RA-bahy*)   A religious teacher and man authorized to make decisions on issues of Jewish law.

Rashi (*RAH-shee*)   Rabbi Shlomo Yitzchaki, one of the greatest medieval Jewish scholars.

rebbe (*REB-bee*)   Usu. translated "Grand Rabbi." The leader of a Hasidic community, often believed to have special, mystical power. Also called a *Tzaddik.*

Rebbetzin (*REB-i-tsin*)   The wife of a rabbi.

Rosh Chodesh (*ROHSH CHOH-desh*)   Lit. first of the month. The first day of a month, on which the first sliver of the new moon appears.

Rosh Hashanah (*ROHSH hah SHAH-nuh*; *RUSH-uh SHAH-nuh*)   Lit. first of the year. The new year for the purpose of counting years.

sages   Refers generally to the greatest Jewish minds of all times.

Sandek (*SAN-dek*)   The person given the honor of holding a baby during a ritual circumcision. Sometimes referred to as a godfather.

Sarah   Wife of Abraham. Mother of Isaac. One of the matriarchs of Judaism.

Scriptures   The Jewish Bible, also referred to as the Tanach. Contains all the books commonly referred to by Christians as the Old Testament.

second day of holidays   An extra day is added to many holidays because in ancient times, there was doubt as to which day was the correct day.

Seder (*SAY-d'r*)   Lit. order. (1) The family home ritual conducted as part of the Passover observance. (2) A division of the Mishna and Talmud.

Sephardic Jews (*s'-FAHR-dic*)   Jews from Spain, Portugal, North Africa, and the Middle East and their descendants.

Shabbat (*shah-BAT*; *SHAH-bis*)   Lit. end, cease, rest. The Jewish Sabbath, a day of rest and spiritual enrichment.

Shacharit (*SHAHKH-reet*)   Morning prayer services.

shalach manos (*SHAH-lahkh MAH-nohs*)   Lit. sending out portions. The custom of sending gifts of food or candy to friends during Purim.

Shammus (*SHAH-mis*)   Lit. servant. (1) The candle that is used to light other Hanukkah candles; (2) the caretaker of a synagogue.

Shavuot (*shuh-VOO-oht*; *shah-VOO-uhs*)   Lit. weeks. A festival commemorating the giving of the Torah and the harvest of the first fruits.

Shechitah (*sh'-KHEE-tuh*)   Kosher slaughter.

Shema (*sh'-MAH*)   One of the basic Jewish prayers.

Shemoneh Esrei (*sh'MOH-nuh ES-ray*)   Lit. eighteen. A prayer that is the center of any Jewish religious service. Also known as the Amidah or the T'filah.

Shevarim (*she-vahr-EEM*)   One of four characteristic blasts of the shofar (ram's horn). *See* Rosh Hashanah.

Shiva (*SHI-vuh*)   Lit. seven. The seven-day period of mourning after the burial of a close relative.

Shochet (*SHOH-khet*)   Kosher slaughterer.

shofar (*sho-FAHR*)   A ram's horn, blown like a trumpet as a call to repentance.

Shul (*SHOOL*)   The Yiddish term for a Jewish house of worship. The term is used primarily by Orthodox Jews.

Siddur (*SID-r*; *sid-AWR*)   Lit. order. Prayer book.

Sidrah (*SID-ruh*)   Lit. order. A weekly Torah portion read in synagogue.

Simkhat Torah (*SIM-khat TOH-ruh*)   Lit. rejoicing in the law. A holiday celebrating the end and beginning of the cycle of weekly Torah readings.

Sivan   The third month of the Jewish year, occurring in May/June.

Sukkah (*SUK-uh*)   Lit. booth. The temporary dwellings we live in during the holiday of Sukkot.

Sukkot (*soo-KOHT*; *SUK-uhs*)   Lit. booths. A festival commemorating the wandering in the desert and the final harvest.

synagogue (*SIN-uh-gahg*)   From a Greek root meaning "assembly." The most widely accepted term for a Jewish house of worship. The Jewish equivalent of a church, mosque, or temple.

Tabernacles   A festival commemorating the wandering in the desert and the final harvest, known to Jews as Sukkot.

Taharat Ha-Mishpachah (*tah-HAH-raht hah-meesh-PAH-khah*)   Lit. family purity. Laws relating to the separation of husband and wife during the woman's menstrual period. Also referred to as the laws of niddah.

Takkanah (*t'-KAH-nuh*)   A law instituted by the rabbis and not derived from any biblical commandment.

tallit (*TAH-lit; TAH-lis*)   A shawl-like garment worn during morning services, with *tzitzit* (long fringes) attached to the corners as a reminder of the commandments. Sometimes called a prayer shawl.

tallit katan (*TAH-lit kuh-TAHN*)   Lit. small tallit. A four-cornered, poncho-like garment worn under a shirt so that we may have the opportunity to fulfill the commandment to put *tzitzit* (fringes) on the corners of our garments.

Talmud (*TAHL-mud*)   The most significant collection of the Jewish oral tradition interpreting the Torah.

Tammuz   The fourth month of the Jewish year, occurring in June/July.

Tanach (*tuhn-AHKH*)   Acronym of Torah (Law), *Neviim* (Prophets) and *Ketuvim* (Writings). Written Torah; what non-Jews call the Old Testament.

Tashlich (*TAHSH-likh*)   Lit. casting off. A custom of going to a river and symbolically casting off one's sins. *See* Rosh Hashanah.

T'filah (*t'-FEE-luh*)   Prayer. Sometimes refers specifically to the Shemoneh Esrei prayer.

Tefillin (*t'-FIL-lin*)   Phylacteries. Leather pouches containing scrolls with passages of scripture, used to fulfill the commandment to bind the commandments to our hands and between our eyes.

Tekiah (*t'-KEE-uh*)   One of four characteristic long blasts of the shofar (ram's horn).

Temple   The central place of worship in ancient Jerusalem, where sacrifices were offered, destroyed in 70 C.E. Reform Jews commonly use the term *temple* to refer to their houses of worship.

Teruah (*t'-ROO-uh*)   One of nine characteristic short blasts of the shofar (ram's horn).

Teshuva (*t'-SHOO-vuh*)   Lit. return, repentance.

Tevet   The tenth month of the Jewish year, occurring in December/January.

Tisha B'Av (*TISH-uh BAHV*)   Lit. Ninth of Av. A fast day commemorating the destruction of the First and Second Temples, as well as other tragedies.

Tishri   The seventh month of the Jewish year, during which many important holidays occur.

Torah (*TOH-ruh*)   In its narrowest sense, Torah, the first five books of the Bible: Genesis, Exodus, Leviticus, Numbers, and Deuteronomy, sometimes called the Pentateuch. In its broadest sense, Torah is the entire body of Jewish teachings.

Torah readings   Each week, a different portion of the Torah and the Prophets are read in synagogue.

Torah scroll   The Torah (Bible) that is read in synagogue is written on parchment on scrolls.

Tractate   A subdivision of the Mishna and Talmud.

treif (*TRAYF*)   Lit. torn. Food that is not kosher.

Trope   Cantillation. The distinctive melodies used for chanting readings from the Torah and Haphtarah.

Tu B'Shevat (*TOO bish-VAHT*)   Lit. Fifteenth of Shevat. The new year for the purpose of counting the age of trees for purposes of tithing.

Tzaddik (*TSAH-deek*)   Lit. righteous person. The leader of a Hasidic community, often believed to have special, mystical power. Also called a *rebbe*.

Tzedakah (*tsi-DUH-kuh*)   Lit. righteous. Generally refers to charity.

Tzimmes (*TSIM-is*)   Yiddish. A sweet stew. (The word can also refer to making a big fuss over something.)

tzitzit (*TZIT-sit*)   Fringes attached to the corners of garments as a reminder of the commandments.

Ufruf (*UF-ruf*)   The groom's aliyah on the Shabbat before his wedding.

Western Wall   The western retaining wall of the ancient Temple in Jerusalem, which is as close to the site of the original Sanctuary as Jews can go today. Formerly known as the Wailing Wall.

Ya'akov   Jacob (Israel). Son of Isaac. Father of twelve sons, who represent the twelve tribes of Judaism. One of the three Patriarchs of Judaism.

Yad (*YAHD*)   Lit. hand. Hand-shaped pointer used while reading from Torah scrolls.

Yahrzeit (*YAHR-tsahyt*)   Yiddish: lit. anniversary. The anniversary of the death of a close relative.

yarmulke (*YAH-mi-kuh*)   From Tartar for skullcap or from Aramaic *yirei malka* (fear of the King). The skullcap head covering worn by Jews during services and by some Jews at all times. Also known as a *kippah*.

Yitzhok   Isaac. Son and spiritual heir of Abraham. Father of Jacob (Israel). One of the three patriarchs of Judaism.

Yizkor (*YIZ-kawr*)   Lit. may He remember …. Prayers said on certain holidays in honor of deceased close relatives.

Yom Ha-Atzma'ut (*YOHM hah ahts-mah-OOT*)   Israeli Independence Day.

Yom Ha-Shoah (*YOHM hah shoh-AH*)   Holocaust Remembrance Day.

Yom Kippur (*YOHM ki-PAWR*)   Lit. Day of Atonement. A day set aside for fasting, depriving oneself of pleasures, and repenting from the sins of the previous year.

Yom Yerushalayim (*YOHM y'-roo-shah-LAH-yeem*)   Holiday celebrating the reunification of Jerusalem in the hands of the modern state of Israel.

Zohar (*zoh-HAHR*)   The primary written work in the mystical tradition of Kabbalah.

B

Your Guide to the Best Jewish Websites

The prophets predicted that a time would come when the knowledge of Torah would be spread round the world. That day is here! With the blessing of online accessibility, everything you ever wanted to know (almost) about Judaism is available on the Internet. All you have to know is where to find it. So here's a list of some of my favorites that should get you started:

Akhlah: The Jewish Children's Learning Network
www.akhlah.com
Learn the Aleph Bet and the Hebrew Phrase of the Day with streaming audio, Full Torah Parsha for Children, Torah Heroes just for Jewish kids.

All Jewish Torah Discussion Board
www.jewishchicago.com/torah/board.html
Share your Torah ideas with others on their Jewish message discussion board. What better way to use your time online than by talking Torah and discussion of Judaism with others.

Being Jewish
www.beingjewish.com
Very extensive archive of answers to basic questions on Judaism, help in exploring observance, and understanding Jewish practices.

BlueThread
www.exo.net/bluethread
"A neutral space to study the Torah, Mitzvot and their meaning to Reform Jews," searching for a common thread of knowledge, belief, and practice that

can be agreed upon and used to unify Orthodox, Conservative, and Reform Jews. The site provides resources to beginning students of biblical Hebrew and Torah.

Chochmat Yavneh Page
www.kby.org/torah/torah.html
This is a collection of articles and shiurim from the faculty of the Kerem B'Yavneh Yeshiva in Israel.

***Come to Torah* Video!**
torahvideo.com
Hundreds of hours of Jewish learning in streaming video for Jews of all levels and backgrounds!

Daat
www.daat.ac.il
A major resource of curriculum and teaching material on most areas of Jewish study, arranged by topic. Language: Hebrew.

Darche Noam Institutions, Jerusalem
www.darchenoam.org
A Jewish learning resource from Yeshivat Darche Noam. Includes short audios on Parshat Shavua, online class on Middot Character in Judaism, Business Ethics.

Hebrew College Online
www.hebrewcollege.org/online
Five online courses are conducted via the web and e-mail; these courses may be taken for credit or noncredit.

Jewish Interactive Studies
www.jewishstudies.org/
Free online courses. One on Genesis, one on the holidays, and one on Basics of Judaism. Requires registration.

Jewish Online studies, Torah, Kabbalah, Talmud, Laws
www.foreveryjew.com/index.html
Online step-by-step guided courses, based on translated and annotated texts, including Torah, Talmud, Halacha, Kabbalistic thought, and Mussar.

Jewish Torah Audio
www.613.org
Collection of RealAudio tapes of Torah classes and instructional music, in English and Hebrew, from dozens of speakers. Also has RealPlayer videos. The quality of the tapes varies, which is usually indicated before download.

JewishPath: Cyberspace Learning
www.jewishpath.org
Jewish and Torah Learning, Weekly Parsha, Gematria, Hebrew Yiddish Glossary, Mysticism, Responses to other Religions, Divorce, Intermarriage Conflict, and Self Improvement, blended with stories and humor.

JIS Educators

www.jiseducators.org

JIS Educators offers BJE (Board of Jewish Education) accredited online courses to Jewish educators in relevant Jewish topics that stress personalized attention and in-depth classical sources.

Judaism for Today

Aish HaTorah

www.aish.edu

Aish HaTorah is an international network of Jewish educational centers. Our classes assume little or no Jewish background and have achieved a worldwide reputation for making Judaism exciting, relevant, and user-friendly.

Kitah Babayit Hebrew Home School

www.creativesoftwareinc.com/hhs

Hebrew Home School curriculum for Hebrew language, Basic Judaism, and Bar/Bat Mitzvah training customized to individual learning needs for youth and adults.

learn.jtsa.edu

learn.jtsa.edu

Offers courses, children's materials, essays, exhibits, music, and more, from the Jewish Theological Seminary.

Mesora

Torah elucidation

www.mesora.org

Dedicated to Scriptural and Rabbinic Verification of Jewish beliefs and practices.

Project Genesis

www.torah.org

Disseminates traditional Torah learning by sponsoring a number of online classes and discussion groups, many of which require no previous educational background. Most classes are archived. There are links to other Torah-learning resources.

Sephardic Torah Center

www.torahcenter.com

RealAudio classes on Tanach, Mishna, ethics, halacha, and contemporary Torah thought by Rabbi Mansour, and other Sephardic Rabbis. Weekly Torah mailing lists.

Shema Yisrael Torah Network

www.shemayisrael.co.il/

A fairly comprehensive program of study on a variety of Torah themes.

Surf a Little Torah

www.vbm-torah.org/salt.htm

SALT provides a new short five-minute dvarTorah every day, onscreen.

Talmud Torah

Basic Jewish Education

members.aol.com/LazerA

Includes essays on various mitzvot (commandments), prayers, and philosophical concepts. This site also has a collection of biographies of prominent Jewish leaders. Plus a Torah chat room, questions answered, etc.

The Museum of the Bais Hamikdash
www.campsci.com/museum/
A virtual tour of the Bais Hamikdash with photographs, illustrations, and detailed explanations.

The Ohr Somayach International Home Page
www.ohr.org.il/
Ohr Somayach Tanenbaum College, founded in Jerusalem in 1972, is an active initiator of new and innovative educational programs around the world.

The Virtual Beit Midrash
Torah Web Yeshiva
www.vbm-torah.org
Collection of weekly e-mail classes in Torah and Judaism, for beginner and advanced levels. Areas include Tanach (Bible), philosophy, law, and Talmud. There is also an extensive archive of articles on various topics, daily short messages, and holiday journals. Level: Most classes are based on active study on the part of students.

Think Jewish International
www.thinkjewish.com/
An extensive assortment of online (RealAudio) courses, including studies of the talks of the Lubavitcher Rebbe.

Torah Net
www.torah.net/
Offers classes in English, Hebrew, and French.

Torah To Go
torahtogo.org
Many different classes on topics in modern Judaism. Also short daily Torah and audio lectures.

TorahToday
www.torahtoday.com/
One minute daily Torah message, sent as streaming audio, to your mailbox.

TorahWeb.org
www.torahweb.org
An archive of original weekly divrei Torah written by the world-renowned Rabbis of Yeshiva University. (Weekly posting began February 1999.)

Yeshivat Beit El
www.yeshiva.org.il
Torah lessons, on Gemara, Parshat Shavua, holidays, Emuna.

Yeshivat Brisk
Yerushalayim Ir Ha-Kodesh
www.realbrisk.com

Video broadcast of shiurim of R. Yosef Soloveichik from Jerusalem. Both Hebrew and English.

Yeshivat Sha'alvim Online Torah lists
www.shaalvim.org/torahome.html
Weekly and biweekly mailing lists in Torah, from Yeshivat Sha'alvim.

Yiddishkeit.org
www.Yiddishkeit.org
Collection of Torah resources on the web including Gemara, Kabbalah, sichos of the Lubavitcher rebbe, and basic Judaism.

And if you're interested in websites that deal specifically with study of Torah (remember Chapter 30), bookmark some of these:

A Collection of Divrei Torah on the Weekly Sedra
www.campsci.com/dvar/index.htm
Divrei Torah on the Parsha of the week written by Rabbi Eli Teitelbaum. Inspiring words to illuminate your Shabbat.

A Taste of Torah
www.hir.org/torah/rabbi
Rabbi Avi Weiss of the Riverdale Jewish Center.

Akhlah: Children's Parsha
www.akhlah.com/parsha/parisha.asp
Children's versions of the Torah portions for each week. All five books of the Torah.

Anshe Emes Parsha Page
www.anshe.org/parsha.htm
Parsha thoughts from Gadolei Yisroel compiled by Fred Toczek. Perfect for printing and use at your Shabbes tisch.

Chumash
Intelligent Concept Search
www.mnemotrix.com/texis/vtx/chumash
Search tool for words (English) and synonyms in the text of the Torah and Rashi's commentary (plus additional text notes).

Divrei Beit Hillel Torah
dolphin.upenn.edu/~dbh
The weekly parsha publication of the students at the University of Pennsylvania.

Divrei Torah—Commentaries
shamash.org/tanach/dvar.html
Shamash's archived divrei Torah.

Hadrash Ve-Haiyun
Weekly Torah Parsha Page
members.aol.com/EYLevine/
Torah insights on the weekly parsha, by Efraim Levine.

Hamaayan: The Torah Spring
www.acoast.com/~sehc/hamaayan/
Essays on the weekly parsha.

HaReshima: Parsha Resources
www.hareshima.com/study/DivreiTorah.asp
A comprehensive list of Divrei Torah and weekly comments on parsha. This list contains sites from rabbis and Torah scholars from all over the world.

Jacobs Shabbat Learning Center
www.ou.org/torah/shabbat
A master index to parsha-based Torah learning on the internet. Has subject, author, and parsha index to dozens of sites and resources.

Jewish Stuff
www.jewishstuf.com/
Online newsletter of divrei Torah, as well as links to additional sites of Jewish interest are provided.

Navigating the Bible
bible.ort.org/
Translation, with commentary, in English, Spanish, and Russian. Also has audio files of Torah reading, haftorot, Biblical Atlas, and more resources.

Nechama Leibowitz—weekly parsha sheets
www.torahcc.org/nechama/index.htm
Weekly "gilyonot," previously unpublished, from one of the premier teachers of the century. Includes worksheets and sample answers.

Nechama Leibowtz gilyonot
www.kkl.org.il/mekorot/english/5759.htm
Gilyonot and study guides, with answers, to parshat hashavua, from the work of Nechama Leibowitz. Includes answers.

NER Educational Publications
www.shamash.org/nerncsy/publications/index.html
Archive of short parsha notes
NCSY

Owings Mills Torah Center parsha page
www.omtc.org/torah.html
Parsha thoughts, from the Rabbis of the Owings Mills Torah Center

Parshat HaShavuah Archive
learn.jtsa.edu/topics/parashah/archive.shtml
Ismar Schorsch of the Jewish Theological Seminary (Conservative), including multiple-year archives, some haftrot, and holidays. Includes Torah and haftara text translation.

Parsha Archives of the VBM
www.vbm-torah.org/a-parsha.htm
Collection of parsha articles originally mailed by the Virtual Beit Midrash, written by faculty of Yeshivat Har Etzion. The basic orientation is text-analysis.

Parshat HaShavua

www.uahc.org/torah/hashavua.html

Various articles about this week's Torah reading. From the UAHC (Reform). Updated weekly.

Rabbi Ari Kahn

Weekly Parsha Sheet

www.jewishsoftware.com/kahn/index.html

A shiur on Parshat HaShavua, based on Midrash and Zohar. The author teaches at Bar Ilan University.

Rashi Yomi

www.rashiyomi.com/

This site's goal is to explain all 8000 Rashis on Chumash using database methods. We fully defend all Rashis using simple grammatical rules.

Rav Kook on the Weekly Torah Portion, Holidays, & Tehillim

www.geocities.com/m_yericho/ravkook/index.html

Thoughts and insights taken from the writings of Rav A. I. Kook, and organized according to the Weekly Torah Portion, Tehillim (Psalms), and Jewish Holidays.

Sermons the Year 'Round by Rabbi Bernard L. Berzon

www.jr.co.il/books/rberzon/index.html

Full-text of sermon book on all parshiot of the Torah.

Shma Yisrael Parshas HaShavua Collection

www.shemayisrael.co.il/parsha/index.htm

A collection of 19 different weekly parsha commentaries, from a variety of different approaches.

Shurim of Rav Soloveitchik on parshat hashavua

www.shamash.org/listarchives/mj-ravtorah/

A collection of transcribed tapes from public lectures of Rav Yosef Dov Soloveitchik, the leading scholar of Modern Orthodox American Judaism. The transcriptions vary in quality.

Thoughts on the Weekly Torah Reading

www.jewishamerica.com/aftertho.htm

Traditional commentary on the weekly parsha.

Torah from Dixie, Inc.

www.tfdixie.com/

Thoughts on the weekly Torah portion and Festivals by the Jewish community of Atlanta, Georgia.

Torah Portion of the Week

by Reb Yosef

www.mazornet.com/jewishcl/Torah/torahportions.htm

Weekly thoughts on the Torah portion of the week.

Torah.net
Parshiot
torah.net/eng/parsha/index.htm
Divrei Torah on each Parsha as well as the Parshas read on Yom Tovim (holidays).

Weekly Dvar
www.weeklydvar.com/
A collection of short, practical Dvar Torahs on the weekly Parsha.

Weekly Parsha from Yeshiva Ohr Somayach
www.ohr.org.il/thisweek.htm
Site includes Parsha, Parsha Q&A, and other weekly publications.

Yeshivat HaMivtar Parsha
www.yhol.org.il/parsha/rcbparsha.htm
A parsha and Rashi class by Rabbi Brovender, emphasizing how to read and understand the commentary.

Online Courses

www.uj.edu
The University of California at Davis offers a course, Introduction to Judaism.

www.ceu.hu/jewish_studies.html
The Academic Jewish Studies Project offers several services including H-Judaic, Jewish Studies Online Directory, and the JSJ eJournal. Another Academic Jewish Studies Internet Directory offers further links.

listserv.lehigh.edu/lists/ioudaios-review/
The IOUDAIOS Review is an online journal devoted to the study of early Judaism.

homepages.ed.ac.uk/dreimer/SAHD/
The Semantics of Ancient Hebrew Database Project web page at Oxford University describes the project's work creating a new thesaurus of ancient Hebrew.

orion.mscc.huji.ac.il/
The Orion Center for the study of the Dead Sea Scrolls and Associated Literature, at the Hebrew University of Jerusalem's Institute of Jewish Studies, has information on the scrolls and about Judaism during the Second Temple period.

www.ethnologue.com
The Ethnologue Database at the Summer Institute of Linguistics, has information on the languages of Israel.

www.jewish-languages.org
The Jewish Language Research website has resources about the various distinctive languages spoken by Jews.

babel.uoregon.edu
The Yamada Language Center at the University of Oregon, Eugene, has a page on the Hebrew language.

www.columbia.edu/cu/lweb/indiv/mideast/cuvlj/index.html
The Center for Israel & Jewish Studies at Columbia University has a web page describing its programs.

www.du.edu/~sward/institut.html
The Institute for Islamic-Judaic Studies at the University of Denver has a web page describing its work.

www.colby.edu/rel
The Department of Religious Studies at Colby College in Waterville, Maine, has a paper on the Location and Identification of the Shikhin available in hypertext format.

www.glasnet.ru/~heritage
The Jewish Heritage Society in Moscow, Russia, does research into the Jewish history of the Russian Empire and former Soviet Union.

www.huc.edu/aja
The American Jewish Archives has a website with information about their collections, exhibitions, and programs.

www.meru.org
The Meru Foundation has information on its research into the essential structure of Hebrew letter forms.

www.aish.com
Torah Codes info, from Aish Hatorah. A skeptical view may be found at Brendan McKay's Torah Codes web page.

servercc.oakton.edu/~friend/chinajews.html
The China Judaic Studies Association has a web page with information on its work and programs, including study of the history of Jews in China and Chinese research on Judaism.

faculty.smu.edu/dbinder/index.html
Donald D. Binder of Southern Methodist University has a website devoted to the study of Second Temple Synagogues.

www.fordham.edu/halsall
Paul Halsall of Fordham University has compiled an Internet Jewish History Sourcebook.

Museums and Exhibitions

Interested in museums? Want to know where—around the world—you can get the best firsthand information about Judaism?

This list (with much thanks to Andrew Tannenbaum for permission to reprint it from his website) will be invaluable to you. Save it for when you travel.

The National Museum of American Jewish History has a good directory of Jewish Museums.

IlMuseums.com has an extensive list of museums and exhibitions in Israel.

- **Yad Vashem,** *Jerusalem*
- **The Israel Museum,** *Jerusalem*
- **Jerusalem Mosaic,** *Hebrew University of Jerusalem*
- **The Chagall Windows,** *Hadassah Hospital, Jerusalem*
- **Tower of David Museum,** *Jerusalem*
- **The Chavi Feldman Art Gallery,** *Jerusalem*
- **From Israel to the World—Isabelle Bos,** *Jerusalem*
- **The Tel Aviv Museum of Art,** *Tel Aviv*
- **Beth Hatefutsoth—Nahum Goldmann Museum of the Jewish Diasporah,** *Tel Aviv*
- **The Israel National Museum of Science,** *Haifa*
- **The Hecht Museum,** *University of Haifa*
- **Archaeological Museum,** *Kibbutz Ein Dor*
- **Babylonian Jewry Museum,** *Or-Yehuda, Israel*

- The United States Holocaust Memorial Museum, *Washington, D.C.*
- Yiddish Play Scripts, *The Library of Congress, Washington, D.C.*
- The Museum of Tolerance, *Los Angeles, California*
- The Judah L. Magnes Museum, *Berkeley, California*
- Israeli Artists Gallery, *ArtNet, Palo Alto, California*
- Franz Rosenzweig, His Life and Works, *Vanderbilt University, Nashville, Tennessee*
- The Dead Sea Scrolls, *University of North Carolina, Chapel Hill*
- The Bloom Southwest Jewish Archives, *University of Arizona, Tucson*
- Harvard Semitic Museum, *Cambridge, Massachusetts*
- The American Jewish Historical Society, *Waltham, Massachusetts*
- Center for Jewish History, *New York, New York*
- The Jewish Museum, *New York, New York*
- Museum of Jewish Heritage, *New York, New York*
- National Museum of American Jewish History, *Philadelphia, Pennsylvania*
- The Sydney Jewish Museum, *Sydney, Australia*
- The Jewish Museum, *St. Kilda, Victoria, Australia*
- The Austrian Jewish Museum, *Vienna, Austria*
- The Jewish Museum of Vienna, *Vienna, Austria*
- Jacob M. Lowy Collection, *National Library of Canada, Ottawa*
- The Jewish Museum, *Prague, Czech Republic*
- The Jewish Museum, *London, England*
- Jewish Museum Berlin, *Berlin, Germany*
- The Jewish Museum of Greece, *Athens, Greece*
- The Jewish Museum of Franconia, *Fuerth, Germany*
- The Jewish Historical Museum, *Amsterdam, Holland*
- The Jewish Museum, *Venice, Italy*
- The Queen's Park Synagogue Windows, *Glasgow, Scotland*
- The Sephardic Museum, *Toledo, Spain*

Jewish Organizations

(With thanks again to Andrew Tannenbaum for permission to reprint.)

There are websites for the various branches of the North American Jewish religious community, Conservative, Humanistic, Orthodox, Reconstructionist, Reform, and Young Israel, as well as organizations including B'nai B'rith, Hillel, JCC, and NCSY.

The World ORT Union in London has a web server with information about its many interesting projects.

The European Union of Jewish Students has programs and information for Jewish students throughout Europe.

The American Jewish Committee, Anti-Defamation League, Hadassah, Jewish Agency, Jewish National Fund, United Jewish Communities (UJA and CJF), World Zionist Organization, and Zionist Organization of America have websites with info on their organizations.

Jewish Women International (a.k.a. B'nai B'rith Women) has a website with news and information about its organization.

Na'amat has a website with information about its Women's Labor Zionist organization.

The Center for Business Ethics and Social Responsibility at the Jerusalem College of Technology offers resources related to Jewish business ethics, including the weekly column, "The Jewish Ethicist," which is cosponsored by aish.com.

Volunteers for Israel (Sar-El) runs programs where Diaspora Jews can do volunteer work in Israel.

The Center For Jewish History in New York City is headquarters for organizations including the American Jewish Historical Society, American Sephardi Federation, Leo Baeck Institute, Yeshiva University Museum, and the YIVO Institute for Jewish Research.

The New Israel Fund advocates tikkun olam, democracy, and social justice in Israel.

The Jewish Defense League fights to defend Jews and Judaism by any means necessary.

The Mosaic Outdoor Clubs of America has a website describing its organization and activities.

The National Jewish Committee on Scouting has a web page at Shamash that describes Scouting opportunities for Jewish youth.

The Jewish War Veterans of the USA has a web page with information about its work and history.

The American Physicians Fellowship for Medicine in Israel is an organization of North American physicians and other health professionals dedicated to advancing the state of medical education, research, and care in Israel.

The Jewish Deaf Community Center and the Jewish Braille Institute provide resources for the deaf and blind.

Jews for Judaism fights against missionary cult groups that try to draw Jews away from Judaism.

The Congress of Secular Jewish Organizations is dedicated to the study and preservation of Jewish history and culture.

AIPAC has a website with information on its pro-Israel activism in the United States of America.

NCSJ advocates on behalf of Jews in Russia, Ukraine, the Baltic States, and Eurasia.

JINSA has a website with information on its pro-Israel defense-oriented think tank.

The American Israeli Cooperative Enterprise develops social and educational programs between the United States and Israel. The organization sponsors the Jewish Virtual Library (formerly JSOURCE) website with resources for Jewish students.

Keshet Ga'avah, the World Congress of Gay and Lesbian, Bisexual, and Transgender Jews has a website with information on its activities.

Maccabi USA sponsors the USA team to the World Maccabiah Games. It also keeps a list of Jewish Sports websites.

The International Jewish Sports Hall of Fame has a website with information about its organization and members.

JewishSports.com has a website with current news stories on Jews in sports.

The Krav Maga Association of America has information on Israeli martial art.

Books I Highly Recommend to Start a Jewish Library of Your Own

Congratulations! You've taken the first step by reading this book. The journey to a true understanding of Judaism is long and arduous. Don't plan on completing it quickly! To do it well would take you a lifetime. But one of the things Judaism teaches you is not to get discouraged by the immensity of the task. A journey of 1,000 miles begins with a single step; a voyage of religious discovery moves from one book to another as you expand your wisdom and vision.

Where do you begin? Of course, with the most basic text itself, the Bible. The most commonly used Jewish translation into English is the one put out by the Jewish Publication Society: *Tanakh: A New Translation of the Holy Scriptures*. A more recent and much more user-friendly translation is the Stone *Tanakh*.

For wonderful selections from the Midrash and Talmud try any of these:

◆ *The Book of Legends: Legends from the Talmud and Midrash* by Hayim Nahman Bialik and Yehoshua Hana Ravinitzky

◆ *The Talmud: Selected Writings* by Ben Zion Bokser and Baruch Bokser

◆ *Every Man's Talmud* by A. Cohen

◆ *Hammer on the Rock: A Midrash Reader* by Nahum Glatzer

◆ *Our Masters Taught: Rabbinic Stories and Sayings* by Jakob Petuchowski

◆ *Insights: A Talmudic Treasury* by Sol Weiss

For excellent overviews of Judaism, I recommend the following:

- *Basic Judaism* by Milton Steinberg
- *To Be a Jew* by Hayim Donin
- *This Is My God* by Herman Wouk
- *Judaism and Christianity: The Differences* by Trude Weiss Rosmarin
- *The Jewish Catalog Series* (3 vols.), by Richard Siegel, et al.

Also, in alphabetical order by author, here's a list of works that probably belong in the "not-to-be-missed" category of Jewish books:

- Bleich, J. David. *Contemporary Halachic Problems*
- Bunim, Irving. *Ethics from Sinai* (3 vols.), a wide-ranging commentary on *Ethics of the Fathers*
- Chill, Abraham. *The Mitzvot*, a listing as well as an explanation of all 613 mitzvot
- Heschel, Abraham Joshua. *The Earth Is The Lord's: The Inner World of the Jew in Eastern Europe*
- Heschel, Abraham Joshua. *Man's Quest for God: Studies in Prayer and Symbolism*
- Heschel, Abraham Joshua. *A Passion for Truth*
- Jacobs, Louis. *Jewish Law*
- Jacobs, Louis. *Principles of the Jewish Faith*
- Jacobs, Louis. *What Does Judaism Say About …?*
- Klagsbrun, Francine. *Voices of Wisdom: Jewish Ideals and Ethics for Everyday Living*
- Lamm, Maurice. *The Jewish Way in Love and Marriage*
- Lamm, Maurice. *The Jewish Way in Death and Mourning*
- Lamm, Norman. *Faith and Doubt: Studies in Traditional Jewish Thought*
- Newman, Louis. *The Hassidic Anthology: Tales and Teachings of the Hassidim*
- Prager, Dennis, and Telushkin, Joseph. *The Nine Questions People Ask About Judaism*
- Scholem, Gershom. *Zohar, The Book of Splendor: Basic Readings From the Kabbalah*
- Silver, Abba Hillel. *Where Judaism Differed*
- Steinberg, Milton. *Anatomy of Faith*
- Telushkin, Joseph. *Jewish Wisdom: Ethical, Spiritual and Historical Lessons from the Great Works and Thinkers*
- Zevin, Shlomo. *A Treasury of Hassidic Tales on the Torah*

Oh, and please don't let me forget two more important books:

- *The Complete Idiot's Guide to Jewish History and Culture* is a good introduction to the Jewish people, their story, and the contributions they have made over the centuries.
- And also *Understanding Judaism: The Basics of Deed and Creed*, which serves as an advanced text for this one.

If you enjoyed this book, I'm sure you'll enjoy these two as well—because I wrote them!

Index

Z

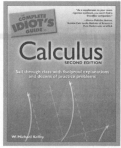